THE NEW PROVINCE FOR LAW AND ORDER

The Commonwealth of Australia was federated in 1901. Only three short years later the Federal Government established a court system to arbitrate over industrial disputes in a young country that already had a history of half a century of organised labour.

This book is a thematic history of an important Australian institution, the federal conciliation and arbitration system, on the occasion of its centenary. The various chapters written by leading scholars deal with the system's political history, the work of the tribunal, the legal framework, economic and social effects, the effects on indigenous and women workers, the role of employers associations and unions, and the management of industrial conflict.

It is a story rich in drama involving strikes, lockouts, imprisonment of union officials, noisy protests in courtrooms and in the streets, momentous High Court judgments, and the rise and fall of governments. The book is heavily illustrated with cartoons and photographs recording some of the most memorable moments.

The institution itself has undergone many changes – in name, jurisdiction, functions, procedures, style, composition and structure. The contributors propose no single, comprehensive explanation of its durability but they offer insights into its operation and its capacity to adapt to a constantly changing environment.

Joe Isaac is a professorial fellow in the Department of Management at the University of Melbourne and a former Deputy President of the Australian Industrial Relations Commission and a leading researcher in industrial relations and labour economics.

Stuart Macintyre is Ernest Scott Professor of History at the University of Melbourne. He is the author of many books including *The Concise History of Australia* (now in a second edition), and a leading researcher in Australian industrial and labour history.

THE NEW PROVINCE FOR LAW AND ORDER

100 YEARS OF AUSTRALIAN INDUSTRIAL CONCILIATION AND ARBITRATION

EDITED BY

JOE ISAAC AND
STUART MACINTYRE

CAMBRIDGE UNIVERSITY PRESS
Cambridge, New York, Melbourne, Madrid, Cape Town, Singapore, São Paulo, Delhi

Cambridge University Press
The Edinburgh Building, Cambridge CB2 8RU, UK

Published in the United States of America by Cambridge University Press, New York

www.cambridge.org
Information on this title: www.cambridge.org/9780521120579

First published by Cambridge University Press 2004
This digitally printed version 2009

A catalogue record for this publication is available from the British Library

National Library of Australia Cataloguing in Publication data

Isaac, Joseph, 1922–.
The new province for law and order : 100 years of Australian industrial conciliation and arbitration.
Bibliography.
Includes index.
ISBN 0 521 84289 1.
1. Arbitration, Industrial – Australia – History.   2. Arbitration and award – Australia – History.
3. Mediation and conciliation, Industrial – Australia – History.   I. Macintyre, Stuart, 1947–.
II. Title.
344.940189143

ISBN 978-0-521-84289-1 hardback
ISBN 978-0-521-12057-9 paperback

CONTENTS

FOREWORD

The Constitution of the Commonwealth of Australia enacted by the British Parliament in 1900 made provision for the parliament of the new Commonwealth to make laws with respect to conciliation and arbitration for the prevention and settlement of industrial disputes extending beyond the limits of any one State. By the *Conciliation and Arbitration Act of 1904* the parliament established the Commonwealth Court of Conciliation and Arbitration. The high purpose of the new court was to protect the public from the effects of industrial disputation by requiring that industrial disputes be subject to compulsory conciliation and arbitration as a substitute for strikes and lockouts. While the concept of compulsory arbitration had already been adopted in some of the States and the need for a federal industrial arbitration system was generally acknowledged by the members of the Commonwealth Parliament, the form the system should take and the powers the new Court should exercise gave rise to controversy.

A Conciliation and Arbitration Bill was introduced into the first parliament in 1903. Three governments failed to procure the passage of the bill and two prime ministers resigned as a direct result of unsuccessful efforts to do so. In 1903 Sir Alfred Deakin abandoned the bill over the contentious question of whether State industries, in particular State railways, should be subject to the authority of the proposed Court. The bill was revived in 1904, early in the second parliament. In April of that year, it was amended in the House to bring employees in State industries within the Court's jurisdiction. This was the issue which had led to the withdrawal of the bill the year before. Having been defeated on the issue for a second time, Deakin resigned. A Labor Party government was then formed with Chris Watson as prime minister. Watson attempted to get the bill through in an amended form which included provision for union preference. When the bill was defeated on the issue of union preference in August 1904, Watson also resigned. The bill was eventually passed in December 1904.

It can be said without exaggeration that the passage of that historic piece of legislation was accompanied by political upheaval. And over the decades attempts to alter the system of industrial arbitration have also attracted controversy. This is because of the economic and social importance of major industrial relations issues and the political considerations that make the resolution of those issues so challenging.

Ever since 1904 there has been a national body independent of parliament and the executive government charged with the responsibility for the prevention and settlement by conciliation and arbitration of industrial disputes extending beyond the limits of any one State. In 1956, the Court was abolished and its conciliation and arbitration functions were conferred on the Commonwealth Conciliation and Arbitration Commission, which exercised those powers until the establishment of the Australian Industrial Relations Commission in 1988.

Between 1904 and 2004, the jurisdiction of the national industrial tribunal changed in a variety of ways. While the industrial conciliation and arbitration powers remain at the heart of the jurisdiction, it now extends to many disputes which are not interstate in character in industries such as the maritime, air transport and waterfront industries, employees in the Australian public sector, in the Commonwealth Territories and on Cocos and Christmas Islands. The Commission's jurisdiction was enlarged significantly in the 1990s to include the power to make orders in some important areas such as equal remuneration for work of equal value, parental leave and individual disputes in relation to termination of employment. As well, the Commission has power to certify a range of agreements made with corporations at the enterprise level. Nevertheless, the bulk of the Commission's work, and the focus for this book, is conciliation and arbitration, particularly arbitration. The Commission's awards have played an important practical role in the establishment and maintenance of living standards for employees and will continue to do so. While the number of employees directly reliant on awards has declined with the spread of enterprise-based bargaining, for millions of employees, and particularly those who are unable to bargain for their labour, the Commission's awards constitute a tangible safety net of considerable importance.

The chapters of this book chronicle many significant events in the history of conciliation and arbitration and many ways in which the national dispute-settling body has influenced the first century of our nation's development.

Each of the chapters has been commissioned specifically for this centenary work. The result is a unique collection of historical material and commentary which is an eloquent tribute to the many members of the Court and the Commission whose work it deals with. For those with only a passing interest in the history of conciliation and arbitration in Australia this book will be a valuable resource. Readers with a substantial interest will find in the pages a fascinating mix of history, politics, law, sociology and economics, reflecting the nature of industrial relations and the central place it has had in our national consciousness from its inception.

The book had its origins in an approach to Professor Joe Isaac, himself a former Deputy President of the Commission. He in turn invited Professor Stuart Macintyre to join with him in commissioning chapters from leading scholars. The project was then discussed with an Editorial Board, consisting of members of the Commission and representatives of the employers, the Australian Council of Trade Unions and the Department of Employment and Workplace Relations. Some members of the Editorial Board attended a workshop in 2002 where the contributors presented drafts of their chapters. While the book has benefited from the advice and assistance of members of the working group, the editors and contributors have of course exercised their own judgment in the interpretation of the subject.

I would like to express my admiration for the scholarship and dedication of all of the contributors and to thank them for their industry and the many fresh insights which can be found in each chapter. In particular, thanks are due to the joint editors, the indefatigable Professor Joe Isaac and Professor Stuart Macintyre. Theirs has been largely a labour of love. It is to be hoped that seeing this ambitious project brought by their endeavours to such a satisfactory conclusion will bring them great pleasure and will be at least partial recompense for their efforts.

Finally, I would like to acknowledge all of those who have served on the Commission and its predecessors over the years – names such as Richard O'Connor, Henry Higgins, Sir Richard Kirby, Sir John Moore and Barry Maddern loom large in the memory. For a century, judges, presidential members and commissioners have applied the concepts of equity, good conscience and the substantial merits of the case to the disputes coming before them. In doing so they have created a strong tradition of service to the parties and to the public which is an example and an inspiration to us who are currently charged with that responsibility.

Geoffrey Giudice

President

Australian Industrial Relations Commission

FIGURES

ILLUSTRATIONS

ABBREVIATIONS

AAPA	Australian Air Pilots Association
ABS	Australian Bureau of Statistics
ACCI	Australian Chamber of Commerce and Industry
ACEF	Australian Council of Employers' Federations
ACIRRT	Australian Centre for Industrial Relations Research and Training
ACM	Australian Chamber of Manufactures
ACMA	Associated Chambers of Manufactures of Australia
ACSPA	Australian Consumer and Specialty Products Association
ACTU	Australasian (later Australian) Council of Trade Unions
AEU	Amalgamated Engineering Union
AFAP	Australian Federation of Air Pilots
AFE	Australian Federation of Employers
AGPS	Australian Government Publishing Service
AIR	Australian Industrial Registry
AIRC	Australian Industrial Relations Commission
ALP	Australian Labor Party
AMH	Australian Meat Holdings
ARTF	Australian Road Transport Federation
ATSIC	Aboriginal and Torres Strait Islander Commission
AWA	Australian Workplace Agreement
AWIRS	Australian Workplace Industrial Relations Survey
AWU	Australian Workers' Union

BCA	Business Council of Australia
BHP	Broken Hill Proprietary Company
BLF	Builders Labourers' Federation
BWIU	Building Workers' Industrial Union
CAEP	Council of Action for Equal Pay
CAGEO	Council of Australian Government Employees Organisations
CAI	Confederation of Australian Industry
CAR	Commonwealth Arbitration Reports
CBCS	Commonwealth Bureau of Census and Statistics
CCEA	Central Council of Employers of Australia
CDEP	Community Development Employment Projects
CIS	Central Industrial Secretariat
CLR	Commonwealth Law Reports
CPD	*Commonwealth Parliamentary Debates*
CPP	*Commonwealth Parliamentary Papers*
CRAIRLS	Committee of Review into Australian Industrial Relations Law and Systems
DEIR	Department of Employment and Industrial Relations
EFNSW	Employers' Federation of New South Wales
FEDFA	Federated Engine Drivers and Firemen's Association
FLR	Federal Law Reports
GFCA	Graziers' Federal Council of Australia
ILO	International Labour Organisation/Office
IWW	Industrial Workers of the World
MATFA	Meat and Allied Trades Federation of Australia
MRA	Minimum Rates Adjustment
MSU	Machine Shearers' Union
MTIA	Metal Trades Industry Association
MUA	Maritime Union of Australia
NEA	National Employers' Associations
NECC	National Employers' Consultative Committee
NEICe	National Employers' Industrial Committee
NEICl	National Employers' Industrial Council
NEPC	National Employers' Policy Committee

NFF	National Farmers' Federation
NOHSC	National Occupational Health and Safety Commission
NSWCM	New South Wales Chamber of Manufactures
OBU	One Big Union
OECD	Organisation for Economic Cooperation and Development
QEF	Queensland Employers' Federation
RBA	Reserve Bank of Australia
RULC	Real Unit Labour Cost
SAIR	South Australian Industrial Reports
SPSF	State Public Services Federation
UAW	United Associations of Women
VCM	Victorian Chamber of Manufactures
VEF	Victorian Employers' Federation
WEB	Women's Employment Board
WEL	Women's Electoral Lobby
WWF	Waterside Workers' Federation

CONTRIBUTORS

Grant Belchamber	Senior Research Officer, Australian Council of Trade Unions
Breen Creighton	Senior Partner, Corrs Chambers Westgarth Lawyers, Professorial Fellow, The University of Melbourne
Keith Hancock	Emeritus Professor of Economics, The Flinders University of South Australia, Professorial Fellow, National Institute of Labour Studies, Honorary Visiting Fellow, School of Economics, The University of Adelaide
Bill Harley	Associate Professor, Department of Management, The University of Melbourne
Steven Kates	Chief Economist, Australian Chamber of Commerce and Industry
The Hon. Justice Michael Kirby AC CMG	Justice of the High Court of Australia and former Deputy President of the Australian Conciliation and Arbitration Commission
Stuart Macintyre	Dean of the Faculty of Arts and Laureate Professor of History, The University of Melbourne
David Plowman	Professor, Graduate School of Management, The University of Western Australia
Sue Richardson	Director of the National Institute of Labour Studies, Professor of Labour Economics, The Flinders University of South Australia

Malcolm Rimmer	Professor of Human Resource Management, Deakin University
Tim Rowse	Senior Research Fellow, Research School of Social Sciences, The Australian National University
Gillian Whitehouse	Associate Professor in the School of Political Science and International Studies, The University of Queensland

EDITORIAL BOARD

ACKNOWLEDGEMENTS

This centenary history began at the invitation of the President of the Australian Industrial Relations Commission, Justice Geoffrey Giudice, who has provided invaluable assistance and encouragement. The Editorial Board was formed to guide its development and we thank all of its members, not least for giving us a free hand to determine the contents of the book. Grant Belchamber and Steven Kates helped gather testimony from union and employer representatives. The contributors have been generous with their time and patience. A preliminary workshop was held in 2002, with financial support provided by the Commission. Wayne Geering undertook research on the members of the Court and the Commission, Andrew Tierney gave editorial assistance and Simon Booth helped with pictorial research. Helen Coulson, the Archivist, Judy Hughes, Media Liaison Officer, and Peter O'Rourke, Librarian of the National Australian Industrial Registry, assisted us with archival material and answered all of our queries with unfailing courtesy and enthusiasm. We are also indebted to Jane Gibbons, Brendan Hower and Vicki Ashwin of the Australian Industrial Registry for assistance in compiling the membership list of the Commission.

INTRODUCTION

On 15 December 1904 *An Act relating to Conciliation and Arbitration for the Prevention and Settlement of Industrial Disputes extending beyond the Limits of any one State* received assent, establishing the Commonwealth Court of Conciliation and Arbitration. The passage of a century in the life of an important Australian institution, and one that is almost unique in the world, is a suitable occasion to reflect on its history. It is a story rich in drama involving strikes, lockouts, imprisonment of union officials, noisy protests in courtrooms and in the streets, momentous High Court judgments, and the rise and fall of governments. Some of the States were ahead of the Commonwealth in industrial regulation. Victoria had set up the wages board system in 1896; Western Australia established compulsory arbitration in 1900, to be followed by New South Wales in 1901. But as time passed, the federal body led the others in many important decisions and took centre-stage in industrial relations. It has been a subject of controversy through most of its existence and an enormous literature, popular and academic, has grown about it.

This volume draws on a number of distinguished scholars to present a thematic history of the federal system. Each tells a story of change and the adaptive evolution of the institution at the centre of the system. That institution itself has undergone many changes – in name, jurisdiction, functions, procedures, style, composition and structure. Its path over 100 years has been anything but smooth. It has been buffeted by powerful social and political forces, by major stoppages and economic problems – mass unemployment, high inflation, balance of payments crises – that have challenged its operation. It has met with opposition from all sides – unions, employers and government – sometimes singly and sometimes in combination. It has been challenged in the courts and in the field on numerous occasions. Referenda to extend its powers have been rejected repeatedly, although the single attempt to abolish it failed.

What is the secret of its continued survival? Is it, as one employer quoted by Plowman put it, because 'the arbitration tree is rooted in the community', a way of industrial life? Is it because of the Australian belief in the prospect of 'a fair and reasonable' decision from the umpire despite the frequent disappointment of one side or another with the umpire's decision? Can we measure the contribution the system has made to the country's economic performance? Can we disentangle its influence from those of other forces? Has the system contributed significantly to industrial peace, one of the main hopes of its founders? Has its ability to adapt chameleon-like to the changing environment in which it operates been an important factor in its survival?

The contributors propose no single, comprehensive explanation of the durability of the system, but they offer instructive insights into its operation. From different perspectives they reveal that the limited expectations of those who established the institution were soon overtaken. Those who were responsible for its operation came to see new functions as necessary and desirable in pursuit of its charter to secure industrial peace and protect the public interest; the parties that appeared before the tribunal sought further outcomes; the High Court read and re-read the broadly phrased provision of its constitutional foundation, and federal governments repeatedly altered its charter.

Each chapter takes up a theme of federal conciliation and arbitration, and explores it over 100 years of change. In some cases, the authors describe changes that have altered the system dramatically; in others, they follow developments that have taken it back almost full circle to its original design. Because the authors are all concerned with different aspects of the same institution, it is inevitable and indeed desirable that the chapters share common ground.

Tim Rowse deals with the political history of conciliation and arbitration. He provides an account of the original debates on the novel principle of industrial arbitration, the tortuous passage of the arbitration bill through parliament, the participants in this protracted argument and their points of difference – whether seamen on foreign vessels in coastal shipping and State public servants should be covered, and whether union preference should be available. Two new governments had to be formed before the bill became law. There was no agreement on the need for such a system and opposition continued to its early operation; this reluctance to accept a system of conciliation and arbitration has resurfaced periodically and is revealed by Rowse as inherent in its very nature: 'The legislative history of the Commonwealth's arbitration law is an exploration of the restless marriage between capitalism and liberal democracy, a restlessness manifest in the strivings of Australian politics to reform arbitration'. Trade unions, employers and the political parties have all exhibited an ambivalence about the requirements of the system. Rowse takes the reader through the century, highlighting the times of trouble for the system in the constantly changing economic, social and political climate.

In speaking to the Conciliation and Arbitration Bill in 1903, Deakin said that 'The Bill has been drawn from first to last, looking at the employer and employee with equal eyes, with a view to bringing them before the Bar of the tribunal where . . . they shall have meted out to them evenhanded justice' (*CPD* 30 July 1903: 2883). Rowse claims that this 'middle ground' eluded the system. One of the underlying issues he identifies in the early life of the system, which has returned in more recent times with the *Workplace Relations Act 1996*, is whether the employer–employee relationship 'is a contract between equals' or whether 'it is deeply and radically unequal'.

Stuart Macintyre provides an account of arbitration in action. This chapter is concerned with the structure, composition and operation of the tribunal. It follows the repeated reconstitution of the original Court of Conciliation and Arbitration into the present Industrial Relations Commission. (The change from a Court to a Commission occurred in 1956, and the contributors use these specific titles to refer to the tribunal in the respective periods as well as that generic term.) Macintyre examines the personnel who composed the tribunal and how they conducted their work. He also describes the work of the Registrar and other officials who contributed to the operation of the system, and he traces its growth from a makeshift institution conducted by part-time officers into a large and complex organisation. Attention is paid to its distinctive practices and customs, the efforts to rationalise its operation and to constrain its independence. The Australian system of conciliation and arbitration emerges from this chapter as a place of routine and drama, an instrument of adjudication and a forum where claims were argued and central aspects of industrial and working life were determined.

One of the themes in this chapter is the tribunal's mode of operation. It was established as a Court but was to operate 'without regard to technicalities or legal forms'. It was to combine conciliation and arbitration of industrial disputes, but a characteristic of the system was that, when conciliation failed, arbitration was compulsory and the Court's awards binding. A senior judge presided, and unlike the systems created in New Zealand and the Australian States, there was no provision for representatives of employers and unions to sit alongside him. Throughout the early decades there was persistent argument over the role of lawyers in the system: employers wanted legal representation, unions resisted their appearance and the technicalities they raised. In a characteristically pragmatic solution, the system developed along dual lines of Court hearings of major cases, with counsel present, and other matters going to lay Commissioners who operated more informally. The judicial tendencies reached a peak under the autocratic Chief Judge Kelly in the 1950s, and led to the reconstitution of the system in 1956. The new Commission dispensed with many of the earlier judicial trappings and developed closer coordination with the work of the lay Commissioners.

In telling the legal story, Michael Kirby and Breen Creighton begin with a discussion of theories of constitutional interpretation. They note that the area of constitutional law dealing with the federal arbitration 'illustrates more vividly than most the impact upon constitutional exposition of the forces of history, economics, national values and survival as well as the forces of changing legal doctrine and political and social needs'. The restrictive approach of the High Court's early interpretation of the Commonwealth's industrial power gave way progressively to a view granting wider jurisdiction to the tribunal, giving it power going well beyond the founding fathers' assumption that it would be used 'in exceptional circumstances such as the disputes of the 1890s'. As noted by Kirby and Creighton, and also David Plowman, the legal challenges by the employers to the jurisdiction resulted paradoxically in its extension. On the other hand, the High Court has maintained its insistence on the separation of powers, and on two occasions – in 1918 (*Waterside Workers* case, 25 CLR 434) and in 1956 (*Boilermakers* case, 94 CLR 254) forced reconstitution of the tribunal. By the time the remaining important limitation on the tribunal's national coverage was removed in the 1985 *Social Welfare Union* case by the High Court's abandonment of the esoteric meaning given to the term 'industrial disputes', federal legislation confined the scope for centralised determinations to the 'safety net'. Collective bargaining at the enterprise level came to apply to nearly 80 per cent of those under federal coverage.

The role of the tribunal as a maker of economic and social policy is assessed by Keith Hancock and Sue Richardson against a range of economic statistics for most of the century. Those who set the system in motion in the early years of the twentieth century intended it to prevent and settle industrial disputes, and they hardly envisaged it would exercise such a wide influence on the economy. Much of that expansion of its economic role was not based on deliberate choice, despite a great deal of tinkering with the legal and structural basis of the system. What was expected to be a minor adjunct of collective bargaining became, as a result of unfolding events, an instrument of economic and social policy.

The process began with Henry Bournes Higgins, the second president of the Court of Conciliation and Arbitration and one of the leading proponents of 'a new province for law and order', as he was to characterise the system. He formulated principles that continued to be applied long after he had departed from the scene. But other developments were far from his contemplation, and these are amply discussed in a number of the chapters that follow. He was initially reluctant 'to devise great principles of action as between great classes, or to lay down what is fair or reasonable as between contending interests', since he held that 'it is the function of the Legislature, not the Judiciary, to deal with social and economic problems' (*Harvester* case, *Ex parte HV McKay* (1907) 2 CAR 1). Before long, however, he reached the conclusion that 'One cannot conceive of industrial peace unless the employee has secured to him wages sufficient for the essentials of human existence' (Higgins 1922b: 6). This provided the rationale for the basic wage and it had an important social content. But, as Hancock and

Richardson show, the elusive meaning of the 'minimum needs' of a family unit did not deter Higgins from determining such a minimum wage as a first call on industry. In time, with family endowment and other benefits being provided outside the wage system, this concept lost currency.

It is worth noting in passing that Higgins did not invent the concept of the basic wage. It would appear from the wording of some of his pronouncements that he drew from the Papal Encyclical *Rerum Novarum* of 1891, which said that 'there is a dictate of nature more imperious and more ancient than any bargain between man and man, that the remuneration must be enough to support the wage-earner in reasonable and frugal comfort' (Timbs 1963: 24). The same concept had been proposed by Sir Samuel Griffith in a bill to the Queensland Parliament in 1890, while Higgins' counterpart in the New South Wales tribunal had provided a similar justification for a family basic wage in 1905, two years ahead of him.

The basic wage as determined by Higgins was not only the minimum for 'purely' unskilled work, it became the 'foundational' component of all award wages: an additional amount, the 'margin' or the 'secondary wage', was awarded for skill, responsibility and other job requirements beyond 'purely' unskilled work. The effect of this classification of wages was momentous because an increase or decrease in the basic wage set in motion a national wage movement affecting a considerable part of the national wages bill. Such movements, often reinforced by corresponding changes in State basic wages, had economic implications going beyond considerations of 'minimum family needs'. The capacity of the economy to support such wage increases became a vital element for consideration. Consequently, the tribunal had become an arm of economic policy-making, not intentionally but by the accident of its early wage principles. This was reinforced when, before long, the margin of the basic tradesman classification in the metal industry became the yardstick for other categories of skills, and on the principle of 'fairness', this margin became the source of general increases in margins. By the 1960s, the two sources of wage movements, relying on similar national economic considerations, were compounded into one, and in 1966 the 'total wage' concept came into existence. The basic wage came to an end, its place taken by the 'national minimum wage', now no longer a foundational element but a 'wage floor'. And so it has been ever since.

Institutions that are given a broad charter in wage policy have the potential to be swept in unexpected directions, like the Sorcerer's Apprentice, by the forces they unleash. At least that is how it must have seemed to employers in the early life of the system, as narrated by David Plowman. But in truth, an industrial tribunal of the kind under discussion, with substantial statutory discretion available to it, must perforce work in a world of change, often unforeseen and unforeseeable. In such circumstances its functions must be expected to evolve so that it can discharge the essential terms of its broad charter, namely settling industrial disputes in the public interest. In this connection, the somewhat anomalous 'judicial' approach taken by the institutions in the first half-century of its existence gave way to a more realistic understanding of how it operated, namely as a quasi-legislative body adjudicating on wages and conditions of work.

In formulating its principles, the tribunal has found it necessary to search for standards of 'justice' not from the common law or earlier determinations, but from community values and the expressions of such values from the submissions of those who appear before it. While such values must obviously be considered in conjunction with economic considerations, it is no use devising principles that are unacceptable to a large section of the industrial community. The circumstances of mass unemployment in the 1930s were different from those of full employment in an economy largely sheltered from international competition during the 1960s and 1970s, and different again from the circumstances of the 1990s of less than full employment in an open economy. Each presented different industrial relations problems calling for different approaches from the tribunals.

Sir Richard Kirby understood this; hence his willingness to practise 'accommodative' arbitration, as did his successor Sir John Moore, setting the standard practice for the future. In Kirby's words (1970: 4):

> . . . there will be a better understanding of the workings of the
> Commonwealth conciliation and arbitration system, if we look at the
> Commission as a key-stone of our industrial relations system, rather than
> as a legal institution or an economic policy maker . . . the Commission
> should not attempt to impose unacceptable solutions on the parties
> involved simply because of its legal position.

This is evident from the various cases discussed by Keith Hancock and Sue Richardson, who point out that 'the tribunal from time to time found it necessary to adapt its policies to the limitations of its *de facto* power'.

The rampant wage inflation of the 1960s and early 1970s brought an even more difficult national wage policy role for the Commission. It became, not by legal power but by the substantial consensus among the parties and governments, part of a set of economic policy instruments to tame the destructive effects, on employees no less than on employers, of wage inflation. But its part depended not only on economic considerations of the kind that the Reserve Bank or the Treasury, for example, saw as desirable, but also on what was possible without industrial upheaval of an order that would negate the desired economic benefits. To this end, on assurances from the parties and the ACTU in particular, about their commitment to wage restraint, it formulated new principles which included indexation intended to be applied generally, including to those covered by State tribunals. The federal tribunal was now sitting on the very peak of centralised industrial determination, not so much as a policy-maker but more as a vital facilitator – or, to use Hancock and Richardson's term, an 'industrial policeman' working by consent of the parties. The short-lived success of this policy was followed later by the Accord, which returned the Commission to a centralised role, again short-lived.

These developments are narrated and analysed by Hancock and Richardson and need not be repeated here. The Acts of 1993 and 1996 effectively marked an end to this role and set in motion a 'bifurcated wage system' – decentralised enterprise-based collective bargaining and a limited centralised function for the Commission to determine a 'safety net' for a small minority, 'a disadvantaged class of wage earners', still clutching at the awards of the system because of their weakness in collective bargaining. In an undefined and unquantifiable form, the social wage concept lingers on within the safety net. For section 88B of the current *Workplace Relations Act 1996* requires the Commission to 'ensure that a safety net of fair minimum wages and conditions of employment is established and maintained', having regard among other things 'to the needs of the low paid'. In a sense, the tribunal has come back to something close to Higgins' view of its function, but now with greater statutory restriction on its discretion and in circumstances of greatly weakened union power. For those employees with limited capacity to engage in collective bargaining, the tribunal remains a significant guardian of their living standards.

A review of the tribunal's part in wage policy over a century prompts the question of how it has contributed to the economy's performance. Hancock and Richardson, after a close analysis, are unable to give an unambiguous answer to this question. There are too many interacting forces at work to allow the tribunal's actions to be isolated with much confidence. On the issue of employment and unemployment, they maintain that 'There are few suggestions that the catastrophe of 1929–34 was significantly due to wage policy . . . It is unlikely that tribunal policies go far toward explaining either the low unemployment levels of the 1940s, 1950s and 1960s or the high levels of the 1930s and the last quarter of the century'. The net contribution of federal arbitration to inflation is 'unanswerable', but they admit that it may have a short-term role as during the Accord years. They also discount the contribution of the system to productivity movements, including the recent productivity growth accompanying enterprise bargaining.

Has the system produced greater wage equality? International comparisons would suggest an affirmative answer, but would rest on 'heroic' assumptions. In this connection they refer to the findings of Borland and Woodbridge (1999: 109) that 'the Australian system has reduced inequality of earnings, particularly by raising the relative pay of low paid workers; that female, part-time, immigrant and young workers have particularly benefited from the Australian system, in terms of wages'. They further refer to the study of Gregory and Duncan (1981) that the Commission's equal pay decisions of 1969 and 1972 caused a marked compression in gender-related pay differences.

Thus, the system's overall economic contributions remain unresolved, although this does not mean that Hancock and Richardson imply that the system could be abolished without adverse economic consequences. Moreover, they see the reduced award-making role of the Commission in recent years as having produced a divided society, which allows the industrially strong and those with scarce skills to do well, leaving a 'disadvantaged class of wage earners' reliant on the safety net and the protection of social security which, 'however generous cannot replace the tribunal's historic role in enforcing a fair day's pay for a fair day's work'.

The 'greater prospects of the establishment of social justice and the removal of inequalities' envisaged by Deakin came late for Indigenous and women workers, an aspect of 'wage justice' explored by Gillian Whitehouse. Higgins applied the concept early in the life of arbitration to male workers, the breadwinners as he saw them. Women he regarded as temporary participants in the workforce, holding that their proper place was as carers of households, and the measure of wage justice based on that tenuous logic produced a lower female wage for equal or even superior economic performance. However, where women offered competition to male workers and threatened the latter's livelihood, they were to be paid the same wages as men. It was a tidy industrial world: there were traditional male jobs and female jobs, male rates and female rates. Labour scarcity during two world wars and technological changes opened up increasing employment opportunities for women, making a dent in this logic, but it generally applied well into the second half of the twentieth century.

Discrimination against Indigenous workers occurred in other ways, although much of it was outside the wage determination system. Where it did come within the system, it occurred mainly in the exclusion of Indigenous stockmen in Northern Australia from award protection.

For women, significant change came eventually in 1972. The Commission conceded the principle of 'equal pay for work of equal value' even before Australia had ratified the International Labour Organisation's Discrimination (Employment and Occupation) Convention (No. 111) and the Equal Remuneration Convention (No. 100) in 1973 and 1974, respectively. For Indigenous stockmen, the paternalistic view of the tribunal in 1944 that 'it would be inadvisable and even cruel to pay [Indigenous workers] for the work they can do at the wage standards found appropriate for civilized "whites"' (53 CAR 212, 215) was superseded by the decision of the bench of 1966: 'We consider that overwhelming industrial justice requires us to put aboriginal employees in the Northern Territory on the same basis as white employees . . .' (113 CAR 651, 666–9). In both cases, there were concerns about the unemployment consequences of equal treatment. But by the 1960s consistency in the application of wage justice dominated the tribunal's concern; unemployment was a matter for other authorities to rectify.

However, as Whitehouse points out at the end of her chapter, the move to enterprise bargaining by statutory direction since the 1990s has brought another source of inequity to those, disproportionately women workers, who are disadvantaged by the way the new system operates. Her conclusion, that 'for both women and Indigenous workers, there remain risks in a system that grants a formal equality in the absence of broader notions of wage justice', reminds us of the unfulfilled promise made by Deakin in the debates of 1903 quoted above. Reflecting on this chapter, some may be tempted to ask: How are we to judge tribunals who did not see discrimination in pay and work as a violation of human rights? Should they be judged on the basis of the accepted social values of the times or on the basis of an absolute standard of fairness? And are economic considerations relating to the employment opportunities of the subjects of discrimination relevant in such judgments?

Trade unions have been leading players in the system, which in its original design relied administratively on workers being represented by organisations. The question explored by Malcolm Rimmer is why Australian trade unions have accepted, even if with varying degrees of ambivalence, a compulsory arbitration system when unions in most other developed countries have opposed such a system. He finds no complete answer from those who espouse a version of either the 'capture' theory or the 'dependency' theory. The former maintain that the tribunal, by various decisions sympathetic to union claims, has essentially carried out the main objectives of the unions; the latter argue that the unions, out of weakness or incompetence, have in effect sub-contracted their main function to the system, becoming tame quasi-unions, relying on the tribunal to deliver benefits to their members.

Tracing the history of unionism over the century, Rimmer shows that the relationship between unions and the tribunal has varied over time and has been essentially pragmatic. In the early period, the union attitude was generally one of support for arbitration, in contrast to that of employers. Union power was weak, the system offered unions legal status; it gave them security when this was sought and warranted; it provided the protection of awards, and, as noted in several other chapters, the unions enjoyed the sympathetic approach of Higgins who said that 'the Act was designed for the benefit of employees' (Higgins 1922b: 3). Until removed in 1996, the Act had as one of its objectives the encouragement of unions; and the progressive extension of the jurisdiction of the federal system, discussed by Kirby and Creighton, was also very much to the liking of unions.

However, there have been occasions when unions have felt let down by the system – such as in the strikes during and after the First World War, and the economic depression of the late 1920s and early 1930s – and received no comfort from it. But they were sometimes able to use concessions, usually on hours of work, made by one or more compliant State Labor governments to spearhead a flow of such benefits to State and federal tribunals. High employment in the years after the Second World War gave them renewed strength, and they were able to use it in collective bargaining to supplement awards. The less legalistically inclined Commission of the 1960s tolerated such gains with accommodative arbitration that maintained its authority and relevance. The continued support of the union movement for the system was manifest in the early phases of indexation agreed to by the Commission in the 1970s and in its administration of the Accord in the 1980s. But things went sour after that. By 1990 the relationship between the unions and the Commission 'was at breaking point' because the Commission refused to comply with the claim for greater freedom from the wage restraints imposed by the Commission in its application of the Accord, and for other reasons detailed by Rimmer.

The move to enterprise bargaining promoted by the Acts of 1993 and 1996, the latter further limiting the award-making jurisdiction of the Commission, widened the distance between unions and the Commission. Less than a quarter of the workforce was now beholden to the awards of the Commission. The 1996 Act was also less friendly to unions. It removed the Act's objective, which had been there since 1904 to encourage trade unionism, and promoted individual bargaining. Union preference was no longer available and compulsory unionism became illegal. In the face of sharply declining union density and weakened bargaining power in an economy now more open to global competition, Rimmer quotes with agreement the observation that 'unions are facing their most difficult challenges for at least 60 and possibly 100 years' (Lee and Peetz 1998: 19). This conclusion is consistent with that reached by Rowse: 'The fates of arbitration and of unions are linked now, as they were at the inception of Commonwealth arbitration'.

With changes in the economic environment and in the jurisdiction and person-nel of the tribunal, the policy of employers went through several stages of change. As might have been expected, employers were initially opposed to compulsory arbitration. The unions had been badly bruised in the strikes of the 1890s and the employers saw arbitration as weakening their own bargaining power. David Plowman recounts their attempts through employer associations to frustrate the passage of compulsory arbitration legislation at both federal and State levels. The employers' fears were justified, particularly when Higgins became President in 1907. They sought his removal through parliament and took legal action designed to limit the power of federal arbitration. But these tactics rebounded on them because they resulted in the High Court's confirmation of wide federal jurisdiction, as recounted by Kirby and Creighton.

After changes in membership of the tribunal and changed economic conditions that gave unions greater bargaining power, employers accepted the system and at times depended on it. By 1937 one employer group was able to say that the system 'had become part of the life of our democratic country'. Once they were reconciled to the system, the greater centralisation arising from its enlarged jurisdiction called for greater coordination of the various employer associations. After experimenting with various coordinating mechanisms, they eventually established in 1977, largely through the leadership of George Polites, a centralised body, the Confederation of Australian Industry.

However, the advent in 1983 of a new body representing big business, the Business Council of Australia, provided the push towards enterprise bargaining which resulted in the Labor government's 1993 Act and was further developed by the Coalition's 1996 Act. The 1980s also saw opposition to the federal system from the HR Nicholls Society, which Rowse, Macintyre and other contributors discuss. With the reduced authority of the Commission in limiting wage increases in collective bargaining settlements in 1991, the Confederation of Australian Industry, previously a strong supporter of the centralised system, became reconciled to enterprise bargaining. The Metal Trades Industry Association, which had been a persistent dissenter in the ranks of employer bodies, seeing benefit from potential wage restraint from the centralised indexation packages of the 1970s and the Accord, also ultimately fell into line on enterprise bargaining. These changed circumstances saw old alliances of employer associations giving way to new ones. Plowman believes that, as in the past, employers could be expected to 'act in both reactive and adaptive ways' to any future changes.

A number of contributors to this book refer to the great strikes of the 1890s as the main force behind the establishment of the federal arbitration system. This

'new province for law and order', as one of the main proponents of the system was
to describe it, was to substitute 'the crude and barbarous processes of strike and
lockout' by 'conciliation, with arbitration in the background' (Higgins 1922b: 2).
'The extension of the nation's power to industrial conflict will suppress, we
may hope, the private wars between the great employers and the great unions'
(Higgins 1922b: 150). The hope was based on an idealistic perception that failed
to materialise, as Higgins was to see for himself before he resigned from the Court
in 1921. And he was not innocent of the fact that, despite a large area of common
interest, there is generally latent conflict in the employer–employee relationship
arising from opposed interests on pay and conditions of work.

Nevertheless, the tribunal has had to wrestle with the difficult problem of
punitive measures against strikes available within the system on the initiative of
employers. In many cases, this deterred or shortened industrial action; on the
other hand, in times of full employment, as in the 1960s and 1970s, it provoked defiance. From time to time employers have had recourse to the common law, established long before collective bargaining was dreamt of, to claim
heavy damages from striking unions. Later it would become apparent that there
is inconsistency inherent in a system that encourages collective bargaining but
makes any strikes or lockouts liable to punitive measures. Collective bargaining
is not an effective process for resolving industrial differences without the parties having the *right* to apply coercive pressures on each other, at least within
limits necessary to protect the public interest. It was not until 1993 that this
fact was recognised formally when the Act provided for protected strike action
during the bargaining period and, in so doing, met to a limited extent the right
to strike inherent in the ILO's Convention No. 87 (Freedom of Association and
Protection of the Right to Organise) and the complementary Convention No. 98
(the Right to Organise and Collective Bargaining) which Australia had ratified in
1973.

In the light of these considerations, Bill Harley attempts to evaluate the federal system's role in managing conflict. This turns out to be a difficult task.
There is no counterfactual argument available against which to test the system;
the Australian statistical material does not separate industrial actions originating
in the federal and State jurisdictions; and international comparisons are unsatisfactory because different definitions are used. Further, since some industries

are more strike-prone than others, variation in the industrial composition of countries will produce a biased picture irrespective of the method of dispute settlement.

Harley shows that the frequency, magnitude and duration of stoppages, in most cases strikes, vary from one period to another depending on the forces and issues operating, which affect the balance of power between unions and employers. A significant fact is that most stoppages are of a protest nature, lasting a day or less without the intervention of industrial tribunals. The average loss of productive time from strikes has been less than one day a year per employee. This does not include the indirect loss of production, which can be considerable; nor does it allow for a catch-up of production following a stoppage. Overall, the loss of of productivity from strikes is substantially smaller than the loss from industrial accidents and absenteeism. Yet strikes create considerable media excitement, often adverse to unions and usually regardless of the issues involved.

Harley concludes that while it is not possible to answer the question whether the system has been the best possible mechanism for managing conflict, the system has been successful on many counts. Its conciliation process has generally been important in resolving disputes without protracted strikes; it has assisted in rectifying the power balance between the parties; and it has contributed to channelling class conflict into 'orderly processing of issues'. There have been occasions when the tribunal has had difficulty dealing with intractable issues without government intervention as, for example, in the coal mining disputes of the 1940s and the airline pilots dispute of 1991. But these have been exceptions.

What of the future? There are political forces that would like to see the end of the system or at least to reduce its jurisdiction even further. Some of the contributors have ventured into prediction. Kirby and Creighton, while anticipating further changes to the functions of the system, maintain that 'there will continue to be a need for a national tribunal of some kind to supplement and modify the outcomes of unregulated market forces'. Although noting that 'One hundred years after the introduction of the Arbitration Act, employers' associations are again seeking to contain and constrain industrial tribunals', Plowman sees no significant change in the system so long as the Coalition does not command a majority in the Senate. The 'more open nature of the Australian economy would restrict moves to re-centralise industrial relations', ensuring the survival of the present system under future Labor governments, although a change of government might see an expansion of the jurisdiction of the Commission. Plowman's contention on protection and centralisation is disputed by Hancock and Richardson, who argue that 'the assertion that the demise of protection removed an essential underpinning of arbitration elevates historical event into historical necessity. The linked contention that freedom of trade necessitates "market" determination of wages and conditions is a massive *non sequitur*'. Harley maintains that 'the institutional arrangements regulating conflict in Australia will continue to change, but it is unlikely that a time will come in the foreseeable future when they will no longer be needed. The force of long history on institutional arrangements should not be discounted'.

The persistence of industrial conciliation and arbitration over a century is no guarantee of its future. When we look back on the history of this distinctive Australian institution, we are struck by its persistence. The frequent changes attest to dissatisfaction with its operation and contestation of its authority, but they also indicate an attachment to the basic principles it embodies. It began in the early years of the Australian Commonwealth as a remedy for the industrial warfare that a new nation sought to avoid; it soon took on a new role of securing wage justice and at times determined national wage policy. The reduction in the Commission's award-making powers following the 1996 Act has not prevented it from finding an extended role, effectively of private arbitration, in connection with the dispute resolution clauses of registered collective agreements (Giudice 2001).

This new province for law and order was created out of a protracted political argument and its boundaries have never been settled. None of the parties that come before the tribunal has ever submitted fully to its authority. Yet all attempts to abolish it have failed. If Henry Higgins announced his resignation more than eighty years ago with the explanation that the Court's 'public usefulness' had been 'fatally injured', those who came after him have kept it alive.

1

ELUSIVE MIDDLE GROUND: A POLITICAL HISTORY

Tim Rowse

Around the beginning of the twentieth century, Australian legislators made class warfare into a legal process in which the rules have since been contestable and subject to amendment. Compulsory arbitration secured the influence of Australian employees, organised as trade unionists, over their wages and conditions. That is, arbitration shaped the way that capitalists in Australia purchased labour power. They have had to deal with the sellers of labour as powerful collectives. In return for being allowed to structure the wage–labour relationship in this way, trade unions have been required to accept certain disciplines over the terms and the manner of their bargaining. Under compulsory arbitration, trade unions have been the instruments both of employees' self-assertion and of their self-discipline.

This duality in the way that trade unions are implicated in arbitration has affected the Australian political party system by making it difficult to define the 'middle ground' of Australian politics. On the one side, the Australian Labor Party, as the political representative of the trade union movement, has found it difficult to stabilise the terms of its long commitment to compulsory arbitration. Labor has championed the trade unionist both in their right to direct actions such as strikes and in their obligation to abide by the arbitration process and the arbitrated rule. On the other side, the non-Labor parties, known under a series of names since Federation, have been ambivalent about trade unionism itself. Non-Labor political thought has sometimes apprehended the trade union as a monopolistic intrusion into wage bargaining and, worse, as the breeding ground of anti-capitalist thought and action. A more pragmatic strand of non-Labor thought concedes a place for the trade union as the employer's civil interlocutor, contributing form and stability to industrial relations.

These ambivalences within both the Labor and the non-Labor ideological traditions have a common source: the intrinsic difficulty of settling the social forms of a capitalist economy. The central feature of the capitalist economy is the wage–labour relationship and that relationship is ever open to two competing interpretations: that it is a contract between equals; and that it is deeply and radically unequal. An irresolvable debate over the nature of the wage–labour relationship is implicit in Australian attempts to regulate it. The legislative history of the Commonwealth's arbitration law is an exploration of the restless marriage between capitalism and liberal democracy, a restlessness manifest in the strivings of both sides of Australian politics to reform arbitration.

MAKING THE CONSTITUTIONAL POWER

The early advocates of a Commonwealth power of conciliation and arbitration included liberals who sympathised with the labour movement, such as Charles Cameron Kingston and Henry Bournes Higgins, and others who were not so partisan with the working class, horrified at the 'barbarism' emerging in their ostensibly 'civilised' society. These were the terms in which Australian leaders made sense of a decade that was both blighted, by the social divisions exacerbated by economic depression and by massive strikes in the early 1890s, and blessed, by the popular movement towards a national federation of six colonies.

Kingston unsuccessfully proposed a Commonwealth arbitration power at the 1891 National Federation Convention in Sydney. His critics included Samuel Griffith, who defended 'freedom of contract' between employer and employee. Kingston was again defeated at the meeting of the convention's Constitutional Committee in Adelaide in 1897. In that forum, he invoked the shearers' strikes of 1891 and 1894, the Maritime Strike of 1890, and the Broken Hill miners' strike of 1892. He assumed that his audience agreed that they had been preventable disasters. The Maritime Strike was Higgins' illustration for his argument that some strikes were not simply 'local' and so made necessary a federal power to prevent and settle industrial disputes. For those worried that the new national government would override State powers, Higgins clarified that federal jurisdiction would apply only 'where the dispute extends outside the limits of one colony' (Australasian Convention 1897: 792). John Downer, while saluting conciliation in principle, foresaw practical difficulties in defining such disputes. Bernhard Wise (Australasian Convention 1897: 786), although a supporter of arbitration, asked whether 'the working classes of this country' would 'surrender the right of local self-government over industrial disputes'. At the end of this debate, Higgins' motion was defeated by 22 votes to 12.

Higgins tried again at the Sydney session of the convention in September 1897. Finally, at the Melbourne session of January 1898, he found the support of John Forrest, controller of the West Australian delegation, and by 22 votes to 19, the makers of the Australian Constitution gave the federal government the power to legislate 'conciliation and arbitration for the prevention and settlement of industrial disputes extending beyond the limits of any one State' (section 51(xxxv)).

The terms of the Melbourne debate show that by 1898 the pros and cons of a Commonwealth role in arbitration had become familiar to each side. Opponents of a federal arbitration power worried about the threat to the States' powers and opposed the alleged subversion of freedom of contract. George Reid said that a federal tribunal would give one party to the dispute an incentive to widen it so as to take advantage of federal jurisdiction. Josiah Symon challenged liberals who romanticised 'conciliation'. Would their law compel settlement? Both Deakin and Kingston conceded that compulsion was a likely ingredient of any legislation. The advocates of the Commonwealth power were eloquent on the miseries of not having a framework for conciliation. Kingston referred to 'strikes and lock-outs' as 'barbarous modes of settling differences'. He pointed to beneficial results of conciliation laws in South Australia (1890) and New Zealand (1894). Labor politician and unionist William Trenwith, speaking as an 'active participator in the disastrous maritime strike of 1888'[1] (though at odds with a great many unionists), agreed that where there had been conciliation disputes 'have vanished into thin air and left nothing behind'. A federal tribunal comprising people of intellectual

CHARLES KINGSTON

Charles Cameron Kingston was the inventor of the Australian system of industrial conciliation and arbitration. He was not the first person to conceive of such a system – conciliation and arbitration were familiar methods of dispute resolution and proposals to apply them to industrial relations had been presented to various colonial parliaments. Kingston, however, was the first to hit upon the idea of a permanent tribunal with powers to make binding awards.

He drafted a bill to create such a tribunal, recommended it to the New South Wales Royal Commission on the Maritime Strike and introduced it to the South Australian Parliament late in 1890. He was at that time a backbencher and even though he became Premier in 1893, was unable to get the legislation past the conservative Legislative Council without crippling amendments. Similar legislation was enacted in New Zealand in 1894, then taken up by other Australian colonies and finally the new Commonwealth.

Kingston himself was remarkably unconciliatory. The son of a Speaker of the South Australian Parliament, he was an unruly child and an accomplished but rough Australian Rules footballer. His admission to the South Australian bar was challenged on the grounds that he had seduced his future wife. Shortly before he became Premier, the police arrested him when he went to Victoria Square to fight a duel. While Premier, he wrestled a riding crop from an assailant, snapped it in two and set upon the other man with his fists.

Kingston was an advanced liberal, sympathetic to trade unions, and he enjoyed the support of the new Labor Party. He proposed at the first Federal Convention in 1891 that the Commonwealth be given the power to establish courts of conciliation and arbitration, and failed; he tried again at the Adelaide session of the second convention in 1897, and again failed. Henry Higgins revived the proposal at the Melbourne session in 1898, and this time it narrowly succeeded.

Kingston became Minister for Trade and Customs in the first Commonwealth ministry, and the program of the ministry included the establishment of a Court of Conciliation and Arbitration. He was a controversial minister, strict in his application of the customs regulations and scathing in criticism of businessmen who failed to observe them. A warm friend and an implacable enemy, he bullied his staff and brooked no contradiction. When he presented his draft bill to the Cabinet in mid-1903, he wanted it to include seamen on foreign vessels that worked on the coastal trade (who were

Charles Cameron Kingston, the inventor of the Australian system of industrial conciliation and arbitration.

usually paid far less than crews of Australian vessels). When the Cabinet refused to include these workers, he resigned. He spoke at passionate length in the subsequent parliamentary debates on the measure, but his health broke down in 1904 and he died four years later.

A statue of Kingston was made, showing him in the court dress of a Privy Councillor, but positioned in Victoria Square so that he faced his working-class electorate of West Adelaide. He achieved much in his own State but the Court of Conciliation and Arbitration was his lasting national monument.

and moral authority would 'inspire the people with confidence', he predicted. Higgins agreed with Trenwith that the public esteem of the arbiters was vital. He conjectured that employers would soon appreciate the certainty that such men would bring (Australasian Convention 1898: 185, 193–6, 201–3, 209, 210–12).

Some Australian conservatives could find such arguments appealing. The liberals' arguments would not have prevailed in Melbourne had not Western Australia's John Forrest thrown his weight behind them. John La Nauze (1972: 208) has commented that Western Australia's delegates were, at that time, the least concerned with the problems and the tensions of the industrial society that had emerged in the eastern colonies. The liberals' rhetoric – of civilising incipient barbarism – voiced the conservatives' apprehensions of modernity. Thus, Forrest and others warmed to legislation in the Commonwealth Parliament on the ground that it would be less likely to be influenced by the 'party feeling' that was afflicting State legislatures (1898: 210).

When the first federal parliament turned its attention to the design of the Commonwealth statute, these Founding Fathers differed over the particulars and the urgency of their legislation. When Prime Minister Barton promised a federal law during the first federal election campaign in January 1901, he presented it with less enthusiasm than the Protectionist colleagues who had written it into his platform. His biographer, Geoffrey Bolton, contrasts Barton with Higgins and Isaacs, who saw arbitration legislation as a creative opportunity for the new Commonwealth to civilise capitalism (Bolton 2000: 308). Two of Barton's ministers, Deakin and Kingston, could not agree about whether the bill should cover seamen on foreign vessels engaged in coastal shipping, and Labor's Andrew Fisher could not win Deakin's support for coverage of Commonwealth and State public servants. When a Labor amendment to include State railway workers was carried with the support of Free Trade members in 1903, the Barton government abandoned the bill. Deakin, having succeeded Barton as Prime Minister in September 1903, revived it in the second parliament in 1904 but he would not accept Labor's amendment to extend coverage to State public servants. Division on this point brought Labor briefly to office, from April to August 1904, but the Watson government could not command support from Free Trade and Protectionist MPs for one feature of the bill to which Labor MPs were bound: allowing employment preference to the members of trade unions. In December 1904, the succeeding Free Trade–Protectionist coalition government, led by George

Reid and Allan McLean and lacking Deakin and other pro-Labor Protectionists, legislated a version of the much-harried bill. Reid, at first an opponent of arbitration, had moderated his opposition to state intervention in order to broaden his conservative constituency to include more anti-Labor Protectionists. And so the *Commonwealth Conciliation and Arbitration Act 1904* became law.

The Act established a Federal Court of Conciliation and Arbitration, whose President would be selected from the High Court bench, with a seven-year appointment. The Court's compulsory awards would settle disputes that crossed State borders. Organisations of employers and employees were to be registered, and their complaints would initiate proceedings. Collective agreements arising from conciliated disputes could be registered and be as binding as awards. Strikes, lockouts and the flouting of awards were to be subject to penalties. In the period of the parliament's deliberations, there had been three, and then with a split in the Protectionists, four, groupings in the legislature (Rickard 1984: 138). In the tactical manoeuvres among Free Trade, Protectionist and Labor members, the two most important issues had been the Act's coverage of employees of the States and the Court's discretion to compel employers to prefer employees who were members of trade unions.

Historical interpretations differ in the degree to which the Act can be credited to the labour movement. There is no doubting the intensity of Labor's interest. Labor represented a class defeated in the great industrial disputes of the 1890s: the Maritime Strike of 1890; the shearers in 1891 and 1894; the metal miners in 1892; the seamen in 1893; and the coal-miners in 1894, 1895 and 1896 (Markey 1989: 156). Trade unions, reeling from these blows, had resolved that if they were to win better wages and conditions they would have to secure the means of collective self-representation. In the 1890s, economic depression had stimulated competition for jobs and thus undermined unionism. Many employers and conservative MPs, building on this rebuff to organised labour, liked to insist on their freedom to contract with each individual worker. Labor leaders saw compulsory arbitration as a way to secure trade unions as the employees' collective negotiator. Men such as Thomas McGowen, William Hughes and William Holman led the push for arbitration in New South Wales in the 1890s, encouraged by New Zealand's 1894 experiment in making awards enforceable public law. Compulsory state arbitration became the policy of the New South Wales labour movement in 1898–99, and the New South Wales Act was passed in 1901.

ALFRED DEAKIN

Charles Kingston resigned from the Barton ministry in July 1903 when the Cabinet altered his Conciliation and Arbitration Bill. Alfred Deakin, the Attorney-General, assumed responsibility for its passage through the parliament.

Deakin had a strong commitment to state action and a warm sympathy for the rights of labour. 'Instead of the State being regarded any longer as an object of hostility to the labourer', he wrote in 1890, 'it should now become identified with an interest in his works, and in all workers, extending to them its sympathy and protection, watching over their welfare and prosperity' (*Age* 10 June 1890). As a young Victorian minister in 1885, he had introduced a Factories and Shops Bill to protect female and juvenile wage-earners from exploitation, and saw the Legislative Council water down its provisions. A decade later, the anti-sweating movement secured the establishment of wages boards in Victoria to lay down minimum conditions for factory workers.

The wages boards were restricted to regulating employment and had no role in dispute settlement. Deakin was formed in the Victorian protectionist tradition, which nurtured social harmony but had little sympathy for those who disturbed it by resorting to industrial conflict: as Chief Secretary he had called out the militia against union pickets during the Maritime Strike of 1890. Still, he supported Higgins and Kingston when they secured the inclusion of conciliation and arbitration as a Commonwealth power at the final session of the Federal Convention, and Deakin persuaded a reluctant Barton to include industrial arbitration in the program of the Liberal Protectionists for the first Commonwealth elections in 1901.

The Conciliation and Arbitration Bill was Kingston's. As Deakin noted in his diary, the South Australian was 'desperate' that it be enacted, and in his own introduction of the legislation he paid handsome tribute to his friend and former colleague. Even by his own standards, Deakin's second reading speech was fulsome. He presented the new Court as a 'transfer to the realm of reason and argument those industrial convulsions which have hitherto involved, not only loss of capital, but loss of life, liberty, comfort, and opportunities of well-being' (*CPD* 30 July 1903: 2864). An Opposition member jibed that the Attorney-General imagined a world 'in which everybody is happy, and life a sort of perpetual harvesting; in which men and women do little else but walk about with rakes adorned with a pretty little piece of ribbon' (*CPD* 12 August 1903: 3455).

Alfred Deakin, who supported Kingston in his advocacy of conciliation and arbitration.

The passage of the measure was less tranquil. Deakin, who became Prime Minister when Barton went to the High Court in September 1903, refused to accept a Labor amendment. Lacking a parliamentary majority, he put Labor in office; this, the first Labor government anywhere in the world, fell when it could not carry its version of the bill. Next, he installed the Free Trade Party, which did enact the legislation but was then removed so that Deakin could form his second ministry. In 1906, he was therefore able to introduce his 'New Protection', which tied tariff protection of Australian industry to fair wages for workers. In his *Harvester* judgment, Higgins established the meaning of a 'fair and reasonable wage', and while the High Court disallowed the Excise Tariff Act, the principles he had set out in that judgment became the yardstick of the basic wage.

Deakin had not foreseen the way that arbitration would develop, and subsequently regretted that instead of securing industrial peace it had become 'an additional weapon of strife' (*CPD* 18 October 1911: 1528). Yet he above all others enunciated the principle it embodied: 'Loth as we are to take any steps which would seem to imperil the prospects of employment and profits, yet there are some considerations vital to the national life which cannot be subordinated even to them' (*CPD* 30 July 1903: 2858).

Granting the federal Labor leadership's clear interest in compulsory arbitration, Macintyre (1989: 192) points out that 'Labor's attempt to dictate the ambit of the Court was . . . unsuccessful'. Not only was Labor unable to get federal coverage of State railway employees, but Deakin rallied non-Labor MPs to defeat the Watson government on the issue of employment preference for unionists. That 'preference' should divide Labor from its liberal allies helps to clarify the limits of the appeal of arbitration to those non-Labor MPs whose support Labor required. 'Insofar as arbitration was meant to mediate class relations in industry', writes Macintyre (1989: 193), 'it was more likely to gain acceptance where class antagonism had not become the organising principle of political life'. To make it easy for the Court to compel preference was to turn compulsory arbitration into an instrument for building up the trade union movement; that would surely help to promote 'class antagonism' as 'the organising principle of political life'. Deakinite liberals were sure of their commitment to conciliating class disaffection but ambivalent about securing the solidarity of working persons.

1904–1921: ESTABLISHING THE COURT'S SCOPE AND AUTHORITY

Though Justice Richard O'Connor was the founding President of the Court from 1905 to 1907, the story of the Court's emerging presence within Australian political life had better begin with its second President, H B Higgins, who served from 1907 to 1921. Higgins' pursuit of what he considered to be social justice eventually illustrated the limits of government tolerance for the Arbitration Court's independence.

Relations with government started well. The second Protectionist government, led by Deakin (1905–08), sought to link the protection of Australian industry with Australian employers' willingness to pay a certain level of wages. The *Excise Tariff Act 1906* was quickly declared to be unconstitutional by the High Court, but while it was in force, a number of employers took advantage of its procedures. That is, in order to obtain tariff protection from competitive imports they applied to the Arbitration Court to have their wage rates declared to be 'fair and reasonable'. This gave Higgins the opportunity to define 'fair and reasonable' and to declare that minimum to be sacrosanct. Whatever happened to the Excise

Tariff Act, Higgins now had his own clear test of what was minimally equitable between employer and employee. Applying that standard, the basic wage became essential to his settlement of disputes from 1907. In 1913, Higgins began to adjust upward this minimum rate in order to take into account rises in the cost of living, measured from 1912 by the Commonwealth Statistician. In this and other clarifications of what 'conciliation and arbitration' meant in practice, Higgins had the sympathy of short-lived progressive governments (Protectionist 1905–08, Labor 1908–09, Fusion 1909–10) and then the Fisher Labor government (1910–13). When Fisher extended the Act's coverage to domestic servants and agricultural employees in 1910, he noted his opponents' ambivalence to the growing jurisdiction. Those who

Sir Richard Edward O'Connor, the first President of the Commonwealth Court of Conciliation and Arbitration (1905–1907).

had feared the Act's effects on 'the whole of the industries of Australia' and on the 'prosperity of the Commonwealth' were now 'coo-ing like doves. They now say that the principle is an ideal one, only we must beware that we do not carry it too far' (*CPD* 27 July 1910: 772).

'Too far' meant, for some Members of Parliament, making it easier for the President of the Court to include in his awards the condition that employers must prefer employees who were trade unionists. Attorney-General (and former officer of the Waterside Workers' Federation) WM Hughes defended this amendment by saying that it would encourage unions to register themselves as parties bound by the Act: '[I]t is infinitely better that they should look to the Court rather than sharpen their swords and resort to violence' (*CPD* 27 July

1910: 751). His Labor colleague (and former leader of the Australian Workers' Union), WG Spence, argued that preference rewarded unionists for giving up the strike and for submitting 'their interests to the arbitrament of one man – a man not of their class, no matter how able he may be'. It was non-unionised labour that employers should fear, he added; to make the new jurisdiction more inclusive was to mop up the remaining pools of indiscipline (*CPD* 27 July 1910: 841). Non-Labor members were not persuaded. The labour movement – assertive in the workplace and successful in the electorate – was beginning to worry them. Deakin argued that from 1904 to 1909 legislators had remained true to the Act's purpose in their amendments. Labor's amendments in 1910 and 1911 strayed from that heritage. 'Instead of being the prize offered to those who conform to the law and assist in the maintenance of peace', complained Deakin, the Act 'becomes an additional weapon of strife' (*CPD* 18 October 1911: 1528). In April 1911 and May 1913, the Fisher government sought, by referendum, Australia-wide power to control wages and conditions of employment and to settle industrial disputes. Contested by non-Labor, the measures were rejected by the electorate (by a narrower margin in 1913 than in 1911), leaving a problem of dual jurisdiction that would eventually, in the 1920s, threaten the very existence of the federal statute. In a 1914 decision, the High Court (minus Higgins) defined 'interstate' in such a way that any well-organised trade union could position its dispute, if it chose, under federal jurisdiction.[2] For Hughes, 'the tendency of labour organisations, and also of organisations of capital, to cover a wider and still wider area' was a feature of modern life – so why should this not be matched by the Court's widening jurisdiction (*CPD* 17 October 1911: 1441)?

Though President Higgins was a 'man not of their class', as Spence said, trade unionists saw him as their champion. Unemployed wharf labourers cheered Higgins when he arrived by ship in Sydney in 1914. They saw, as he did, the asymmetry of the wage–labour relationship. Higgins had asserted in a 1909 judgment that that relationship privileged the capitalist. Displeasing the Broken Hill Proprietary Company, he remarked that 'the power of the employer to withhold bread is a much more effective weapon than the power of the employee to refuse to labour' (Rickard 1984: 185). The second Fisher government reappointed Higgins as President, for a second seven-year term, the day after it took office on 18 September 1914. Higgins was cautious in his use of the 'preference' power conferred on him by section 40 of the Act, however. In 1913, he stated that the principle governing his award of preference was defensive. If he was sure that an employer would not discriminate against union members or officials, he would not order that employer to prefer trade unionists (Anderson 1929: 69).

The First World War polarised Australians along lines of religion and class. An inflationary war economy meant that workers who did not enlist for combat would contribute to the war effort nonetheless by incurring a fall in the purchasing power of their wages – by 10 per cent between 1914 and 1915. Many thought that the Labor government, under WM Hughes from October 1915, could have done more to curb price rises. In 1916, there were many days lost through strikes in key industries. As well, the Labor Party was divided over whether the Hughes' government should conscript to military service. Breaking with Labor, Hughes formed a 'National Labor' government (November 1916 to February 1917) and a 'Nationalist' government (February 1917 to January 1918). In 1916 and 1917, rank-and-file militancy on the wharves, in the railways, in metal fabrication and in the mines exceeded moderate union leaders' control. The popular perception that working-class families were fuelling the war with their money and their blood threatened the authority of any arbiter. Hughes began to doubt that his government should leave so much of industrial relations to Higgins' tribunal.

For Higgins, centralised union authority was essential to arbitration. Could that discipline be fortified? Hughes relished the exercise of executive power; he had less confidence than Higgins in the subtle mixture of mutual trust and mutual discipline that connected rank and file to union official and union official to arbitration judge. In 1916, Hughes appealed to metal and coal workers to take their grievances to Higgins, hinting that Higgins would give them what they wanted. When Higgins resisted the miners' case, Hughes used wartime powers to appoint a special tribunal that gave them what they wanted. Higgins was more in line with government wishes during the New South Wales 'general strike' of 1917 when he cancelled employment preference for some Sydney branches of the Waterside Workers' Federation that refused to return to work. However, Higgins then angered Hughes by refusing to deregister the Federation. Hughes barred Higgins from accepting Queensland Premier Ryan's invitation that

Higgins mediate a railway workers' dispute in Townsville. Higgins and the Hughes government again found themselves at cross-purposes in their responses in 1919 to a long strike by seamen. Higgins won bourgeois approval with his rejection of the strikers' demands, while Hughes, by now contemptuous of the Arbitration Court, negotiated with the seamen in terms that implied both the irrelevance and the pliancy of its procedures (see Turner 1965: 155–8; Rickard 1984: 231–41). Hughes would have liked to have extended his executive power but in a December 1919 referendum he failed to persuade voters to give the Commonwealth temporary powers over industrial matters.

Returning from the Paris Peace Conference in 1920, Hughes introduced two Industrial Peace Bills to overcome the 'cumbrous procedure of the Court' (*CPD* 29 July 1920: 3106). They gave the Prime Minister power to constitute tribunals 'flexible, convenient, expeditious and economical . . . not to supersede but merely to supplement, the Arbitration Court' (*CPD* 29 July 1920: 3106). Though Hughes and Higgins had agreed on something like these proposals in 1918, the bitter 1920 debate on the bills consummated their public adversity;

Henry Bournes Higgins, the second President of the Court (1907–1921).

Higgins' critique of Hughes elicited much loyalty to the sixteen-year-old Act (Fitzhardinge 1979: 443). Former Australian Workers' Union (AWU) official Arthur Blakeley accused Hughes of wishing to 'settle' Justice Higgins. He predicted that the legislation would inspire some AWU members to take direct action and to win a 44-hour week (*CPD* 4 October 1920: 3225–6). That was one way to frighten conservative MPs uneasy at Hughes' style. Higgins himself objected that 'a tribunal of reason cannot do its work side by side with executive tribunals of panic' (cited in Macintyre 1986: 184). Though Hughes' bills were passed, he appointed few tribunals (mostly in the coal industry). The debate on the *Industrial Peace Act 1920* elicited widely based affirmations of the Arbitration Court's value, including from most Nationalists. So the first era of this history concluded with the exposure of what Rickard (1984: 258) describes as 'the grudging consensus which underlay the system'.

1921–1939: THE LIMITS OF NON-LABOR REFORM

Industrial (in)discipline was one of the central issues of Australian politics in the 1920s. In Brian Fitzpatrick's view (1940a: 153), the government 'overtly took the employers' side'. The Nationalists, in office from 1918 to 1929 (from 1923, in coalition with the Country Party), were preoccupied with and frustrated by several features of arbitration, including the overlapping jurisdictions of State and federal tribunals and the ineffectiveness of sanctions against a combative trade union movement. Towards the end of the decade, as enterprises became less profitable, as overseas loans became more difficult to repay, and as unemployment rose, the Bruce government came under pressure to see arbitration as the principal obstacle to economic reform.

In Bruce's first general election as Prime Minister, in November 1925, he addressed the voters as if they were fed up with industrial lawlessness and fearful of the Bolshevik affiliations of militants. His *Crimes Act 1926* was understood, for good or ill, as an assault on trade union militancy. Apart from the frequency of strikes and lockouts in the early 1920s, the most pressing industrial issue was the length of the standard working week. With Labor governments in every State except Victoria, some State awards were leading the push for a working week of 44 hours instead of 48 hours. Bruce sought to strengthen his management of the nation's industrial relations by a 1926 constitutional referendum. By giving the national parliament the authority to determine the States' arbitration powers, the government would end the jurisdictional overlap and unions would no longer select the jurisdiction most favourable to their cause. Bruce envisaged a Federal Court that would make an award a 'common rule', would be allowed to make an award where no dispute existed, and would acquire the judicial power to enforce penalties and to interpret its own awards. In a concession to Labor, all trusts and

Sir Charles Powers, the third President of the Court (1921–1926).

combinations in restraint of trade, and not only trade unions, would be subject to the new federal powers of regulation. However, in a separate constitutional amendment obnoxious to Labor, the Commonwealth would be given authority to legislate to prevent the disruption of 'any essential service'. In September 1926, the electorate denied the Commonwealth these powers.

Apart from its firm rejection of the proposed 'essential services' power, the Labor Party had been disunited. State Labor governments had dissented from the Federal Parliamentary Labor Party's preference for increasing the authority of the national government. Labor supporters of Bruce's solution to jurisdictional overlap thought that it substantially resembled Fisher's May 1913 bid for enhanced Commonwealth powers. On the other side, the proposed power to regulate trusts and combinations inspired in 'a powerful segment of the Australian business community . . . much fear and resentment'. Bruce was beholden to a variety of interests in the composition of his mixed referendum package, including to federal Labor (Wildavsky 1958: 80, 114–15).

Bruce did not give up; he included 'arbitration' in the terms of reference of a Royal Commission on the Constitution appointed in August 1927. By legislative amendment in 1928, the Coalition sought to minimise State and federal overlap; to permit employers to lock out employees on partial strike; to hold workers' organisations responsible for the actions of branches; to compel secret ballots; to outlaw the usual forms of union action against non-union labourers; to define the offence of contempt of court; and to regulate the rules and financial administration of unions. These measures provoked a parliamentary debate about the social responsibilities of trade unions. According to John Latham, the Attorney-General, Labor did not understand arbitration, in that it did not embrace unreservedly its most important tenet – 'conciliation and arbitration in place of direct action'. The Act could not work without trade unions, Latham conceded, but they must be imbued with a spirit of obedience. To demonstrate that there really were recalcitrants among trade union leaders, he quoted from union literature that explicitly rejected the 'chloroforming effects of arbitration courts' (*CPD* 29 May 1928: 5279, 5282). Labor MPs parried the amendments by declaring their confidence in most trade unionists' moderation and respect for process. Norman Makin, the member for Hindmarsh and an official of the Amalgamated Engineering Union, depicted an unholy alliance between 'the militant extremists who regard themselves as the advance guard of revolutionary labour' and the 'reactionary employers' who seek to 'rid the country of the system of compulsory arbitration and revert to untrammeled direct action' (*CPD* 7 May 1928: 4995). Labor was 'embarrassed' by Latham and Bruce, according to Sawer (1956: 276), because Labor 'disliked the tactics of the maritime and wharf unions, while supporting their industrial claims'. Though favouring arbitration over strikes, no Labor MP could renounce the *right* to strike.

Behind Bruce and Latham stood those on the non-Labor side who remained hostile to the very idea of compulsory arbitration. 'By making the worker a docile and sometimes unwilling unit in a great organisation', argued the 'ultra-conservative' anti-Protectionist Henry Gregory, compulsory arbitration 'strikes at the root' of Australian democracy (*CPD* 22 May 1928: 5078; Davies 1983: 98). Gregory spoke for a strand of conservative thought that was particularly strong in rural districts, with their self-reliant ethos and their dependence, as traders, on rail, wharf and sea workers. Over twenty years of federal arbitration had not completely uprooted conservative feelings against the very idea of trade unionism. In October 1928, the Central Council of Employers' Federations resolved that compulsory arbitration be abolished. A British Economic Mission, reporting in January 1929 on the Australian economy, argued that the nexus between tariffs and arbitration was at the heart of the Australian malaise; they added that arbitration consolidated class antagonism. If it could not be abolished, the visitors prescribed, it must be reformed so that judges would take into account the 'economic effects' of higher wages and shorter hours.

By the middle of 1929, Bruce despaired of reforming arbitration to make it a federal instrument of economic recovery. Since the failed referendum of 1926,

BRUCE: "Come! What about taking the hand of peace?"
LABOR: "What about YOU taking that other hand from behind my back?"

The Prime Minister stabs the worker in the back: this cartoon from the labour press shows Stanley Melbourne Bruce offering the olive branch of an industrial peace conference while amending the Conciliation and Arbitration Act to strengthen the Court's powers over unions.

strikes on the waterfront and in the timber industry had demonstrated to conservatives that arbitration, as currently constituted, was no discipline. Other disciplinary legislation, such as the *Immigration Act 1925* and the *Transport Workers Act 1929*, had been no more effective. In Latham's words, 'Federal arbitration has no real, loyal support anywhere. By Federal arbitration I mean arbitration with an unqualified obligation to obey valid awards.' He cited labour movement expressions of hostility to the determinations of the Federal Court (Carboch 1958: 195). If wages were to fall, as the non-Labor Coalition now thought they must, then ridding industrial relations of duplicate jurisdiction would knock one weapon of resistance out of the hand of the labour movement. The Coalition's Maritime Industries Bill, introduced in August 1929, would end federal arbitration except in coastal shipping, to be regulated under the 'interstate and foreign commerce power' (section 51(i)), and in federal territories and federal public service employment. Now Labor was on stronger ground, accusing the Bruce–Page government of being against arbitration per se. Labor could point out that the problem of dual jurisdiction, no less a thorn in a Labor government's flesh as Fisher had acknowledged in 1913, did not have to be solved by a measure that effectively punished many federally registered workers for the indiscipline of a minority. Labor accused Bruce of planning an assault on workers' living standards. Some government MPs, including WM Hughes, opposed Bruce's bill. In committee, Hughes' amendment that it be subject to a referendum or general election was carried by one vote and Bruce resigned. His own and his government's defeat at the ensuing general election seemed to place the Commonwealth Conciliation and Arbitration Act beyond repeal. No matter how fed up conservatives might be with the Court, they would henceforth prefer reform over abolition.

In 1929, Labor, led by James Scullin, inherited the economic crisis that Bruce had begun to face. Scullin removed many penal provisions from the Act in 1930 and upgraded the powers of Conciliation Commissioners, an office introduced by Bruce in 1926. However, the more momentous development in arbitration was not in legislation but in the Court's reinterpretation of its responsibility for 'social justice'. In January 1931, the Court ordered a 10 per cent reduction in the basic wage. The Scullin government, in a state of 'near panic', applied without success for the Court to delay by three months the implementation of that decision

(Schedvin 1970: 217). At the December 1931 election, Scullin promised an inquiry into the basic wage; however, his government was defeated by the United Australia Party.

The new Prime Minister, former Labor Postmaster-General Joseph Lyons, had promised to 'confine federal industrial arbitration to general standards and leave detailed disputes to "local" (meaning probably State) authorities' (Sawer 1963: 41). However, his period as Prime Minister, 1932–39, is remarkable for its legislative inactivity as far as arbitration is concerned. Lyons' Labor opponent in the 1934 election, Scullin, promised the restoration of wages cut in 1931, while, in 1937, Curtin undertook to reform the calculation of the basic wage. In these promises, they echoed trade union submissions to the Court in June 1932, May 1933 and January 1934, 'for the restoration of the Harvester standard'. In 1934, the Court ceased to apply the 10 per cent reduction in basic wage and margins that it had imposed in January 1931 (Fitzpatrick 1949: 335–56).

Was the writ of Higgins torn up or affirmed in the years 1929–39? Electorally, it was resoundingly affirmed; since Bruce's humiliation in 1929, no federal politician has ever suggested that the national government's constitutional power was not also its public obligation. As well, because the cost of living fell during the Depression, the impact of the cut in the basic wage was nominal. According to statistical series calculated by Gregory and others in the 1980s, *the real value* of the basic wage and of 'the arithmetic average of nominal weekly rates of award wages payable to adult male workers for a full week's work' did not fall (or fluctuated above and below a horizontal line) in the six years following the 1931 wage cut (see Chapter 4). Though high unemployment caused widespread hardship for the working class, for those who retained their jobs 'the Commonwealth Court system could not deliver a real wage reduction. Real wages were held up by forces outside the Court' (Gregory et al. 1988: 230).

CHIFLEY AND ARBITRATION

Though there were no amendments to the Act between 1934 and 1947, governments did not neglect industrial relations issues. During the Second World War, temporary defence powers enabled the Menzies and Curtin governments to change the framework of conciliation and arbitration by Regulations under the

National Security Act 1939. For example, such Regulations pegged a maximum wage. The Federal Court gained extra powers, including some that Bruce would liked to have given it in 1926 – 'the right specifically to grant a common rule, to make awards not limited to the ambit of matters in dispute, to deal with intra-state disputes, to deal with industrial unrest before official disputes arose, and to speed up its working by cutting out inessential formalities' (Sheridan 1989: 10). As well, the wartime governments used their temporary powers to intervene directly in fixing wages for certain vital industries such as munitions. Special tribunals were set up for the stevedoring, maritime and coal industries. In order to set rates for women workers in industries where no 'female' rate had ever been established, the government instituted a Women's Employment Board.

The Labor government sought to extend these useful powers into peacetime. However, in two referenda, 1944 and 1946, the electorate denied the Curtin and Chifley governments the power to legislate on employment and unemployment in 1944 and over the terms and conditions of employment in industry in 1946. If Labor was to reform arbitration, it must live within the constitutional limits that had bound its predecessors. Chifley's Cabinet now feared inflation as much as unemployment, yet the instruments for suppressing a wage–price spiral were slipping from their grasp. It faced a trade union movement keen to enjoy such foreshadowed rewards as shorter hours, higher pay, penalty rates for weekend work, and more annual leave. Meanwhile, in October 1947, the wartime powers to control wages returned to the Court, and, in May 1948, the electorate refused Labor's referendum seeking the power to control rents and prices.

As it happened, the Labor government found a weapon against inflation. The Court's slow processes delayed the introduction of the 40-hour week, from October 1946, when the Court committed itself in principle to implementation on 1 January 1948 – by which time, employees working under New South Wales awards had already had it for six months. Meanwhile, workers, advantaged by labour shortages and by their organisational discipline, were determined to win pay above their awards. In 1945 and 1946, the number of working days lost through strikes was more than double the total for 1944. Printers, power workers, coal-miners, seamen and wharf labourers were particularly militant. In Victoria, metal workers and management endured six months of lockouts and strikes in 1947 before they agreed to new margins (the award levels in excess of the basic wage, recognising the skill and responsibility associated with a particular form of employment). When coal-miners struck in 1949, the Chifley government mobilised the capitalist press and the army to defeat them.

Labor's 1947 amendments to the Act were crafted to find a new balance between conciliating militant workers and maintaining a national policy on the cost of labour. Building on the wartime experiment with Conciliation Commissioners, Chifley gave the Court more Commissioners and enabled them to specialise in certain industries. To keep consistency among their decisions, they would meet three times per year under the counsel of the Chief Judge. A Chief Commissioner would allocate their duties and report annually to parliament. In favouring conciliation over arbitration, the Chifley government was in accord with the ACTU. That body sought a less legalistic process, trusting in the strength of trade union mobilisation, industry by industry, in a booming economy. Although Chifley left some large issues in the hands of judges – standard hours, the basic wage, annual leave and female rates – in their determination of margins the seventeen Commissioners would enjoy a very significant power. The Opposition objected that Labor would appoint Commissioners who favoured unions. The conservatives wanted Commissioners' decisions to be appellable. In 1948 and 1949, after seeing what some Commissioners were doing, some ACTU delegates agreed that right of appeal was necessary (Sheridan 1989: 156). Chifley preserved the Act's disciplines over trade unions: the powers to deregister organisations; to order secret strike ballots; to cancel or suspend awards; and to impose penalties for breach of awards.

FULL EMPLOYMENT AND ARBITRATION'S AUTHORITY

Full employment elevated trade unions' bargaining power and tested Arbitration Court authority over wage levels. Australia's inflation rate between 1948 and 1952 provoked a re-examination of both the basic wage and margins. Under Chifley's reforms, margins were to be decided by Conciliation Commissioners, while the basic wage was a matter for the full bench of the Court. The Menzies government amended the Act in 1952 to facilitate appeals against the Commissioners and to provide for a matter to be transferred from a Commissioner to a Judge.

A more potent reform questioned the fixation of the basic wage. In 1949, Judge Raymond Kelly became Chief Judge of the Commonwealth Court of Conciliation and Arbitration. Up to 1941, he had been President of the South Australian Industrial Court, a jurisdiction where the basic wage was adjusted at the Court's discretion. In the 1949–50 Basic Wage Case, Kelly argued that an increase would fuel inflation and that the basic wage should accommodate the capacity of the economy to pay. His fellow judges outvoted him, granting a larger rise than he thought wise. However, in the 1952–53 Basic Wage Case, his view prevailed and the Court terminated quarterly adjustments to the basic wage. For the next eight years, 'wage changes were discussed mainly in economic terms and little attention was given to the effects of rising prices on real wages' (Hancock 1969: 28).

In the 1961 Basic Wage Case, the Arbitration Commission renewed its commitment to raising wages to compensate for price rises. The Commission was not turning its back on 'productivity' criteria, merely demonstrating that it took seriously *both* employees' purchasing power *and* employers' capacity to pay.

Employers soon began to promote the idea that the Commission's consideration of the basic wage and of margins should be combined as a 'total wage' determination. The unions' case, they thought, had benefited from opportunities to argue for corrections of the relativities between basic wage and margins. In the 1967 National Wage Case, the Commission accepted the employers' concept of a total wage and the High Court upheld their right to do so. But how 'total' was the 'total wage' if, in buoyant and standard-setting industries such as metal fabrication, a significant proportion of employers' labour costs continued to be made up of over-award payments negotiated with assertive unions? By 1966, the extent of this 'earnings drift' had rendered irreconcilable the 'widely professed goals of stable prices and full employment', declared one economist (Hancock 1966: 155). The Commission presented a solution in its report on the Metal Trades Work Value Inquiry of 1966–67. Determining new marginal rates, it told employers that if they were already paying above the award, they could absorb that 'excess' within the stipulated rises in margins. This effectively cancelled much of the 'over-award' payments that had been characteristic of metal fabrication industries since the war. So vigorous was the 1968 metal workers' campaign against 'absorption', abetted by many employers who preferred to conciliate their employees, that the Commission effectively lost control of wage-setting (d'Alpuget 1977).

Union militancy in the late 1960s highlighted the issue of the Act's 'penal powers'. The Menzies government had added penal powers to the Act in 1951 and it had continued the powers in the Commonwealth Industrial Court in the 1956 amendments that had created that body. Commissioners were empowered to insert 'bans' clauses into awards. However, such awards were not common in the 1950s and unions were rarely fined. Confronted in the early 1960s with strikes in support of over-award payments, employers became more committed to using the Act's disciplinary provisions. By 1964, 'a national strike over the penal clauses was a distinct possibility' (Hagan 1981: 222). The Menzies government amended the Act (section 109a) so as to require a 'cooling off' period before a punitive order could be sought from the Industrial Court, but this was largely ineffective. The unions' militancy of the late 1960s made good use of the opportunity provided by the government's conciliatory approach.

Would penal powers be effective if trade unions did not respect the Commission and Court? In 1956, one observer had wondered whether 'workers might seek to take advantage of the strong bargaining position conferred on them by full employment . . . and so set off wage-induced inflation'. Not yet, he thought, but 'it is a potential danger'. To meet that threat, he advised, the Commission must try to retain 'prestige, authority and respect' and not 'fritter[ed] away its position in a futile attempt to stem current inflationary pressures which are the responsibility of the Government and the Commonwealth Bank' (Downing 1956: 61). The Commission had continued to contribute to anti-inflationary policy through its wage discipline and by the 1970s some commentators suggested that full employment, by giving 'the economic whiphand to the unions', had indeed undermined the authority of arbitration (Woodward 1970: 115–16). Since employees felt 'less and less of the psychological dependence on the Commission as a bulwark against unknown economic horrors', the Commission had lost its 'oracular role in the community' and now 'unions and employers are prepared to contemplate the possibility of getting along without compulsory arbitration' (Wootten 1970: 139). The McMahon government's 1972 amendments to the Act gave the impression of a restoration of the Commission's and the Court's lost authority, but the disciplinary crisis was too deep. In the 1970s, the Court and the Commission were challenged to find new ways to be relevant to industrial relations.

THE WHITLAM GOVERNMENT FINDS
AN INCOMES POLICY

The new Labor government's Minister for Industrial Relations, Clyde Cameron, wanted to recognise that there was now a dual system of wage determination. Under his proposal, the Commission would set or ratify national wage and minimum conditions. Union actions in support of variations in these minima would not be subject to penalties. Complementary to these awards, unions and employers would negotiate over-award wages and conditions on an industry or enterprise basis and penalties would enforce them. Cameron was unable to legislate this scheme. The Opposition-dominated Senate threw out his amendments in late 1974 and early 1975. The Liberals did not want collective bargaining and did not trust unions enough to agree to a relaxation of penal powers.

A conservative Senate thus contributed to the Whitlam government's rethinking of how to adapt compulsory arbitration to the threat of unionists' militancy. Severe inflation from 1973 to 1975 was the other spur to Labor's policy innovation. Even before the Senate had its way, Labor had begun in 1974 to discuss an alternative to Cameron's model of self-disciplining, decentralised wage-setting. In 1974, the government made the Kirribilli Accord, an agreement with the ACTU to reintroduce wage indexation. It took a year to negotiate the precise indexation formula. Thus, the Whitlam government determined the role of the Arbitration Commission not by legislation that would have recognised the effective limits, under conditions of full employment, of its domain, but by negotiating the trade unions' renewed submission to the Commission's revived authority.

To reassert the Commission's centrality to wage fixation required the Labor government explicitly to repudiate some trade union ambitions. After the National Wage decision of March 1975 set out eight principles of wage indexation, a number of unions continued to pursue wage claims through collective bargaining. Cameron's successor as Minister for Labour, Jim McClelland (1988: 158), recalls that he quickly acquired a reputation as a 'union basher' as he 'barnstormed the country', explaining why the government would oppose such claims, to 'hoots and catcalls' from unionists. McClelland also sought to limit the discretion of Arbitration Commissioners to settle industrial disputes in ways that breached the full bench's indexation framework. McClelland's amendments to the Act, announced in August 1975, would have made Commissioners more accountable to the full bench and would have given the minister a right of appeal against a consent award or a certification of agreement. The ACTU felt 'menaced' by McClelland's amendments (Yerbury 1981: 220). His colleague, Treasurer Bill Hayden, has since recalled with admiration the way that McClelland 'remorselessly set upon the unions'. His 'startling departure from Labor traditions . . . commenced the roll-back of the cozy, old *industrial relations establishment* way of doing things' (Hayden 1992: 456–7, emphasis in original).

Labor lost office at the end of 1975 in circumstances that allowed no one to gauge the extent of non-Labor support for McClelland's approach. The succeeding Fraser government, inheriting wage indexation, presented to the Commission a series of arguments for zero or discounted indexation. In twelve out of fifteen National Wage cases between 1976 and 1981, the Commission awarded partial indexation and thus pulled real wages back towards their 1973 level (Bennett and Cole 1989: 184–5). Unemployment was rising, undermining employees' bargaining power. The Commission's slow reduction of the real wage reduced the living standards of workers with low bargaining power, but did not prevent strong unions from bargaining over-award payments. Singleton (1990: 57) has described the latter industry-based campaigns as 'the safety valve that allowed union support for wage indexation to be maintained'. However, this 'safety valve' became so prominent that it supplanted that which it was helping to protect. The Commission abandoned wage indexation in July 1981, condemning trade unions' and employers' indiscipline.

Finding a cure for unemployment remained an incentive for unions to remain interested in a broad-based incomes policy based on centralised wage-fixing (Bennett and Cole 1989: 93). However, to discuss such issues with the trade unions was not on Prime Minister Fraser's agenda. While the government was watering down and then losing the wage indexation remnant of Whitlam's incomes policy, it was also amending the Conciliation and Arbitration Act so as to intensify discipline over trade unions. Fraser's 1975 policy speech had borrowed selectively from the rhetoric of Clyde Cameron (whose reforms of democratic processes within trade unions had fallen foul of the Senate) in portraying 'militant union leaders dictating to their rank and file memberships' (Bennett and Cole 1989: 188). The Coalition government's 'Industrial Relations Bureau',

legislated in June 1977, was to be the 'industrial police' and facilitate the enforcement of the Act's disciplinary powers (Wood 1979). As well, Fraser passed laws
to protect the rights of individuals, the right not to take industrial action, and the
right of independent contractors not to join a union. His legislation promoted
secret ballots and democratic control of unions; it provided for the deregistration of unions, and his amendments to the *Trade Practices Act 1974* outlawed
unions' secondary boycotts. In 1979, the Fraser government amended the Act
to prevent the Commission from awarding strike pay and to extend the Commonwealth's right to argue issues before the Commission to include requesting a
review, on 'public interest' grounds, of an award or certification of agreement. In
the interests of providing greater consistency, the Fraser government legislated to
promote closer cooperation between State and federal tribunals. It also required
a Commissioner to consult with a Deputy President before making or varying an
award relating to wages and conditions; and it confirmed the President's powers
to allocate work within the Commission.

Much of Fraser's legislation had been foreshadowed in McClelland's 1975
proposals. Both Labor and non-Labor governments saw that in order to centralise
wage fixation it would be necessary to centralise the Commission itself – that is, to
intensify full-bench authority over the Commissioners and secure the cooperation
of the State tribunals. In the second half of the 1970s, the answer to union
militancy had become largely bipartisan.

ESTABLISHING THE ACCORD

With the breakdown of wage indexation in July 1981, the Labor Party began to
differentiate itself more from the Coalition. In 1980, Labor's shadow Minister for
Economic Affairs and former ACTU research officer (1960–69) and advocate
(1970–72), Ralph Willis, had begun to negotiate an incomes policy blueprint
with the ACTU, announcing 'the Accord' in August 1982.

The Fraser government, in one view, had compromised the Commission's
authority over trade unions by making wage indexation an instrument of real
wage reduction, though this had won the approval of economists and politicians
who believed that employees, by 1975, were taking home more than their share of
the national product. The disciplines of such 'faux indexation' had been exhausted

by July 1981. The Commission complained of a lack of commitment to indexation by both the Fraser government and the trade unions. Not long after that critical observation, the ACTU and the ALP were able to present a reformed and viable vision of indexation. It suited both the Accord partners and the Commission if the electorate credited the ACTU and the ALP with the restoration of a disciplined incomes policy framework whose defining public forum was the Commission's annual National Wage Case. The Commission had been demanding 'responsibility' of government and unions since 1974; in 1983, they got it in the form of 'the Accord' (Dabscheck 1994: 154–5).

The Accord made the ALP electorally competitive with the Coalition and distanced ALP leaders such as Hayden from what they referred to as the economic incompetence of not only the Fraser but also the Whitlam government. The ACTU declared itself to have matured through the inflation–unemployment crisis of the 1970s. Indeed, it was organisationally stronger. The amalgamation of the white-collar peak councils, the Australian Consumer and Specialty Products Association and the Council of Australian Government Employees Organizations, to the ACTU in 1979 and 1981 had increased its representative coverage. The recruitment of a large research staff, complemented by a rise in the number and quality of research staff in some affiliate unions, and the novel challenges of 'stagflation' had stimulated the ACTU's strategic reassessment. Three interests converged in the Accord: the Commission's desire to be the forum for a disciplined national wages framework; the ACTU's ambition to become a force in the making of national economic policy; and the ALP's need to win voters from the Coalition.

From 1983 to 1993 there were seven versions of the Accord. The Commission (after 1988, the Industrial Relations Commission) responded in nine National Wage decisions (September 1983, June 1986, December 1986, March 1987, February 1988, August 1988, August 1989, April 1991 and August 1994) to joint government–ACTU submissions. Wage indexation was the Accord's principal feature from 1983 to 1986, though in 1985 the index-based rise was discounted (with tax cuts and superannuation as sweeteners).

From 1987 the philosophy of the Accord began to shift from centralisation to decentralisation. To enable that change became the most important political impulse in legislation, starting with the *Industrial Relations Act 1988*. The speed and extent of this transformation of the Accord was remarkable. In January 1983, then assistant secretary of the ACTU Bill Kelty declared the ACTU's hostility to 'a decentralised wage system' based on 'free collective bargaining'. He scorned as 'pious nonsense and academic trivia' any suggestion that the trade union movement would abandon its collective responsibility for an incomes policy. He conceded that this commitment bound the strongest unions to 'forfeiting some of their rights for a prices and incomes approach to work on a uniform and egalitarian basis'. But anything less than a centralised approach 'would destroy the whole fabric of the trade union movement' (Kelty 1984: 45–6). Within three years, Kelty was singing a very different tune.

In 1987, the Commission accepted a submission by the government and the ACTU (substantially supported by employers) that wages could henceforth be raised in two ways. They would get not only rises decreed for all by the Commission in the National Wage Case, but also productivity-based rises wherever they could be negotiated, and then ratified by the Commission if they remained within stipulated maxima. The Industrial Relations Act provided for enterprise-based agreements. Subsequent versions of the Accord linked negotiated wage rises to the restructuring of awards. In 1988 and 1989, the Commission promoted the review of awards under what it called the 'structural efficiency' principle. The ACTU agreed not to make a national wage claim in 1989–90, pursuing instead the restructuring of awards according to this principle. In 1993, former Prime Minister (1983–91) Bob Hawke (1993: 476) expressed satisfaction that 'in the last decade the industrial relations system has undergone more change than it has experienced since Federation'.

What was the Commission's contribution to that change? Looking back at the shift to the 'structural efficiency' principle in 1991, Isaac (1994: 86) characterised the Commission as the fourth player in what he saw as a 'process of quadripartite consultation and cooperation'.[3] No doubt that was so, but the high degree of consensus between the Commission and the representatives of capital, labour and government both underwrote the Commission's authority and fostered a threat to that authority. That is, some critics of the Accord began to say that it was the creature of an 'Industrial Relations Club' that dogmatically excluded alternative neo-liberal (or deregulationist) approaches to Australia's political economy. Gerard Henderson had used the 'club' phrase in a much-quoted *Bulletin* article of September 1983 to condemn the ways in which the interests of certain government and trade union officials, lawyers and business figures converged in the maintenance of a regulated labour market. It would be good for the Australian economy, Henderson argued, if the 'club' were disbanded. A series of incidents gave currency to that damaging 'club' perception.

One was the situation of Justice Staples. Staples, appointed to the Commission by Labor in 1975, had made decisions displeasing to the Fraser government. In 1977 he had been sent overseas on an extended study of human rights. He returned with his eagerness for public debate undimmed. When he publicly criticised the full bench for upholding an appeal against one of his decisions, it seemed to senior personnel of the Commission that Staples was violating one of the essential procedural rules of the machinery of arbitration. The Court's President, Sir John Moore, relieved him of many duties in May 1980. Labor's Accord rested on a high degree of policy cohesion within the Commission and Justice Maddern, Labor's 1985 appointment to the presidency, would entrust to Staples no cases at all. Staples' appointment was terminated when Labor legislated the Industrial Relations Commission in 1988 to replace the Conciliation and Arbitration Commission. Some observers argued that as the new body simply did not include Staples, he had been sacked, effectively, in an attack on judicial independence. Told as a story of a laudable heretic crushed by an intolerant industrial relations clerisy, the Staples affair helped to circulate the phrase 'Industrial Relations Club' (Kirby 1989: 357–61). Staples was no advocate of labour market deregulation but his victim status, in one perspective, made him an individual victim of the 'club' just as individuals who did not want to join unions could be presented as victims of unionism. The Staples case illustrated the ideological vulnerability of a national incomes policy that exalted centralised decisions over decentralised ones, organisations over individuals.

The Hawke government's defence of the Accord was no less sparing of errant unions than of outspoken judges. When airline pilots refused to channel their demands through the Accord's procedures in 1989, Hawke took them on, to the astonished delight of employers and conservative politicians. Liberal MP John Howard (1990: 40) later relished the irony:

In 1985 the members of the Committee of Review of Australian
Industrial Relations Law and Systems – the Hancock Committee – could
state with collectively straight face that trade unions could not be made
subject to the ordinary courts because they could not be expected to obey
the directions of those courts. Yet only four years later the Prime
Minister, a former president of the ACTU, was exhorting airline
companies to sue the Australian Federation of Airline Pilots.

Howard was prominent in a new tendency within Liberal politics and its business
allies: a push for a radical questioning of the entire tradition of compulsory arbitration and of such contemporary manifestations of that tradition as the Accord.
Paul Kelly (1992) has labelled this tendency as 'the attack on Justice Higgins'.
The HR Nicholls Society, a network of businessmen, politicians and economists
formed in 1986, promoted a revisionist liberalism that condemned the legal 'privilege' of trade unions. In the late 1970s and early 1980s, the National Farmers
Federation had shown that direct action by unions could be defeated by using
parts of the Trade Practices Act (legislated by the Fraser government). The NFF
and the HR Nicholls Society began to be influential within the Liberal Party
through figures such as John Howard and Peter Costello. Between 1984 and
1986, Howard triumphed over Ian McPhee – a former industrial advocate for
employers and thus a member of the 'Industrial Relations Club' – as the shaper
of Liberal Party industrial relations policy.

In a series of platform changes culminating in the October 1992 statement
'Jobsback', the Coalition promised that industrial tribunals would no longer play
a part in resolving disputes and determining wages and conditions and that the
enterprise (rather than the industry or sector) would be the unit at which wages
and conditions would be negotiated. Most important, for the radical liberals, was
that trade unions would not be necessary vehicles of such bargaining. Howard
advocated voluntary unionism, arguing that compulsory membership denied 'an
individual's basic human right to associate or not associate'. Guaranteeing that
right would 'promote voluntary agreements between employers and individual
employees by reducing trade union membership'. It would be the end of '"closed
shop" arrangements and union preferences' (Howard 1990: 37). These radical
liberals' confidence that unions could be dispensed with was boosted by a series

The HR Nicholls Society announced itself with an inaugural conference early in 1986, and the
proceedings were subsequently published as Arbitration in Contempt. *Geoff Pryor's cartoon*
shows John Stone the former head of Treasury, at the rostrum. Geoffrey Blainey stands on his
right while the light relief is a colourful depiction of John Howard, who was then the Leader of
the Opposition.

of disputes (South East Queensland Electricity Board, Mudginberri meat works
and Dollar Sweets) in the 1980s in which employees proved willing to work
under conditions not sanctioned by their unions. The radical liberals were also
buoyed by data on falling union membership.

This shift within the Liberal Party was strongly supported by the Business
Council of Australia, a coalition of big business that made industrial relations a
focus of study and discussion in the 1980s. Three BCA-commissioned reports,
in 1989, 1991 and 1993, advocated enterprise bargaining in place of compulsory
arbitration. Legislation should be amended so that enterprises and their employees could agree to leave the award system and to make their own agreement about
the enforcement and adjustment of their contract, and employees could choose
representatives other than registered unions and be protected by nothing more
than statutory minimum conditions.

The Labor government's response to this persistent advocacy of enterprise
bargaining put to the test Isaac's model of the Accord as a 'quadripartite'

negotiation. Could the Commission put its own views without damaging its standing as one of the four players? The Accord partners' submission to the 1991 National Wage Case (Accord Mark VI) sought to accelerate the transition towards enterprise bargaining by a change that the Commission found worrying. Under the ACTU–ALP proposed 'enterprise bargaining principle', any employer–union agreement should be certified by the Commission without reference to a prescribed ceiling on wage increases and without the 'public interest' test. In April 1991, the Commission set out principles that it wished to see embodied in enterprise bargains and it called for further discussion of the proposal. The Commission wished to retain the 'public interest' test, that is, its power to refuse the certification of any agreement that, by disturbing relativities among awards, would stimulate inflationary wage claims.

Commission personnel were surprised when the ACTU and the Labor government responded to its criticism of Accord Mark VI by publicly lambasting the Commission. Looking back in 1999, union leader George Campbell recalled that the ACTU had then good reason to be concerned at the Commission's stance. When it had supported the shift to enterprise bargaining in 1991, the ACTU had been trying to deal with 'an upsurge of rancorous strikes over claims which fell outside the IRC's [award restructuring] guidelines'. By opposing this shift, the Commission had contributed to the erosion of its own authority, Campbell suggested (1999: 54). Among those advising the Keating government, there was jubilation at the stiff ACTU–ALP rebuke to the Commission. Treasury officials welcomed the dispute over Accord Mark VI as a turning point in Labor's income strategy. 'Thereafter we were in a new world', a happy Keating adviser recalled, 'The commission would not again be asked to make single decisions for the entire workforce' (Edwards 1996: 421). In October 1991, the Commission reluctantly acceded to the enterprise bargaining principle sought by the ACTU and Labor, but by then the damage to the 'quadripartite' process was irreparable.

THE 'NEW WORLD' OF KEATING AND HOWARD

As long as he had trade union support for his changes to the Accord's agenda, Prime Minister Keating was emboldened to press on. The Keating government amended the Industrial Relations Act in June 1992 to remove the Commission's 'public interest' powers to intervene in agreements bargained at the enterprise level. When asked to ratify a single-enterprise agreement, the Commission could no longer invoke such considerations as whether it would 'distort the wage structure, cause industrial relations problems in other enterprises, exacerbate unemployment or add to inflationary pressures' (Hancock and Rawson 1993: 500). Commenting on this amendment, Ludeke (1992) pointed out that its role from 1986 had been steadily diminishing as the Accord gave more scope to wage determination at the enterprise level. With the latest truncation of Commission responsibility, the Labor Party was now pursuing the BCA/Liberal agenda, he surmised. Having made the Commission a subordinate player in the Accord, would the Labor government turn next on the ACTU? Under the Accord up to 1992, the ACTU had enjoyed 'a measure of authority and an importance in economic policy-making never experienced before', wrote Isaac in 1991. Yet, in the eyes of some employers (the Confederation of Australian Industry) this was 'the most dangerous aspect of the entire package known as the Accord' (Isaac 1994: 92).

Keating's 1992 legislation indeed brought Labor policy closer to that of the Opposition. Accord Mark VII, in March 1993, was dedicated to reviving employment, while setting limits to inflation. That Accord made it explicit that the responsibility for formulating wage policy did not lie with the Industrial Relations Commission but with the government and the unions. To its own surprise, Labor won the March 1993 election, led by Paul Keating, and warmly supported by a trade union movement repelled by what they perceived as the anti-unionism of the Coalition's policy – exemplified in Victoria in 1992 by the Kennett government's reforms to industrial law. Keating made much of his remaining differences with non-Labor. There were both real and imagined differences. Spokesperson on industrial relations John Howard (1990: 37) suggested that while the Keating government was burdened by still wanting Commission approval of enterprise agreements (a debatable description of Keating's stance by then), the Opposition looked forward to ending the Commission's oversight. The trade union movement's horror at the looming 'New Right' gave Keating space in which to manoeuvre. Moderation had been redefined; it now meant being less antagonistic than Howard to the Commission and to the ACTU. A month after the election, Keating dismayed his Accord partners by outlining to the Institute of Company Directors legislative amendments that followed the BCA model. Keating's speech-writer, Don Watson (2002: 369), recalls that Keating hoped that the unions would continue to be motivated by their apprehensions about a future Liberal government and so support, however grudgingly, the next round of reforms. The 1993 amendments to the Industrial Relations Act made awards a safety net beneath what was now to be the main means for wage fixation – the enterprise agreement. The Commission would periodically adjust the safety net. Invoking Deakin, Minister for Industrial Relations Laurie Brereton claimed that his amending bill changed the 'methodology' but not the 'principle' of Australia's approach to industrial relations. He also hailed it as 'the culmination of the government's break with the past'. The new 'enterprise flexibility agreements' could be generated without either an interstate dispute or a union, but a union could be a party to any Commission hearing into whether such an agreement respected award minima (*CPD* 28 October 1993: 2778).

By such steps, Keating practically minimised the difference between Labor and the radical liberals of the Coalition. Between 1993 and 1996, the Keating government consolidated this shift to what it called 'bargaining at the workplace level within a framework of minimum standards provided by arbitral tribunals' (cited in Hancock and Rawson 1993: 502). The ACTU had difficulty accepting Keating's proposal that wage agreements made by non-union workers could be ratified before the Commission, but its posture was defensive, given the high likelihood of a Coalition victory in the next election. The Commission was in an even more vulnerable position. John Edwards, who was one of Prime Minister Paul Keating's advisers, recalls ACTU President Kelty, once a champion of centralised wage fixation, speculating that the Commission would have to concede that it now had no function other than to define the safety net. 'If they knock it back', Edwards (1996: 491) recalls Kelty saying, 'we abolish the fucking Commission'. His 'we' was the Accord's potent remnant.

From the point of view of non-Labor, Keating was taking industrial relations in the right direction but not far or fast enough. Howard was confident that the Keating government had alienated many employees from their unions by using the Accord to reduce wages, while not reducing unemployment, and by speeding up the process of union amalgamation. He and his colleagues continued to say that the government's policy protected an 'industrial relations club' that held back the performance of the Australian economy (Howard 1990: 41). In 1996, the Coalition won government, giving John Howard his chance to legislate the radical liberal vision. Under the *Workplace Relations and Other Legislation Amendments Act 1996*, Australian Workplace Agreements would be negotiable without union involvement. However, such agreements could not undercut awards, defined in terms of: pay rates; annual leave; long service leave; public holidays; penalty rates; redundancy pay and hours of work; superannuation; variations in work hours and breaks; career paths. The new government's last few years in Opposition had taught it that the public might not yet be ready for the abolition of the safety net; and their negotiations with Democrat senators (for the Coalition had no majority in that chamber) confirmed such caution (Singleton 1997).

The shrinking of the Commission's role has been mostly an effect of Labor's legislation in 1992 and 1993, rather than Howard's in 1996. Unions were more the focus of the *Workplace Relations Act 1996*. They were excluded from negotiating Australian Workplace Agreements. An Office of Employment Advocate would substitute for unions' oversight of individual wage bargaining. Agreements made with unions can be overturned by a majority of employees in a workplace. The Act upheld employees' rights not to belong to unions, or their right to start their own unions, should they choose. Penalties for strikes, lockouts and secondary boycotts were strengthened, though consumer and environmental boycotts were permitted.

When the Coalition government tested the new legal framework against the Maritime Union of Australia (MUA) in 1997–98, it became clear that the Industrial Relations Commission had become marginal to dispute settlement. The MUA's response to Patrick Stevedores was to litigate through the Federal Court, alleging that Patrick's structuring of its enterprise amounted to a conspiracy to dismiss union members. The MUA also found ways to fight the employer by alleging breaches of freedom of association and of employment contracts. The Workplace Relations Act was the legal basis of some of the relief that the Federal Court granted to the MUA.

THE ECLIPSE OF TRADE UNIONISM?

Trade unions have flourished under Australia's system of compulsory arbitration. As Foenander (1937: 10–11) wrote:

[A]t the very foundation of the Act there lies the implication that the
trade union is an integral in the modern industrial structure . . . The
factory or workshop of the employer is . . . no longer unreservedly his
castle . . . The Court is conscious of the shortcomings of unionism; but
as a principle, it believes that those defects are outweighed by the utility
of unionism and its possibility of social uplift.

By reconciling Australian employers to trade unionism, compulsory arbitration made pragmatists of non-Labor politicians. They might not have endorsed
Spence's 1910 declaration that 'Every organisation, whether it is a trade union
or not, is a good thing. A man who becomes a member of a group is always made
better by it' (*CPD* 29 July 1910: 841). But Australian political conservatives, until
the 1980s, learned to accept trade unions. It now seems remarkable that, after
one of the least compliant moments of Australian trade unions' history, the Liberal Party's Philip Lynch (1971: 243) would concede in 1971 that 'We . . . need
a strong trade union movement dedicated to furthering, by legitimate means, the
interests of its members, while at the same time recognising and respecting the
rights of others'.

One result of this conservative habituation to a strong trade union movement
was the extent and the resilience of the 'closed shop', the accumulated outcome of
a regulatory regime that favoured 'preference'. Zappala's review of studies of the
extent of 'closed shop' suggests that in the 1980s – that is, even after the demise
of the full employment economy – in many occupations and industries trade
unions have been able to maintain the established principle, essential to collective
employee strength, that all employees are in the union. The research shows that
many Australian employers (including governments) have been acquiescent and
even supportive of such arrangements (Zappala 1992). In the early versions of the
Accord, the ACTU and some members of the Hawke government attempted to
build on that solid industrial base a political edifice whose most cogent expression
was *Australia Reconstructed* (1987): an industry and incomes policy that aspired
to institutionalise trade union influence over the planning of Australian capitalism.

The Labor Party of Hawke and particularly of Keating proved to be not 'true
believers' in that vision of Australian government. Obituaries for the Accord cite
the influence of neo-liberal economists over not only business leaders but also
Labor politicians. They mention also the Labor leadership's primary valuation of

the Accord as an instrument for managing elections; the ambition of strong trade unions to accept workplace reform as the central measure of 'reconstruction' in exchange for greater scope for their collective bargaining; the importance of the ACTU as a career path for aspirant Labor MPs; and the difficulty of securing a popular valuation of the 'social' (as opposed to the 'money') wage (Higgins 1994; Bray 1994; Hampson 1996). Keating favoured an account of the Australian economy's flaws that highlighted 'inflexibility' in labour markets. Following the prescriptions of a business elite for the 'globalisation' of Australian society, his government shrank the domain of compulsory arbitration. Keating's innovations may have been intended to forestall the radical liberals. Certainly his successor, John Howard, has warmly endorsed their direction; he looks forward to the day when a non-Labor Senate majority might allow him to terminate compulsory arbitration.

In the 2001 election, Labor promised to legislate to compel employers to bargain 'in good faith' with unions. It would also have increased the number of strands of the 'safety net' under enterprise bargains. Labor would have put an end to the Employee Advocate (the Coalition's alternative to union advocacy of members' interests) and it would have done away with Australian Workplace Agreements. Under Labor, 'secondary boycotts' would be transferred from the sphere of civil law to the Commission's increased jurisdiction.

Labor did not win in 2001. At the time of writing, the Coalition seeks further reform of Australia's industrial relations framework. In limiting the authority of arbitration and the scope for trade union representation, their 1996 legislation reprises the nineteenth-century conservative ideal of the employer–employee contract as a relation among equals that is not to be fettered by monopolistic intermediaries. In that notion of 'freedom', Coalition policy further challenges the diminished eminence of trade unions. The fates of arbitration and of unions are linked now, as they were at the inception of Commonwealth arbitration.

2

ARBITRATION IN ACTION

Stuart Macintyre

The Commonwealth Court of Conciliation and Arbitration heard its first case on 5 November 1906.[1] The Merchant Service Guild, representing ships' officers, had lodged a claim for an award and the Commonwealth Steamship Owners Association responded on behalf of the various shipping companies that operated out of Australian ports. Billy Hughes, the Labor member for West Sydney in the Commonwealth Parliament and secretary of the Waterside Workers' Federation, appeared for the union; he had qualified for the Bar three years earlier. Arthur James Kelynack appeared for the employers; he had a substantial practice in common law.

The two parties had already conferred in the Sydney chambers of the Court's President, Mr Justice O'Connor, who wanted to see if it was possible to arrive at an 'amicable settlement'. They remained at odds over terms of engagement, levels of remuneration, hours of duty, classification levels and other matters. When the case came before the Court for arbitration, the President searched for some basis of determination, for he was conscious that he was creating a precedent for later claims. The Act that established the Court had laid down no principle other than that the Court should decide 'according to equity, good conscience and the substantial merits of the case'. O'Connor rejected the argument put to him by Hughes that the Court should ensure that all ships' officers were paid a 'living wage' that would support a family and household; he held that these employees already enjoyed such a level of remuneration. In the end he decided 'that the

Court is in each case to make such settlement of the matters in dispute as shall be fair and reasonable between the parties'. Having applied this yardstick to the claim of the Merchant Service Guild, he embodied the terms of their employment into an award that became their legal entitlement (1906 1 CAR 1–54).

The case occupied the Court for sixteen days of evidence and argument, and was completed on 12 December. The creation of the Court, by contrast, had exercised the Commonwealth Parliament for the best part of a year. The eventual Act established this new federal court, to consist of a President appointed for a seven-year term from among one of the three Justices of the High Court. The Court was empowered to make compulsory awards prescribing terms of employment so as to settle industrial disputes extending beyond the limits of any one State. The Court would register organisations of employers and employees, and proceed on plaints initiated by them; it could also register collective agreements to give these the force of awards, and it was charged to provide preliminary conciliation of disputes. The distinctive character of this system of industrial arbitration – for there were many precedents for arbitrating disputes between employers and employees – rested on the element of compulsion vested in a permanent and independent government tribunal. The procedure could be invoked by either party and the respondent was forced to participate; an award was binding, with a machinery to enforce awards, and prohibition of strikes and lockouts (Mitchell 1989).

Such was the initial design of an institution that would undergo repeated change and yet persist in recognisable form up to the present. Other chapters of this book relate how the Commonwealth system of industrial arbitration was shaped by politics and the courts, the approaches taken to it by the employers and the unions, its record in securing industrial peace, and its social and economic effects. This chapter is more particularly concerned with the structure, composition and operation of the tribunal. It follows the alteration and reconstitution of the original Court of Conciliation and Arbitration into the present Industrial Relations Commission. It examines the personnel who composed it and how they conducted their work. It considers the tribunal as an organisation with distinctive practices and customs, as a place of routine and drama, an instrument of adjudication and a forum where claims were argued and central aspects of industrial and working life were determined.

ESTABLISHMENT

Compulsory arbitration had been devised by the South Australian politician, Charles Kingston, as a response to the Maritime Strike of 1890. That strike, which drew in many other industries and brought economic activity to a standstill, began when the shipping companies refused to permit their maritime officers to affiliate to a body of trade unions. The ensuing confrontation turned on the rival claims of national combinations of employers and workers, and raised the spectre of violent class conflict. Kingston, along with other progressive liberals, sought a remedy that would resolve the antagonism and protect the public interest. A friend of labour, he accepted the legitimacy of workers combining to pursue their mutual interests. A lawyer and progressive politician in an advanced democracy, he therefore sought to bring the conduct of industrial relations into the ambit of a public tribunal.

Kingston was unable to implement his scheme in his own colony: the tribunals that were introduced there and in other Australian colonies during the 1890s lacked the powers to effect compulsory arbitration. The final session of the Australasian Convention in Melbourne in 1898 agreed narrowly to include arbitration of interstate disputes as a power of the Commonwealth (La Nauze 1972: 207–8). By then, the practicality of Kingston's invention had been demonstrated on the other side of the Tasman. The Liberal government of New Zealand had enacted legislation in 1894 that followed Kingston's original draft bill both in its structure and in much of its content. New South Wales in turn followed New Zealand closely for its Arbitration Act of 1901, while Western Australia adopted a similar model for the Arbitration Court it established in two legislative stages in 1900 and 1902. Victoria, on the other hand, had struck out in a different direction with boards that determined wages but had no role in dispute settlement (Mitchell 1989).

When the Commonwealth created its own Court of Conciliation and Arbitration, it was thus able to draw on working examples of compulsory arbitration for both institutional design and operational procedures. The New Zealand Court was a court of equity, empowered to summon witnesses and take evidence; the Commonwealth Court had the same authority. The President was a judge of the jurisdiction's highest court, though in New Zealand and in New South Wales he was assisted by two assessors, one representing the unions and one the employers; the Commonwealth Court relied on a single judge. The Victorian wages boards were also composed of elected representatives of employers and workers under an independent chairman. The absence of lay members emphasised the judicial character of the new Commonwealth Court, as did another distinguishing feature of the federal scheme. New Zealand created separate procedures for conciliation by appointing boards composed of union and employer representatives (Holt 1986: 41); the Commonwealth put both conciliation and arbitration in the hands of the judge who presided over this new federal court.

This emphasis upon the dual function of the Court was in keeping with its overriding purpose: to settle disputes and maintain industrial peace. Well before Henry Higgins characterised his jurisdiction as a 'new province for law and order', arbitration was described as a necessary extension of the rule of law. In his second reading speech on the original bill in 1903, Alfred Deakin anticipated Higgins in likening the substitution of industrial litigation for the reign of violence to the replacement of baronial wars by the King's Peace. Deakin saw this step as marking a process of social development from primitive lawlessness to advanced civilisation, and remarked that 'our remote ancestors' had once lived in a time of private feuds like the natives of Papua. The leader of the Opposition, George Reid, interjected: 'There were no lawyers amongst them then'. Deakin replied that 'The appearance of lawyers marks one of the first stages in social development' (*CPD* 30 July 1903: 2862–3).

This was an insiders' joke, for Reid, Deakin and Kingston (who had drafted the bill) were all barristers. Others were less sure that professional advocates would facilitate the operation of an industrial tribunal. The Commonwealth therefore followed its forerunners in allowing legal representation only with the consent of both parties – for, as Reeves (1902a: 2, 118) put it, 'The exclusion of barristers from the conduct of cases was an undoubted advantage, irrelevant and long-winded as a few of the lay agents and union officers were occasionally found to be'. Similarly, the legislation specified that the new Court would operate 'without regard to technicalities or legal forms, and shall not be bound by any rules of evidence, but may inform its mind on any matter in such manner as it thinks fit' (section 25), a provision that continues to the present day.

This left the office of president to be filled from the judiciary. Strictly, that arrangement was required if the new tribunal was to exercise the powers of a court of record, and there was already an Australian habit of removing contentious issues from the hazards of a trial of strength to determination by an independent body (Parker 1965; Hughes 1980). The shearers' leader, WG Spence, had told the New South Wales Royal Commission on the Maritime Strike (which itself was an illustration of the national proclivity) in 1891 that he thought any dispute-settling agency would require a chairman 'who has a trained mind and none are better than our judges'. Besides, Spence added, 'he would be impartial' (Bray and Rimmer 1989: 71).

The difficulty was to persuade a member of the High Court to undertake the additional duties. The Attorney-General, Josiah Symon, was in bitter dispute with the judges when he wrote to Richard O'Connor to ask that he accept nomination. Since Symon loathed the Chief Justice, Griffiths, and despised his colleague, Barton, the choice was limited – though O'Connor had little experience in industrial relations and less interest. He and the Attorney-General were both on summer holidays, so their letters and telegrams bypassed each other until on 1 February 1905 O'Connor wrote that he had consulted his colleagues and was willing to accept the office, on condition that he could resign if he found the new duties interfered with his work on the High Court. Symon insisted he could accept no such condition since it was a matter for the executive branch of government, and the argument, conducted with stately courtesy, remained unresolved when O'Connor's appointment was gazetted on 10 February 1905 (*CPP* 1905).

In fact, the presidency made little demand on O'Connor's time. After hearing the first application for an award in 1906, he had one more to consider in that year and just two in the following year – together they occupied twenty-six days of sittings – along with a number of shorter hearings of procedural matters. It was rather that O'Connor's duties on the High Court left him little time to arbitrate, so that the Merchant Service Guild had to wait for most of 1906 for its case to be heard.

A court requires premises, personnel and procedures. Following the passage of the *Commonwealth Conciliation and Arbitration Act 1904*, officers of the Attorney-General's Department drafted and gazetted the regulations that would

enable it to operate. A Registry was established in the Commonwealth's temporary capital, Melbourne, and district registries in the five other State capitals.
A Registrar was appointed in January 1905, GH Castle, who was already Chief
Clerk of the Attorney-General's Department and Registrar of the High Court.
The increasing demands of the High Court duties led to his replacement two years
later by Alexander Murdoch Stewart. He would serve as the Industrial Registrar
for two formative decades and eventually become a Conciliation Commissioner,
but for the time being he simply added his new responsibilities to those as Chief
Clerk of the High Court, and received no additional payment for them (NAA
A432 1929/2656; A432 1929/3456, part 3).

The arrangements for the Deputy Industrial Registrars were even more rudi-
mentary. The Commonwealth simply asked the States to provide an appropriate
officer to act in a part-time and unsalaried capacity. The States obliged, offering
the Registrar of the Supreme Court in three cases and officials of the State's arbitration courts in the case of New South Wales and Western Australia (NAA A432
1929/3456, part 1). This was meant to be a temporary arrangement until the
volume of work became evident, but it continued into the 1920s. The duties of the
Deputy Industrial Registrar in New South Wales were the most onerous because
of the volume of business there. Several incumbents resigned, and another withdrew on the insistence of his minister. A replacement was assisted by a chief
clerk (and the Commonwealth compensated the New South Wales government
for a portion of their salaries), yet they too were available on a part-time basis
only (NAA A432 1929/3456, parts 2 and 20). Indeed, the very first sitting of
the Court on 9 November 1905 was delayed by a failure of these arrangements.
The President travelled to Sydney to hear the appeal of a union over registration
only to discover that no Deputy Industrial Registrar had been appointed and no
papers had been sent from Melbourne (NAA A432 1929/3456, part 8).

All of the officers of the fledgling tribunal were thus working on a part-time
basis as they fashioned its procedures. They took over a familiar method of operation. A plaintiff served a log of claims on a respondent and the Court initially
tried to negotiate a settlement of them. The remaining matters were taken to arbitration, the arguments presented in adversarial fashion, the evidence presented,
witnesses examined and cross-examined, and a decision handed down and made
binding.

The Registrar exercised a further responsibility. A union seeking access to the Court had to provide the Registrar with details of the organisation, its constitution and rules, and submit annual returns of membership along with financial records. Registration gave the union coverage of a particular occupation and allowed it to serve claims on employers, who were required to respond. The system of industrial arbitration transformed unions from associations tolerated by the state into protected organisations that the Court recognised, assisted and regulated. The employers, who generally resisted this new dispensation, were themselves drawn into the Court's ambit and responded with their own arrangements.

The fledgling system of industrial arbitration thus brought employers and wage-earners into a new relationship that, in turn, shaped their own forms of industrial and political activity. It fostered the formation of unions and employers' associations, as parties to the Court's awards, as litigants in appeals against its decisions, and as political interest groups seeking legislative amendment of the Court's operation. Arbitration was also a subject of keen public interest. Even as the original legislation was being prepared, a journalist working for the Melbourne *Age* obtained and published a full outline of the bill. Its eventual enactment allowed the formation of the Australian Journalists' Association (Lloyd 1985: 55). Industrial arbitration was the most celebrated of the state experiments, bringing overseas investigators to Australia in the early years of the twentieth century. It was the most influential and durable feature of the arrangements devised by the Commonwealth to reconcile the social and economic objectives of nationhood.

HIGGINS' COURT

O'Connor's unwilling presidency did not last long. Legislation in 1906 created two more positions on the High Court, and in October Henry Higgins and Isaac Isaacs were appointed to them. It was understood that Higgins would replace O'Connor as President of the Court of Conciliation and Arbitration. Since Higgins had served as Attorney-General in the recent Labor ministry, and thought he should not proceed so quickly 'from my advocacy of labour claims as a member into a position in which I should have to drop wholly the attitude of a partisan', he asked Alfred Deakin, his friend and the Prime Minister, for a year's grace (Rickard 1984: 150). Higgins therefore succeeded to the presidency on 14 September 1907. Reappointed for a further seven-year term in 1914, he resigned on 29 June 1921, less than three months before the expiry of that term. His fourteen years at the helm established the Court as a major national institution.

'I had to learn the business', Higgins wrote, 'with no book of instructions, no teacher other than experience, no kindly light except for the pole star of justice' (Higgins 1922a: v). An immigrant youth of a genteel but impoverished family, he had worked as a teacher while training for his profession and built up a lucrative equity practice at the Melbourne bar. A friend of labour, he had represented a working-class electorate in the Commonwealth Parliament and served in a Labor government, but he was not a member of the Labor Party and formed no intimate friendships with its members. He had known the pinch of poverty but not the sweat and grind of manual toil, the aching limbs and shortened breath – his hands were smooth. He developed his jurisdiction, 'his new province for law and order' as he styled it, with a lawyer's regard for order and consistency. Each case had to be decided on its merits, according to the evidence and the law. A finding established a precedent for later cases, marking out the paths for those who came before his Court.

Higgins was presented in the first case that came before his Court with the opportunity to expand its scope from the settlement of disputes to the determination of wage standards. As part of its effort to foster economic growth and social harmony, and with the support of the Labor Party, Deakin's Liberal ministry had elevated the protection of local industries by tariffs into the doctrine of New Protection. Excise duties were imposed on local manufactures equivalent to the tariff duties on the imported product, but the excise duties would be waived if the President of the Arbitration Court certified that the manufacturer was paying 'fair and reasonable wages' to his workers. O'Connor had readily granted certificates of exemption to a number of manufacturers of agricultural machinery, but Higgins chose as a test case the application of a large employer, HV McKay of Sunshine, which was opposed by the unionists he employed.

In the hearing of what became known as the *Harvester* case, Higgins enunciated the principles he would use. A fair and reasonable wage could not be what was determined by ordinary bargaining, for the legislation clearly intended something more than 'the higgling of the market'. Nor could a fair and reasonable wage depend upon the level of profits; it should be regarded as a first charge and if an enterprise could not afford to pay an adequate wage, it was better abandoned. Higgins decided that the minimum wage should enable a male worker to live as 'a human being in a civilized community' and to keep his family in frugal comfort. Using some family budgets as evidence for the cost of living, he fixed the minimum wage at 7 shillings per day and refused McKay's application (1907 2 CAR 2–3).

The *Harvester* judgment was quickly established as a landmark of Australian social democracy. It provided the basis for the system of wage determination based on the cost of living that spread to take in the majority of Australian workers; and it gave institutional force to the privileged position of the male breadwinner. But McKay appealed against the decision and the High Court decided (with Higgins and Isaacs dissenting) that the Excise Tariff Act was invalid. This was just the first of many occasions when Higgins' colleagues in the High Court, usually on application by employers, overturned his decisions and trenched the operation of his Court. The principal cases are discussed elsewhere, and here the concern is with their effect on his work.

In a series of public statements, Higgins protested at the restrictions that were imposed on his jurisdiction: 'the approach to the Court is through a veritable Serbonian bog of technicalities; and the bog is extending' (1909 4 CAR 42). In the face of these restrictions, Higgins consolidated the procedures of his Court. It would hear a case on a plaint brought by either side in a dispute, and Higgins' initial step was usually to try to resolve the dispute in conference. If conciliation failed, the preliminary hearing was usually occupied by arguments over the nature of the dispute and whether the Court had jurisdiction. When Higgins had resolved this question to his own satisfaction (if not the High Court's), he would hear evidence on the matters in dispute in order to make a determination that would then be incorporated into an award. The award set out duties, rates of payment, hours and other conditions of employment in a comprehensive document that was binding on the parties. His Court sat wherever was most convenient for the case under consideration, borrowing chambers in the State capitals from the courts there. It travelled further afield, to inland towns and distant factories and mines, so that the President could inspect workplaces and get a better sense of working conditions.

The volume of business was increasing. In its first five years, the Court made just six awards, but it registered 61 organisations, and in the following decade a further 116 (Griffin and Scarcebrook 1990: 25). There was also a rise in the use of the Court to register agreements – just 9 were filed in the first five years, 24 in 1910, and no less than 94 in 1911 (*CPP* 1914–17). A Deputy President operated from 1913 but there were long delays in processing applications for awards. Meanwhile, the increasing use of boards of reference placed greater strains on the Registrar and Deputy Registrars.

The cost of arbitration was considerable. While the Court's charges were modest, a union had to outlay hundreds of pounds to serve claims on a large number of respondents, gather evidence and muster witnesses – and if the employers appealed to the High Court, the cost of defending an award might prove prohibitive. Unions seldom briefed barristers, though they usually retained solicitors. Sometimes the unions accepted the appearance of counsel for the employers; increasingly, they objected. Even then, Higgins usually ruled that the barristers could stay while preliminary legal issues were argued. Wrestling with a difficult procedural issue, he remarked: 'This is just the kind of difficulty in which I confess I would like to have the assistance of counsel skilful in the methods of the law, so that we might by pressure on both sides crack the nut and get the kernel' (*Argus* 6 December 1910). At the same time, he expressed vexation with the issues these lawyers raised. 'I have been exceedingly patient with you', he chastised a leading practitioner, 'but the more I see the lines on which you are going, the more I see that you are trying to find a technical flaw where there is an actual, practical and humane dispute that has to be dealt with' (*Argus* 31 May 1913).

Higgins conducted his Court with a minimum of formality. He dispensed with judicial robes and disdained the rituals of 'the lofty and inaccessible temple in which the mysteries of the law are stored' (Rickard 1984: 193). Yet he brooked no disrespect for his jurisdiction. In a case involving the Builders Labourers' Federation, the secretary of a bogus union was threatened with imprisonment for refusing to give evidence; having submitted to the authority of the Court, he was excused from doing so (*Argus* 25 October 1913). Recalcitrant employers and

One of the union complaints in the early years of conciliation and arbitration concerned the costs of registering and obtaining an award. The Boot Trade Employees' Federation kept this photograph of its witnesses who attended the Court in 1909.

union officers alike were admonished for impugning the integrity of the arbitration system. Higgins looked severely on employers who victimised workers for giving evidence. He took particular exception to parties that divulged confidential proceedings to the press or prejudiced hearings with public commentary. The conciliation process depended on privacy: 'It is obvious that in trying to get conflicting parties to any agreement it is often essential to keep the conference private, so that representatives may speak their minds freely, and discuss freely suggested concessions' (1910 CAR 5 45). It was just as obvious to him that those who made partisan claims on matters before the Court for arbitration were at fault, and he secured apologies from more than one employer's representative for such prejudicial conduct (*Argus* 23 May 1917, 18 May 1918).

HR NICHOLLS AND ARBITRATION IN CONTEMPT

The HR Nicholls Society was established in 1985 by a group of prominent Australians who held the arbitration system in contempt. At its inaugural seminar early in 1986, a number of speakers recalled Nicholls as a forthright defender of 'the liberty of the subject faced with the tyranny of arbitrary power' who had protested against 'the pollution of the real law, and the real courts, by politicised judges and over-powerful unions' (HR Nicholls Society 1986: 13, 156).

Henry Richard Nicholls was born in London in 1830 and under the influence of his socialist father was prominent in the Chartist reform movement. He migrated to Melbourne in 1853 and his brother joined him in Ballarat in the following year. The two enrolled at the Eureka stockade but left before troops overran it. Charles went into mining, Henry into journalism, and their progressive sympathies weakened as their business ventures prospered. Henry Nicholls contributed to the *Argus*, owned the *Ballarat Star* and became editor of the Hobart *Mercury* in 1883.

His editorial on 7 April 1911 was prompted by an angry exchange in the Court of Conciliation and Arbitration between Higgins and Hayden Starke, a leader at the Melbourne bar and afterwards a colleague of Higgins on the High Court bench. Starke, appearing for the employers, alleged that the Broken Hill miners were encouraged in their breaches of agreements by the unions and the government. Higgins refused to countenance such language: 'I will not allow you to speak in that form of a Government of the country and those above us. If you do not comply with my rules you will leave the Court.'

In calling Higgins a political judge appointed for his political services, the *Mercury* said he would not allow any reflections 'on those to whom he may be said to be indebted for his judgeship'. There was a Labor government at the time and Nicholls seems to have been under the misapprehension that Higgins had been appointed to his post by an earlier one.

Nicholls did not appear when the case was heard in Melbourne; his doctor said he was too frail at the age of 82 (he was in fact 81) to make the journey. The Crown's case was that the leader was calculated to bring a judge of the High Court into disrepute. The Chief Justice dismissed the case on the grounds that the words complained of were not calculated to interfere with the course of justice in the High Court. He noted, however, that the 'respondent has very properly expressed his regret for having used something which is capable of being construed as a disrespectful comment, which he did not intend' (*Argus* 23 May, 8 June 1911; Rickard 1984: 185–7). HR Nicholls, it seems, was a reluctant martyr.

In his early years, Higgins received many abusive letters, unsigned but nearly all of them 'from partisans of the employers' (Higgins 1922a: 40). His observations on the inequity of the wage relationship were a particular provocation. For Higgins, the employer was in a much stronger position than the individual employee, for whom the catchcry of freedom of contract amounted in practice to 'despotism in contract'. The worker, he remarked on one occasion, 'is in the same position, in principle, as Esau, when he surrendered his birthright for a square meal, or as a traveller, when he had to give up his money to a highwayman for the privilege of life' (Rickard 1984: 185–6). A storm of criticism followed these remarks, which was scarcely mollified when Higgins had his judgment printed and made available so that those with 'impartial minds' could see how the press had misrepresented it (*Argus* 19 May 1911). More than once, he delivered statements from the bench in response to 'slovenly, reckless and untrustworthy' newspaper reports on his work (*Argus* 21 August 1917).

The *Argus*, a conservative Melbourne daily, was the chief offender, though it was the editor of the Hobart *Mercury* who stung Higgins to an unwise overreaction. Commenting on an exchange in the Court between Higgins and counsel for the employers, the *Mercury* described Higgins as 'a political judge', who had been appointed for his political services and continued to serve those who appointed him (*Mercury* 7 April 1911). At Higgins' behest, a charge of contempt was brought against HR Nicholls, the aged editor of the *Mercury*. The High Court dismissed the charge, making a hero of Nicholls in his home town and providing later critics of arbitration with an illustrious martyr (*Argus* 19 and 23 May, 8 June 1918; 1918 25 CLR 280–6).

The Court of Conciliation and Arbitration, it seemed, was an anomalous national institution, operating both as a legislature and a court. It was a legislature in the sense that it created new laws – awards – that governed industry. It was also a court in that it interpreted its awards, enforced them and punished violations. As a lawmaker, it was subject to public commentary and often virulent criticism of its actions; as a court, it was supposedly a separate branch of government, removed from the ruck of partisan interests. The combination of functions created some of Higgins' difficulties but more of them followed from the fact that his Court lacked the full power of either agency. It was a subordinate legislature, subject to the strictures of the legislators who had created it, and it was something less than a court because of the restrictions imposed by the High Court.

In 1914, the Labor Attorney-General, Billy Hughes, complained that the inability of the Court to arbitrate except in the case of a genuine dispute (the existence of which only the High Court could determine) was nullifying its capacity to maintain industrial peace. He suggested that the Court should have inscribed over its portals 'None who will not strike may enter here'. The problem was compounded by the insistence of the President that he would not hear an application from any union whose members were on strike. 'It serves to disgust unions with arbitration', Hughes complained, 'it is intolerable and it cannot be permitted to continue' (*Argus* 29 October 1914). Within a year, Hughes had succeeded Andrew Fisher as leader of the wartime Labor government, and he quickly used the extraordinary provisions of the Wartime Precautions Act to impose his will on all aspects of national government. Thwarted by his party over his determination to introduce conscription for overseas service, he formed a new government that was more submissive. Billy Hughes, who had previously appeared before the Court on behalf of unions, now acted as a law unto himself. He soon came into collision with the fiercely independent Higgins.

The question at issue was the independence of the Court in a period of national sacrifice, when industrial dislocation jeopardised the war effort. In 1915, Higgins was prepared to accommodate the government when members of the Waterside Workers' Federation refused to accept an award (1915 9 CAR 298–304). This extenuation of the union's apparent breach of an award infuriated the conservative press and alarmed Higgins' deputy, Mr Justice Powers, who had to be dissuaded from resigning.

In 1916, Hughes approached the Registrar to suggest appeasement of another recalcitrant union in a vital industry. The coal-miners were demanding an eight-hour day and Higgins would not hear their claim while they remained on strike. Hughes proposed that Higgins concede the union's claims as a commissioner acting under the Wartime Precautions Act. Higgins was reluctantly prepared to use these powers to hear the case but insisted he should be free to judge the merits of the claim, so Hughes turned instead to a New South Wales judge who did as the Prime Minister asked (*Argus* 14 September, 13 and 28 October 1916, 23 October, 7–13 November 1917; Fitzhardinge 1979: 220–5).

In the following year, the two men were again at odds. A dispute among railway workers in New South Wales spread to the maritime industry and Hughes decided to break the union he had once led by applying to the Court for the

The recent decision of Mr. Justice Higgins in the Waterside Workers' case (which he refused to de-register) caused the Hughes Ministry to talk of reviewing his position as an Arbitration Court Judge.

THE ONE MAN.

AUSTRALIA (to Judge Higgins): "Thanks—to you, at least, I can look for justice."

Higgins' refusal to cancel the registration of the Waterside Workers' Federation when it stopped work in 1917 brought to a head his insistence that the Court should not operate at the bidding of the prime minister. His dignified appearance as he receives the gratitude of a feminine Australia evokes the earlier depiction of George Higinbotham, a judge Higgins took as his model. Hughes is represented as a diminutive imp who clings to the sword of power.

registration of the Waterside Workers' Federation to be cancelled. At the same time, he gazetted a regulation under the Wartime Precautions Act to give the Governor-General in council the power to deregister any striking union. Higgins denounced this regulation as 'a sword hanging over me' and refused the application for deregistration. Several weeks later, Higgins revealed Hughes' actions in the earlier coal dispute, and the Prime Minister's denials ('It is a deliberate and monstrous fabrication') occasioned a lengthy exchange that did little to restore his credibility. Characteristically, Higgins had the entire exchange published in the reports of his Court (1917 11 CAR 994–1002).

Finally, in 1919, the government intervened once more in an effort to resolve a dispute in the maritime industry. The Seamen's Union refused to work under an award recently handed down by Higgins, which he was reluctant to improve. The government tried compulsory conferences in the Court and then private negotiations with the union to reach a settlement. Meanwhile, the High Court had decided in 1918 that the Arbitration Court was not a court (on the grounds that its President was not appointed for life), so that its powers to enforce awards were invalid (1918 25 CLR 434). When the government passed an Industrial Peace Act, which allowed it to create special tribunals for the settlement of particular disputes, Higgins declared that 'a tribunal of reason cannot do its work side by side with executive tribunals of panic', and announced his resignation (Higgins 1922a: 176). This time, the government did not allow him to publish his statement in the Court's reports (Higgins 1924: 15) and he therefore combined it with some earlier articles on the work of the Court in a book that became his testament. *A New Province for Law and Order: Being a Review, by its Late President for fourteen years, of the Australian Court of Conciliation and Arbitration* concluded with his pronouncement that 'the public usefulness of the Court has been fatally injured' (Higgins 1922a: 176).

BETWEEN THE WARS

Yet the Court survived. Hughes did not proceed with the provisions of his Industrial Peace Act, but instead ended the exclusive authority of the President. Higgins had recently granted an application for a 44-hour week, and the Act was amended in 1920 to stipulate that in future three judges would be needed to alter the length of the working week. (In the same year, public servants were removed from the

"THE WRECKER."

Judge Higgins says the public usefulness of the Arbitration Court has been fatally injured, and caustically blames the Prime Minister for it.

AUSTRALIAN UNIONIST (to Hughes): "You may know something about mending umbrellas—but you've made a wreck of a real good car."

In announcing his resignation from the Court, Higgins said that its public usefulness had been fatally injured. This cartoon from the labour press lays the blame on the prime minister.

Court's jurisdiction and a separate Public Service Arbitrator created.) In place of Higgins the government selected Charles Powers, the least distinguished member of the High Court, to preside over the Arbitration Court. Various other members of the High Court served as deputy presidents until two permanent appointments were made in 1922; one of them, John Quick, had been a member of the Commonwealth Parliament, and the other, Noel Webb, had previously served on the South Australian Arbitration Court. Thus assisted, Powers restored the 48-hour week to Commonwealth awards in 1922.

Charles Powers had been a solicitor in rural Queensland, then a barrister and State parliamentarian, the Crown Solicitor for Queensland and finally for the Commonwealth before appointment to the High Court in 1913. Although a Labor appointee, he was proud of his conservative industrial record: when he wrote to the Attorney-General in 1925 asking for a knighthood, he drew attention to his restoration of the 48 hours, his refusal to implement the recommendations of Piddington's Royal Commission on the basic wage, and other rebuffs to union claims (Fricke 2001). He had, however, introduced the practice of automatic indexation of the basic wage for changes in the cost of living. Powers' Court was subjected to criticism from both sides of industry, yet the volume of business continued to increase as its coverage expanded to take in most of the major industries: there were 261 applications for awards in 1920 and 1921, 460 in 1924 and 1925 (Powers 1926). This was a period of overlapping coverage when unions used the most favourable jurisdiction, but by the end of the decade half of all trade unionists worked under federal awards (Frazer 2001: 116).

Following its return to office, the government sought to extend the federal industrial power by removing the restriction of conciliation and arbitration to interstate disputes. The constitutional referendum failed, as did a further proposal to give the Commonwealth control of essential services. The government had meanwhile reconstructed the Court by a new Conciliation and Arbitration Act in 1926. Ever since the High Court decision of 1918, the Court had lacked judicial authority and relied on the magistrates' courts for enforcement of its decisions. Now the Court was to consist of judges appointed for life and therefore able to exercise a judicial function to police its awards. Provision was also made for the appointment of Conciliation Commissioners, to facilitate the settlement of disputes and ease the congestion of the Court.

George James Dethridge, the first Chief Judge of the Commonwealth Court of Conciliation and Arbitration (1926–1938).

The labour movement was generally supportive of these changes, which held out the prospect of officers with greater expertise working on a full-time basis to improve the Court's operation. There were reservations about strengthening the judicial nature of arbitration. Percy Coleman, the Labor member for Reid and secretary of a public service union, spoke for many when he suggested the Court should 'set aside purely legal considerations and adjudicate upon the conflicting claims'. Not unreasonably, a senior Nationalist asked, 'How does the honourable member expect a bench of lawyers to put aside legal considerations and procedures?' (*CPD* 17 June 1926: 3038–9).

In 1927, the first Chief Judge of the new Court expressed his regret that the Act maintained the restriction on the appearance of counsel. It was, he said, a policy of 'penny wise, pound foolish' (*Argus* 14 September 1927). Later in the same year, John Latham, the Attorney-General, introduced new amendments to the Act, and among them one that allowed lawyers to appear at the leave of the Court in applications for interpretation or variation of awards. A Labor member remarked that 'These lawyers are non-unionists'. Latham replied that 'The lawyers' union at least gives a guarantee of a certain amount of training, which is some guarantee of efficacy' (*CPD* 15 December 1927: 3285). By this time, arbitration had spawned a growing legal practice, and barristers were beginning to specialise in industrial advocacy.

The reconstitution of the Arbitration Court in 1926 increased its formality. An application from the Amalgamated Engineering Union in 1926 for a 44-hour week brought no less than 25 advocates, 543 exhibits and 145 witnesses before the Court. They included expert witnesses: JT Sutcliffe of the Commonwealth Bureau of Census and Statistics and Frederic Benham, a lecturer in economics at the University of Sydney, provided conflicting advice on the capacity of the economy to bear the reduction in hours. The hearing lasted four months and, with Judge Lukin dissenting, the Court granted the claim (Foenander 1928). Such lengthy hearings increased the congestion of the Court; by 1928 there were nine applicants for awards who had been waiting longer than two years (Anderson 1929: 42).

The easing of restrictions on the appearance of counsel was part of a series of further changes made in the *Commonwealth Conciliation and Arbitration Act 1928* that were designed to strengthen the Court's powers over union militancy. Henceforth, a union would be responsible for strikes called by its branches or even unauthorised stoppages by members; the Court could order a secret ballot for election of union officials at the request of just ten members, and on its own initiative order a secret ballot on any issue that arose in the course of a dispute. The 1928 Act made it an offence to prevent any person from working in accordance with an award, and the Court was given a general power to punish contempt (Sawer 1956: 269–70). Coupled with these draconian measures were amendments made to the Crimes Act in 1926 that were designed to prevent unions from escaping the Court's discipline. While technically the new provisions merely extended to unregistered unions, the penalties that the Arbitration Court could impose on registered ones, the inclusion of strike action in a statute dealing with serious criminal offences, caused particular affront.

So too did the appointments to the reconstituted Court. The Chief Judge was George Dethridge, previously a judge of the Victorian County Court. He was scrupulous in attention to detail and gained respect for his willingness to listen. The two Judges, on the other hand, were regarded as inimical to labour. George Beeby had been a pioneer of the Labor Party in New South Wales, but broke away to form his own Progressive Party in 1912 and became an alarmist critic of industrial unrest. Upright and formal, painfully aloof, he would stand on his dignity. The third Judge was Lionel Lukin, an outspoken conservative from the Supreme Court of Queensland who had clashed repeatedly with the Labor premiers of that State. They were joined in 1927 by Edmund Drake-Brockman, who until the previous year had been a Nationalist senator and president of the Australian Employers' Federation.

Speaking during the debate on the Conciliation and Arbitration Act of 1928, Matt Charlton, until recently the leader of the Labor Party, warned that the government had made 'a declaration of war against the organised workers of Australia' (*CPD* 16 May 1928: 4892). The Bruce–Page government restructured, recomposed and strengthened the Court as it grappled with a deteriorating economy. The country had borrowed heavily to finance development projects and financiers were concerned that the foreign capital was being used to prop up an unsustainable standard of living. In 1928, a British Economic Mission warned that the cost structure of Australian industry was too high and that 'the combined operation of the tariff and of the Arbitration Acts has raised costs to a level which has laid an excessive and possibly even a dangerous load upon the unsheltered primary industries' (*CPP* 1929).

In a series of decisions that began in the same year, the Court used its new powers to reduce the burden of labour costs. In August 1928, Judge Beeby handed down a new award for the Waterside Workers' Federation that reduced overtime rates and required attendance at a second daily pick-up. The federation was fined when some branches refused to work under the award, and the government used the Transport Workers' Act to license strike-breakers. Then Judge Lukin made a new award for the Timber Workers' Union that increased hours and reduced wages; again the government used its strengthened powers to break union resistance. Finally, in March 1929, the coal-owners locked out the mining unions for refusing to accept a cut in hewing rates. While Judge Beeby made an interim award restoring the old rates, the owners appealed successfully to the High Court, which struck down the award; meanwhile, the government withdrew prosecution of a leading coal-owner for locking out his workers. The aggrieved miners were starved into submission (Hagan 1981: 91–3; Macintyre 1986: 247–8).

These events brought protest and open defiance. In 1927, the secretary of the New South Wales Labor Council led a march of the Amalgamated Engineering Union on a Court sitting in Sydney when Beeby provided for piecework and daily hiring; the union members chanted, 'One in gaol, all in gaol' (Hagan 1981:

84). After Lukin ordered a ballot of the striking timber workers, they burned the ballot papers issued by the Court along with an effigy of the judge (Dixson 1963). In February 1929, the ACTU passed a resolution 'that all unions now before the Federal Arbitration Court be urged not to proceed with their claims' (*Sydney Morning Herald* 11 February 1929).

Yet when Bruce proposed to abandon the field of industrial relations to the States, the labour movement rallied behind the arbitration system. In an atmosphere of imminent economic crisis, Bruce had clearly despaired of the Court's capacity to make the adjustments to wage levels he thought necessary, and arbitration had manifestly failed to maintain industrial peace. In advising business leaders of his intention to abolish arbitration, he warned them that it would be impolitic if the public announcement 'were greeted with paeans of joy and triumph by the employers' federations' (Macintyre 1986: 249).

With the assistance of the vengeful Billy Hughes and other government rebels, the Labor Party defeated Bruce's proposal in the parliament in September 1929 and then won the ensuing election that was effectively a plebiscite on the issue. Labor's victory ensured the maintenance of the Court as a national institution, albeit one that vexed both sides of industry. The unions were enraged when the Court decided in January 1931 to cut the basic wage and all wage rates by 10 per cent. After the judges handed down their decision, cries of 'thieves' were heard in the Court and unionists gathered round the table occupied by their representatives to sing 'The Red Flag'. The secretary of the ACTU, who was the chief union advocate, called for three cheers for the social revolution (*Sydney Morning Herald* 23 January 1931). But the following ACTU congress rejected a motion calling for abandonment of arbitration.

The Labor government was committed to substantial reform of the Court and the ACTU urged it to 'provide for a system of sound business-like arbitration, free from the entangling legalisms of the Law Court . . . to ensure equitable expeditious and less costly methods of dealing with industrial matters' (Hagan 1981: 96). The government obliged in 1930 with a bill that removed many of the penalty provisions in the Act, restored the restrictions on representation by lawyers, gave the Conciliation Commissioners award-making powers, and created Conciliation Committees (consisting of representatives of employers and unions, as in New Zealand) to work with them. The High Court disallowed the

powers given to the Conciliation Committees, while the Senate weakened the
other changes; henceforth lawyers could appear subject to approval by the Court
and agreement of the parties (Sawer 1963: 13–17).

There were no further changes to the Court itself, other than the retirement
of Lukin in 1930 to become federal judge in bankruptcy (the failure of the Labor
government to make a more congenial replacement is surprising) and the appointments in 1938 and 1939 of two new judges. Harold Piper was a South Australian
lawyer and company director, a member of both the Adelaide and Melbourne
Clubs. Thomas O'Mara had worked in the Attorney-General's Department of
New South Wales and the Department of Labour and Industry before he practised industrial law, usually appearing for the employers. Chief Judge Dethridge
died in 1938 and was succeeded in that post by Judge Beeby.

This was the Court that the secretary of the New South Wales branch of the
Australian Railways Union recalled:

> I never forget my first experience in an Arbitration Court, it was before a
> Full Bench hearing. The judges were arrayed in wigs and gowns, and
> there was a full exhibition of Court conduct and paraphernalia. My own
> impression was that it was an awe-inspiring spectacle designed to force
> its attitude and decisions rather than to serve justice in respect of claims
> put forward on behalf of workers. (Walker 1970: 86)

In 1932, 1933 and 1934, the ACTU and the unions approached the Court
seeking restoration of the 10 per cent cut in the basic wage. ACTU officers
would present the union case, arguing both on economic grounds and by appeal
to Higgins' principle of entitlement. On each occasion, the employers' advocates
opposed any increase and the full bench of the Court affirmed its new criterion
of industry's capacity to pay. Taking advice from economists, the Court awarded
a limited increase in 1934. A further increase in 1937 still fell short of the union
claim. Victoria in 1934 and New South Wales in 1937 required their tribunals
to apply the Commonwealth decisions, and while a majority of wage-earners still
worked under State awards, the Commonwealth Court was exercising increasing
control over national wage policy. Unions with communist leadership – which by
the later 1930s included the Seamen's Union, the Waterside Workers' Federation,

the Miners' Federation, the Federated Ironworkers' Association and the powerful New South Wales branch of the Australian Railways Union – challenged these constraints with industrial campaigns that wrested limited concessions from the federal and State tribunals.

RECONSTRUCTION

During the Second World War, the government assumed a large measure of direct control over industrial relations. Regulations gazetted under the National Security Act controlled wages. The government used its manpower regulations to direct labour to essential industries and provide higher rates for those working in them. Through the Women's Employment Board it determined wages in industries where there was no award for female workers. The stevedoring, maritime and coal mining industries were placed under the control of special tribunals. This left the Arbitration Court with the task of settling disputes, and further wartime regulations enlarged its powers to do so.

In its last month in office in August 1941, the Menzies government was presented with the opportunity to make further appointments to the Court when George Beeby retired as Chief Judge. It appointed Harold Piper to the position. Raymond Kelly, who for the past decade had been President of the South Australian Industrial Court, filled the vacancy on the bench. Scholarly, gentle, dogmatic and authoritarian, Kelly would become a lightning rod for discontent with the Court. The Curtin government made just one wartime appointment, Alfred Foster, who chaired the Women's Employment Board until he joined the Arbitration Court in

Sir George Stephenson Beeby, the second Chief Judge of the Court (1939–1941).

October 1944. Foster had been a member of the Victorian Socialist Party, like Curtin, then a labour lawyer, and from 1928 a judge of the Victorian County Court. A rationalist and civil libertarian, outspoken and domineering in manner, he was soon at odds with Kelly.

At the end of the war, the Chifley government reconstructed the Court. Simplification of arbitration was a long-standing objective of the labour movement and the Labor government's control of both houses of federal parliament offered the opportunity of achieving it. The ACTU wanted the existing Court to be replaced by a new one with a purely judicial function and a single judge; that would leave the settlement of disputes and making of awards to the Conciliation Commissioners (Sheridan 1989: 151). The government had no intention of passing control over wages and hours to these lay officers. There were already claims for an increase in the basic wage and a reduction of the working week to forty hours. Preoccupied with the danger of inflation in a period of post-war reconstruction, Chifley would resist these claims for as long as he could. Meanwhile, the impatience of militant unions brought a sharp rise in industrial disputes; Chifley was determined to maintain the authority of the Court. His Commonwealth Conciliation and Arbitration Act of 1947 made the Arbitration Court a superior court of record with power to impose penalties for contempt of its orders.

The Act kept the Court to arbitrate on hours and wages, while increasing the number of Conciliation Commissioners and giving them power to make binding awards on other matters. There was no appeal from decisions by these Commissioners, who were not required to possess legal qualifications, and lawyers were virtually excluded from their hearings. While the Chief Judge allocated their duties aided by the new Chief Commissioner, there was clear potential for inconsistency between the two arms. This became apparent before the end of the year when the Chief Commissioner granted increases in the margins of metal trades that the Full Court had refused just a few months earlier. The Act was amended in 1952 to allow for appeals and references from the Commissioners to the judges, and also from the Public Service Arbitrator to the Court.

Of the sixteen Conciliation Commissioners initially appointed under the 1947 Act, six were former trade union officials, two had Labor Party backgrounds, four had worked in arbitration (chiefly on the registry side), two were public servants and two were lawyers (Foenander 1952: 222). If the unions expected more sympathetic treatment from these 'dilutee judges', however, they were quickly disappointed (Sheridan 1989: 156–7). Meanwhile, the government appointed Judge Drake-Brockman Chief Judge following the resignation of Chief Judge Piper in 1947, and Kelly succeeded the ailing Drake-Brockman on his death two years later. Judge O'Mara died in 1946. Several new appointments were made. Bernard Sugerman, a Sydney barrister, was a judge for a year but left in 1947 to join the New South Wales Supreme Court. He was replaced by Richard Kirby, who had become part of the circle of labour lawyers that formed around Bert Evatt in Sydney. In 1949, as relations between the Chifley government and the communist unions broke down completely, it added Edward Dunphy, the head of the Western Australian Arbitration Court and a devoted anti-communist. Kelly gave Dunphy responsibility for supervising union ballots, a task he relished and conducted openly as a campaign against the left-wing influence in unions (CCCA 1951).

The Court could not avoid becoming involved in this confrontation, which was played out against the international and domestic background of the Cold War, since the strength of the Australian Communist Party (which had reached a peak membership of 23 000 at the end of 1944) lay in the unions. The communist hostility to arbitration, always less absolute than its declarations suggested, found expression in this period in a series of campaigns to win by industrial action what the Court would not grant. When a communist union official who represented the Federated Ironworkers' Association in the Basic Wage Case that began in 1949 said as much – 'This issue will be decided outside the Arbitration Court. We do not trust the people in charge of the court to play the game' – he was charged with contempt and punished by the Full Court with a month's imprisonment. Later in the year, Chief Judge Kelly sentenced a miner's official to the same term for refusing to divulge where the union funds, which the Court had ordered to be paid to the Industrial Registrar, had gone. Judge Foster subsequently increased the sentence to a year and extended it to a number of communist union leaders after members of the Waterside Workers' Federation assembled outside the Court and counted him out (Larmour 1985: 194–9).

The antagonism was exacerbated by the conviction of the Chief Judge that industrial disputation was unnecessary. Drawn to the corporatist program of Catholic Action, in 1952 Kelly took the extraordinary step of issuing a letter to employers and unions that set out his vision of an organic peasant society, proclaimed that 'contentment and peace and happiness are only to be found in the acceptance of authority', and suggested a wage reduction. On hearing of Kelly's letter, the Prime Minister was reported to have exclaimed, 'God save me from my friends!' (d'Alpuget 1977: 128, 139).

Kelly was a remarkably impolitic Chief Judge. He wanted to deny any increase in the Basic Wage Case of 1949–50. Judge Foster, with whom he no longer communicated, wanted to award a large increase of £1 (or 15 per cent). Judge Dunphy was closer in sympathy to Kelly than Foster, but felt some increase was required. Since his two senior colleagues would not compromise, he found no alternative but to side with Foster and leave the Chief Judge in the minority. The Court was similarly divided over the unions' claim for equal pay for women: Kelly saw no reason to alter the old rate of 54 per cent of the male wage; Foster favoured 75 per cent and Dunphy followed him (Larmour 1985: 204–9). This case, which occupied twenty-two months, involved 225 witnesses and ran to more than 8000 pages of transcript, indicated that the reconstructed Court was no less cumbrous than its predecessor. A subsequent case involving the Professional Engineers extended over no less than eight years and their award cost them £100 000 (CCAC 1960: 20; Hutson 1966: 71).

The Commonwealth Court of Conciliation and Arbitration in 1952. From left to right: Justices McIntyre, Dunphy and Foster, Chief Judge Sir Raymond Kelly, Justices Kirby and Wright. The Industrial Registrar, J.E. Taylor, is seated at a lower level in front.

The next Basic Wage Case began in 1952 before an enlarged bench of seven. The Coalition government, returned to office at the end of 1949, appointed the new judges: Sydney Wright, a distinguished employers' advocate who, upon appointment, revealed his sympathy for the working class (d'Alpuget 1977: 150); 'Bunny' McIntyre, the only solicitor ever appointed to the Court; and Edward Morgan, who had succeeded Kelly as head of the South Australian Industrial Court and held views similar to those of his predecessor. Kelly wanted to abandon the system of automatic quarterly indexation and was assisted when first Wright, then Foster, withdrew from the hearing; Foster's withdrawal, after nine months of hearings, caused particular controversy as Kelly insisted the case must begin again. The High Court disagreed and late in 1953 Kelly finally obtained his object of abolishing indexation of the basic wage (d'Alpuget 1977: 128–38; Dabscheck 1995: 143–8).

The decision brought a storm of protest. Albert Monk, the ACTU president had already described the Court as 'a Frankenstein monster', and a decision by the full bench in the following year not to increase margins caused the ACTU executive to call it 'a menace to the industrial peace' (d'Alpuget 1977: 140; Hagan 1981: 290). The impatience of the ACTU president with the Court's inflexibility was shared by Harold Holt, the Minister for Labour, and his powerful departmental secretary, Henry Bland, who sought closer relations with the union peak body.

Morale was not assisted by the Court's dilapidated and cramped facilities. The fact that the Commissioners were housed several blocks away exacerbated their discontent. Kelly, who resented the enhancement of their authority in the 1947 Act, made little effort to assist them. The Chief Judge placed great emphasis on the formality of his Court; he objected to lay advocates and in 1951 secured an unfettered discretion to admit counsel, including to hearings by the Commissioners. In the same year, he gained the title of 'Honourable' for the members of his Court, and for himself assumed the more prestigious designation of Chief Justice, which he had inscribed on his wig tin. When the tin was presented by mistake to the Chief Justice of the High Court, the latter was not amused (d'Alpuget 1977: 117). An appeal from the Boilermakers' Society against fines imposed by the Arbitration Court allowed Sir Owen Dixon to quash the pretensions of the

'ROSTELLA'

The Court of Conciliation and Arbitration began with part-time officers and borrowed premises; the first Registry was accommodated in the Attorney-General's Department in Spring Street, Melbourne. A growing volume of business after the First World War made its President anxious to obtain a separate building in Melbourne.

In 1920, Mr Justice Powers learned that the Navy Board was vacating a building at the western end of Lonsdale Street, close to the Law Courts, and asked Robert Garran, the Commonwealth Solicitor General, to inspect it with him.

The building was named 'Rostella', a freestanding Victorian mansion of three storeys. It had been built in 1868–69 for Sir Thomas Fitzgerald, a leading surgeon, who added a tower in 1885. Among his collection of fine pictures was Lefebvre's *Chloe*, which is now displayed in Young and Jackson's hotel (Macdonald 1972).

'Rostella' was designed for gracious living. The massive arcaded loggia gave entrance to a grand vestibule and spiral staircase, with spacious formal rooms on the ground floor. Powers was especially excited by the ballroom and its dais, as he thought this would make an excellent Bench for his Court. He did notice the motto inscribed at the back of the dais by the Naval Board — 'Strike first, strike hard, strike often!' — and insisted that it be painted out before the Press was admitted to the new premises (Garran 1958: 282).

The Court remained at 'Rostella' for the next forty years. Selby Hastings, who would become a Deputy Registrar and later a Commissioner, commenced work there in 1940, standing before a slope-topped ledger desk and inscribing notification of disputes into a leather-bound register. His early duties also included rolling empty beer kegs down the spiral staircase after a Christmas party (Hastings 2001).

'Rostella' allowed a straitened grandeur. Coal burned in marble fireplaces in the judges' chambers, but there was no room for their associates. There were baths of Olympian proportion but the sanitary arrangements were primitive. The annual reports of the 1950s paint a plaintive picture of judges three to a chamber, a Registry forced out into another building, and counsel squeezed into the hopelessly cramped and inadequate former ballroom. The Court had to use the High Court's second Melbourne courtroom when it was available and even hold hearings at the Hawthorn Town Hall (*CPP* 1952: 1207).

The staff endured these privations until 1958, when they moved into new, purpose-built premises in 451 Little Bourke Street. Within a decade, the Commission was spilling out of them, and in 1979 it moved to Nauru House. It served for the next quarter-century and the Commission will shortly move again to another new building at the southern end of Exhibition Street.

An exterior view of 'Rostella' shows the colonnade, pediment and tower of the mansion that Powers obtained for the Court.

subordinate tribunal. By a narrow majority, his bench decided that the Arbitration Act had no power to punish contempt on the grounds that, since its primary function was arbitral, it could not be invested with judicial functions.

THE COMMISSION

The government took the opportunity to separate the two activities and remove Kelly to a far more limited role. It established an Industrial Court to perform the judicial functions and a Conciliation and Arbitration Commission to carry out the essential business of resolving disputes and making awards. Kelly was to be the Chief Judge of the new Court, with Dunphy and Morgan as its two other members, but Kelly died before the appointment was made and the senior post was instead taken by John Spicer, who as Attorney-General had informed the members of the old court that it was to be broken up.

The judges were indignant at the apparent loss of status attached to the new Commission since the government wanted to dispense with the legal formality that it saw as encumbering its operation. Foster protested publicly that the government's legislation would make him 'just Mr Alfred William Foster', and Kirby drafted a petition to Menzies on behalf of the aggrieved judges that explained the 'personal humiliation' they would feel to have the wigs 'removed from their heads by Act of Parliament' (Larmour 1985: 223; d'Alpuget 1977: 147–8).

A compromise was reached: the four members who transferred to the Commission (Foster, Kirby, Wright and Ashburner) retained their titles and life tenure but agreed to give up their wigs and gowns except on ceremonial occasions. Various legalistic remnants were retained and remain to this day in formal hearings: the bar table, the raised platform, bowing to the Commissioners as they enter the chamber. The presidential members retained their associates and tipstaffs.

The legislation laid down that these presidential members of the Commission would have legal qualifications, and maintained the distinction between them and the lay Commissioners, whose numbers were halved and supplemented by three specialist Conciliators (a position abolished in 1974). The process of conciliation allowed for greater informality. Jackets were worn and surnames used in hearings of the Commission; arguments were addressed to the bench. During conciliation, the jackets came off, cigarettes were lit and participants addressed each other by their first names.

While the lay Commissioners continued to arbitrate within the industries to which they were allocated, the new structure made systematic provision for reference or appeal of cases to the presidential members or a mixed bench of presidential and lay Commissioners. Relations improved further when the entire staff of the Commission was brought together in 1958 in a new building in Little Bourke Street. The Commission was far more responsive to local needs and in its first year conducted proceedings in Launceston and Devonport, Newcastle and Port Kembla, Lithgow and Orange, as well as the capital cities (CCAC 1958: 12).

It took longer to resolve antagonisms on the bench. Alfred Foster was the senior member but the presidency of the Commission went to the more conciliatory Richard Kirby; Foster's estrangement effectively removed him from major cases for several years. Sydney Wright was close to Foster while Richard Ashburner, who was appointed to the Court in 1954, had been a leading advocate for the employers. Subsequent appointments to the Commission were Frank Gallagher, who had presided over the Coal Industry Tribunal at the time of the 1949 dispute, and John Moore, who had previously appeared for the Commonwealth. Both were more congenial to Kirby, who made free use of his authority to compose the bench for major cases.

By far the most important were the Basic Wage cases, which the Commission conducted annually. Since changes in the basic wage flowed into the pay packets of the great majority of Australian wage-earners, there was keen public interest in these proceedings. With its decisions, the Commission largely determined the aggregate wage level, a crucial variable in the national economy at a time when the Commonwealth government exercised an unprecedented control of macroeconomic policy. Its willingness to allow such a large measure of autonomy to an independent wage tribunal was remarkable, and perhaps that was a necessary concession to secure acceptance of centralised wage determination.

To be sure, the Commission was guided by the principle of the capacity of industry to pay, and ever since 1926 the Commonwealth had the power to intervene in Basic Wage cases. Counsel for the Crown regularly appeared in these cases to tender economic evidence and make submissions. Even so, the Menzies government frequently affirmed the independence of the national tribunal: the Prime

Minister himself told the House of Representatives in 1952 that 'The Government has made it abundantly clear that all questions which are now pending, such as quarterly adjustment of the basic wage, are within the sole jurisdiction of the Arbitration Court' (*CPD* 6 August 1952: 66). Moreover, the government indicated a preference for a particular amount in only four out of the nineteen cases that were conducted between 1953 and 1972 (Brereton 1989: 92). It was Kirby's habit to notify the Minister for Labour of Basic Wage decisions the night before they were announced, so that the government could make an immediate response (d'Alpuget 1977: 192). Beyond that courtesy, his Commission controlled wage policy.

The Basic Wage cases were conducted as arguments between the unions and the employers, each buttressing its arguments with expert witnesses to persuade the bench of their claims about the economic consequences of a wage increase. As an economist who appeared for the unions remarked in 1951, 'Each party to a dispute will endeavour to prove that expert witnesses called by the other party are incompetents, liars and cheats' (Walker 1970: 88). Horrie Brown of the Australian National University suffered a heart attack after he appeared for the ACTU in the 1953 case (d'Alpuget 1977: 159), while James Perkins of the University of Melbourne refused to give evidence in the 1961 case unless cross-examination was limited (Kerr 1961). It was frequently observed that the presidential members of the Commission, as well as the counsel who addressed them, while expert in the law were lay economists.

The stakes in these cases were high, however, and there was no lack of economic advice. Kirby himself drew on conversations with a range of economists, from 'Nugget' Coombs (then the Governor of the Reserve Bank) to academics such as Dick Downing and Joe Isaac. It was in this period that labour economists turned their attention to wage policy as a vital component of national economic management (Fisher 1983: 98–104) and brought greater precision to the measurement of productivity. The work of the Commission attracted increasing academic attention and the Industrial Relations Society provided researchers and practitioners with a forum for informed discussion, a development Kirby encouraged as patron of the Victorian Society.

With his aggressive style and flair for publicity, Bob Hawke brought a new edge to the Basic Wage cases after 1959. The employers responded by strengthening their own organisation, with George Polites taking control of the preparation and Jim Robinson, a young Adelaide barrister, jousting with Hawke in the Commission. The ensuing cases brought success to one side, then the other, until in 1966 the Commission took the fateful decision to consider the basic wage together with the margins paid for skill, which until then had been decided separately. With this decision, a familiar ritual assumed a new name: the Commission no longer conducted Basic Wage cases but, rather, National Wage cases.

In amalgamating the two wage components into a total wage, the Commission took the bold step of altering some of the margins. In attempting further to absorb over-award payments into the total wage, it provoked powerful unions into a campaign of rolling stoppages. In resorting to penalties against these unions, it created a head-on confrontation. As is related elsewhere, the union campaign against these penalties culminated in national action during 1969 following the imprisonment of Clarrie O'Shea of the Tramways Union for refusal to pay fines imposed for his contempt of court. Faced with mass protest, the government capitulated. An anonymous benefactor paid O'Shea's fines and the Attorney-General's Department instructed Justice Kerr of the Industrial Court to free him (d'Alpuget 1977: 234).

These dramatic battles were accompanied by a deteriorating relationship between the Commission and the Commonwealth government, and personal difficulties within the Commission. Kirby was distressed by the growing criticism of his Commission and unforgiving of the colleagues who had seized the initiative from him. He did not appoint two of his colleagues to a full bench for eighteen months after they prevailed over his judgment in the 1965 Basic Wage Case, and in 1969 had them removed to the Industrial Court. Public controversy overshadowed the Aboriginal stockmen's award of 1966 (discussed in Chapter 5), in which Kirby took justified pride, while ill health prevented him from sitting on the Equal Pay Case of 1969, which he might well have guided to a better outcome.

For all of the criticism it attracted, the Commission worked with greater efficiency. The number of sitting days for Basic Wage cases fell from over 100 in the early 1950s to as few as 25 by the 1960s. A study of 600 hearings in 1968–69 showed that three-quarters were completed within a month. Lawyers still appeared in most full-bench cases but 90 per cent of those that came before

Commissioners involved no counsel (Isaac 1976: 334). In 1972, the requirement that presidential members have legal qualifications was removed. With Wright's death in 1970, Gallagher's retirement in 1971 and an increased turnover of new appointees, two new presidential members joined the Commission in 1969, two more in 1970, another in 1971 and another two in 1972 (one of them had been Public Service Arbitrator and was the first non-lawyer). Kirby himself retired in 1973 on grounds of ill health from the Commission he had shaped and sustained.

It therefore fell to the new Labor government to appoint his successor. The Prime Minister and his Minister for Labour and National Service wanted Jack Sweeney, a labour lawyer, but Bob Hawke, by now the president of the ACTU, pressed for the senior member of the Commission, John Moore (Cameron 1990: 31). While Hawke prevailed on this occasion, the government quickly put its stamp on the Commission. A change of name in 1973 to the Australian Conciliation and Arbitration Commission expressed Whitlam's expansive view of the national government. The minister was Clyde Cameron, who as president of the South Australian branch of the Australian Workers' Union had extensive experience with arbitration and strong views on how it should be improved. To implement them he replaced the head of his department with Ian Sharp, previously the Registrar of the Commission. This was a sharp break with tradition as Industrial Registrars had previously ended their careers within the tribunal, typically as Commissioners.

The government intervened in the National Wage Case in 1973 to support equal pay for women and chose Mary Gaudron to present its submission (Guy 1999: 254–5). It appointed Elizabeth Evatt as the first female presidential member and Joe Isaac as the first with a background in economics. In its first two years the Labor government secured substantial increases in the minimum wage, and allowed further increases outside the arbitration system. In its last year, with the onset of an international recession, the government persuaded the Commission to reintroduce wage indexation in a belated attempt to contain inflation.

Clyde Cameron recorded a conversation in his diary that took place in October 1975, while Malcolm Fraser was using his numbers in the Senate to block supply and bring down the Whitlam ministry. Cameron, who by this time had been sacked from the ministry, was seated at a table in the dining room at Parliament House adjoining that of the Opposition leader, and heard Fraser in his cups boast to colleagues how he had been to see Robert Menzies and received advice on the fruits of office: 'It's not the laws – laws you can change; it's appointments that matter' (Cameron 1990: 236). Fraser made many appointments to the Commission after he secured office, and they were as carefully chosen as those made by the Whitlam government between 1972 and 1975.

They did not, however, secure the Commission's compliance with his government's wage policy. Wage indexation lasted for the next six years, despite regular government submissions either for partial indexation or that no increase be awarded because of the country's economic difficulties – it was not until a further recession in 1982 that the Commission agreed to a temporary wage freeze. Until then, it took a cautious approach, sometimes giving only part of the increase recorded in the price index and sometimes restricting the full increase to lower-paid workers.

With unions pressing against these constraints, the government used its legislative powers to introduce new measures against union militancy. In its eight years in office, the Fraser government enacted no less than fourteen amendments to the Conciliation and Arbitration Act. These included a requirement that the Commission consider the effects of wages on inflation and unemployment; provision for the Commonwealth to seek a full-bench review of any award or agreement; and establishment of an Industrial Relations Bureau to instigate proceedings for breaches of awards (Deery et al. 1997: 243–6). A further legislative change, the provision in the *Trade Practices Act 1977* for sanctions against industrial action, was particularly significant since it allowed employers to seek remedies outside the arbitration system altogether. In a further change, the separate Industrial Court was abandoned in 1976 and its functions absorbed by the Federal Court.

It was fortunate that Moore presided over the Commission during this testing period. He had worked closely with Kirby and shared his predecessor's extensive familiarity with the jurisdiction. Courteous and reserved, Moore commanded general respect for his integrity. He was a practical reformer. In 1976, he initiated regular meetings with the heads of the State industrial tribunals to foster greater cooperation with them. His practice of holding discussions of full-bench cases before the members prepared their decision did much to improve collegiality and cohesion.

Under Moore's leadership, the Commission picked a careful path to maintain its independence. Like Kirby, he pursued an approach described as 'accommodative arbitration' (Yerbury and Isaac 1971), seeking practical agreements on wage-fixing principles acceptable to the parties, mindful of, but not subservient to, government policy. In accepting this more limited role, it no longer claimed to be guided solely by Higgins' pole star of wage justice: it was more a 'facilitator' than a 'prime mover' (Isaac 1989). Some saw this more pragmatic approach as detracting from the prestige of the jurisdiction: when Michael Kirby accepted appointment to the Commission in December 1974, a leading advocate asked him, 'Michael, why would you do this? You will sink like a stone out of sight without a trace' (Kirby 2001b).

Much of the Commission's work was done unobtrusively. Its style of dispute resolution was captured in a novel published at this time by a pseudonymous practitioner believed to be a member of the Commission. It depicted a fanatical left-wing union officer foiled in his attempt to paralyse the nation's economy, and a headstrong American boss who comes to appreciate that the Commission provides a necessary forum for resolving differences. The company executive, along with the federal minister and the union advocate, celebrate the settlement in a pub. The novel is also notable for its use of the phrase 'the industrial relations club' (O'Charley 1978).

A further change of address by the Commission was also suggestive of its evolving nature. By the time Moore retired in 1985, there were modern premises in every State and Territory that provided for District Registries, offices for the members of the Commission and their staff, along with facilities for conferences and hearings. At the end of 1979, the Commission moved its base of operations in Melbourne from the building it had occupied at the west end of Little Bourke Street to several upper floors of Nauru House, the tallest of the office blocks in the eastern precinct of the city. The move doubled the Commission's workspace, testifying to the increase of business and expansion of staff numbers: when Moore retired, there were twelve Deputy Presidents, twenty-seven Commissioners and nearly a hundred support staff in Melbourne alone. What had begun as a makeshift court in a borrowed chamber was now a tenant in the central business district.

THE COMMISSION CONSTRAINED

The election of the Hawke Labor government in 1983 brought the implementation of the Accord, whereby the government and the ACTU agreed to restore wage indexation and forgo further claims as part of a program of economic reconstruction. Subsequent refinements of the Accord discounted wage increases for improvements in the social wage and superannuation benefits, then linked them to a simplification of award classifications and productivity improvements. These arrangements, which were negotiated between the government and the unions, and then submitted to National Wage hearings, seemed to reduce the Commission's role.

The government had in any case established a committee of inquiry into the federal system of conciliation and arbitration. It was chaired by Keith Hancock, a labour economist, and made a number of recommendations designed to improve the system's operation, but was adamant that 'conciliation and arbitration should remain the mechanism for regulating industrial relations in Australia' (Hancock 1985, Volume 1: 2). This finding heightened rather than stilled the criticisms of the system. In 1983, when John Howard had called for deregulation of industrial relations, he drew on an article written by Gerard Henderson (who would join his staff in the following year) criticising the collusion of the Commission and the parties that came before it in what he called an 'Industrial Relations Club' (Rawson 1984). PP McGuinness, who was then the editor of the *Australian Financial Review*, laid claim to authorship of this epithet when he attacked Hancock's committee as 'paid-up life members of the industrial relations club, the mutual admiration society of practitioners and experts in industrial relations'. McGuinness described the centralised wage-fixing system as a 'shambles' and alleged that its practitioners were 'hopelessly corrupt' (McGuinness 1985: 1–2). These critics were followed by the members of the HR Nicholls Society, who held an inaugural meeting in 1986 and published the proceedings with a foreword from John Stone, the former head of the Treasury, describing the operation of the Commission as an 'irrelevant charade' (HR Nicholls Society 1986: 15).

Such rhetoric was matched by the increasingly impatient secretary of the ACTU, Bill Kelty. Late in 1987, when the Commission delayed a decision in a National Wage Case, Kelty said the Bench had behaved like 'a bunch of clowns' (Dabscheck 1995: 54). Kelty was coming under increasing pressure from member unions seeking larger wage increases. The Accord partners attempted to relieve this pressure by providing for increases in particular industries based on award restructuring and improved efficiency; by the end of the decade they were ready to embrace bargaining at the enterprise level.

The government had followed the Hancock inquiry in 1988 by turning the Conciliation and Arbitration Commission into an Industrial Relations Commission. Hancock suggested the new designation to emphasise the centrality of the tribunal in the wider system of industrial relations; the government used it to indicate the limits of centralised wage determination, and its Act included a provision for enterprise bargaining. Additional legislation in 1993 took this further by establishing two divisions within the Commission, one concerned with awards and one with bargaining: the role of the latter was to approve enterprise agreements. By this time, the Commission had two Vice-Presidents and its other presidential members were classified as Senior Deputy Presidents and Deputy Presidents. Joint Deputy Presidents (who also held senior appointments with State tribunals) were now added as well as Joint Commissioners (who also held State appointments) alongside the Conciliation and Arbitration Commissioners. The government also re-established a separate Industrial Relations Court in 1994.

If the Accord reduced the role of the Commission in wage policy and the intemperate denigration by members of the HR Nicholls Society undermined respect for its integrity, then the government did little to enhance the Commission's standing as an independent authority. There was disquiet when a presidential member of the Conciliation and Arbitration Commission, Jim Staples, was not appointed to the Industrial Relations Commission, as this seemed to violate the principle of tenure of office. John Moore had relieved Staples of many of his duties after he publicly criticised the full bench, but Moore's successor had given him no cases at all after 1985. Barry Maddern, the new President, seemed an unlikely Labor appointment since before his appointment he had appeared as an advocate for employers in many cases.

Maddern had to deal with insistent pressures. Following Bill Kelty's criticism of the Commission, the government legislated to break the link between salaries of presidential members and judges of the Federal Court. Maddern criticised 'the downgrading of the Commission's standing and status' (AIRC Annual Report 1990: 3–4). Shortly after the government fixed the new salaries, the Commission rejected its proposals for enterprise bargaining, which were supported by the unions and most of the employers, on the grounds that 'the parties to industrial relations still have to develop the maturity necessary' for enterprise bargaining to operate (Dabscheck 1995: 70–1). Kelty lashed out angrily (*Australian* 2 May 1991).

In the following year, Kelty claimed that National Wage cases were 'rigged' to favour employers. Kelty referred here to the role of the President in composing the bench for such cases. By his reckoning, there were fifteen members with employer backgrounds, seventeen with union backgrounds and thirteen 'independents', yet he found that those with employer backgrounds made up a majority of the bench in nearly half of the National Wage cases. An anonymous former member of the Commission responded with an attack on 'yuppie graduates who work for a few years in the ACTU office and then expect a deputy presidential position as a God-given right' (*Sydney Morning Herald* 1 September 1992). That the argument could be conducted in such reckless terms, and that independence was regarded as a residual category of the Commission's membership, was a symptom of its difficulties.

When Maddern died, his successor was appointed from outside the ranks of the Commission. Deirdre O'Connor had served on a number of Commonwealth tribunals but had no experience in industrial arbitration when she took up the presidency. She had to deal with a change of government and a further change to the Commission's powers. The *Workplace Relations Act 1996* placed the principal responsibility for determining employment matters upon 'employer and employees at the workplace or enterprise level' (section 3b). It promoted bargaining as the preferred mode of dispute settlement, individual agreements as the preferred outcome. The Act reduced both the arbitral and award-making powers of the Commission. It restricted the scope of awards to a limited range of provisions, and placed greater emphasis on conciliation, with arbitration now to occur 'as a last resort' (section 89a). A separate Office of the Employment

Advocate was created to oversee the new Australian Workplace Agreements, and in 1997 the jurisdiction of the Industrial Relations Court was transferred back to the Federal Court.

Union membership shrank, and the proportion of the workforce covered by federal awards dwindled. A 1999 survey found that 42 per cent of employees were covered by enterprise agreements, 22 per cent by awards and a further 22 per cent by a combination of collective agreements and over-award arrangements (Forsyth 2001: 7). (There are no recent figures to measure the Commission's share of those who continue to work under federal and State awards and agreements, but it had been 40 per cent in 1990 (ABS 1990) and is probably still around that level.) On the other hand, there was no rush to individual agreements and just 130 000 of them were in operation by the end of 2002 (Mitchell and Fetter 2003: 304). The Commission has continued to set what its new President, Geoffrey Giudice, called in 1998 'fair minimum standards' for the national workforce (Norington 1998: 347).

Since the changes made in 1993 and 1996 allowed for industrial action as part of enterprise bargaining, the Commission is no longer expected to enforce the peace. It continues nevertheless to play an active role in dispute settlement. Although the workload of the Commission has continued to increase, the 1993 and 1996 legislative changes have had a significant effect on the distribution of its work. The reduced scope for arbitration, confined mainly to safety net matters, has been offset by increased conciliation activity in enterprise bargaining. The low level of industrial action in recent years has relieved the Commission for dealing with such action.

One of the more significant changes has come from the new provision relating to termination of employment, more commonly referred to as unfair dismissal. Between 1997–98 and 2002–03, annual applications relating to this matter increased from 452 to 7121 (AIRC Annual Reports 1997–98 to 2002–03). Although a large number of applications were withdrawn or lapsed for various reasons, the rest have added substantially to the Commission's work. Of these, on average more than half have been settled by conciliation and about one-fifth by arbitration, while a smaller proportion have gone on appeal to full benches.

The membership of the present Commission attests to the volume of business. It consists of a President, two Vice-Presidents, thirteen Senior Deputy

Presidents, five Deputy Presidents and twenty-seven Commissioners, with an additional fourteen Deputy Presidents and thirteen Commissioners who are members of State Tribunals holding dual appointments. As it approaches its centenary, the Commission is to shift its Melbourne premises once again, to a new building in Exhibition Street, which will provide improved facilities and once again will have its own entrance.

It remains an indispensable part of the Australian system of industrial relations, partly because the Howard government's lack of a majority in the Senate has forced compromise, and partly because it provides a means of facilitating agreements, resolving disputes, protecting entitlements and maintaining a safety net for wage and salary earners. The ambit of this province for law and order has been reduced. It no longer endeavours in the way it once did to enforce industrial peace on powerful antagonists; nor do its wage decisions have such wide effect. Its work is seldom reported as closely as Higgins' Court or Kirby's and Moore's Commission. It continues, however, as a recognisable legacy of a bold experiment and distinctively Australian institution.

3

THE LAW OF CONCILIATION AND ARBITRATION

Michael Kirby and Breen Creighton

The Parliament shall, subject to this Constitution, have power to make laws for the peace, order and good government of the Commonwealth with respect to:-

Conciliation and arbitration for the prevention and settlement of industrial disputes extending beyond the limits of any one State.

Constitution of Australia, section 51(xxxv)

The story of the law of conciliation and arbitration in Australia is, to a large extent, a story of constitutional interpretation. One of the key issues that arises in any study of constitutional law in a country like Australia with a written constitution concerns the theory that will be adopted in giving meaning to the constitutional text. Obviously, the judges of a final court who have the responsibility of assigning that meaning could do so on the basis of considerations such as their impressions, intuitive feelings or the consultation of a good dictionary or two. On the other hand, the judges might, for consistency, try to develop a more sophisticated analysis of the constitutional charter and of their function in interpreting it.

Thus, the judges could follow an approach that insists upon assigning to disputed constitutional words a meaning derived from the perceived meaning of those words at the time the Constitution was adopted as law. This is the so-called 'originalist' approach to constitutional interpretation. As will appear, in the assignment of meaning to the words of the Australian Constitution that include the conciliation and arbitration power, the foundation and early Justices of the High Court of Australia sometimes embraced this originalist doctrine. They could readily do so because all of the early Justices had been participants in the Constitutional Conventions that resulted in the final language in which, for the most part, the Constitution passed into law.[1]

With the passage of time, however, it was no longer possible for the members of the High Court to rely on their own memories and recollections of what had transpired in the years before 1900. After that point, the adoption of the 'originalist' approach to interpretation, including for the meaning of section 51(xxxv) of the Constitution, became more problematic. This change coincided substantially with the decision of the High Court in 1920 in the *Engineers* case.[2] As will be shown, that decision represented a watershed in the Court's constitutional exposition.

Since that time, the struggle to give meaning to the constitutional text has taken several forms. They have included what Justice Scalia of the Supreme Court of the United States (an exponent of originalism in constitutional interpretation) has called 'faint-hearted' originalism (Scalia 1995: 142). But they have also ranged through other theories or explanations such as the 'living force' doctrine of constitutional meaning embraced by Deane J and some of his predecessors and successors.[3]

The debates over theories of constitutional interpretation have attracted vigorous expressions of opinion in the High Court in recent times.[4] Many scholarly articles have been written analysing the conflicting approaches, their viability and the consistency of their application.[5] Despite this, there is no area of constitutional discourse which more clearly demonstrates that, during the first century of the Constitution, the High Court has failed consistently to apply an originalist construction (robust or faint-hearted) to the federal legislative powers than the Court's approach to the interpretation of the industrial conciliation and arbitration power. Indeed, this area of constitutional law illustrates more vividly than most the impact upon constitutional exposition of the forces of history, economics, national values and survival, as well as the forces of changing legal doctrine and political and social needs.

MARY GAUDRON

Mary Gaudron was Deputy President of the Commission from 1974 to 1979. She was appointed at the behest of Clyde Cameron, the Minister for Labour and Immigration, who had first met her in the mid-1960s when she was appearing as junior counsel to Jim Staples, who was representing Pat Mackie, the leader of the Mount Isa miners. Cameron had chosen Mary Gaudron to present the government's case for equal pay in 1973.

In urging Mary Gaudron's appointment on the Prime Minister, Gough Whitlam, Cameron stressed her outstanding legal credentials, which would take her subsequently to the position of Solicitor-General of New South Wales and then to the High Court. In proposing her to Cabinet colleagues, he dwelt on her origins as the daughter of a railway worker who had completed her law degree at the University of Sydney on scholarships. Cameron perhaps embellished these family origins and claimed that she had been born in a tent. Gough Whitlam, who was already convinced, broke in: 'Oh, for Christ's sake, comrade, you'll be telling us soon that she was born in a bloody manger' (Guy 1999: 257).

In a speech delivered at a dinner of the Industrial Relations Commission to mark the Centenary of Federation, Mary Gaudron (2001) recalled some of the earthier exchanges in the courtroom:

> 'Change.' It is the word on everyone's lips. And certainly there have been dramatic changes affecting the Commission and its work. There was a time, probably right up to the decision in the *Boilermakers* case, that the Conciliation and Arbitration Court was the most respected and influential body in the country.
>
> Thus Henry Bournes Higgins could write in 1920: 'Lawyer as I am – or ought to be – I feel the work [of the High Court] has not a tenth of the importance of the work in the Court of Conciliation'.
>
> I do not think that either Michael Kirby or I, both of us having served on the Commission and the High Court, could say the same today. We would, however, probably have no hesitation in saying that our time on the Commission was infinitely more fun.

Justice Mary Gaudron was Deputy President of the Commission from 1974 to 1979, and a Justice of the High Court from 1987 to 2003.

Sometimes, it was even fun for those caught up in the Commission's processes. At least that was the impression I received from an AWU member who solemnly swore in proceedings relating to the Pastoral Industry Award that his name was 'Crutching Jack' and who, when I thanked him for his attendance, volunteered with equal solemnity that he hadn't 'had so much fun since Mum caught her tit in the mangle'.

Crutching Jack's evidence was led in support of a claim for a travelling allowance for suburban shearers. The claim, although made well after metrication, was, as was only to be expected, expressed in cents per mile. When I inquired whether the award should be expressed in cents per kilometre, I was advised by the union advocate: 'Your Honour can do whatever your Honour likes, but I think it only fair to warn you that my members still pay one and thruppence for their combs and cutters'.

In this chapter we will illustrate, by reference to the constitutional powers relevant to the law of industrial arbitration, the way in which the High Court of Australia, and other Australian courts, have developed the sparse words of the Constitution to apply to an area of society's activities that has changed more over the century than most others. The history of the High Court's response to the very large number of cases challenging the invocation of the federal power over industrial arbitration demonstrates the unacceptability of simplistic demands that constitutional courts should simply apply the words of the constitutional text as if, without more, those words alone were sufficient to solve all of the problems. If this chapter shows nothing else, it is that choices must be made in constitutional interpretation. The real question is whether those choices are made candidly and transparently, by reference to the real reasons that lay behind them – or explained in words that deny the choices and obscure the reasons.

COMMON RULE AND REGISTERED ORGANISATIONS

Writing in 1898, Sidney and Beatrice Webb noted that 'the Device of the Common Rule' was a 'universal feature of Trade Unionism' and that 'the assumption on which it is based is held from one end of the Trade Union world to the other'. The 'assumption' to which the Webbs referred was that, 'in the absence of any Common Rule, the conditions of employment are left to "free competition", this always means, in practice, that they are arrived at by Individual Bargaining between parties of very unequal bargaining strength' (Webb and Webb 1898: 561, 560).

By 'common rule', the Webbs meant the fixing of terms and conditions of employment that applied to 'whole bodies of workers' in a given trade or industry. In principle, such rules could be imposed by means of collective bargaining. However, for the Webbs, the distribution of power in a capitalist system was such that 'the only available method of securing a Common Rule is Legal Enactment – difficult in the face of interests so powerful for the Trade Unions to obtain, but once obtained . . . easy of application and enforcement' (Webb and Webb 1898: 554).

This logic clearly constituted part of the conceptual underpinning of the conciliation and arbitration and wages board systems that were adopted in the Australian colonies/States in the late nineteenth and early twentieth centuries (Reeves 1902a: 69–181; Mitchell 1989; Creighton and Stewart 2000: 36–9). It also found expression in section 38(f) of the original *Commonwealth Conciliation and Arbitration Act 1904*. This empowered the Commonwealth Court of Conciliation and Arbitration 'to declare by any award or order that any practice, regulation, rule, custom, term of agreement, condition of employment or dealing whatsoever determined by an award in relation to an industrial matter shall be a common rule of any industry in connection with which the dispute (i.e. the dispute which gives rise to the award) arises'. In the intellectual context of the day, it is easy to understand how it might be assumed that the technique of the common rule was consistent with both the letter and the spirit of the new province for law and order which was to be ushered in by the 1904 Act.[6] But it is equally easy to understand why the use of this technique might be seen as highly controversial.

Given the initial general hostility of the business community towards the conciliation and arbitration system (see Plowman and Smith 1986; Plowman 1989a, 1989b: chs 1 and 2), it is hardly surprising that the constitutional validity of this provision should have been put at issue at an early stage in the history of the system. The challenge duly occurred in 1910 in the *Whybrow* case.[7]

This was actually the third case to reach the High Court in that year involving Whybrow & Co. Earlier, in *Australian Boot Trade Employees Federation v Whybrow & Co*,[8] the High Court, in reliance upon the 'reserved State powers' doctrine, had ruled that the Commonwealth Court of Conciliation and Arbitration lacked the power to make an award that was inconsistent with a State law. At issue in this instance were determinations of tribunals in New South Wales, Queensland, South Australia and Victoria. But the Court also determined that 'inconsistency' did not arise for this purpose where it was possible to give effect to both the State law and the federal law.[9] In the second case in the sequence, *The King v Commonwealth Court of Conciliation and Arbitration; Ex parte Whybrow & Co*,[10] the High Court unanimously rejected an argument to the effect that the 'compulsory' aspects of the regime established by the 1904 Act

QUITE SAFE.

THE PIGMY: "These stilts give me a fine chance to throw mud, and there's no danger, for the giant cannot hit back."

Employers disgruntled with the decisions of Higgins' Court used parliamentary privilege to attack the President. While the cartoonist presents Higgins as unable to respond, in fact he used his bench to deliver some stinging rebukes.

were unconstitutional because they were inconsistent with the essentially 'voluntary' character of arbitration at common law. Plowman and Smith (1986: 214) observe that this decision shows that the three original members of the Court – Griffith CJ, Barton and O'Connor JJ – 'were prepared to adhere to canons of constitutional interpretation even though this resulted in the preservation of aspects of the arbitration system to which they were personally opposed'.

The third case in the *Whybrow* trilogy saw a rather different outcome. In this instance, all five members of the Court found that section 38(f) of the 1904 Act was beyond the power of the federal parliament acting in reliance upon section 51(xxxv). Griffith CJ put the matter thus:

> I adhere to the opinion which I expressed in the *Woodworkers' Case*[11] that the term 'dispute' connotes the existence of parties taking opposite sides, to which I would add that the word 'arbitration' connotes the same idea. In the nature of things, an industrial dispute may be prevented from coming into existence by various means, but the only means which the Parliament is authorised to employ are conciliation and, perhaps, arbitration. If, therefore, the state of things is such that there are no ascertainable parties between whom an ascertainable difference capable of being composed exists the basis of arbitration is wanting. *A fortiori* if all the parties concerned are contented.[12]

Griffith CJ, Barton and O'Connor JJ all proceeded from the assumption that it simply was not possible for the parliament to pass a law in reliance upon section 51(xxxv) that permitted the making of common rule awards. In separate judgments, Higgins and Isaacs JJ agreed that section 38(g), as it then stood, was invalid. However, they both left open the possibility that differently worded provisions might be found to fall within the power conferred by section 51(xxxv), so long as they relied upon techniques of conciliation and arbitration.[13] The legislature made no attempt to explore these possibilities for almost forty years,[14] and, when it did do so, it again foundered on the rocks described in the reasoning in *Whybrow*.[15] The consequence is that the principal focus of the system for virtually all of its first century was upon the settlement of disputes, with little attempt to explore the possibilities afforded by the concept of prevention.[16]

It is not entirely surprising that Griffith CJ and Barton and O'Connor JJ should have been uncomfortable with provisions enabling the making of common rule awards. For most of the founders of the Constitution, including the three original members of the High Court, it was expected that the conciliation and arbitration power would be invoked in only highly exceptional circumstances such as those which had arisen in the early 1890s. Principal responsibility for industrial relations was to remain with the States. The concept of common rule awards must have appeared inimical to this original view of the 'federal balance'. Taken to its logical conclusion, the availability of such awards could have had the effect of entirely displacing State regulation by ensuring that federal common rule awards operated in all sectors of the economy – especially if the federal instruments had the effect of entirely displacing any inconsistent State provisions dealing with the same issue. Obviously, the foundation Justices of the High Court thought that such an operation of the power in section 51(xxxv) of the Constitution would exceed the paragraph and also that it was inconsistent with the implied relationship between the federal and State law-making authorities.

The *Whybrow* litigation ensured that this did not happen. The first case appeared to establish that the Commonwealth Court of Conciliation and Arbitration could not make any award that was inconsistent with a law of a State – although that principle did not survive the demise of the reserved State powers doctrine in the *Engineers* case in 1920.[17] Of more lasting consequence was the decision in the third case to the effect that section 51(xxxv) did not provide authority for the making of common rule awards and that the federal tribunal could deal only with disputes to which there were identifiable parties. As indicated, this not only helped to preserve the autonomy of the State systems, but also severely circumscribed the development of the prevention power in the federal sphere. This, in turn, meant that the development of the system as a whole had to depend on the highly artificial and increasingly unwieldy concept of the industrial 'dispute'.

Although the decision in the third *Whybrow* case undoubtedly served to inhibit the development of the federal system of conciliation and arbitration, its practical impact was much less marked than might have been anticipated simply by taking the decision at face value. This can be attributed to a number of factors, among the most important of which were the decisions of the High Court in the *Burwood Cinema*[18] and *Metal Trades* cases.[19]

The first of these cases, in 1925, enabled registered trade unions to generate industrial disputes with employers who did not presently employ any members of the union and irrespective of whether their existing employees were satisfied with their terms and conditions of employment. This decision was based on the premise that unions were parties-principal to disputes in their own right, and not just as agents for their members. This reasoning meant that unions could generate disputes on behalf of persons who were presently neither employees nor members, but who might become their members in the future. Furthermore, they could do this by service upon employers of demands set out in written logs of claims. If the employer rejected or ignored these demands, or put a counter-offer, that was sufficient to create a 'dispute' for purposes of attracting the jurisdiction of the federal tribunal, even though the dispute existed only 'on paper'.[20] Ten years later, in *Metal Trades*, a majority of the High Court took this reasoning a stage further by determining that unions could also generate disputes about the terms and conditions of non-members who were presently employed by employer parties.[21] An award made in settlement of such a dispute could require the employer party to observe the terms and conditions set out therein in respect of both members and non-members, but could not impose obligations upon those non-members by reason of the fact that they were not party to the dispute and were not members of an organisation that was such a party.[22]

The logic of *Metal Trades* also led to the result that awards could be binding upon all members of a registered organisation of employers that was a party to an industrial dispute, even though that member was not itself a party to the dispute.[23] It followed that employers who wished to escape the reach of awards could endeavour to do so either by resigning from an organisation that had been made party to a relevant dispute or by not joining an organisation in the first place.[24] Yet this avoidance strategy would be ineffectual in circumstances where a union elected to generate an entirely new dispute with the employer or to 'rope' them into an existing award. This latter technique generally involved the union creating a dispute by serving a log of claims upon the employer demanding that they observe the terms of the award that was attached to the log. An award made in settlement of any such dispute would then bind the employer to observe the terms of the original award.[25]

The constraints imposed by *Whybrow* were also mitigated by the provisions of the 1904 Act which dealt with the continuing operation of awards in circumstances where there has been a transmission of business by an employer who was respondent to an award to another employer entity who was not respondent to that particular award, or who was not respondent to any award. The constitutionality of these provisions was upheld in 1923 in *George Hudson*.[26] Although they have generated relatively little litigation over the years,[27] they did serve to maintain the integrity of the federal system by ensuring that employers could not escape award coverage simply by transferring their business to another entity that was not party to an industrial dispute, and consequently was covered by an award.

The combined effect of the decisions in *Burwood Cinema, Metal Trades* and *George Hudson* was to enable the federal system of conciliation and arbitration to maintain and to extend its reach, notwithstanding the constraints imposed by the third *Whybrow* decision. These decisions were the product of the expanded and reconstituted High Court. However, their practical impact would have been significantly less profound had it not been for what some might regard as a counter-intuitive decision of the Court while the founding members were still in the majority.

Jumbunna Coal Mine NL v Victorian Coal Miners' Association[28] arose out of a judgment of Higgins J as President of the Commonwealth Court of Conciliation and Arbitration to uphold a decision of the Industrial Registrar to register a union of Victorian coal-miners under the 1904 Act. The 1908 case raised three principal issues: whether a trade union all of whose members were in one State had the capacity to engage in an interstate industrial dispute, thereby triggering the jurisdiction of the federal tribunal; whether those provisions of the Act which provided for the registration and regulation of trade unions and employer associations, including the conferral of corporate status upon registered bodies, were within the scope of the conciliation and arbitration and incidental powers; and whether the expansive definition of 'industrial dispute' in the 1904 Act was within the legislative competence of the parliament.

The Court, comprising Griffith CJ, Barton, O'Connor and Isaacs JJ, unanimously upheld Higgins J's decision to register the applicant union and, in doing so, rejected all of the arguments put forward by the employers to the effect that the registration provisions of the 1904 Act were beyond the legislative powers of the parliament under section 51(xxxv). The Court was also unanimous in rejecting employer arguments that the definition of 'industrial dispute' in section 4 of the 1904 Act was beyond its power.

The decision in *Jumbunna* played a crucial role in the development of the federal system of industrial regulation over the ensuing decades. For example, it helped to legitimate provisions intended to protect the organisational security of registered organisations and to give such organisations the capacity to gain access to the Court by agitating disputes as representative of their members and (post–*Burwood Cinema*) as parties

Harold Bayard Piper, the third Chief Judge of the Court (1941–1947).

principal in their own right. It also helped to expand and consolidate the jurisdiction of the federal tribunal by permitting the legislature to adopt an expansive approach to the range of matters that could be made subject to conciliation and arbitration – although, as will appear, the jurisprudence in this area took some curious twists and turns over the years.

In the course of their reasons in *Jumbunna*, several members of the Court exhibited a very real appreciation of the logic of collective bargaining and of the central role of representative organisations in that process. For example, O'Connor J observed that:

It may well be conceded that there is no general power to prevent and settle industrial disputes by any means the legislature may think fit to adopt. The power is restricted to prevention and settlement by conciliation and arbitration. Any attempt to effectively prevent and settle industrial disputes by either of these means would be idle if individual workmen and employees only could be dealt with. The application of the 'principle of collective bargaining', not long in use at the time of the passing of the Constitution, is essential to bind the body of workers in a trade and to ensure anything like permanence in the settlement. Some system was therefore essential by which the powers of the Act could be made to operate on representatives of workmen, and on bodies of workmen, instead of on individuals only. But if such representatives were merely chosen for the occasion without any permanent status before the Court [of Conciliation and Arbitration], it is difficult to see how the permanency of the settlement of the dispute could be assured.[29]

This awareness of the nature of collective bargaining and sensitivity to the need for representative organisations of employees and (to a lesser extent) employers helps to explain a decision that may, at first blush, appear to be somewhat at odds with the views of the three original members of the High Court concerning the implied constitutional limitations on the power of the federal parliament to enact laws or authorise the making of awards intruding upon the sphere of State legal regulation. Although both Barton and O'Connor JJ (and Griffith CJ, less overtly) had opposed the inclusion of the conciliation and arbitration power in the Constitution, they would have been fully aware of the reasons for its inclusion. As such, they were clearly prepared to countenance the enactment of legislation which was apt to, and indeed essential for, the achievement of that purpose.[30] Subsequent developments have clearly demonstrated that, having in *Jumbunna* permitted the genie of conciliation and arbitration to escape from the bottle of section 51(xxxv), it was quite impossible, particularly where that power was enhanced by the express and implied incidental powers, to restore its status as a means of last resort where collective bargaining had proved to be ineffectual or impossible. After the *Engineers* case,[31] comparatively few cases have been argued before the High Court in an attempt to revive the notion that the Constitution itself imported an implied federal restriction on the Commonwealth's law-making. None has attempted to reverse the historic ruling in *Jumbunna*.

THE INDUSTRY REQUIREMENT

The dispute must be in an industry

The employers' challenge to the validity of the 1904 Act in *Jumbunna* was based, in part, on the assertion that the definition of 'industrial dispute' in section 4 of that Act, and the criteria for registration as an organisation set out in section 55, encompassed disputes and organisations who were engaged in activities that did not fall within the meaning of 'industry' as that term is used in section 51(xxxv) of the Constitution. O'Connor J dealt with this issue in a straightforward and commonsense manner:

> The words ['industrial dispute'] are free from ambiguity, and must be construed with their ordinary grammatical meaning. So construed, the definition includes within the term 'industry' every kind of employment for pay, hire, advantage, or reward . . . 'Industrial dispute' was not, when the Constitution was framed, a technical or legal expression. It had not then, nor has it now, any acquired meaning. It meant just what the two English words in their ordinary meaning conveyed to ordinary persons . . .[32]

This expansive approach to the concept of 'industry' survived for some considerable time. For example, in 1919 in the *Municipal Employees* case,[33] a majority of the High Court decided that manual workers employed by local government authorities were engaged in industry in the requisite sense. In the course of his reasons, Higgins J expressly rejected the proposition that only manual employees could be so engaged:

> It is true that up to the present most of the disputes are disputes with manual workers; but we are discussing a remedial power conferred on Parliament for all time; and we have no right to limit the meaning of the words to manual disputes, even if it were true that when the Constitution became law there had been no disputes with non-manual workers as to their conditions of labour . . .[34]

Gavan Duffy J, in dissent, saw the matter rather differently:

> In my opinion an 'industrial dispute' within the meaning of section
> 51 (xxxv) of the Constitution is one in which a number of employees
> organised or united together are in contest with their employer or
> employers with respect to the remuneration of the employees, or with
> respect to any matter directly affecting them in the performance of their
> duties, in an undertaking or undertakings carried on for the purpose of
> gain and wholly or mainly by means of manual labour.[35]

These observations of Gavan Duffy J neatly encapsulate the tensions that were to bedevil the interpretation of the 'industrial dispute' concept for more than sixty years: the notion that white-collar workers in general, and professional staff in particular, could not engage in 'industrial' disputation for purposes of attracting the jurisdiction of the federal tribunal; that 'industrial' disputes could only arise in situations where business was undertaken for purposes of profit; and that, even where the parties were engaged in an 'industry' in the relevant sense, the range of matters in relation to which they could engage in disputation was limited to 'remuneration' and to 'any matter directly affecting them in the performance of their duties'.

White-collar employment was found to be within the reach of the federal tribunal in the *Insurance Staff* and *Bank Officials* cases in 1923.[36] This was essentially on the basis that the activities of banks and insurance companies were ancillary to the functioning of industry, and as such could be regarded as 'incidental' to industry for purposes of access to the conciliation and arbitration system.[37] However, the High Court adopted a rather different approach in the *State Teachers* case in 1929.[38] In that case it was held that school teachers employed in State schools were not engaged in industry in the relevant sense. In the course of their joint reasons, Knox CJ and Gavan Duffy and Starke JJ ((1929) 41 CLR 576) found that the educational activities of the States could not constitute an industry:

> They bear no resemblance whatever to an ordinary trade, business or
> industry. They are not connected directly with, or attendant upon, the
> production or distribution of wealth; and there is no cooperation of
> capital and labour, in any relevant sense, for a great public scheme of
> education is forced upon the communities of the States by law.

Furthermore: 'If carrying on a system of public education is not within the sphere of industrialism, those who confine their efforts to that activity cannot be engaged in an industry or in an industrial occupation or pursuit' ((1929) 41 CLR 575–6). In the course of a vigorous dissent, Isaacs J (at 588) made it clear that he saw the matter in a very different light:

> Education, cultural and vocational, is now and is daily becoming as much the artisan's capital and tool, and to a great extent his safeguard against unemployment, as the employers' banking credit and insurance policy are part of his means to carry on the business. There is at least as much reason for including the educational establishments in the constitutional power as 'labour' services, as there is to include insurance companies as 'capital' services.

Despite the force of this logic, over the next fifty years the High Court handed down a series of decisions which had the effect that some groups of workers were adjudged to be engaged in 'industry' in the relevant sense, while others, in apparently similar situations, were found not to be so engaged. For example, in the *Professional Engineers* case,[39] professional engineers employed by State government departments and authorities were found to be engaged in an 'industry' in the relevant sense. The same was the case for credit union clerks,[40] for insurance clerks employed by the Tasmanian Motor Accidents Insurance Board,[41] and for clerks employed by health funds in Victoria.[42] By way of contrast, clerical officers employed by State governments were found not to be employed in an 'industry' in the *State Public Servants* case.[43] Clerical workers employed by the Commissioner for Motor Transport of New South Wales,[44] fire-fighters,[45] and university teachers all met a similar fate.[46]

The end result of these decisions was that, by 1983, it was impossible to predict with any degree of certainty whether any given group of employees would or would not be regarded as being engaged in an 'industry' for purposes of accessing the jurisdiction of the federal tribunal. Creighton, Ford and Mitchell (1993: 443) have suggested that to the extent that it is possible to derive any principles of general application from the decided cases, it was to the effect that a dispute could be regarded as requisitely industrial if:

(a)   the activity of the employers directly involved the production or distribution of material wealth ('tangible goods and commodities');

(b)   regardless of the activity of the employers, the work of the relevant employees was indistinguishable in character from work performed by other employees directly engaged in the production and distribution of material wealth;

(c)   the activity of the employers, whilst not of itself directly productive of material wealth, was so closely associated with it as to be 'incidental' or 'ancillary' to industry proper. The closeness of the connection required was a matter of degree.[47]

Obviously, the notion that 'industry' was confined to manual labour must be taken to have been rejected by the time *Professional Engineers* was decided in 1959. Furthermore, with the passage of time, and the increasing integration of the modern economy, the dissenting opinion of Isaacs J in the *State Teachers* case became more and more compelling.

The subject matter of the dispute must be industrial in character

It was noted earlier that, in the course of his dissenting reasons in the *Municipal Employees* case, Gavan Duffy J had indicated that in his opinion 'industrial disputes' within the meaning of section 51 (xxxv) were disputes with respect to the remuneration of employees or to 'any matter directly affecting them in the performance of their duties'. This form of words clearly suggests that Gavan Duffy J considered that the jurisdiction of the federal tribunal did not extend to 'disputes' that had only an indirect bearing upon the performance of work by the employees to whom the alleged dispute related.

This reasoning is also evident in the opinion of O'Connor J in *Clancy*,[48] an early case involving the interpretation of the *Industrial Arbitration Act 1901* (NSW). The case turned upon whether the definition of 'industrial matter' in the 1901 Act extended to regulation of the closing hours of butchers' shops. O'Connor J ((1904) 1 CLR 207) stated that:

> The construction of the section must be controlled by the subject matter, and the general intention of the Act. The subject matter is to regulate the relations between employers and employees . . . If we confine the effect

of the sections to matters directly affecting industries, its scope and intention can be carried out. But once we begin to introduce and include in its scope matters indirectly affecting work in the industry, it becomes very difficult to draw any line so as to prevent the power of the Arbitration Court from being extended to the regulation and control of businesses and industries in every part.

The views of Gavan Duffy J (in the *Municipal Employees* case) and O'Connor J (in *Clancy*) stand in marked contrast to those of Isaacs and Rich JJ in the *Union Badge* case in 1913:

The words of the Constitution 'industrial disputes' stand unabridged by any specified subject matter of disputes; they fit themselves to every phase of industrial growth, and look only to the single fact of an industrial dispute. Parliament, shaping the national policy in accordance with the predominant political ideas for the time being, may or may not restrict causes upon which public intervention shall proceed; but unless it does so, we are unable to see how the court can impose any limitations on the matters which, at any given moment in the life of the Commonwealth, do in fact, and by their practical operation, affect at some stage interrelations of employers and employed so as to give rise to what would then be regarded as an industrial dispute.[49]

Isaacs and Rich JJ clearly contemplated that the legislature could place restrictions upon the range of matters that could properly be made the subject matter of arbitral disputes. But they were equally clearly of the view that no such restrictions were inherent in the words 'industrial disputes' in section 51(xxxv) itself.

This distinction between inherent constitutional constraints upon the subject matter of industrial disputes and those imposed by the legislature became a constant refrain in the decisions of the High Court over the years following the *Municipal Employees* case. In some instances, the Court simply did not make clear whether it was dealing with the interpretation of the statutory definition of the term 'industrial dispute', or with the metes and bounds of what was permissible in terms of section 51(xxxv). In other cases, it seemed to elide the two concepts. On either view, the High Court's doctrine on this subject was unclear and open to the criticism that it lacked consistency.

In particular, the Court appeared for a time to vacillate between an apparent desire to respect the principle of 'managerial prerogatives' and an acceptance that parties that stand in an industrial relationship may properly engage in a dispute about any subject matter that pertains to that relationship – and that it is for the legislature to decide whether or not to invest the tribunal with the capacity to prevent and settle such disputes by conciliation and arbitration. This, in turn, helped to highlight the reality that if industrial parties chose to dispute in relation to a given subject matter, it served little practical purpose to determine that that subject matter stood outside the realm of arbitral disputes. Arguably, the fact that a given issue could not form the subject matter of an arbitral dispute might make disputation in relation to that issue less likely, because such disputation had been 'delegitimated'. More prosaically, a restrictive approach to the permissible subject matter of dispute simply served to put the parties beyond the reach of the umpire.

One of the most vigorous proponents of the view that matters of 'managerial prerogative' stood outside the realm of arbitrable disputes was Barwick CJ. For example, in *Tramways No 2* in 1966, his Honour put the matter thus:

> Whilst it is a truism that industrial disputes and awards made in their settlement may consequentially have an impact upon the management of an enterprise and upon otherwise unfettered managerial discretions, the management of the enterprise is not itself the subject matter of an industrial dispute.[50]

On the facts of that case, the High Court unanimously came to the view that it was not possible to have an arbitrable dispute over whether tram or bus services operated by a two-person crew should be converted to one-person operation. The Australian Tramway and Motor Omnibus Employees' Association had formulated its demands in this way, following an earlier majority decision of the High Court to the effect that a demand that all trams and buses operated by the respondents be staffed by both a driver and a conductor and that no existing two-person tram or bus operation be converted to one-person operation without the consent of the union or an order of the Commission did not constitute an 'industrial' matter in the requisite sense.[51]

Following the decision in the 1966 case, the union reformulated its claim yet again. This time, it demanded that employees should not be required to drive trams or buses without the assistance of a conductor. By a majority of 3:2, the High Court determined that this demand *did* operate to create an arbitrable dispute.[52] Just two years later, in *Gallagher*, the Court had to determine whether an arbitrable dispute could arise from a demand that the crew of a ship called the *Cellana* should include the three cooks claimed by the relevant union or the two proposed by the ship-owner. In a unanimous judgment, the Court stated that:

> We should have thought that it was beyond argument that a dispute on such a subject matter is an industrial dispute and that it clearly relates to the relations between employer and employees and to work done or to be done by employees.[53]

The twin concepts of managerial prerogative and the requirement that the subject matter of a dispute should bear directly upon the relations of employers and employees permeated decisions of the High Court for many years. This resulted in a broad range of matters being adjudged to be beyond the reach of the tribunal. In addition to shop trading hours[54] and staffing levels on buses, trams and aeroplanes,[55] they included: compulsory unionism;[56] occupational superannuation;[57] use of outworkers;[58] reinstatement of dismissed employees;[59] decisions on compulsory redundancy of airline pilots;[60] and direct deduction of trade union dues.[61] However, just as there were many examples of restrictive interpretations either of the statutory definition of industrial matter or of section 51(xxxv), there were also many instances, especially in the 1970s, where the Court evinced a preparedness to adopt a more expansive approach than had been evident in cases such as the *Tramways* trilogy.[62] Nevertheless, by the early 1980s there was a clear need for a reassessment of an extensive and confusing body of learning on the industrial matter requirement, as with the requirement that for a dispute to be arbitrable the parties must be engaged in an industry.[63]

'What the two English words in their ordinary meaning conveyed to ordinary persons'

From a number of decisions in the 1970s and early 1980s, it was clear that members of the High Court were becoming increasingly uncomfortable with the 'veritable Serbonian bog of technicalities' in which the interpretation of the term 'industrial dispute' was then mired.[64] For example, in *Darvall*,[65] all members of the Court seemed somewhat frustrated by the fact that the applicant association of university teachers had chosen to try to establish that universities were engaged in activities that could properly be regarded as ancillary or incidental to industry, rather than seeking to reassert the authority of the approach adopted by Griffith CJ and O'Connor J in *Jumbunna*.[66]

In the following year, in the *Social Welfare* case,[67] the Court was unanimous in sweeping away a line of authority dating back to the decision in *State Teachers* in 1929.[68] In doing so, it affirmed the correctness of the

Edmund Alfred Drake-Brockman, the fourth Chief Judge of the Court (1947–1949)

approach expounded by Griffith CJ and O'Connor J in *Jumbunna*, and by Higgins J in the *Municipal Employees* case[69] and in the *Insurance Staffs* case.[70] Their Honours had no doubt that 'The words ["industrial disputes"] are not a technical or legal expression. They have to be given their popular meaning – what they convey to the man in the street. And that is essentially a question of fact' ((1983) 153 CLR 297, 312). They continued:

> It is, we think, beyond question that the popular meaning of 'industrial disputes' includes disputes between employees and employers about the terms of

employment and the conditions of work . . . We reject any notion that the adjective 'industrial' imports some restriction which confines the constitutional conception of 'industrial disputes' to disputes in productive industry and organised business carried on for the purpose of making profits. The popular meaning of the expression no doubt extends more widely to embrace disputes between parties other than employer and employee, such as demarcation disputes, but just how widely it may extend is not a matter of present concern. ((1983) 153 CLR 312–13)

This last observation clearly indicated that there was still some unfinished business in terms of the permissible subject matter of industrial disputes, despite the radical reassessment of the position relating to the range of persons who could engage in such disputes. Even here, however, the High Court did not discard the established doctrine in its entirety:

It has been generally accepted . . . that the power conferred by s 51(xxxv) is inapplicable to the administrative services of the States . . . The implications which are necessarily drawn from the federal structure of the Constitution itself impose certain limitation on the legislative power of the Commonwealth to enact laws which affect the States (and vice versa). The nature of those limitations was discussed in *Melbourne Corporation v The Commonwealth*,[71] *Victoria v The Commonwealth* (the *Pay-roll Tax Case*)[72] . . . If at least some of the views expressed in those cases are accepted, a Commonwealth law which permitted an instrumentality of the Commonwealth to control the pay, hours of work and conditions of all State public servants could not be sustained as valid, but . . . the limitations have not been completely and precisely formulated and for present purposes the question need not be further examined. ((1983) 153 CLR 297, 313)

The question was 'further examined' three years later in *Re Lee*,[73] where the Court unanimously rejected arguments put by the State of Queensland to the effect that State and private school teachers were not engaged in an 'industry' in the relevant sense, and that teachers in State schools were involved in the administrative services of a State or in activities that were inherently a state activity. The approach adopted by the Court in that case meant that it was not necessary for it to express any decided view as to the existence or extent of the exclusion from the reach of the conciliation and arbitration system of employees of a State engaged in the administrative services of that State. Nevertheless, the members of the Court did see fit to express some preliminary views on that issue. For example:

> There is . . . much to be said for the proposition that, assuming that there is no discrimination against a State or singling out . . . the exercise of the arbitration power in the ordinary course of events will not transgress the implied limitations on Commonwealth legislative power. The exercise by the [Australian Conciliation and Arbitration] Commission of its authority with respect to the employment relationship between a State and its employees in the course of settling an interstate industrial dispute appears to fall within s 51(xxxv). Although the purpose of the implied limitations is to impose some limit on the exercise of Commonwealth power in the interest of preserving the States as constituent elements in the federation, the implied limitations must be read to the express provision of the Constitution.[74]

In *SPSF*,[75] the Court again took the view that it was not necessary to pronounce upon the nature and extent of the implied limitation in the case then before it.[76] However, the Court was finally called upon to express a decided view on this issue in *Re Australian Education Union*.[77]

This case arose out of a wide-ranging challenge by the State of Victoria (supported by several other States) to various aspects of federal industrial relations legislation as it applied to the State public sector in Victoria. The Court reaffirmed the preliminary position expressed in *Re Lee* and, in doing so, identified two practical impacts of the implied limitation upon the operation of the federal system.[78] First:

> It seems to us that critical to that capacity of a State [i.e. the capacity to function as a government] is the government's right to determine the number and identity of the persons whom it wishes to employ, the term

of appointment of such persons and, as well, the number and identity of the persons whom it wishes to dismiss with or without notice from its employment on redundancy grounds. An impairment of a State's rights in these respects would, in our view, constitute an infringement of the implied limitation. On this view, the prescription by a federal award of minimum wages and working conditions would not infringe the implied limitation, at least if it takes appropriate account of any special functions or responsibilities which attach to the employees in question. ((1995) 184 CLR 188, 232)

In other words, federal regulation of core terms and conditions of State employees would not of itself run foul of the implied limitation, but regulation of the numbers and identity of such employees would not be within the federal power. However, the Court went on to identify a second category of State employees whose core terms and conditions could not be subject to any measure of federal regulation:

In our view, also critical to a State's capacity to function as a government is its ability, not only to determine the number and identity of those whom it wishes to engage at the higher levels of government, but also to determine the terms and conditions on which those persons shall be engaged. Hence, ministers, ministerial assistants and advisers, heads of departments and high level statutory office holders, parliamentary officers and judges would clearly fall within this group. The implied limitation would protect the States from the exercise by the [Australian Industrial Relations] Commission of power to fix minimum wages and working conditions in respect of such persons and possibly others as well. ((1995) 184 CLR 188, 232)

The net effect of these decisions is that the only employees who fall outside the reach of the conciliation and arbitration power are a somewhat imprecisely defined group of senior State public servants and office holders and, in respect of certain issues, some less senior employees of the States. It remains to consider the range of matters in relation to which the federal tribunal may exercise powers of conciliation and arbitration.

It will be recalled that in *Social Welfare* the High Court had expressly reserved the question of the extent to which the conciliation and arbitration power would extend to disputes between parties other than employer and employee, 'such as demarcation disputes'. By implication, it had also reserved reconsideration of the 'industrial matter' concept. Manifestly, however, the existing decisional law in this area could not long survive a reversion to a broader view of the concept of 'industrial dispute' defined by reference to what the 'man in the street' would understand by the term.[79]

That this was indeed the case was evident from two 1984 decisions concerning the powers of the (then) Victorian tribunal. First, in the *Federated Clerks* case,[80] a majority of the High Court determined that the concept of 'industrial matter', as used in the *Industrial Relations Act 1979* (Vic), could encompass a demand for the insertion in an industrial instrument of a clause requiring notification and consultation in advance of technological change, where that change might have 'material effects' such as 'termination of employment, the elimination or diminution of job opportunities, promotional opportunities, job tenure or the use of skills, the alteration of hours of work, and the need for retraining or transfer of employees to other work locations'. In the course of his reasons, Mason J clearly signalled that at least some members of the Court were prepared to countenance a reconsideration of the notion that managerial prerogatives fell outside the realm of industrial matters:

Whether the concept of management or managerial decisions can be sustained as an absolute independent criterion of jurisdiction . . . is an important question that may require future consideration . . . The prospect of industrial tribunals regularly reviewing business policy decisions made by employers, and thereby controlling the economy to a substantial extent, is indeed a daunting one. On the other hand, the popular understanding of an industrial dispute extends to any dispute between employees and employers that may result in the dislocation of industrial relations . . . What is more, reflection on the serious impact on

the community of industrial dislocation suggests that the scope and
purpose of statutes regulating conciliation and arbitration and industrial
relations extend to the conferment of jurisdiction on industrial tribunals
in relation to industrial disputes in their broadest conception. ((1984)
154 CLR 491)

As will appear presently, the foreshadowed reconsideration did not take long
in coming. Further evidence of its imminence was furnished by the decision in
the second of the 1984 Victorian cases, *Slonim v Fellows* ((1984) 154 CLR
505). That case arose out of a decision by the Chairman of a Conciliation and
Arbitration Board, subsequently affirmed by the Full Court of the Supreme Court
of Victoria, that the Board did not have the capacity to deal with a dispute between
a trade union and an employer concerning the reinstatement of a member of the
union who had been dismissed by the employer. The High Court unanimously
found that such a dispute did relate to an industrial matter in the relevant sense,
although the Court also expressed some reservations as to whether there could
be an arbitrable dispute about reinstatement between a dismissed employee and
their former employer, since by definition the employer–employee nexus would
have been broken by the dismissal.[81]

Further erosion of the notion that decisions concerning termination of
employment and reinstatement fell outside the realm of arbitrable matters came
with the 1987 decision in *Ranger Uranium*,[82] although the importance of ensuring that claims in this area are made in the proper form is clearly evidenced by
Wooldumpers.[83]

Meanwhile, any doubt as to whether claims for payment into an occupational
superannuation fund could constitute an industrial matter was put to rest by the
decision in *Manufacturing Grocers*.[84] In the course of its decision, the High Court
had this to say about the need for a 'relevant connection' between the subject
matter of a purported dispute and the relationship of employer and employee:

For present purposes, it is sufficient to say that a matter must be
connected with the relationship between an employer in his capacity as
an employer and an employee in his capacity as an employee in a way

which is direct and not merely consequential for it to be an industrial matter capable of being the subject of an industrial dispute. ((1986) 160 CLR 353)

These observations constituted the starting point for the Court's rejection of managerial prerogatives as an inherent restriction on the jurisdiction of the tribunal in *Re Cram*.[85] That case arose out of a dispute in the mining industry over staffing levels and recruitment. The Colliery Proprietors' Association argued that such matters could not properly be made the subject of an industrial dispute because they did not directly affect the relationship between employer and employee as such, rather it 'is a dispute about the policy and procedure to be adopted by the employer in the management of his business enterprise and thus falls within the scope of managerial prerogatives' ((1987) 163 CLR 133). In a joint judgment, the High Court decisively rejected this argument:

we reject the suggestion . . . that managerial decisions stand wholly outside the area of industrial disputes and industrial matters. There is no basis for making such an implication. It is an implication which is so imprecise as to be incapable of yielding any satisfactory criterion of jurisdiction . . . ((1987) 163 CLR 135)

The Court was not unmindful of the concerns expressed by O'Connor J in *Clancy* about the jurisdiction of the tribunal being extended 'to the regulation and control of businesses and industries in every part'. Their Honours acknowledged that these observations 'probably echoed . . . what was received doctrine at an earlier time'. However:

Over the years that climate of opinion has changed quite radically, perhaps partly as a result of the extended definition of 'industrial matters' in s 4 of the *Conciliation and Arbitration Act* and partly a result of a change in community attitudes to the relationship between employer and employee . . . No doubt our traditional system of industrial conciliation and arbitration has itself contributed to a growing recognition that management and labour have a mutual interest in many aspects of the operation of a business enterprise. Many management decisions, once regarded as the sole prerogative of management, are now correctly seen as directly affecting the relationship of employer and employee and constituting an 'industrial matter'. ((1987) 163 CLR 135)

This did not mean that the cautionary note sounded by O'Connor J in 1904 should be disregarded entirely. On the contrary, while managerial prerogative did not go to the jurisdiction of the tribunal:

... it is an argument why an industrial tribunal should exercise caution before it makes an award in settlement of a dispute where that award amounts to a substantial interference with the autonomy of management to decide how the business enterprise shall be efficiently conducted. The evident importance of arming such tribunals with power to settle industrial disputes capable of disrupting industry is a powerful reason for refusing to read down the wide and general definition of 'industrial matters' in the Commonwealth and State Acts by reference to any notion of managerial prerogatives as such. ((1987) 163 CLR 136–7)

By the late 1980s, therefore, it appeared that the integrity of the approach to the definition of 'industrial disputes' adopted by Griffith CJ and O'Connor J in *Jumbunna* had effectively been restored. With a limited exception in respect of senior State public servants, no group of employees was placed beyond the reach of the system of conciliation and arbitration by reason only of the nature of the work they performed or of their employer's business. Furthermore, the range of matters in relation to which parties could legitimately engage in disputation was to be constrained, not by artificial constructs such as the managerial prerogative doctrine, but rather by the need for an appropriate degree of connection to the employment relationship, and by what the parliament considered could appropriately be the subject of regulation through conciliation and arbitration.

The importance of this last proposition is neatly illustrated by the 1994 decision in *Alcan*.[86] In that case, the High Court determined that, although it was now clear that there was no constitutional impediment to making an award provision concerning the direct debit of trade union dues, at any rate where the employee concerned had authorised the deduction,[87] the fact that the legislature had not changed the definition of 'industrial matter' since the 1972 decision in *Portus*[88] must be taken to evince an intention that the matter should remain outside the realm of arbitrable matters. Even more importantly, the *Workplace Relations and Other Legislation Amendment Act 1996* renamed and amended the former *Industrial Relations Act 1988*. Among the most significant of the amendments effected by that measure was the introduction of what is now section 89A of the *Workplace Relations Act 1996*. In simple terms, this has the effect that the Australian Industrial Relations Commission now has power to make arbitrated awards only in relation to a list of 20 'allowable award matters'. To a large extent, this list mirrors the range of matters that was traditionally regarded as falling outside the scope of 'managerial prerogative' and, thus, to be within the jurisdiction of the tribunal.[89]

Put differently, matters of managerial prerogative have once again effectively been put beyond the reach of the award-making powers of the federal tribunal, having clearly been recognised to be within its constitutionally permissible jurisdiction only in 1987. This time the exclusion is by statute, rather than interpretation of section 51(xxxv). Obviously, if the legislation were to be changed again, the state of constitutional authority would presumably remain that set out in *Clancy* and *Alcan*.

THE SEPARATION OF POWERS DOCTRINE

It is clear from the opening words of section 51 of the Constitution that the legislative powers conferred upon the federal parliament under that section must be exercised subject to the other provisions of the Constitution – express and implied. The 'implied limitation' that constrains the jurisdiction of the federal tribunal in relation to certain categories of employees engaged in the administration of the States furnishes an interesting example of the impact of an implied constitutional principle of general application upon the operation of the system of conciliation and arbitration. An even more dramatic illustration of this impact is provided by the doctrine of separation of powers as applied by the High Court (in 1956) and the Judicial Committee of the Privy Council (in 1957) in the *Boilermakers* case.[90]

Prior to 1919, members of the Commonwealth Court of Conciliation and Arbitration were appointed for fixed, renewable terms of seven years. In *Alexander's* case,[91] the High Court cast doubt upon whether it was permissible in constitutional terms for the judicial power of the Commonwealth to be vested in a tribunal, the members of which did not enjoy judicial tenure. This resulted in the 1904 Act being amended in 1919 to provide that judges of the Commonwealth Court of Conciliation and Arbitration had the same security of tenure as the members of all other courts established under Chapter III of the Constitution. There the matter rested until 1956.

Boilermakers arose out of a challenge to the power of the Commonwealth Court of Conciliation and Arbitration to include provisions in awards banning the taking of industrial action and then to impose fines for failure to observe those same orders. The Boilermakers' Society argued that the enforcement of the bans clauses involved the exercise of a judicial power of the Commonwealth and that it was not constitutionally permissible for those powers to be vested in a body that also exercised arbitral functions. This challenge was upheld by the High Court by a majority of 4:3. In the course of this decision, the majority said:

> It is difficult to see what escape there can be from the conclusion that the Arbitration Court . . . is established as an arbitral tribunal which cannot constitutionally combine with its dominant purpose and essential functions the exercise of any part of the strictly judicial power of the Commonwealth. The basal reason why such a combination is constitutionally inadmissible is that Chapter III does not allow powers which are foreign to the judicial power to be attached to the courts created by or under that chapter for the exercise of the judicial power of the Commonwealth.[92]

'MEMORIAL FROM THE JUDGES'

On 2 March 1956, the High Court upheld an appeal by the Boilermakers' Society against a fine imposed by the Commonwealth Court of Conciliation and Arbitration. The High Court determined that the Arbitration Court could not exercise both arbitral and judicial functions.

While the Commonwealth government appealed to the Privy Council against the High Court decision, it had already decided to break the Arbitration Court tribunal into two separate tribunals, a Conciliation and Arbitration Commission and an Industrial Court. On the morning of Friday 6 April, the Attorney-General met the judges and told them of this decision. He explained that three of them would go to the Industrial Court and the remaining four to the Commission; the latter group would lose their life tenure and judicial trappings.

Even though the Attorney-General assured them that the Commission would be the more important body, the judges felt strongly that the new arrangements would demean their status. They decided accordingly to petition the Prime Minister, since Robert Menzies was known for his attachment to legal traditions. Richard Kirby took the lead in drafting this 'Memorial from the Judges', which was submitted on the following Monday (d'Alpuget 1977: 145–6).

The Memorial begins by thanking the Attorney-General for meeting with them, expressing concern that the government seemed likely to implement its proposals almost immediately and asking that their petition be considered by the Prime Minister. If the government was determined to create two separate tribunals, then the Memorial suggested that it would be better if both were designated courts. The judges were especially unhappy with the suggestion that the judges appointed to the Commission 'would be prohibited from the wearing of robes and forbidden the assistance of counsel except by permission of the parties'.

'The Judges', they said, 'have worn the wigs of judges for many years. It would naturally involve them in some personal humiliation to have those wigs removed from their heads by Act of Parliament.' From their experience, they advised 'that they could not adequately perform the task of adjudicating, which must of course be performed judicially, with the denial of the best assistance available to them'. They made a strong defence of their existing procedures:

The Judges have heard from time to time the suggestions that the lack of formality, absence of what is called legalism and the presence of lay advocates alone to assist the Court, would in some undefined manner assist in the process of arbitrating . . . The experience of the judges at the Bar and on the Bench forces them to reject these suggestions. They assert that their proceedings are not conducted with undue formality and that the matters which require their adjudication require not only the devotion of trained minds to the task but the assistance of trained minds.

They noted that five of their number had given up other judicial offices to accept appointment to the Court of Conciliation and Arbitration, while others 'relinquished large and remunerative legal practices'. Had they known that the Court was to be abolished and some of its members appointed 'to a body which would not be a Court', then they would not have accepted their original appointments to the Court. More than this, 'they would find it extremely difficult to feel that a strong sense of duty would compel them to accept appointment to the Commission if it were set up in the manner and with the title and prohibitions proposed' (NAA M1505/27).

There is no record of Menzies' reaction to the Memorial. His government proceeded with the new arrangements, though it did allow the judges appointed to the Commission to retain their titles and judicial status. Richard Kirby also reached a compromise on the question of judicial dress: as President of the new Commission, he determined that wigs would be abandoned.

Various members of the High Court have suggested from time to time that *Boilermakers* may have been incorrectly decided or that it introduced an unnecessary rigidity that might need to be reconsidered. Of particular interest in this regard are the observations of Barwick CJ in the *BLF* case:

> The principal conclusion of the *Boilermakers' Case* was
> unnecessary . . . for the effective working of the Australian Constitution
> or for the maintenance of the separation of the judicial power or for the
> protection of the independence of courts exercising that power. The
> decision leads to excessive subtlety and technicality in the operation of
> the Constitution without . . . any compensating benefit. But none the less
> and notwithstanding the unprofitable inconveniences it entails it may be
> proper that it should continue to be followed. On the other hand, it may
> be thought so unsuited to the working of the Constitution in the
> circumstances of the nation that there should now be a departure from
> some or all of its conclusions.[93]

In recent years, the High Court has on several occasions reaffirmed that the principle of separation of powers is a fundamental tenet of the Constitution.[94] Amongst other things, this has led it to strike down decisions of industrial tribunals which were adjudged to have stepped over the line of what was constitutionally permissible by reason of the *Boilermakers* principle.[95]

The Commonwealth's immediate response to the decision in *Boilermakers* was to legislate retrospectively to validate decisions handed down by the Commonwealth Court of Conciliation and Arbitration over the previous decades, which technically had been rendered invalid by the decision of the High Court. The Commonwealth also moved to separate the judicial and non-judicial functions of the Court of Conciliation and Arbitration. The former were initially vested in the Commonwealth Industrial Court. In 1976, they were transferred to the newly established Federal Court of Australia.[96] In 1993, these powers were again transferred, this time to the Industrial Relations Court of Australia. However, in 1996, they were returned to the Federal Court where they presently reside. In accordance with invariable federal convention, none of the Commonwealth Court of

Conciliation and Arbitration, the Commonwealth Industrial Court or the Australian Industrial Court was abolished while there remained any member of the Court who had not resigned. Consistent with this convention, the Industrial Relations Court remains in being, even though its substantive jurisdiction is now vested in the Federal Court.

In 1956, the non-judicial powers were vested in the Commonwealth (later Australian) Conciliation and Arbitration Commission, where they remained until that body was abolished in 1988, and replaced by the Australian Industrial Relations Commission.[97]

It is not easy to assess the practical impact of the application of the *Boilermakers* principle in the context of the law of conciliation and arbitration. Of course, there was an immediate and direct result in terms of the restructuring of the tribunal. But beyond that it is difficult to express any very definite view. In part, this stems from the fact that it is impossible precisely to define what constitute judicial, as opposed to non-judicial, functions.[98] Nevertheless, it does seem reasonable to suppose that the power to enforce legislation and definitively to pronounce upon its meaning are core elements of the judicial function. The same might be said for making a definitive determination of the rights and duties of parties vis-à-vis each other, although this adjudicative function inevitably merges into the quasi-legislative function of creating new rights through the processes of conciliation and arbitration.

As indicated, the entire *Boilermakers* episode stemmed from a challenge to the capacity of the Commonwealth Court of Conciliation and Arbitration to enforce its own decisions. Manifestly, the newly created Conciliation and Arbitration Commission lacked the power to do this. There are some who would argue that the standing of the tribunal was diminished in consequence. On the other hand, the Commonwealth Industrial Court was invested with extensive powers of enforcement, and it might equally be said that the effective demise of those powers in the aftermath of the Clarrie O'Shea episode in 1969 had a rather greater effect upon the standing of the institutions of the system than the separation of dispute-resolution and enforcement after 1956. Nevertheless, had the enforcement powers been vested in a tribunal that was rather more in tune with the sensitivities and nuances of industrial relations, the O'Shea debacle might have been avoided.[99]

Sir William Raymond Kelly, the fifth Chief Judge of the Court (1949–1956)

There is little reason to suppose that the loss of the power to interpret awards has had any great impact upon the functioning of the federal industrial tribunal. Only a very small number of cases involving the interpretation of awards have come before the courts over the years. Instead, it has been common practice for such matters to be brought before the Commission, which then determines what the award *ought* to mean in light of the representations of the parties and then proceeds to give effect to its decision, where necessary, by varying the instrument in the appropriate manner. In a polity governed by the rule of law, it is inevitable that the AIRC will regularly be required to give meaning not only to awards but to statutes (including its own constituent statute) and to the Constitution itself.

The most vexed issues that arise in this area concern the line between adjudication on existing rights and the creation of new ones. Just how fine the line between the two can be is illustrated by the following passage from the decision of the High Court in *Ranger Uranium*:

> A finding that a dismissal is harsh, unjust or unreasonable involves the finding of relevant facts and the formation and expression of a value judgment in the context of the facts so found. Although findings of fact are a common ingredient in the exercise of judicial power, such findings may also be an element in the exercise of administrative, executive and arbitral powers . . . So too with the formation and expression of value judgments.
>
> In our view the fact that the Commission is involved in making a determination of matters that could have been made by a court in the

course of proceedings instituted under . . . the Act does not ipso facto mean that the Commission has usurped judicial power, for the purpose of inquiry and determination is necessarily different depending on whether the task is undertaken by the Commission or by a court. The purpose of the Commission's inquiry is to determine whether rights and obligations should be created. The purpose of a court's inquiry and determination is to decide whether a pre-existing legal obligation has been breached, and if so, what penalty should attach to the breach. ((1987) 163 CLR 656, 665–6)

FUTURE DIRECTIONS

The industrial conciliation and arbitration power in section 51(xxxv) of the Australian Constitution was the product of a very particular set of historical circumstances. It seems safe to assume that most of those who supported the inclusion of section 51(xxxv) in the Constitution, and probably all of those who opposed its inclusion, envisaged that the power to legislate in reliance upon this provision should be used, if at all, only in highly exceptional circumstances, such as the disputes of the 1890s.

The reality has proved rather different. From its first sitting, the parliament evinced an intention that the power be utilised to a substantial extent. The system established in reliance upon that power, together with tariff protection and the 'White Australia' policy, became one of the three pillars of social policy in Australia for the greater part of the first century of Federation. The Commonwealth's expansionary ambitions were also evidenced by a number of unsuccessful attempts to extend the reach of the power by constitutional amendment.[100]

The High Court was initially inclined to adopt a restrictive approach to the interpretation of section 51(xxxv) and of legislation enacted in reliance upon it. This was especially evident during the early years of the twentieth century when the Court was comprised of Justices who had been involved in the debates leading to the adoption of the Constitution, a majority of whom were particularly sensitive about the need to maintain the 'federal balance'. Nevertheless, even during this phase in its history, the High Court handed down a number of decisions that sowed the seeds of the later dominance of the federal system of conciliation and arbitration. The most important of these was *Jumbunna*,[101] which not only legitimated the legislative provisions that provided the basis for the registration and operation of organisations of employers and employees, but also endorsed a view of the concept of an 'industrial dispute' that subsequently provided a basis for federal regulation of almost all aspects of the employment relationship and in respect of a very large cohort of the Australian workforce.

Following significant changes in its size and composition in 1913, the High Court adopted a more consistently expansive approach to the interpretation of section 51(xxxv) and of the *Commonwealth Conciliation and Arbitration Act 1904*. In certain instances, this entailed overruling some of the earlier restrictive interpretations.[102] In others, it involved breaking new ground.[103] The result was that, by 1935, the federal system of conciliation and arbitration was well on its way to becoming the dominant force in social and economic regulation that it remained until almost the end of the twentieth century.

Just as the High Court handed down 'expansionary' decisions during its early 'restrictive' period, so it continued to adopt 'restrictive' interpretations of aspects of section 51(xxxv) and the 1904 Act even during its more expansive phase. In large measure, this reflected a continuing tension between those members of the Court who were concerned to preserve the 'federal balance' and those who took the view that the regulation of work relations was an integral part of regulation of the national economy, and that, as such, it should be subject to national regula-tion. It also reflected a tension between those who took an expansive view of the range of matters that could properly be the subject matter of contention between employees, employers and their respective organisations, and those who took a more restrictive approach to such issues.

Despite such tensions, the system evolved in such a way that, by the out-break of the Second World War, it constituted the basis for the regulation of the core terms and conditions of employment of the great majority of the Australian workforce – whether through direct coverage by the federal tribunal or through flow-on into the State systems.

Yet, by the time the High Court seemed at last to be willing and able to adopt a consistent view of the nature and extent of the conciliation and arbitration power under the Constitution, the traditional system was becoming increasingly unfash-ionable. In particular, from the late 1980s onwards there was increasing pressure for a move away from the determination of terms and conditions of employment through centralised processes of third party conciliation and arbitration in favour of the direct negotiation of terms and conditions at the level of the enterprise. These pressures have resulted in significant changes to the legislative framework – notably in 1993 and 1996. To some extent, the reaction, evident in the legislation introduced by successive governments of differing political complexions, may have reflected both the impact of the dynamic of global economic forces upon Australia and a belief that the highly regulated system of conciliation and arbitration, eventually endorsed by the High Court, was now out of harmony with the needs of the Australian economy and the best interests of employers and employees alike.

The reasons for this shift of emphasis are beyond the scope of this chapter. But the emergence of enterprise bargaining has most assuredly had a profound impact upon the use to which the conciliation and arbitration power is now put and the use to which it is likely to be put in the foreseeable future.

As noted earlier, the federal system of conciliation and arbitration was originally conceived as a support mechanism for collective bargaining, with arbitrated outcomes being imposed upon the parties only where collective bargaining, assisted by conciliation where appropriate, proved incapable of preventing or settling the differences between the parties. Gradually, conciliation and arbitration became the norm. But it is important to appreciate that they never entirely displaced collective bargaining – rather, collective bargaining assumed forms which do not conform to the traditional North American or (to a lesser extent) European concept of that phenomenon.[104] The changes of the last fifteen years have seen a reversion to collective bargaining as the centrepiece of the system with conciliation and arbitration as a kind of default or 'safety net'.[105] In many respects, these legislative changes have reflected, and further stimulated, modifications that were already occurring in a changing marketplace.

The early attempts to encourage enterprise bargaining – such as those contained in sections 112–17 of the *Industrial Relations Act 1988*, and their replacement in Division 3A of Part VI of the 1988 Act – all drew upon the conciliation and arbitration power for their constitutional underpinning. However, the *Industrial Relations Reform Act 1993* represented a radical break from the past in this respect. While the principal enterprise bargaining stream still relied

During the late 1970s the Commission maintained a policy of partial wage indexation, while the stronger unions pursued additional increases. This cartoon shows Cliff Dolan, the president of the ACTU, carrying a reluctant partner towards the bridal bed where the siren collective bargaining waits; two months later the Commission abandoned wage indexation.

mainly upon the conciliation and arbitration power, a new stream of 'enterprise flexibility agreements' drew upon the corporations power in section 51(xx) of the Constitution and provisions recognising (for the first time in federal law) a limited right to strike drew, in part, upon the external affairs power in section 51(xxix).[106]

This shift away from reliance upon the conciliation and arbitration power gained further momentum with the passage of the *Workplace Relations and Other Legislation Amendment Act 1996*. As noted earlier, this measure renamed the 1988 Act as the Workplace Relations Act. It further consolidated the shift to enterprise bargaining, and introduced an individualised bargaining option in the form of Australian Workplace Agreements (AWAs).[107] It is still possible to enter into certified agreements to prevent or settle interstate industrial disputes.[108] However, the great majority of agreements are now made between corporations and registered unions or between corporations and their employees under

Division 2 of Part VIB of the Workplace Relations Act. The provisions relating to AWAs also rely for their constitutional validity upon the corporations power.

The year 1996 saw another major development in the evolution of the federal system of industrial regulation. For the first time, one of the States, Victoria, referred a significant part of its power to legislate with respect to industrial relations to the Commonwealth in reliance upon section 51(xxxvii) of the Constitution. So far, no other State has followed this lead. However, the Victorian referral clearly has the effect that for that jurisdiction it is not necessary to draw upon the conciliation and arbitration, corporations or external affairs power as a basis for federal regulation of referred matters.[109] In respect of Victoria, subject to the Constitution, the federal parliament enjoys both referred State and federal legislative powers.

It would be erroneous to suppose that the conciliation and arbitration power has been rendered redundant by these legislative and economic changes. Awards made in reliance upon that power still play a crucial role in the federal industrial relations system, whether as the basis for the no-disadvantage test which must be satisfied by every certified agreement or AWA,[110] or as the basis for regulating terms and conditions of employment for those employees who, for one reason or another, are not covered by a certified agreement or an AWA. Important issues of social policy and safety net wage increases are still dealt with through test cases in the Australian Industrial Relations Commission.[111] Furthermore, the federal tribunal still plays an important role in the day-to-day operation of the industrial relations system – for example, by means of conciliation to facilitate the making of certified agreements.

Nevertheless, it seems clear that laws enacted in reliance upon the conciliation and arbitration power will never resume their former dominant role in the regulation of work relations in Australia.[112] Yet, it is equally clear that the history of the national industrial relations tribunal over the first century of its existence has been one of remarkable resilience, persistence and adaptability. That history has reflected the expanding concept of Australian nationhood; the stable and changing features of the applicable federal legislation; the evolving constitutional doctrines of the High Court concerning the relevant heads of legislative power; the interpretative principles of constitutional law to be applied in fathoming the depths of these powers; the alterations that have occurred in the national and international economies; the changing educational and training levels of the Australian workforce; fluctuating levels of union membership; increasing challenges to the very nature of work; and differing political fashions.

There seems to be no doubt that the national industrial relations tribunal will continue to adapt and change both in its functions and in its methods of operation. After a century, the impediments to such adaptation and change now seem less likely to be constitutional in character and more likely to be the emergence within the economy and the institutions of federal government of a different vision for the role of the tribunal in its second century.

If the history of the first century is any guide, only two things can be said of the future with a fair degree of certainty. First, even though there will inevitably be less reliance upon the conciliation and arbitration power in the second century of federation, there will continue to be a need for a national tribunal of some kind to supplement and moderate the outcomes of unregulated market forces. And second, the alteration of the established functions of the tribunal and the accretion of new ones cannot accurately be predicted in a rapidly changing world of economic, social and technological innovation (Kirby 2002: 575–6).

4

ECONOMIC AND SOCIAL EFFECTS

Keith Hancock and Sue Richardson

While an arbitral tribunal deriving its authority under an exercise of the legislative power given by section 51 (xxxv) must confine itself to conciliation and arbitration for the prevention and settlement of industrial disputes including what is incidental thereto and cannot have in its hands the general control or direction of industrial, social or economic policies, it would be absurd to suppose that it was to proceed blindly in its work of industrial arbitration and ignore the industrial, social and economic consequences of what it was invited to do or of what, subject to the power of variation, it had actually done.

Sir Owen Dixon, Chief Justice of the High Court[1]

In this chapter, we focus our attention on the role of the federal industrial tribunal as a maker of economic and social policy. Our treatment of the topic is less than complete in that we do not discuss, except in passing, the institutional factors – constitutional, legislative and political – that affected the development of this role. Much of this context is described in other chapters.[2] We do, however, try to describe the evolution of ideas within the tribunal about its economic and social responsibilities and to locate it in both the changing state of the economy and the society and the emerging opinions about wage policies and their effects.

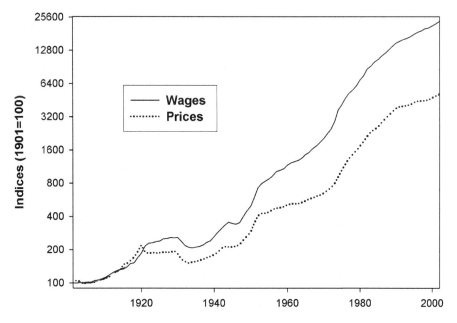

Figure 4.1 Adult male wages and consumer prices, 1901–2002

A CENTURY OF PRICES AND WAGES

This section provides a context for later discussion of tribunal policies and their effects. Figure 4.1, using a logarithmic scale, summarises the rises in full-time male wages and consumer prices between 1901 and 2002.[3] Over the 101-year period, wages rose 236-fold and prices by a factor of 51.

Real wages

We now use the estimates of prices, wages and hours to derive indices of real wages. The two series represented (on a logarithmic scale) in Figure 4.2 are for total and hourly male wages and show their growth in the 101 years from 1901 to 2002.[4] Real wages, unadjusted for working time, grew by a factor of 4.6. Hourly real wages grew 5.3 times. The most striking features of the figure are a decline in real wages over the period 1914–20; a sudden increase in 1920–21; a sustained rise between the late 1940s and the mid-1970s; a stagnation of real

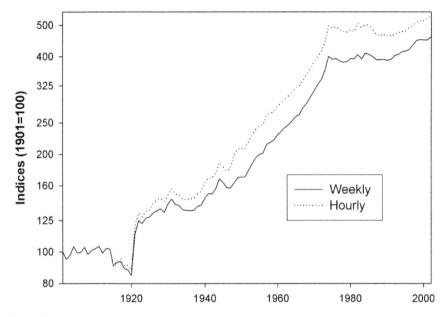

Figure 4.2 Male real wages, 1901–2002

wages between the late 1970s and the early 1990s; and a modest increase over
the decade 1992–2002.

Female wages

With the available data, it would be even more difficult to construct a continuous
index of female wages than it is for male wages. There are, however, various
series (all limited in time) from which female–male relativities can be calculated.
Since the series measure different things, it is to be expected that they will show
different ratios. But they support broad inferences about trends in gender relativities. For Figure 4.3, we use six data series: annual earnings in manufacturing,
1912–68; minimum adult wage rates, 1915–80, shown for five-year intervals;
average weekly earnings (AWE), 1946–81; average weekly earnings (full-time),
1972–84; average weekly ordinary time earnings (AWOTE), 1984–2002; and
'May survey' data, derived from surveys of employers, 1975–2002.[5] Notwithstanding the deficiencies of the data, it is clear that the relative rewards of females

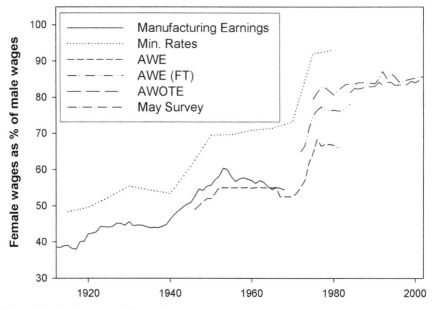

Figure 4.3 Gender wage differentials, 1912–2002

increased substantially across the century. Although the impact of the equal pay decisions of 1969 and 1972 is evident, there was also a longer-term trend towards lesser differences. If male real wages grew 4 to 5 times, the increase in real wages of females may well have been of the order of 6 to 8 times.

The basic wage

The federal basic wage – a 'foundation' component of award wages – began with the *Harvester* decision of 1907, was first incorporated in an award in 1908, and ended in 1967, with the adoption of the 'total wage'. Because of its importance in wage-setting for much of the century, we briefly survey its history. This is a statistical view only: we defer our discussion of arbitral policies. Figure 4.4 shows the course taken by the federal basic wage.[6] It also shows, for comparison, minimum rates (adult males) – an average of rates prescribed in awards, certified agreements and like legal instruments – and the composite wage index constructed for Figure 4.1 and later figures. The three series are all set at

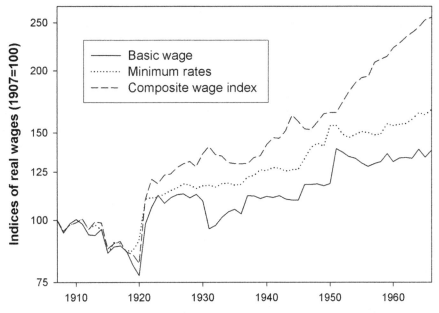

Figure 4.4 The basic wage and other wage measures, 1907–66

100 in 1907 and are converted to real values by means of the composite price index.

By 1920, the real basic wage was more than 20 per cent below the *Harvester* standard.[7] Falling prices in 1920–21 obliterated the deficiency. Through the 1920s, the basic wage exceeded the *Harvester* equivalent, probably because of 'Powers' three shillings',[8] intended as a protection against rising prices but in force at a time of price stability. In the Depression, however, the real basic wage fell, and would have fallen further but for the lag of wage reductions behind falling prices. The real basic wage failed to match the growth of minimum wage rates. Disparate movement of the basic wage and minimum rates would flow from unequal proportional changes in the basic wage and margins. But as the minimum rates series includes wages set under state instruments, unequal movements in the indices were due also to differences between federal and State wage-fixing practices. Until the early 1930s, any difference between the two series was insignificant in the light of the margins of error inherent in the data. With the fall in the basic wage in the Depression, a 'gap' was opened that was never fully closed.

Over the sixty-year period of the figure, the real basic wage grew by an estimated 38 per cent and minimum rates grew by 67 per cent. The composite wage index, constructed to measure actual rather than prescribed wages, rose (in real terms) by 156 per cent. A high proportion of the divergence between the composite index and the other indices is due to the period 1953–66, when the composite index grew by 41 per cent, minimum rates by 14 per cent and the basic wage by 3 per cent (all in real terms). The divergence between actual and prescribed wages represents the 'earnings drift' (discussed later in this chapter).

Concluding comments

Our wage data refer to pre-tax wages. Across the century, the proportion of the GDP absorbed by tax grew from around 6 per cent to about 30 per cent (Hancock and Smith 2001: 1). Had this transfer of spending power been effected by a proportional income tax, we might say that real post-tax wages grew by a factor about 25 per cent less than that indicated by pre-tax data, this 'loss' being offset by 'benefits' in the form of government-provided goods and services and transfer payments. The matter is more complex than this, however, for at least two reasons. One, obviously, is that neither taxes nor benefits are proportional to pre-tax wages. The other is that part of the greater tax burden took the form of indirect taxes, which affect the price indices. For example, the excise on petrol affects the CPI. To this extent, taxes are taken into account *before* the calculation of real wages. Conversion of pre-tax into post-tax real income of wage-earners is difficult, if not impossible.

SOCIAL DIMENSIONS OF WAGE POLICY

Wages and needs[9]

Much of the debate about the social aspects of arbitration has focused on the relation between minimum wages and needs. *Harvester*, and the subsequent applications of the *Harvester* standard, did much to generate that debate. At best, the standard was a crude assessment. But the rhetoric of the decision included significant reference to family needs. The intellectual affinity of the judgment to the papal encyclical *Rerum Novarum*, of 1891, has been widely noted: it includes the use of the term 'frugal comfort' (as in the English-language version of the encyclical) to describe the family living standard that the lowest wage ought to support.

If the basic wage were to support a particular standard of living, it would have to be adjusted for rising prices. Beginning in 1913, the Court, when setting the basic wage in new awards, took account of the movement of prices disclosed by the 'A Series' price index (first published in 1912, retrospective to 1901). But the lag between the rise in prices and the eventual making of a new award caused significant erosions of the real basic wage.

Some of the innate hazards of a needs criterion were exposed – if that was necessary – by the episode of the Piddington Commission. Appointed in late 1919, the Royal Commission was directed to inquire into the needs of a family comprising two adults and three children under 14. It did this by listing the items that such a family 'needed' and pricing them. The amount so determined exceeded the then-prevailing basic wage by more than 50 per cent. The impossibility of implementing such a standard pointed to an inevitable subordination of social criteria to economic constraints. It also raised a question about the relation between wages and social welfare. Piddington, in a personal memorandum, proposed that the basic wage be set at a level sufficient for a childless couple and that child endowment be paid where there were children. This proposal was not adopted – except for the payment of child endowment to Commonwealth public servants (Anderson 1929: 255–6).

The idea of child endowment persisted, however. Higgins (1926: 183) said:

It is obvious, and admitted by the critics, that to prescribe a higher basic wage for a man with ten dependent children than for a man with no dependent children would seriously hamper the former in getting or keeping employment. But these critics want a provision for family endowment – endowment coming from the State or from groups of employers – a direct payment for children and for wives independent of wages . . . Perhaps it is sufficient to say that when I gave what is called

'FAIR AND REASONABLE'

Henry Bournes Higgins, the second President of the Commonwealth Conciliation and Arbitration Court from 1907 to 1921, formulated the principles of wage fixation which dominated Australian wage determination for almost half the life of the tribunal. One of his earliest tasks was to give meaning and a monetary value to the term 'fair and reasonable' in connection with the Excise and Tariff Act in the 1907 *Harvester* case. In an exchange with counsel for the employer, HV McKay, on the meaning of 'fair and reasonable', the following passage reflects his philosophy in the determination of the basic wage:

> His Honour: Can you say that any bargain can be fair which is made by one party on pain of starvation? Take the case of Esau. He is very hungry and he must get something to eat. He sells his inheritance for a mess of potage. Would you call it a fair bargain?
>
> Mr Schutt: Probably not in that case.
>
> His Honour: It may be that, although the words are not worked out elaborately in the minds of the Legislature, still there is something to be said for the view that where you have the two words used they must have separate meanings. It is not enough to be fair, it must be reasonable. It is not enough to be reasonable, but it must be fair. Perhaps the word fair refers to in some sense 'within reasonable limitations, equality of contracting position'. But if one or several men say – 'I take it because I cannot get better, I must live', then the Legislature says that I must look at what would be fair remuneration assuming the two parties were not on the basis of individual bargaining but were upon the basis where each party is as strong as the other. For instance, if the two parties are on a basis of collective bargaining then I can understand them more or less being on a level, a whole army of workmen on one side and a considerable body of employers on the other . . .
>
> Mr Schutt: I do not say that fair and reasonable remuneration for labour includes cases where the remuneration paid is a starvation wage.
>
> His Honour: Perhaps you do not follow me. I say that on pain of starvation he accepts a wage which otherwise he would not . . . Take a man whose wife is

sick and whose children are hungry; he goes to the factory and says: 'I want work'. He has got no money in his pocket. He is told: 'Well, I will put you on at six shillings a day'. Do you mean to say he would not take it? Would that be a fair wage for a tradesman?' . . . The ordinary higgling of the market is not the basis upon which the Legislature treats this thing as fair. The higgling of the market is not a fair basis where two men who are making a bargain are not upon reasonably equivalent foundations. The word fair may have that meaning that you are not to treat the individual bargain that a man is willing to accept as being an indication of what is fair for the purpose of the Act.

Mr Schutt: I do not think it is at all conclusive but it is certainly an element in the matter. The market price of his labour is an element. It may be that owing to the unequal circumstances of the man he is forced to take less remuneration than what he is worth. But apart from that being shown I should say that what his labour is worth in the market is a strong factor in coming to a conclusion as to what is fair to give him under the Act.

His Honour: Do you say the Legislature meant I should base fair and reasonable upon what he can get in the market?

Mr Schutt: Your Honour should take it into account.

His Honour: . . . If the Legislature meant to go upon the market price of a man's labour or a price which he is willing to sell his labour or life for, it would have left it to individual bargaining, because that is in operation and there is no need to go further . . . (*Harvester* case, Transcript 595–7) the 'Harvester Decision' in 1907, fixing a basic wage at 42/- per week, the decision would have been materially different if any such provision existed for wives and children; and in that state of the law no wages could be deemed 'fair and reasonable' which did not, to some extent, allow for this maintenance.

The conflict between uniformity of wages, on the one hand, and the diversity of family composition, on the other, was again noted in the 1934 Basic Wage Case, when the majority judges said that if it were desired to equalise the living standards of families of different size, 'some system of family or child endowment would have to be introduced by competent legislative authority' (Foenander 1941: 159).

The wages policies of the 1930s were explicitly related to economic conditions. Except for the 1940 Basic Wage Case (when the federal government averted a wage increase by introducing child endowment), needs very largely disappeared from the wage-setting agenda. In no decision between the Second World War and 1967 did the Court or the Commission relate the wage levels set to any concept or measure of adequacy for the recipient or a family.

At the time of its decision to abolish the basic wage, the Commission instituted a 'minimum wage', set at a level above, and prevailing over, some lower award rates. Its amount was not founded upon any assessment of needs. The Commission, rather, was alive to the fact that many employees received above-award wages and sought to protect the relative position of the low-paid worker reliant on award rates. In the period between 1967 and the suspension of the 'centralised system' in 1981, national wage increases were translated to the minimum wage as if it were a specific classification in the award structure. It was bypassed, however, in the so-called 'work value' round of 1979–80. Likewise, it was unaffected by the increases secured during the period of 'decentralised' wage determination of 1981–82. Exclusion of the minimum wage from these wage rounds rendered it virtually irrelevant.

Needs returned to the agenda in the 1990s. Their 'rediscovery' was linked to the advent of enterprise bargaining and the relegation of the award system to the role of a 'safety net'. A decreased proportion of wage-earners dependent on award conditions, with safety net increases having a lesser economic impact than did earlier general wage decisions, encouraged greater attention to needs. This change of focus was further encouraged by the requirement of the *Workplace Relations Act 1996* that the Commission, in adjusting the safety net, have regard to 'the needs of the low paid'. 'Safety net' cases have replaced National Wage cases. The Commission, like the parties, has approached them as occasions for protecting the interests of workers unable to benefit directly from bargaining. In 1997, it discussed the meaning of 'needs', distinguishing two approaches: construing needs 'simply as an adjunct of "low paid" without any further attempt to specify or quantify them'; and attempting 'to quantify needs and the cost of meeting them, leading to an endeavour (subject to other constraints, such as economic capacity) to ensure that wages are sufficient to provide for them'. Preferring the former, the Commission said that it entailed 'a general acceptance that the standard of living available to wage-earners is related to (though not wholly determined by) their level of wages; and that low paid wage-earners are more likely than others to experience hardship due to their limited capacity to spend' (AIRC 1997: 65). The Commission introduced a federal minimum wage, equated to the minimum classification rate in the metal industry award and displacing any lower rates in other awards.

In Safety Net cases, the Commonwealth government, with non-Labor governments in the States and Territories (before 2002), has argued for 'capping' increases in award rates. The government advocates this strategy as one that accords with an emphasis on the needs of the low paid. At the same time, it argues for limiting the increases granted to the low paid by questioning the association of low wages and unmet needs. The main cause of household poverty, the government says, is unemployment, which is exacerbated by wage increases. To date, the government has not followed the logic of this reasoning to the point of opposing any safety net increases. Nevertheless, its contentions imply a lack of sympathy for the protective function of awards.

The Commission has not so far adopted this view. In 2000, it (AIRC 2000: 36) said:

> As a result of societal change it is often the case that there are two wage-earners (sometimes more) within a family unit. It is not surprising that it is no longer as simple as it once may have been to view the income

of an employee as an indicator of household income . . . We accept that safety net adjustments are not perfectly targeted to meeting the needs of the low paid. They do, however, assist in meeting those needs.

In 2002, the Commission (AIRC 2002: 55) referred to this statement and said that 'nothing in the material presented on this occasion leads us to alter the view there expressed'.

The award system and social security

Minimum wage prescription may be viewed as averting the emergence of a class of 'working poor'. Inasmuch as it serves this purpose, it alters the set of problems that confront the framers of social security policy. Frank Castles (1985, 1994) has depicted arbitration as a mechanism of social protection that has functioned as a partial substitute for government-funded benefits such as have emerged in other developed countries. Accordingly, he coined the term 'wage-earners' welfare state' to characterise the Australian mixture of interventionist wage-setting and parsimonious social welfare. Ingenious as the idea is, it is almost entirely inferential: examples of policy-makers explicitly attributing the structure and content of social services to the adequacy of wage levels are, to our knowledge, non-existent. Whether wage regulation nullified political pressures that *might* otherwise have emerged for a bigger social security system is unknowable.

The pre-1940 pressures for child endowment, discussed earlier, *were* an attempt to mould one aspect of social security around the wage system, so as to offset the latter's inability to differentiate with respect to the numbers of dependants supported from wages. The incongruities of a 'family wage' had become evident to the tribunals – both federal and State – which identified a role for social welfare as a supplement to wage prescription and progressively downgraded the needs criterion. Child endowment was initially a device to take pressure off the wages system. No other aspect of the social security system has had a similar interaction with wage policy.

Some recent proposals, calling for the wages system to *vacate* territory to social welfare, have the *opposite* implication to that of the wage-earners' welfare state. In Safety Net cases since 1996, the Commonwealth government has tried to persuade the Commission that income enhancement through social security diminishes the need for the Commission to protect the low-paid.[10] Indeed, safety net wage increases are depicted as an inefficient device for alleviating poverty (Commonwealth Submission 2002: 87). To date, the Commission appears not to have accepted this argument, which is taken a stage further by the proposal of the self-styled 'Five Economists' who, since 1998, have advocated a 'freeze' of award wages, with compensation provided to low-paid wage-earners through adjustments to the tax and social service systems (Dawkins and Kelly 2003).

WAGE POLICY AND THE ECONOMY

The advent of 'capacity to pay'

Higgins distinguished between the *sacrosanct* character of the basic wage and the mere *desirability* of preserving rewards for skill. The distinction was expressed in an oft-quoted passage of his 1909 *Broken Hill* decision:

> So long as every employee gets a living wage, I can well understand that workmen of skill might consent to work . . . for less than their proper wages, not only to get present employment, but in order to assist an enterprise which will afford them and their comrades more opportunities for employment hereafter. For this purpose it is advisable to make the demarcation as clear and as definite as possible between that part of the wages which is for mere living and that part of the wages which is due to skill, or to monopoly, or to other considerations. Unless great multitudes of people are to be irretrievably injured in themselves and in their families, unless society is to be perpetually in industrial unrest, it is necessary to keep this living wage sacrosanct, beyond the reach of bargaining. (1909 3 CAR 32)

It was to be expected that any consideration of economic effects would, at that time, be limited to particular employers or, perhaps, industries. By 1920 or thereabouts, the spread of arbitration and the growing significance of the basic wage encouraged a wider view. The report of the Commonwealth Statistician, GH Knibbs, on the Piddington basic wage was, in fact, about the economic limits to aggregate real wages (*CPD* 23 November 1920: 6817). Knibbs may or may not have been correct in saying that raising the basic wage to the Piddington standard would more than absorb the whole national income, but few economic lessons have been as easy for the tribunals to absorb (see, for example, Powers 1921 15 CAR 841). During the 1920s there was a growing economic commentary – mostly critical – on the effects of arbitration. Some of it rested on a concept of 'capacity to pay'. An explicit or implicit assumption was that wage levels exceeding 'capacity' threatened employment. Capacity to pay, in this view, was jointly determined by the volume of production and the prices received for it. Copland (1923: 573), focusing particularly on the volatility of prices, argued that adverse economic consequences had flowed from the poor timing of wage changes. Figure 4.1, which shows the contrary movements of wages and prices in the early 1920s, provides a context for this argument.

In 1924, the economists JT Sutcliffe, RC Mills and JB Brigden were appointed to an Economic Commission on the Basic Wage to advise the Queensland Court of Industrial Arbitration.[11] They too invoked the notion of capacity to pay. This depended upon 'net aggregate production', which was determined by 'the volume of production and the price of a unit' (Sutcliffe et al. 1925: 13). Prices were relevant, not as a synonym for the cost of living, but as a determinant of the flow of funds from which wages were paid. The Economic Commission proposed an index of capacity to pay, representing the value of production (measured in nominal terms) and combining both present data and projections.[12]

After the institution of automatic adjustments (announced in December 1921 and confirmed by an enlarged bench in 1922), the Court did not revisit the basic wage at large until 1930, but various decisions about other matters reflected the difficult economic conditions of the 1920s (Hancock 1979: 136–7). The Depression led to more fundamental rethinking. Debate about the correct response to the 'emergency' was dominated by the professional economists' advocacy of spreading the sacrifice – that is, partially relieving exporters of the effects of depressed prices for their products. Copland's evidence in the 1930 hearing went along these lines and underpinned the Court's decision, in January 1931, to reduce federal award rates by 10 per cent. But the Court had views of its own. Among the three judges who sat on all of the Basic Wage cases of the 1930s (Dethridge, Beeby and Drake-Brockman), there was a perception that the 'right' level of wages represented a balance between opposite forces affecting employment: a *positive* effect of higher wages associated with wage-earners' demand for consumption goods and services; and a *negative* effect related to producers' costs.

When Dethridge announced, in July 1930, that the Full Court would be convened to consider, among other things, the possible necessity of reducing the basic wage below the *Harvester* standard, he alluded to this balancing task (1930 29 CAR 274). It was 'sound economic doctrine' that 'at all times, whether depressed or prosperous, the aggregate of employers and capitalists . . . would profit by distributing in wages as much as possible of the return from industry'. In a closed economy, it might be possible to adjust wages so as to ensure the purchase of the whole of the product. But in an open one, such a policy was constrained by the prices received by exporters. In the circumstances of the time, 'wages must be reduced or the industry must collapse' (1930 29 CAR 267).

In 1934, when the Court cancelled the emergency reduction, Dethridge and Drake-Brockman (1934 33 CAR 150) thought that it 'had assisted many industrial concerns to weather the economic blizzard', but the benefit had been lessened because 'the transferred spending power was not used by employers or capitalists quickly or abundantly'. Their dictum 'that what should be sought is the independent ascertainment of the highest basic wage that can be sustained by the total of industry in all its primary, secondary and ancillary forms' reflected their concept of balancing the favourable and the adverse effects of higher wages.[13]

In the 1937 Basic Wage Case (resulting in the award of 'prosperity loadings'), the Court sought 'the assistance of some trained mind'. WB Reddaway appeared, like Copland in 1930, as a witness of the Court, 'identified with neither side'.[14] He advised the Court that, without an increase in wages, the current expansion of real income would be concentrated on profits and rents and generate a 'most unhealthy' investment-driven boom. A rise in real wages 'would now be extremely valuable as a restraining influence both on the price of existing capital assets and

In the 1934 basic wage case the Court cancelled the reduction it had imposed as an emergency measure three years earlier, but the increase it awarded fell short of the unions' expectations. The original caption read: 'Here's a bit of luck for you. A needle and thread to sew your pants.' Note that this labour cartoon attributes the decision to the United Australia Party government.

the excessive construction of new ones' (Reddaway 1937). The Court saw a need:

> to arrive at a wage level which, while not so high as to prevent the capitalist sector investing all of the 'savings' which come under its control, is not so low as to allow money to pass to the capitalist sector, which may not spend it promptly within the community to buy goods and services. (1937 37 CAR 590)

This reasoning was closer to the Court's earlier notion of 'balance' than to Reddaway's arguments. Nevertheless, the Court adopted his judgment that a wage increase would forestall 'a likely boom and slump'.

Post-war 'prosperity'

'Capacity to pay', before the Second World War, was closely related to employment. In the post-war context of full employment, it was a more vacuous concept. The link between economic data and specific decisions was 'fuzzy'.

Early post-war claims by unions, pertaining to the basic wage, standard hours, annual leave and margins, invited the Court to assume that prosperity justified higher labour costs. The Standard Hours Case, which began in November 1945 and was decided twenty-two months later, was the occasion of a major economic review. The 225 witnesses included the economists HP Brown, Colin Clark, HC Coombs, LF Giblin and SM Wadham. The Court (alluding to the Main Hours Case of 1926, when a general reduction of hours was refused) said that 'it seems to us as it seemed to this Court when it dealt with this problem in 1926 so clear as to be beyond cavil that the appropriate time to add burdens to industry . . . is when industry is booming and nature is bountiful' (1947 59 CAR 599).

Over the next few years, the presumption that prosperity signified increased capacity to pay clashed with concerns about inflation. Raymond Kelly became Chief Judge in 1949. A division of opinion between Kelly and his colleagues Foster and Dunphy marked the Basic Wage inquiry of 1949–50. To Kelly, inflation was an evil to be arrested. 'I am not prepared', he said, 'to take any risks about this matter. There are other steps necessary to be taken by other authorities . . . Their existence, even their inaction, in some regard, to date does not absolve this Court from doing what it understands to be its duty' (1949 68 CAR 775). Foster and, less clearly, Dunphy thought that the worker was entitled to a share of the current prosperity and that inflation was a problem for other authorities. They 'out-voted' Kelly. In 1952, however, Conciliation Commissioner Galvin (in a decision not subject to appeal) refused an application for increases in metal trade margins, expressing views similar to Kelly's (1952 73 CAR 345–63).

The abandonment of automatic basic wage adjustments in 1953 was not expressly intended to counter inflation (which by then had subsided considerably), but the experience of a 'wage–price spiral' in the previous few years influenced the Court's judgment that price increases did not signify greater 'capacity to pay'. The Court set out a set of 'indicators' of capacity: employment, investment, production and productivity, overseas trade, overseas balances, competitive position of secondary industry, and retail trade (1953 77 CAR 509–10). Whatever help this may have been to parties preparing submissions in future cases, or to the tribunal in structuring its published reasons, the 'indicators' suffered the weakness of defying logical translation into wage outcomes (see Isaac 1954).

Prices and productivity

Economists in the 1920s, as we have seen, criticised the arbitration system's failure to preserve a stable relation between the wages bill and 'net aggregate production' (a term used by the Queensland Economic Commission on the Basic Wage). Two aspects of the implied formula are worthy of note: it is about distributive shares, for it entails a stability of the wage share in the value of production; and the average wage rises or falls proportionally to the average value of production per worker; this, in turn, implies that the average wage rises or falls with both the level of real product per worker and the price level.

Wage shares, directly or by implication, were crucial to the wage policy debates of the 1930s. For example, Copland's 1930 evidence called for a reduction of wages to offset the diminished share of exporters in the national product; the 'balancing' model of the Court implied a need to get 'right' the respective shares of labour and capital; and Reddaway's evidence called for an increase in the wage share (and a smaller capital share) to curb over-investment. When, however, unions developed explicit arguments about income shares to support their wage claims, the Court bridled. In the 1940–41 Basic Wage inquiry, the unions argued for a wage increase so as to reverse an alleged decline in the wage share of the national income. Beeby said:

> Again and again, the Court has pointed out that it is not the
> legislature . . . Deliberate re-arrangement of the division of the national
> income amongst the different factors of production is beyond both its

power and its capacity . . . The Court's past decisions undoubtedly have affected the division of national income, but not as preconceived schemes of social reconstruction. (1941 44 CAR 49)

The 1949–50 Basic Wage inquiry was conducted against the background of a 'wool boom' that brought with it higher exporters' incomes. Union arguments included a need to raise the labour share of the national income. A submission of Benjamin Higgins[15] (1950: 9) supported them:

The facts that I have presented do seem to suggest that it might be desirable to raise labour's share of national income to a figure more closely approximating the share received by Australian workers before the war, or by the workers of other countries at the present time. I should also like to suggest . . . that the Court can scarcely avoid making some decision as to what share of national income should be paid to employees as wages and salaries. A decision to do nothing to alter the share is itself a decision that the existing share is appropriate.

Higgins added 'that the exporters are the group whose candidature for a cut in share of national income is strongest'. His submission did not impress the Court. Dunphy said:

It is not a function of the Court . . . to make a deliberate attempt to take a proportion of the income of one wealthy constituent part of the community and transfer it to a poorer group, even if such were a practical possibility. This over-simplified operation seems to have appealed to Professor Higgins . . . but outside of such an action being impracticable and unconstitutional, it raises the question of reciprocity in hard times. (1949 60 CAR 836)

'Reciprocity in hard times' was, in fact, an apt depiction of the wage reductions of 1931.

In the Basic Wage cases of the later 1950s (there was none between 1953 and 1956), unions applied repeatedly for the restoration of automatic adjustments. Initially, much of their argument was directed against the Court's assertion of an inconsistency between the adoption of the capacity-to-pay criterion in the early 1930s and the retention of price-related adjustments. In the case that concluded early in 1957, counsel for the unions was assisted by an analysis of court decisions provided by RJL Hawke. This showed that the Court had consistently dealt with the level of the basic wage on the clear understanding that automatic adjustments would compensate for price movements, leaving the real basic wage for explicit decision. The Commission did not contest this historical analysis, but, in effect, asked 'so what?' It was better for the Commission, acting with reference to the state of the economy, to control wage movements than to impose a formula representing only one aspect of it.

The ACTU confronted squarely the question of wage-fixing criteria in the 1959 Basic Wage Case. Hawke – now ACTU advocate – called two expert witnesses, WEG Salter and EA Russell. Central to their evidence was the concept of 'effective productivity'. This varied with (1) the *per capita* physical productivity of the labour force and (2) the terms of trade. Russell (1959: 1–2) explained:

> If effective productivity increases by a certain percentage it will be possible to increase real wages by the same percentage and (if the level of employment is unchanged) real incomes other than wage incomes will, in the aggregate, increase in the same proportion. (If the level of employment changes certain qualifications must be made.) It is this that we have in mind, I believe, when we say that an increase in productivity increases the capacity of the economy to pay a higher real wage.[16]

Effective productivity, thus defined, was a *real* magnitude, independent of the price level. But it determined the capacity of the economy to pay *real* wages. To achieve the result that real wages rose or fell with effective productivity, it was necessary for money wages to vary with productivity *plus* prices (Russell 1959: 5–6). This wage rule resembled the capacity-to-pay criterion that economists such as Copland and the Queensland Economic Commission had proposed in the 1920s. Underlying both was the objective of stabilising the wage share in the national product. A common element was the assumption that higher prices, along with higher productivity, translated into the capacity to pay higher money wages.[17] Sir Douglas Copland, called as a union witness in 1961, supported the automatic adjustment of the basic wage for price movements. The Commission, in his view, should periodically adjust the *real* basic wage for movements in productivity.

The 'prices plus productivity' criterion in the 1960s met the alternative of 'productivity only'. If prices were rising, this was obviously a recipe for smaller wage increases. The argument was put in different ways, but a common version was that 'mark-ups' – the percentage relation between product prices and labour costs – were either fixed or immune from alteration by rises in money wages. Hence, a money wage increase related to price increases would merely feed through into further price increases of equal proportion, whereas an increase in productivity permitted an increase in money wages of the same proportion *without* upward pressure on prices. Alternatively, constancy of money wages would allow prices to fall proportionally to the gain in productivity. Thus, there was a choice between realising the gain in real wages through higher money wages and doing so through lower prices; but for reasons of practicality and industrial realism, the former was a more probable process.[18]

At the heart of the dispute was the relation between money and real wages. The 'prices plus productivity' rule implied a significant correlation. Adjustment of money wages was necessary to ensure that real wages grew with productivity (and to preserve the wage share in national income). 'Productivity only' represented real and money wages as independent, depicting the battle over money wages as one about the rate of inflation. Opponents of 'prices plus productivity' made the point that, because wage increases caused price increases, there was a self-repeating quality about them. It seemed anomalous that a wage increase today would 'justify' (via its price effects) yet further increases in the future. The argument was also made that attempts to 'distribute', via wages, *past* gains in productivity entailed double-counting. There was no mechanism for 'storing' productivity gains – they had already been distributed, whether in higher money incomes or in lower prices. The only relevance of past productivity growth was as a guide to likely *future* growth.

This conflict of ideas had its counterpart in actual wage policy. The Court, in 1956, and the Commission, in 1957 and 1958, had unanimously rejected applications to restore automatic adjustments of the basic wage. In 1959, the bench was divided.[19] Kirby (then President of the Commission) said that 'the annual

RICHARD KIRBY

Richard Kirby's membership of the Court and the Commission spanned twenty-six years, and his seventeen years as President of the Commission made him the longest-serving head of the tribunal.

Born in Charters Towers in 1904, he was educated at the King's School, Parramatta, and at the University of Sydney. Kirby worked as a solicitor and barrister before serving with the AIF from 1942 to 1944. He described himself as an 'unquestioning Establishment man' until the Depression ended his prosperity and his marriage (d'Alpuget 1977: 20). He then turned to industrial practice and developed a sympathy for the underdog. The New South Wales Labor government appointed him to the District Court in 1944 and he also served as a member of the Australian War Crimes Commission.

In 1947, Kirby became the youngest appointee to the Commonwealth Court of Conciliation and Arbitration. Assigned to the chair of the Stevedoring Industry Commission, he had an immediate baptism of fire. With his senior colleagues on the Court bench bitterly divided, Kirby's prescience was increasingly apparent. The government chose him to head the Conciliation and Arbitration Commission when it reconstituted the arbitration system in 1956, bypassing his more senior colleague, Alfred Foster.

Speaking at his retirement in 1973, Kirby provided an acute summary of the changes he had introduced (Kirby 1973): 'Since taking over in 1956 my policy has been that all members, including the President and the judges, should be freed from the status shackles of the judicial courtroom proper, should be flexible in dealing with problems, readily approachable, and perhaps most importantly work in association together, judge and lay members alike, as a team. I think we have done all those things.'

Kirby accommodated the pressures on his jurisdiction while maintaining its independence. 'Now and then', he recalled, a speech by a government minister 'would perhaps wrongly appear to be aimed at scaring us into a particular decision, and just in case it was I would on occasion make a public reply that we acted only on submissions in actual cases'.

Kirby made the decision to dispense with much of the judicial formality of the old Court. In opening sittings, the Court crier used to say, 'All manner of persons having any business before this honourable Court of Conciliation and Arbitration draw nigh and give their attendance and they shall be heard'. Sittings of the Commission were proclaimed in a much simpler form: 'This Commission is now in session. God Save

Sir Richard Clarence Kirby, the first President of the Commonwealth Conciliation and Arbitration Commission (1956–1973).

the Queen.' An Attorney-General later suggested that the monarchical flourish might be abandoned. Kirby remarked that the exhortation 'God Save Australia' might be misinterpreted.

Blanche d'Alpuget wrote a biography of Sir Richard Kirby and entitled it *Mediator*. It is an illuminating study of his vocation and a tribute to a great Australian.

review of the amount of the basic wage by a presidential session of this Commission is a substitute in every way for arbitrary adjustment by an index which has to do with one factor only of the many making up the economy' (1959 91 CAR 685–6). Foster, dissenting, maintained that a decision about the basic wage was 'a deliberate estimate by an informed tribunal that for the contemplated period of the award . . . the productive capacity of the economy can provide to the basic wage-earner a market basket of determined proportions' (1959 91 CAR 709). There was no explicit discussion of the Russell–Salter formula of 'effective productivity'. Kirby, however, found Salter 'an impressive and interesting witness'; research such as his should be encouraged. Salter's estimates were 'perhaps more definite than the material available now warrants'. Nevertheless, 'I consider that some allowance should be made for the growth of productivity . . . and I have done my best as a matter of judgment to take this factor into account' (1959 91 CAR 691). The increase of 15 shillings granted by the Commission temporarily raised the basic wage to a real value above that of the time when automatic adjustments had ceased.

By 1961, there was a significant movement in the Commission's attitude (1961 97 CAR 376). A reading of the decision in the Basic Wage inquiry suggests Copland's influence. The Commission, in a unanimous decision, said that 'the significant thing for an employee is not how much money he receives but how much money will buy'. It foreshadowed the annual adjustment of the basic wage for price movements, but with an opportunity for opponents of an increase to show reasons why it should not occur. A broader review of the economy 'and in particular of productivity increases' should occur at longer intervals – 'say, every three or four years' (1961 97 CAR 387).

The scheme of annual price-related reviews, with less frequent larger economic reviews, had a short life. In 1964, the Commission abandoned the distinction between the two levels of inquiry. Kirby and Moore denied that the 1961 decision implied a 'prices plus productivity' formula, the disavowal pertaining to productivity rather than prices (106 1964 CAR 629). Their view about the wage increase awarded prevailed over that of Gallagher and Nimmo, who were plainly influenced by the employers' advocacy of a 'productivity only' criterion (Hancock 1964).

In the combined Basic Wage and Margins Case of 1965, Kirby and Moore were a minority. Gallagher, Sweeney and Nimmo decided 'to grant wage increases which we consider will not be inconsistent with price stability because, in our view, any wage increase granted at the present time without due regard to this question would not confer a real or lasting benefit upon wage and salary earners' (1965 110 CAR 257). Moore saw the issue as one of 'competing priorities' – between creating or sustaining 'a favourable economic climate' and resolving 'the problems of industrial relations' (1965 110 CAR 267). The Commission 'should always give priority to problems of industrial relations'. And, if it failed to take account of past price changes, 'not only will industrial injustice be done but also the influence of the Commission in the field of actual wages will probably diminish' (1965 110 CAR 272; Isaac 1965).

What became known as the Kirby–Moore view – one that was generally to prevail – supported the adjustment of wages so as to offset price movements. By 1968, apparently, Gallagher was convinced. The National Wage Case was now about 'total wages'. 'We all agree', said Kirby, Gallagher and Moore, 'that in the present circumstances of full employment and in the absence of an incomes policy it is just not practicable for increases in wages and salaries to be confined within productivity increases' (Hancock 1969: 34).

What had emerged by the late 1960s as the Commission's dominant view included a presumption that in National Wage cases award wages should be adjusted for past price increases. The long-term preservation of real wages could not be left to impersonal market forces. As to factors that might lead to *increases* in the real value of award rates, the Commission's attitude was less definite. Productivity was but one of the economic criteria to be considered.

Earnings drift

A 'prices plus productivity' rule would have been difficult or even impossible to implement because of the wage increases occurring 'outside the Commission'. 'Earnings drift' described the tendency of actual earnings to rise faster than the wage rates prescribed in formal instruments (awards and certified agreements). It had two main causes. One was the growth of over-award payments, due to informal collective bargaining, individual bargaining and unilateral action by employers (responding, perhaps, to 'market forces'). The other was structural change in the labour force, such as a growth in the relative importance of salaried employment (Hancock 1966; Isaac 1967; Horn 1970; Worland 1972).

Earnings drift in the 1950s and the 1960s absorbed much of the growth in real wages. Unless the tribunals could somehow displace it, part of the scope for raising real award wages was pre-empted. The Commission's non-acceptance of a 'prices plus productivity' rule was not due to explicit reasoning along these lines. Rather, reality presented itself to the Commission in the form of limits to the size of wage increases that appeared economically responsible. The earnings drift also gave rise to a continuing debate between employers and unions in major wage cases as to whether wages were 'keeping pace' with productivity growth. The employers argued that real average earnings had risen more or less in line with productivity. The unions, on the other hand, pointed to the lesser growth of the wages directly under review, such as the basic wage.

There was a tradition, dating back to the earliest decades of arbitration, that payments above the award rate demonstrated employers' capacity to sustain higher award rates. This made sense if it was assumed that the award increase would displace the over-award payments. No such assumption was tenable for the 1950s and 1960s. The traditional view gave way to a concern that over-award payments were a source of inequity among wage-earners, encouraged resort to direct action and pre-empted capacity to pay (Hancock 1966). The pragmatic wisdom of 'no absorption' was to be demonstrated in the metal trades 'work value' cases of 1967–68. The Commission, by majority, initially granted increases premised on absorption. When the unions concerned made it plain that absorption would not be tolerated, the Commission retreated, withdrawing the presumption of absorption and deferring part of the increases (Mills 1968). In the 1970 National Wage Case, it said that 'wages actually paid should not have the significance they once had in assessing work value because arbitrators must accept that probably any increases awarded will not be absorbed' (Hughes 1970). The persistent growth of over-award payments called into question the reality of wage policy (Isaac 1973).

Wage policy and inflation again: the wage explosion of 1973–1975

The years 1973–75 were testing for wage policy. As Figure 4.1 shows, inflation re-emerged as a serious economic problem. The interrelation of wages with the escalation of inflation was complex. From one perspective, wage increases granted by the Commission were a likely cause of more rapid price increases. From another, a rising cost of living created pressures for higher wages to which the Commission had to respond. And the task was made more difficult by an increase in the size of wage increases secured outside the framework of National Wage cases.

The first Labor government since 1949 was elected in December 1972. Influenced by the views of the Minister for Labour, Clyde Cameron, it supported for some time deliberate efforts to increase wages (especially those of lower-paid workers) relative to profits. In the National Wage Case concluded in May 1973, the Commonwealth submitted that 'there is scope in the capacity and the flexibility of the Australian economy for an appreciable increase in wages without undesirable inflationary consequences'. The Commission said that it had 'given that statement due weight', noting also that 'the Commonwealth emphasised its role as the arbiter of economic policy and stated that the Government considers it has the responsibility to take account of the effects of the Commission's decisions' (1973 149 CAR 81; Nieuwenhuysen 1973).

The wage increase granted in the National Wage Case raised average minimum wages of adult males by 5.7 per cent, but, for the calendar year, total increases in minimum wages were 12.7 per cent (Nieuwenhuysen 1974). Male average weekly earnings increased by 27.7 per cent between the December quarters of 1973 and 1974 (Dabscheck 1975).[20] Cameron, in November 1974, noted that between the September quarter of 1973 and the June quarter of 1974, the percentage share of employed labour in gross national income had risen from 58.7 to 64.1. This, he said, was 'in line with what the government set out to achieve in its social welfare programme' (McGavin 1985: 17). It was also the basis of what was to become known as the 'real wage overhang'.

In the 1974 National Wage Case, the Commission said that 'in the present conflict between doing justice to groups of wage earners and adding to inflation . . . our duty is to the former' (1974 157 CAR 304). Nevertheless, it expressed concern at the emergence of a 'three-tiered wage system, with increases occurring as a result of National Wage cases, industry awards and agreements, and over-award gains of varying amounts obtained from employers' (1974 157 CAR 301). The metal trades increase of $15 (19 per cent for the fitter) in April 1974 was an example of the industry awards that contributed to wage inflation. Such

JOHN MOORE

John Moore was appointed Deputy President of the Commission in 1959 and succeeded Richard Kirby as President in 1973 until his retirement in 1985. By that time, he was the longest-serving member of the federal tribunal, exceeding Richard Kirby's term by a few months. He worked closely with Kirby and sat on all the major cases during the latter's presidency.

Moore presided over the most centralised industrial relations system in Australian history in which the role of the Commission was pivotal. To deal with the wage explosion of the 1970s, the Commission embarked in 1975 on wage indexation underpinned by a coherent set of wage-fixing principles. After a short interruption in 1981, when the main parties were not able to meet the requirements of the principles, the centralised arrangement was resumed in 1983 under the Accord. The centralised system called for consistency in dealing with industrial claims not only within the Commission but also between the Commission and the State tribunals. To that end, Moore initiated regular conferences with the heads of State tribunals about which he said on his retirement:

> I took it upon myself in 1975 following the first indexation decision to go round all the states and talk to the various state tribunals, to suggest that there should be regular meetings between the heads of each tribunal in Australia. Since the first meeting took place in Adelaide in 1976 there have been regular meetings, first of all on an annual basis and more lately on at least a six-monthly basis.

> Whereas the first of these meetings tended to be somewhat formal and the people at them not only did not know one another but tended to regard members of other tribunals with some suspicion, that has now all disappeared and we conduct informal discussions about general problems which affect us all, such as computerisation, without attempting to dictate to one another how we should deal with any particular problem which is before any tribunal. (ACAC 1985: 28a)

Moore was born in Sydney in 1915. On completing an Arts degree at the University of Sydney, he worked for a short period in the New South Wales Public Service and later, while he did a law course part-time, worked as associate to Judge (later Sir) John Ferguson of the New South Wales Industrial Commission. Of him he was to say:

*Sir John Cochrane Moore, the second
President of the Commission (1973–1985)*

I learned many things from him, the most important being that in industrial
relations one is always dealing with people, whether they be workers or
employers. I also learned from him the desirability of patience when dealing
with their problems and the importance of evolutionary reforms. What I
learned from him has always been basic in my philosophy. (ACAC 1985: 25–6)

In 1940, Moore enlisted in the AIF, and following a serious injury in a flying boat
crash he joined the Department of External Affairs. He was posted to Australia's first
mission to the United Nations in New York during 1946–47. On his return to Australia,
he practised at the Bar, securing a large industrial relations clientele until his appointment to the Commission. For his contribution to industrial relations, he was knighted
in 1976 and made a Companion of the Order of Australia in 1986.

awards were largely by consent and generally signified the successful application of union pressure.

In this environment, the idea of indexing award wages to the CPI gained currency. In 1973, the Department of Labour published a discussion paper: *Wage Indexation for Australia*. To the union movement, indexation had the attraction of maintaining real award wages and 'locking in' the real wage increases recently achieved. For those concerned about the *escalation* of inflation, it had the merit of pre-empting wage demands reflecting *anticipations* of future inflation. To the government, indexation was a means of *limiting* wage increases.[21] The Commonwealth and the ACTU, in the 1974 National Wage Case, proposed automatic indexation. The Commission announced that the President would convene a conference of the principal parties 'to see whether a consensus can be reached on the two interacting issues – wage fixation methods and wage indexation' (1974 157 CAR 307; Nieuwenhuysen 1974).

The ACTU's proposal of automatic quarterly adjustment of award rates was supported by the Commonwealth, but with a 'plateau' at the level of average weekly earnings. During the hearing, the Commission pressed the ACTU and the peak white-collar associations as to whether pay increases outside the package would be kept 'within reasonable economic limits'. Reluctantly, the ACTU gave such an undertaking (Dabscheck 1975). The Commission's adoption of an indexation package in April 1975 was an attempt, within the bounds of industrial realism, both to regain control of the award system and to moderate the growth of wages.

The indexation era

Indexation lasted, with modifications, until July 1981. The modifications included a shift (in 1979) from quarterly to half-yearly adjustments. In various decisions, the Commission granted less than full indexation. Sometimes, the departure took the form of plateau indexation, whereby higher award rates were only partially adjusted. Such decisions were usually responses to unfavourable economic news. On other occasions, adjustments were 'discounted' for special factors that affected the CPI, such as exchange rate devaluation and the 'oil shock' of 1979. One of the 'principles' of the system was that 'each year the Commission will consider what increase in total wage or changes in conditions of employment should be awarded nationally on account of productivity'. This was a gesture to the 'prices plus productivity' rule. In practice, real wage increases were off the national wage agenda.

Opposition to indexation had two conflicting bases. One was the view that the system entrenched a real wage level that was 'too high'. Allied to this was a mounting hostility, especially on the part of the Commonwealth Treasury, to the institutions of wage and employment regulation that were blamed for excessive wages. The other was a resistance within the trade union movement to the system's restraints.

Whereas the Whitlam government, by late 1974, saw indexation as a means of restraining the surge in labour costs, the Fraser government regarded the wage increases generated by indexation as inflationary and (in the prevailing labour market conditions) needless (Dabscheck 1977). By implication, it wished to reverse, at least partially, the real wage increases of the early 1970s. This accorded with the Commonwealth Treasury's perception of the 'real wage overhang' as the main cause of unemployment. Budget Paper 2 for 1976 argued that 'unless and until the real wage is brought down relative to productivity in the process of winding inflation rates back, it will not be possible to restore fully the level of economic activity and to provide sufficient new job opportunities to reduce unemployment significantly' (Commonwealth Treasury 1976: 23). In 1979, Treasury said that the degree of containment of real wages containment effected by the Commission:

> coming as it did after a period in which three years' normal increases in real wages were crammed into one, [had] fallen far short of the contribution to the rectification of the real wage/productivity imbalance – and hence the unemployment problem – that might have been hoped for from our centralised wage determination system. (Commonwealth Treasury 1979: 49)

Becoming more forthright, Treasury (1980: 63) said in 1980 that wage increases below its forecast level 'could only be derived from an assumption that the Conciliation and Arbitration Commission will bring down more economically rational awards than it has in the past'.

In the union movement, there was a tension between the objectives of making indexation work and maintaining the struggle for higher wages. In July 1976, Hawke told a Special Conference of Affiliated Unions that the current goal for unions was 'consolidation of what we have won' and that there had to be 'some sense of responsibility' for the unemployed. In December, Carr (1977: 86) records, 'he couched remarks about a wages pause in similar terms . . . provoking criticism from a group of unions which saw no link between wages militancy and the unemployment figures'. Hawke, sensitive to the limits of union forbearance, denounced partial indexation decisions. In practice, the union movement did not – and perhaps could not – remain for long circumscribed by the indexation system. When some unions breached it, others found it difficult to abstain.[22]

The Commission's principles allowed for award wage increases in recognition of increases in 'work value'. In 1979, the Transport Workers' Union based a successful claim on recent changes in the road transport industry, such as greater traffic densities, increased sophistication of vehicles, the growing use of containers, and carriage of heavier freight (Plowman 1980: 85). The effect was to inaugurate a 'work value' round, wherein many other unions claimed and achieved increases with little basis other than the maintenance of pre-existing relativities. Some arbitrators 'rubber-stamped' agreed increases that had little or nothing to do with changed work value. 'Eight dollars plus' became an accepted 'community standard' (Carr 1980: 99; Wright 1981: 108). That was, if anything, confirmed by the full bench that overturned a decision of Justice Staples, granting $12 in wool stores, and substituted $8.

From the outset, the Commission saw indexation as a 'fragile package'. It repeatedly expressed doubt about the existence of the required attitudes. For example, in its decision of June 1979, it said that 'an orderly system of wage fixation cannot survive on a voluntary basis unless the participants demonstrate a firm commitment to its essential requirements' – a commitment that seemed to be lacking (Plowman 1980). National Wage cases were being delayed by the Commission's refusal to proceed while major strikes were under way. In January 1981, the full bench (cited in Wright 1982: 70) said:

What was envisaged in April 1975 tentatively and cautiously as a co-operative and voluntary venture to deal with a difficult industrial and economic situation in an equitable and orderly way, seems to have worked more or less satisfactorily for some four years. But in the last eighteen months the system has made heavy weather industrially, and we do not believe that it is any longer viable in its present form.

The final review of indexation, leading to its abandonment, was to occur in the midst of a major transport dispute.

As Figure 4.2 shows, the rapid growth of real wages, which characterised the 1960s and early 1970s, was halted in the indexation period. There can be no certainty about the role of wage policy in this process. Previous increases in real wages had compressed profit shares and some recovery of those shares may have been irresistible. It is possible – but by no means certain – that indexation, for a time, was associated with a more rapid increase of money wages, and a smaller reduction of the wage share in GDP, than would have occurred if 'market forces' (including serious unemployment) had prevailed. But by 1979, or 1980 at the latest, the Commission was struggling to avoid being overpowered by 'market forces'. Ultimately, it abandoned the endeavour.

Both the growth of unemployment and the alteration of income shares had implications for the debate about wage-fixing criteria. In contrast with the context wherein the earlier debate about prices, productivity and wages had been conducted, the situation was altered in two significant respects. One was that profit shares were less stable than had been earlier assumed (certainly, by those supporting the employers' arguments and probably, too, by the unions' advisers). The other was the return of unemployment. These changes invited debate about relevant economic relationships.

To the Treasury, excessive real wages were a cause – perhaps *the* cause – of high unemployment. There were three alleged linkages: a simple imbalance between the price of labour and its marginal product; discouragement of investment associated with reduced profitability; and inducement to switch the focus of investment towards labour-saving plant and machinery. These connections were asserted as self-evident truths. Though the depressed profit shares might well have such effects, the *reliance* placed on the real-wage overhang by the Treasury and others as the explanation for contemporary unemployment was questionable. Remembering the earlier presumption that 'excessive' wage increases would merely feed through into higher prices, we wonder *by what mechanism* the excessive increases of the 1970s reduced profit shares. The answer may be that wage increases had a different effect when economic conditions were less buoyant: firms had greater difficulty in 'passing on' higher labour costs to their customers. This, however, requires an explanation *other than* wage increases for less buoyant conditions. A story that large wage increases *intensified* the effect of some other factor or factors in decreasing economic momentum makes sense. But it leaves undetermined the *apportionment* of the economic decline between the primary and the intensifying causes. Given that many other countries also experienced the demise of full employment and that, in Australia, the later elimi-nation of the real-wage overhang did not restore full employment, we are sceptical of the weight accorded to it in the 1970s.

The new wage explosion

The end of indexation reflected the Commission's judgment that the system no longer had the consent of the relevant parties, especially the unions. It retreated from wage policy to dispute management, and the locus of wage determination shifted to collective bargaining. A factor underlying union demands was the goal of offsetting the fall in real wages attributed to partial indexation. A twelve-month agreement between metals unions and the Metal Trades Industry Association, reached in October 1981 and certified in December, produced an initial wage increase of $25 for the fitter, a further increase of $14 in June 1982 (both pro-rated for other grades) and a 38-hour week. A gain to the employers was union commitment to 'no extra claims' for the life of the agreement (Wright 1982: 76; Mulvey 1983: 69). The ACTU tried to generalise these gains through the Com-mission. In the first National Wage Case after the end of indexation, in May 1982, it sought a declaration of approval for case-by-case award adjustments related to the metals standard. It also sought a return to a centralised system based on full indexation. The Commission, unconvinced that the metal industry agreement yet represented a community standard, refused the declaration. It rejected the return to a centralised system, doubting the existence of the consensual basis for acceptance of Commission decisions.[23]

Agreement was reached in the oil industry for wage increases of 7 per cent in August 1982 and a further 8 per cent in January 1983. In October 1982, wage claims were made in metals, transport, building, and storage and packing

(Mulvey 1983: 71). Clearly, the 'wage explosion' had not abated. In this context, government policy changed: Ian Viner, as Minister for Industrial Relations, had shared the Treasury's antipathy to centralised wage determination. He, however, was replaced by Ian Macphee, a strong advocate of the centralised system. This may have contributed, along with the level and success of wage claims, to the government's decision of November 1982 to call for a wage freeze (Mulvey 1983: 72–3). The government legislated a twelve-month wage freeze for its own employees and sought from the Commission a like freeze of wages within its awards. A full bench decided on a six-month freeze, with a review at the end of the period.

There was an obvious similarity between the situations of early 1975 and late 1982. On each occasion, the Commission was called upon to subdue a 'wage explosion' that was the product of collective bargaining. The problem that the Commission attempted to solve was an outcome of its own inability to restrain unions unwilling to forgo the exercise of their market power. A degree of instability, manifesting itself in an alternation of 'on' and 'off' periods for wage policy, was inherent in this system.

Wage policy under the Accords: 1983–90

Accord Mark I was negotiated between the ACTU and the Labor Party before the election of March 1983.[24] Subsequent Accords were negotiated between the Labor government and the ACTU. There were suggestions that participation might be broadened to include employers; but this was not a real possibility. Employer views were channelled through a variety of forums: the Summit conference of 1983; recurrent consultations with government; conferences within the framework of the arbitration system; and submissions to the Commission (Campbell 1996).

There was a potential for tension between the Accord partners' agreements and the Commission's legal duty to exercise an independent discretion with reference to the public interest. This was managed – not without difficulties – until 1991.

Initially, wage policy under the Accords entailed indexation. In the first Accord-era National Wage Case, concluded in September 1983, the Commission adjusted wages for the price movements that had occurred in the first two

In implementing the wage principles of the Accord, the Commission considered anomalies as the basis for additional payments. Alice represents Ralph Willis, the former ACTU advocate and now hapless Minister for Employment and Industrial Relations.

quarters of the year. It again adopted a set of principles. These provided, inter alia, for six-monthly wage adjustments of a uniform percentage amount, based on the CPI, unless the Commission were persuaded otherwise (Mulvey 1984: 117). Wage increases would be allowed only if unions gave 'no extra claims' commitments, an innovation derived from the 1981 metal industries agreement (Polites 1984: 109).

By 1985, the depreciation of the Australian dollar was widely seen as a source of price increases for which wage-earners should not be compensated. In negotiating Accord Mark II, the government and the ACTU agreed on a set of modifications to strict indexation. It included a discounting of wage increases relative to the CPI, tax reductions and the introduction of award provisions for super-annuation contributions by employers (Petridis 1986: 124–7). In the earlier of two National Wage cases in 1986, a discounted wage increase was granted. The Commission also approved productivity bargaining for 'payments' in the form of superannuation contributions.

By the end of 1986, there had been a substantial shift of opinion towards the view that wage increases needed justification on grounds other than price changes. This seems to have been due principally to deterioration in the economy, especially in the terms of trade and the balance of payments. With surprising rapidity, support grew for the doctrine that correction of the external imbalance required an enhancement of 'competitiveness' through higher productivity. Its effect was evident by the time of the later National Wage Case of 1986. Although the ACTU sought CPI-related increases, it proposed the alternative of a two-tier system. In one tier, there would be a uniform flat rate increase; in the other, scope for additional bargained increases up to a determined limit (Petridis 1987: 82). The Commission rejected the indexation claim and, in March 1987, adopted a two-tier system. It allowed, for the first tier, a flat rate increase of $10 (about 2 per cent of average award rates). Later in 1987, consideration would be given to a further increase.[25] In the second tier, increases of up to 4 per cent would be available. Of several alternative routes to a second-tier increase, the most common was to satisfy the Commission of cost-saving changes in work arrangements.

The second tier was a mixed success. In some instances, the parties negotiated important productivity-enhancing changes at the industry or enterprise level. In others, the 'changes' were cosmetic. Looking back on the 'restructuring and efficiency' exercise, in August 1988, the Commission said that there had been successes, but 'some parties have exhausted the usefulness of the principle and it would seem impractical to expect others, who have not yet been capable of applying the principle successfully, to repeat the process'. The Commission would now direct attention to 'the more fundamental, institutionalised elements that operate to reduce the potential for increased productivity and efficiency' (AIRC 1988: 5).

The 'structural efficiency' principle articulated in the 1988 decision required unions to cooperate in a fundamental review of awards. The Commission listed measures to be considered in such a review, such as the establishment of career paths, multi-skilling, more flexible working arrangements and more appropriate wage relativities (AIRC 1988: 6). 'Structural efficiency' was further developed in two 1989 cases (AIRC 1989a, 1989b). In the second, the Commission discerned 'substantial economic grounds for rejecting any notion of wage increases at the present time'. But to take economic factors in isolation might compound rather than reduce the economic difficulties. The Commission allowed wage increases 'for completion of successful exercises under the structural efficiency principle' (AIRC 1989b: 5, 7). In the aftermath of the August 1989 decision, individual Commission members were heavily involved in monitoring compliance with the principle and approving award wage increases consistent with the decision.

Thus, the approach to wage policy that had emerged by the end of 1989 was one wherein traditional economic criteria, including productivity growth already achieved, were supplemented by *facilitation* of productivity enhancement. There was an assumption that reforms of industrial relations arrangements, overseen by the Commission and induced by conditional wage increases, would raise productivity. Absent from the analysis was any quantification of the contribution of labour market inefficiencies to low productivity and any differentiation between one-off increases in productivity and raising the ongoing rate of growth. A sceptical view, such as that of Mitchell (1992: 153), cannot be dismissed out of hand:

> The key to high productivity is a high rate of investment . . . The strong
> productivity growth in the 1950s and 1960s was not a lucky accident but
> a reflection of the high level of policy-managed demand and output
> which accelerated investment. By focusing on wage fixing as a panacea,
> we are being sidetracked by second-order concerns.

Few, if any, submissions to the Commission reflected such doubts. The closest that the Commission came to a recognition of them was a brief section of an appendix – 'The Economic Context' – to its decision of August 1988 (AIRC 1988: 50).

The change of approach in centralised wage determination had the implications that wage increases were not granted at identical times and that, in principle, all or part of the available increases might be withheld. Nevertheless, the system remained a managed one, deviating only marginally from the historic presumption that the benefits of productivity advance were to be distributed evenly across the labour force. The Commission's continued adherence to this presumption was fundamental to its National Wage decision of April 1991.

The period 1983–91 was a bad one for real wage growth – especially for award wages, but even for average earnings. In its August 1988 decision, the Commission referred to Treasury data of real unit labour costs (RULC). On an index basis (1972–73 = 100), RULC in the non-farm sector had fallen from 108.4 in 1982–83 to 99.1 in 1987–88. In other words, the labour cost of a unit of output was about the same in 1987–88 as in the early 1970s. Treasury saw the fall in RULC as a significant cause of reduced unemployment:

> *Real unit labour costs* . . . are now significantly below the average level of the late 1960s and early 1970s. This unwinding of the fundamental imbalances in relative factor shares prevalent throughout most of the 1970s and early 1980s has contributed importantly to the strength of job growth over the past five years. (Commonwealth Treasury 1988: 21)

Two years later, Treasury said:

> Real wage restraint – and related reductions in real unit labour costs – provided a substantial stimulus to employment growth. This operated through increased use of labour in the production process in response to its lower relative cost and through the boost to private investment and output from improved profitability. The effect of real wage restraint on profitability meant that the gross profit share in the late 1980s exceeded the levels of the late 1960s. Over the period 1986 to 1990, private employment growth increased at an annual rate of 3.3 per cent. About one quarter of this growth, or around one quarter of a million jobs, was attributable to real wage restraint . . . (Commonwealth Treasury 1990: para 2.23)

Treasury's confidence belied the complexity of the issue. The very concept of 'real wage restraint' is elusive. Real wages depend on the interaction of money wages and prices. A fall in real wages or of the wage share in aggregate income may be explicable by factors relevant to the adjustment of prices as much as, or more than, the adjustment (or lack of adjustment) of money wages. A *possible* story of the Accord years (to 1990) would see the economic forces driving non-wage shares upward as the primary source of the stagnation of real wages, with money wage restraint merely averting some of the economic 'pain' (especially higher inflation rates) that would otherwise have attended it. Further, the negative correlation between the wage share and employment, if factual,[26] leaves the nature of the connection to be determined. In the Treasury's story, real wages are the independent variable. Again, this is not the only available story. Another ascribes both the rise in employment and the growth in the non-wage share to a third factor: an expansion of aggregate demand, perhaps facilitated by macro-economic policy and the depreciation of the dollar.

The endeavour of the parties and the Commission, after 1986, to link wage policy to productivity enhancement raises the obvious question of whether the restructuring and efficiency principle and the structural efficiency principle did raise productivity.

Bargaining: 1991–2002

The enterprise bargaining proposal that the Commission declined to implement in April 1991 originated in Accord VI, negotiated shortly before the 1990 federal election. Subsequently, there emerged a broadly based agreement that the Commission should approve and assist the adoption of 'enterprise bargaining' as a step beyond structural efficiency. The Commission saw elements of enterprise bargaining in the restructuring and efficiency and the structural efficiency principles. It did not exclude further movement, but doubted that the conditions then existed for instituting an enterprise bargaining principle. The Commission noted a fundamental problem: 'The enterprise bargaining proposals challenge a long established principle of wage fixation in Australia, namely, that the benefits of increased efficiency should be distributed on a national, rather than an industry or an enterprise basis'. Those advocating enterprise bargaining would 'need to inform the Commission of their views as to the future role, if any, of National Wage cases and the criteria that should operate for sanctioning general wage increases within a system whereby increases are also negotiated at the enterprise level' (AIRC 1991: 39–40). But the pressures were irresistible. The Commission relented in October 1991 by formulating an enterprise bargaining principle.

After an early hiatus (from 1991 to 1993), periodic – largely annual – wage reviews have occurred, designated since 1997 as *Safety Net Reviews – Wages*. But a bifurcated wages system has emerged. In 1997, the majority members of the bench said:

Issues surrounding the relation between wages, prices and productivity and the Commission's role in relation to the level of real wages have, in the past, been discussed in the context of the Commission's exerting much influence over the average level of wages. It now has less influence over the average level of wages than for many decades. We thus face the question as to the relative weight to be given to overall wage movements, over which the Commission retains *some* influence, and the interests of those who do depend on awards. (AIRC 1997: 31–2)

Safety Net cases have been contests between the two goals of curbing the growth in the gap between bargained and safety net wages and limiting increases in labour costs. The ACTU and supporting unions have stressed the former; the federal government, non-Labor State governments and most employer groups, the latter. The unions argue that award-dependent workers should share in the benefits of productivity growth. This argument has been supplemented by calculations suggesting that increasing award wages is a low-cost option.[27] Their adversaries say that increasing award wages reduces the incentive to bargain, militating against productivity enhancement, while the economic consequences of award wage increases remain serious. The Commission has given greater weight to economic constraints than the unions think appropriate. It has, at times, implied that the unions (abetted by employers) bear responsibility for the gap by reason of the level of increases secured in enterprise bargaining.[28] The trend of its decisions, however, has been towards more generous 'safety net' increases.

THE WAGE STRUCTURE

'Wage structure' denotes the *relative* amounts paid to workers. Wage policy rarely specifies individuals. Rather, it categorises labour. Categories are constructed from a range of factors, including occupation, industry, formal qualifications, experience, gender, age, location and enterprise. It is convenient here to distinguish: the categories by which workers are differentiated; the location (or 'slotting in') of categories within the structure; and the degree of *dispersion*, or inequality, in the structure. In practice, these overlap, but the distinctions are helpful.

Categories

In the main, the tribunals' role in classifying labour was passive – there was an acceptance of the classifications recognised by the parties to awards. The predominant differentiation was by occupation, but with industry too a significant factor. Required or customary formal qualifications, such as apprenticeships and (later) degrees, were also common defining characteristics. In some awards, salaries (rarely wages) were related to length of service. For most of the century, gender was a major and systematic differentiator. There were, however, exceptions to this passivity. We mention three.

One was the Court's determination – in the face of union resistance – to introduce semi-skilled classifications in the metal awards. A feature of the consolidated Metal Trades Award of 1930 was the process-worker classification, with a margin of 6 shillings (compared with 24 shillings for tradesmen). Beeby, who made the award, saw the growth of 'manufacturing' (contrasted with 'jobbing') as providing scope for routine semi-skilled operations and reduction of costs (Hancock 1979: 137; Cockfield 1993: 25–7). The Court's objective, however, was not so much to act as the *driver* of change as to ensure that the occupational structure of awards did not *obstruct* it. In the long term, 'low margin' classifications would proliferate and were a means by which many workers with limited skills were lifted above the basic wage.

The second exception was the tribunal's priority for consistency between employers and industries. In the first sixty years of arbitration, there had been occasional instances wherein the tribunal took account of the degree of prosperity in the industry, the enterprise or the region. These had generally been decisions affording 'relief' to 'struggling' employers. In a few instances, prosperity produced the opposite result. Such decisions were sporadic. In the main, differentiation resulted from bargaining, and the tribunal's contribution (if any) was the ratification of consent arrangements. The *General-Motors Prosperity Loading* case (1966 115 CAR 931) arose from a union claim for a $6 loading, to 'pass on' to the company's employees some of the high profits then being enjoyed by the company (both in Australia and globally). Rejecting the application, the Commission affirmed its support for the national distribution of productivity gains ('Advocatus' 1966: 301). A similar issue arose, at the industry level, in the *Oil Industry* case (1970 134 CAR 159), when the Commission rebuffed a union claim to allocate to employees a share of the employers' prosperity. The Commission's adherence to the principles of the *General-Motors* and *Oil Industry* cases was an important reason for its critical decision of April 1991 (see above).

The third intervention was the award restructuring exercise associated with the structural efficiency principle. This had its basis in broad agreements reached between the ACTU and particular unions, employer associations and the federal government; but the Commission gave specific effect to these understandings. It was generally accepted that awards had become too complex and detailed, largely through the tribunals' ratifying agreements between industrial parties. Classifications had proliferated. Award restructuring, as it pertained to classification, had two underlying aspects: broadbanding, whereby the number of classifications was reduced (in the case of the metal industry award, from over 300 to 14); and consistency across awards. 'Consistency' involved the identification of key awards and aligning them with wage rates in other awards.

Thus, the tribunals were influenced by concepts of equity, consistency and orderliness in the award wage structure. Over-award payments frustrated, to a degree, the attainment of these objectives in the structure of *actual* wages. If some employers paid above the award, could and should the tribunal redress the seeming inequity to less fortunate employees? And if disputes arose because unions demanded over-award rates that employers would not concede, would the tribunal stand firm on the award rates or make concessions to 'realism'? Compromises with 'reality' included the making of 'paid rate' awards, prescription of a minimum wage above the lowest award rates, supplementary payments for low-paid workers, and making recommendations for the adjustment of over-award payments in the light of national wage decisions.

'Slotting in'

How were the rankings of categories of labour determined? Which classifications were to be treated as equal? On what basis might one be ranked higher and another lower in the structure?

In the earlier decades of arbitration, the Court sometimes relied on existing practice. Higgins said that 'the safest line to follow, for one who is not initiated in the mysteries of the several arts and crafts, is to keep close to the distinctions in grade between the employees as expressed in wages by the employers for many years' (1907 2 CAR 65–7). Kelly, thirty-four years later, said that:

> the Court from its inception has allowed itself to be guided in its
> assessment of 'fair' wages by the evidence of what reasonable employers
> of competent labour have found it desirable to pay and what competent
> workmen have been willing to accept for any particular class of work.
> Such evidence has, in fact, provided the only practicable starting point
> from which to approach the wage-fixing problem. (1941 48 CAR 586)

Often, however, the Court found it necessary to make, and to be seen to make, its own assessments. The normal basis of these was examination of job requirements. Despite his affirmation of the existing-practice principle in *Marine Cooks, Bakers and Butchers* (1907 2 CAR 65), Higgins found that the work of butchers was 'undervalued' relative to that of galley hands. This was the Court's first 'work value' assessment. As the notion of 'work value' developed, the job attributes most often emphasised were the required levels of skill, training and experience. Necessary or usual formal qualifications, such as apprenticeship, were especially important. Informal skill requirements were more problematic, but over time the tribunal recognised gradations of skill below the tradesperson level. It also took account of responsibility, physical strain, the exercise of authority, unavoidable danger and discomfort, and the need for care, intelligence or alertness. Arbitral assessments of work value were more prevalent in the first than in the second half of the century, largely because, by mid-century, award coverage was extensive and much of the 'slotting in' had been done. When federal regulation was extended to new areas, as with professional engineers in the early

1960s and nurses in the 1980s, there *were* both in-depth inquiries into the work performed and innovation in the classification structures.

The ranking of jobs within the award wage structure was increasingly resistant to change. This inflexibility is often characterised as the dominance of 'comparative wage justice'. The tendency for the overall wage structure to move in line with 'metals' emerged as early as 1935, when increases in margins in the metal trades award granted by Beeby were followed in many other awards (Hancock 1979: 145).[29] Margins prescription in the early post-war years (especially 1947) is a complicated story, but the metal industries remained pre-eminent. Test cases in the 1950s and 1960s established formulae that were more or less generally applied. Some members of the bench in the 1967 metal trades margins case hoped to alter the relativity of metal industry wages to other rates, but it was a forlorn hope.

Since the advent of the total wage, few attempts have been made to review the ranking of jobs. The continuing force of comparative wage justice was seen in the so-called 'work value' round of 1979–80 and again in the award changes that occurred in 1981 and 1982. Fear of 'flow-ons' led to restrictive terms in the wage-fixing principles in force between 1975 and 1981 and from 1983 onward. As part of the award-restructuring exercise begun in 1989, some attempt was made to rationalise cross-award relativities. But a reading of the National Wage decision of August 1989 does not disclose any reasoning that led to the chosen relativities (AIRC 1989b: 12–13).

Why was the structure of classifications inflexible? The force of horizontal comparison has frequently been noted and is common to different industrial relations systems. It has, no doubt, a psychological source, and is reinforced by the imperative for trade unions to avoid adverse comparisons of their performances. If considerations of work value did not seriously challenge these conservative influences, a likely reason is the intrinsic subjectivity of the concept. It was difficult to *demonstrate* that a pre-existing relativity was wrong. Would work value have been a more discriminating instrument if allied with quantitative job evaluation? In the 1967 *Metal Trades* case, the Commonwealth argued for systematic evaluation and, drawing upon witness evidence, proffered points scores. Moore and Winter took account of this; but no such technique was employed in the subsequent adjustments of wages outside 'metals' (Woodward 1968: 108). To our knowledge, this was the one occasion when job evaluation played any part – a slight one – in the tribunal's deliberations about work value (see also Isaac 1967: 41–4).

Dispersion

The wage structure, in its *vertical* dimension, had a concertina-like character. The equal tended to remain equal; but the unequal could differ by greater or lesser proportions. Until 1966, disparate movements in the basic wage and margins caused vertical changes in the award wage structure (Hancock and Moore 1972). That the two elements of award wages would have lives of their own was demonstrated during the First World War. For a skilled worker, said Higgins (1916 14 CAR 459), the preservation of a customary living standard was 'essential', but in comparison with safeguarding the living wage 'not so absolutely essential; and in a time of violent disturbances such as the present . . . I do not think it advisable to push matters to an extreme'. In 1921, Higgins began to restore the proportionality of margins to the basic wage that had existed at the time of *Harvester*. A 36-shilling margin for the fitter re-established the 10:7 ratio of the tradesman's to the labourer's wage. After Higgins' departure, however, the Court abandoned this policy: Powers, later in 1921, reduced the fitter's margin to 24 shillings (Hancock 1979: 136).

In the 1930s, price-related reductions of the basic wage under the automatic adjustment system caused proportional increases in skill relativities.[30] This movement towards a less-equal pay structure was accentuated by Beeby's decisions of 1935 and 1937 to increase margins. By raising the tradesman's margin in metals to 30 shillings, Beeby restored the *Harvester* relativity of the tradesman's rate to the basic wage (Hancock 1979: 143–4).

Wartime controls virtually confined wage increases to the automatic adjustment of the basic wage. Basic wage increases, due to automatic adjustments and to court decisions in 1946 and 1950, 'squeezed' differentials, and the increases in margins granted in 1947, were skewed in favour of the semi-skilled. The abolition of automatic adjustments in 1953 brought to an end one source of compression of relativities; and a partial reversal of the earlier compression was effected by the 'two and a half times' formula of 1954. Thereafter, the sequence of basic wage and margins reviews generated less vertical variance in relativities.

General wage adjustments in the eras of the total wage and the safety net have been a mixture of flat rate and proportional increases. Flat rate increases compress the structure of award wages. The Commission has not suggested that compression was a goal to be sought. On the contrary, it has from time to time expressed its misgivings about the reduction of proportional differences. In the Safety Net decision of May 2000, the Commission (AIRC 2000: 40) said that, although it had awarded flat money amounts in the previous six National Wage and Safety Net cases and would do so again on this occasion, the parties should discuss the case for a return to percentage adjustments in the next review. In the 2001 Safety Net Case, the Commission (AIRC 2001a) granted increases in three tiers, with the larger increases applying to higher award rates. In 2002, however, the Commission (AIRC 2002: 56) granted a flat-rate increase, noting that no party had called for larger increases at the higher levels in the pay structure. The 2003 decision brought a reversion to 'tapering', with better-paid workers on award rates receiving lesser dollar increases than the lower-paid (AIRC 2003). Such outcomes seem to be due to the emphasis currently given to 'the needs of the low-paid' rather than a wish to 'engineer' a wage compression.

THE ARBITRATORS AND THE ECONOMY

How has the institution of compulsory arbitration affected Australia's economic experience? There are two broad reasons why this question cannot be answered confidently. One is the counterfactual problem. What is the implicit alternative? In what sense was any such alternative available? If there is an implication of 'historical choice', when was that choice made; by whom; and what were the rejected options? The other is the vast range of influences that contribute to the evolution of any economy and society. It is not simply that there are so many things to be considered, but that they interact. History is a tangled skein. Some commentators have sought to avoid these difficulties by comparing Australia with other countries that are 'similar' except for their industrial relations systems. We do not disparage such comparisons, but no two countries are the same and judgments about the relevance and importance of similarities and differences are subjective. The strongest messages to be taken from international comparison are cautionary: where economic trends observed in Australia are also common elsewhere, the character of the Australian industrial relations system is unlikely to be the major cause of the Australian experience. And it is unwise to set much store by mere shades of difference.

We do not here discuss the presumption of some economists that interference with 'market' processes and outcomes is *ipso facto* damaging to economic performance (see Richardson 1999: chs 1 and 2).

Arbitration and protection

There is a widely held view that arbitration was part of a 'historical compromise', fashioned early in the twentieth century and continued for most of it. Another element of the compromise (or 'settlement') was tariff protection.[31]

New Protection – the legislative basis for *Harvester* – was a political 'deal': Labor's support for tariffs was bought by the promise of intervention to enforce fair wages. It does not follow that tariffs and arbitration were inexorably linked. The drive for arbitration had other and obvious sources: industrial strife, perceptions of unequal bargaining power (exacerbated by judicial decisions adverse to trade unionism), and concerns about low wages and harsh conditions. Neither the insertion of the arbitration power into the Constitution nor the inception of arbitration in New South Wales in 1901 was linked to protection. Support for arbitration could well have gathered enough strength to prevail in its own right (likewise with protection). Of course, tariffs and awards were realities taken into account by the makers of awards and tariffs, respectively. But the assertion that the demise of protection removed an essential underpinning of arbitration elevates historical event into historical necessity. The linked contention that freedom of trade necessitates 'market' determination of wages and conditions is a massive *non sequitur*.[32]

There is, however, another perspective of the twentieth-century Australian economy, described by the Brigden committee (Brigden et al. 1929), wherein arbitration and protection have related roles. In this model, the Australian economy was moving towards a lesser dependence on agriculture and pasture and a greater involvement with manufacture. The transition was linked with the expansion of the population. Tariffs had the twofold role of encouraging manufacture and of 'taxing' farmers and graziers by forcing them to pay more for what they bought on domestic markets. The employment opportunities provided by the growth of secondary industry and the higher wages achieved by transferring income from primary producers facilitated population growth. Brigden and his colleagues (1929: 140) concluded that 'the advantage of protection is in the maintenance of a larger population than could have been expected at the same standard of living without the protective tariff'. Wage regulation played only a minor part in the model. The standard of wages was high primarily because the overall average income was high. But 'there are maximum and minimum payments which can be made for labour, neither of which can be established with certainty . . . and regulation can compel the maximum payments, provided the by-products of regulation have not absorbed too much of the income available' (Brigden et al. 1929: 96). Population size and income distribution were policy concerns, and the Brigden model was both relevant and intellectually coherent. The committee acknowledged risks in yet greater use of tariffs to promote income transfer and population growth. In the last quarter of the century, trade policy was increasingly informed by a judgment that freer trade served Australia's economic interests. Tariffs were removed or reduced. The specific role that the Brigden committee ascribed to industrial regulation ceased to be relevant. But that never was its only, or its main, role.[33]

Wage policy and macroeconomic management

Henry Phelps Brown (1969: 222) described the requirements of an effective incomes policy as 'mainly two: the participation, in the reaching of particular decisions, of a spokesman of the common interest; and an understanding of the grounds on which decisions are reached'. Further, he said:

It may be an accident of history that long before the need for a national incomes policy was apprehended, Australia came to adopt procedures so propitious for one; but that they should now be available to meet the needs of the hour seems to me a precious legacy of their history to the Australian people.

Phelps Brown was not alone in seeing public benefit in having an institution able to influence the growth rate of wages.[34]

We have described some of the stepping stones that led the Court to accord importance to macroeconomic criteria. The existence, from 1922, of a basic wage that was common across awards enhanced the significance of the Court's policies. By the 1930s, the Court was recognised as an important manager of economic affairs. This was in spite of the extensive coverage of State awards, made by tribunals that did not necessarily ascribe a leadership role to the Commonwealth Court.

The Court's major decisions in the 1930s had particular regard to unemployment. For the era of 'full employment' – from the Second World War to the early 1970s – the principal issue relevant to the tribunals' macroeconomic role was the interaction of award wages and inflation. The Court and the Commission were between a rock and a hard place. Their dilemma was at the heart of the disagreement between Kelly and his fellow judges in 1950 and, in the 1960s, the disagreement between members of the Commission as to whether the basic wage should be adjusted for price movements. The idea of giving priority to the prevention of inflation was, to some members of the Court and the Commission, at odds with equity to wage-earners and with the tribunal's statutory responsibilities.

There was another, related, constraint. The Australian labour force was highly unionised; and some unions were in strong bargaining positions. By adhering to a policy dictated solely by economic objectives, the tribunal would have risked a reduction of its own relevance in the labour market. This was underlined by the Commission's futile attempt, in 1967–68, to induce absorption of over-award payments. In the early 1970s, the Commission did lose most of its control to 'market forces'. The realities of the labour market, together with institutional constraints (including the tribunal's statutory duties), led inevitably to compromises.

The wage explosion of the early 1970s was intensified by the Labor government's initial support for large wage increases. This deterred the Commission from attempting to swim against a powerful tide. By 1975, however, a shared concern about inflation and the emergence of serious unemployment enabled the Commission to reassert its role. The indexation package had the potential to *decrease* the momentum of wage inflation. It also had a chance of commanding the required consent of unions. Pursuit of the ideal might have sacrificed the possible. The Commission, by reason of its experience and its direct dealings with the relevant parties, was better placed than the Treasury and other critics to make such a judgment. In the years 1979–81, with the unions' effective withdrawal of consent and the acquiescence of many employers and their associations in their behaviour, wage policy crumbled and finally disintegrated.

Economic and political conditions in 1983 facilitated a return to consensus. From then until 1991, there *was* a wage policy. *Whose* policy was it – the Accord partners' (with some input by employers' associations) or the Commission's? There was a high level of congruence between the various views – the government's, the ACTU's, the employers' and the Commission's. The Commission, at the least, translated policy from the general to the concrete (through its wage-fixing principles) and monitored compliance. Without it, the broadly agreed wage policy may have succumbed to 'free rider' behaviour, with the striking of separate employer–union agreements that, in the aggregate, exceeded the agreed limits. The Commission's capacity to act as industrial policeman was, however, by consent of the major 'players', especially the ACTU and the government. In the 'safety net' era, its role as economic policy maker has unambiguously diminished.

To what extent, then, did arbitration equip Australia with an additional tool of economic management? This question eludes a simple answer. There is a range of subsidiary questions. How far did the tribunal's influence over market wages and conditions extend? How far was it constrained by, rather than in control of, economic forces? What was the level of compliance with its policies and to what extent was it forced to adapt them to secure compliance? How far were the dictates of equity at odds with economically 'sound' policy? What was the tribunal's capacity to understand economic issues and to foresee the consequences of its decisions? These are all difficult issues. But they point to significant limitations on wage policies oriented to macroeconomic goals.

From the present perspective, Phelps Brown's account of the public benefits flowing from a wage policy implemented by an authoritative tribunal was simplistic. From that of 1969 – despite the recent turmoil about absorption of over-award payments – it was understandable. The force whose destructive power was not then fully appreciated was a trade union movement unwilling to commit itself to the kind of system that Phelps Brown (and others) envisaged.

Inflation

What was the net contribution of federal arbitration to the erosion of the value of the Australian pound and dollar? This is another unanswerable question, for the reasons given at the beginning of this section. It affords some perspective, however, to remember that, in the decades after the Second World War, inflation was universal in developed economies. It is also true that, in the 1960s (to lesser degrees in the 1950s and 1970s), incomes policies of various types were widely perceived as an important weapon against inflation; but well before the end of the century, the focus shifted to the behaviour and management of the monetary system. The moderate inflation rates experienced in most countries during the 1990s cannot be attributed to incomes policies, which had fallen out of favour. They may reflect the accuracy of a monetary diagnosis and the enhanced role of central banks, but there are other factors in contention, notably the diminution of trade union power and increased competitive pressures associated with freer world trade.

If we divide the century, somewhat arbitrarily, into ten-year intervals and compare the increases in wages and prices in those periods, we get the result shown in Figure 4.5.[35] The correlation between the rates of change of the two variables[36] says nothing, of course, about causation. Not only does it fail to discriminate between consumer prices and wages as the 'active' force in determining the rate of inflation, it is also consistent with stories wherein both commodity and labour prices respond to other influences, including monetary variables, export and import prices, and the pressure of aggregate demand. It may be a sensible surmise that *if* the rate of growth of wages had been lower, consumer prices would also have risen less; but the converse is also true. In considering the possible role of wage policies, we must also remember that the wage increases shown in Figure 4.5 are not limited to movements in award rates. We have seen, for example, that in the 1950s and 1960s the earnings drift was an important contributor to the rise in average wages.

Agnosticism about the long-term effects of wage regulation on the price level does not necessarily negate a short-term role in altering the rate of increase of wages, with effects on the rate of inflation. There is little doubt that a sequence of decisions of the Court between 1946 and 1950 added momentum to the early

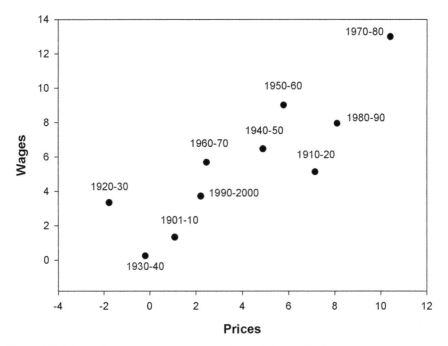

Figure 4.5 Price and wage changes in ten-year intervals (annualised percentages)

post-war inflation. It is arguable that the more restrained wage policies of the period 1953–67 contributed to the 'unwinding' of inflation; and it is likely that the wage restraint implemented by the Commission between 1983 and 1990, in the context of the Accord, alleviated the inflationary forces present at the beginning of the period. What is *not* clear is whether such variations of policy affected much more than the *timing* of wage and price movements. That question raises issues as to the determination of the value of the currency, such as the role of monetary variables, that cannot be debated within the limits of this chapter.

Unemployment

The unemployment rate is an imperfect measure of labour market performance, raising significant issues of definition and measurement. For this chapter, however, it is a useful indicator of labour market imbalance. Figure 4.6 shows its course across the century.[37]

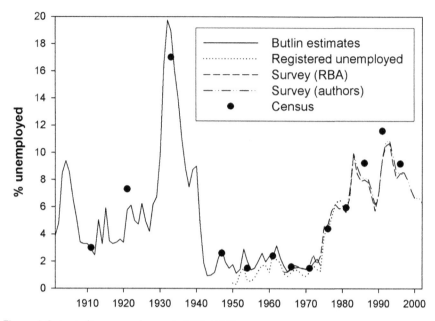

Figure 4.6 Australian unemployment, 1901–2002

Accounting for the features of Figure 4.6 is a complex task. There would be little dispute that the Depression of the 1930s was imported or that the Second World War drove the transition to full employment. But other aspects, including the long continuance of full employment and its disappearance in the last quarter of the century, are problematic. Few economic historians, in interpreting the figure, would ascribe a primary role to industrial regulation. Regulation may, however, have operated to modify – for better or for worse – other influences on the supply of jobs.

Earlier in this chapter we have referred to cases, such as those of the 1930s, when unemployment was a major issue in wage policy. The usual stance of the federal tribunal was to treat unemployment as a ground for curbing labour costs. Its attitudes were often conditioned by recent experience. Thus, the 'prosperity loadings' of 1937 were granted at a time when unemployment was still around 8 per cent, but had fallen, and in the era of 'full employment' the Court and the Commission became concerned about increases in unemployment, even though its level remained below 3 per cent. For most of the century, the tribunal's approach was not informed by any *evidence* of the actual effects on employment of higher or lower wages. In the Safety Net cases of 1996–97 and subsequently, the Commission was taken to studies comparing empirical studies of elasticities of demand for labour in Australia and elsewhere. These studies have not led to any consensus. The Commission's response has essentially been the traditional one of a general but inexact acceptance that avoidance of unemployment calls for restraint.

We also noted earlier the contention of some economists in the 1920s that arbitrated wages had not moved (downward) with capacity to pay and that this militated against the reduction of unemployment. There were few suggestions that the catastrophe of 1929–34 was significantly due to wage policy. Indeed, Copland applauded the Court's decision of 1931 to impose an emergency reduction in federal award wages. In the last quarter of the century, however, there was much controversy about the role of wage policy in the advent and continuance of high unemployment. Critics typically cited two aspects of arbitrated wages as contributors to the problem.

One was the enforcement of average real wage levels that were too high relative to productivity. The Commonwealth Treasury's thesis of the 'real-wage overhang' is the clearest statement of this criticism. As we have seen, Treasury acknowledged that by the late 1980s the real-wage overhang had been eradicated. That unemployment remained high calls into question not so much the validity of the economic model bound up in the real wage overhang as the significance accorded to it. It may be that since the 1970s other changes in the economy had occurred that would require lower real unit labour costs than were consistent with full employment in an earlier era. Unless those changes are identified, however, the argument is tautological – the very existence of unemployment is the 'evidence' that real wages are 'too high'.

The other 'fault' was structural rigidity. Low unemployment, it is said, requires flexibility in the relative rewards of different kinds of labour. Wage-fixing practices that militate against it include the preservation of traditional relativities and the prescription of wages by reference to need. The argument invokes elementary supply-and-demand theory: if external intervention enforces relativities that deviate from equilibrium, excess supplies of the 'over-priced' workers will coexist with excess demand for those who are 'under-priced'. Hence there will be 'structural' unemployment (Evans 1996).

This theory fails to capture important complexities of the labour market. First, the *practical relevance* of simple supply-and-demand analysis depends upon the elasticities of supply of, and demand for, different kinds of labour. The lower these elasticities, the less responsive is employment to relative wages. Second, the supplies of labour for different types of work are affected by the availability of jobs, as well as the going wage rates. The more important the former, the less important is the latter as the mechanism of quantity adjustment. Third, workers – even within a given category – are heterogeneous. Variation in the quality of workers who apply and are selected for specific jobs is one of the ways in which labour markets adjust (Blandy and Richardson 1982). Fourth, wages respond to forces other than those of supply and demand, including perceptions of fairness and the dictates of workplace motivation, harmony and performance. We do not develop these points here (see Hancock 1998), but they suggest reasons why the degree of relative wage flexibility may not be fundamental to the determination of employment and unemployment.

This brief discussion is an insufficient basis for any firm conclusion about the impact of arbitral 'interferences' on employment and unemployment. Figure 4.6, however, calls for a sense of perspective. Other and more powerful forces clearly were at work. It is unlikely that tribunal policies go far towards explaining either the low unemployment levels of the 1940s, 1950s and 1960s or the high levels of the 1930s and the last quarter of the century.

Productive performance

It is uncontroversial that productivity growth, though difficult to measure, was the overwhelmingly dominant source of the growth in real wages discussed earlier. Broadly, the determinants of long-term productivity growth are investment in physical capital, the level and quality of innovation, and the rate of improvement of 'human capital'. There are ways in which industrial relations systems *may* impinge on these sources of dynamism. It is sometimes suggested that the restriction of managerial discretion discourages entrepreneurship, with adverse effects on growth. It may, to the contrary, be argued that institutional pressure on business

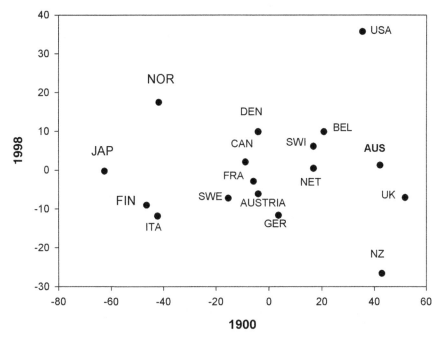

Figure 4.7 Per capita GDPs of seventeen nations, 1900 and 1998

to meet high and rising labour standards encourages a continuous quest for higher productivity, whereas low labour costs induce complacency. But these are mere armchair speculations.

Those who argue that Australia performed badly in the twentieth century often cite the fall in Australia's position in the international 'league table' of income or output. Figure 4.7, derived from Maddison's (1995, 2001) estimates of real GDP per capita, bears upon this argument. It covers seventeen countries that are now within the OECD. The horizontal scale measures relative performances in 1900, with Australia ranking third (behind the United Kingdom and New Zealand). The vertical scale measures relative performance in 1998 (the latest year for which Maddison's estimates are available). By then, Australia's rank had fallen to seventh.[38] The facts that stand out are a negligible degree of correlation between country performances in 1900 and 1998 and a strong convergence towards the mean (the United States being a conspicuous exception).[39] Both may be due largely to differences in the timing of development: countries that were lagging in 1900 had further to travel to reach their potential levels of performance, and most have managed to close the gap. A focus on the change in Australia's relative position may be deceptive. Its seemingly 'good' performance in 1900 may be explicable by the lesser development of other countries (and by the relatively high ratio of prime age males to the population).[40]

Those who are, nevertheless, convinced that Australia's twentieth-century growth record was poor are still left with a diversity of possible reasons. They include the education and training systems; population growth; the propensity to save; the change in economic structure; trade policies; the level and quality of investment in research and development; the declining real prices of commodities exported by Australia; *and* the industrial relations system. Emphasis on the last of these is gratuitous.

For the last third of the century, ABS productivity estimates for the market sector allow clearer identification of the growth path than is possible for earlier decades.[41] Relative to the century as a whole (especially the period before the Second World War), this was a period of strong growth. Between 1965 and 2001, the annual growth rates of labour productivity and multi-factor productivity were 2.3 per cent and 1.1 per cent, respectively. Productivity did not, of course, grow at a constant rate within the thirty-six years, and the variations are of interest. Figure 4.8 shows five-year moving averages of growth rates across the period (beginning with 1965–70 and ending with 1997–2002). Relative to the whole period, productivity growth rose to a high level in the late 1960s and the early 1970s; declined to lower rates in the 1980s and early 1990s; and recovered (though not to the earlier peaks) in the later 1990s.

Whatever explanations for these variations may be found, it would be very difficult to ground them in the industrial relations system. For example, any suggestion that the improvement of the later 1990s was due to the partial dereg-ulation of the labour market raises the question of why the performance was still better in the 1970s, when the labour market was still (as has been alleged) 'sclerotic'. The figure would seem to call for some explanation of productivity behaviour that accounts for the poor performance of the 1980s and early 1990s. It is true that the industrial relations reforms that began in the late 1980s were due partly to concerns about poor productivity growth. The Commission-guided

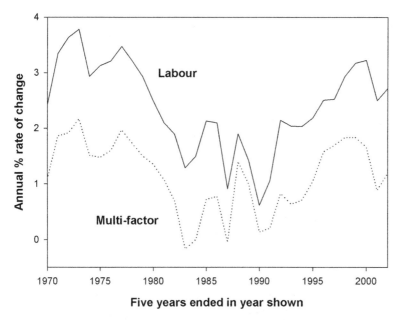

Figure 4.8 Australian market sector productivity growth, 1965–2002

reforms – the restructuring and efficiency and structural efficiency principles – were followed by the shift towards enterprise bargaining, wherein employers could try to trade benefits to employees for better work performance. Loundes, Tseng and Wooden (2003: 256) have recently surveyed the existing research into the effects of enterprise bargaining on productivity. They conclude that 'the available evidence . . . does not enable any strong conclusions to be reached about possible links between enterprise bargaining and productivity'. We are not surprised. The likelihood, in our view, is that any such effects would be submerged by more fundamental forces, especially those of investment and technical change. The United States also experienced, in the 1990s, a productivity surge. Labour market reform has not been identified as a significant cause of that experience: the dominant explanation portrays it as a delayed response to computerisation. A similar effect may have occurred in Australia. Again, Australia's productivity surge may have been due to the pressures on business arising from a more open economy and microeconomic reforms promoting greater competition.

Wage inequality

Has arbitration, with its emphasis on the adequacy of minimum wages and comparative fairness, produced a more or less egalitarian wage structure than would otherwise have existed?

Figure 4.9, derived from data assembled by the OECD (1996) for the early to mid-1990s, lends some perspective to this question. The measure of inequality is the relation of the tenth to the ninetieth percentile in the earnings structure.[42] At the one extreme, the tenth percentile worker in the United States received 4.39 times as much as the ninetieth percentile worker; at the other, Norway had a multiple of 1.98. Australia (2.92) was about mid-field. Countries with strikingly greater degrees of inequality included the United States, Canada and the United Kingdom. If we assumed that, without arbitration, Australia would have been more like these countries, we might infer that arbitration reduced wage dispersion. But the assumption would be heroic.

Borland and Woodbridge (1999) look in detail at the evidence for an impact on the Australian wage structure of the Australian wage-fixing system. They *do* make the heroic assumption that a deregulated Australian system would look much like that of the United States, including in the degree of inequality of wages. On the basis of their own and others' research, they conclude that the Australian system has reduced inequality of earnings, particularly by raising the relative pay of low-paid workers; that female, part-time, immigrant and young workers have particularly benefited from the Australian system, in terms of wages; and that the effect of wage regulation has been 'to increase relative earnings of low-wage workers in Australia by about 15 per cent' (Borland and Woodbridge 1999: 109).

Lydall (1965, 1968) in the 1960s also used percentile analysis to make international comparisons, though with access to less satisfactory data than later research. In 1968, he ranked twenty-five countries, locating Australia and New Zealand in a group of four with the least inequality of pay. Although the data are not directly comparable, a comparison of this finding with the evidence of Figure 4.9 suggests that Australia's relative position may have changed, in the direction of greater dispersion of pay, since the 1960s.

For the period since 1975, data are available about the distribution of earnings in Australia of a kind that did not exist previously or were, at best, available

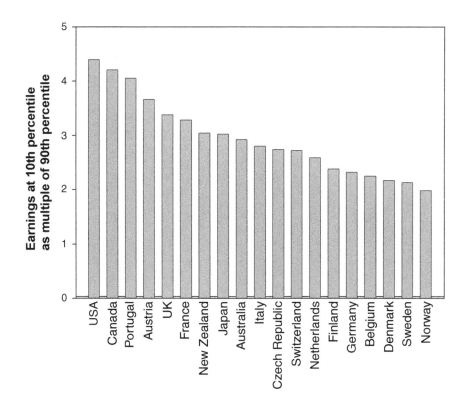

Figure 4.9 Wage inequalities in nineteen OECD countries (various years between 1990 and 1995)

sporadically. These relate to personal earnings.[43] They have supported much economic research.[44] The period was one of growing inequality in the interpersonal distribution of earnings. This is illustrated by Figure 4.10, which shows (for males and females separately and for both sexes combined) the ratio of wages at the tenth percentile (from the top) to those at the ninetieth. (The earnings are those of full-time non-managerial employees.) Clearly, there has been a long-term growth of inequality among wage-earners. In the case of males, there seems to have been some reversal between 2000 and 2002. This is not evident in the 'persons' series, both because female earnings continued the trend to greater inequality and because female pay fell relative to male pay.

Explaining this is a major challenge for Australian labour economists. Much research has been structured on the 'human capital' model of relative pay, wherein

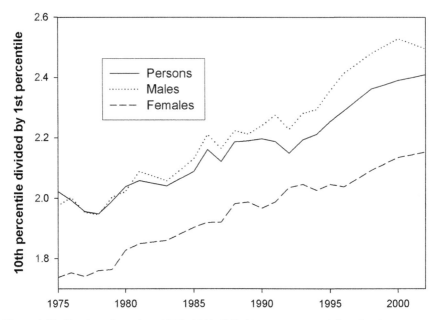

Figure 4.10 Earnings dispersion, 1975–2002 (full-time non-managerial workers)

differences in rewards are an outcome of unequal 'investments' in people. The investments are the direct expenditures in the acquisition of skills plus the income forgone during periods of education and training; and the theoretical presumption is that earnings differentials represent returns on these investments. Most economists who have used econometric techniques to 'explain' pay differences have found that 'investment' variables are insufficient and have added others such as industry, the size, profitability and market strength of the employing enterprise, and union membership. These analyses explain some of the growth of inequality between 1975 and 2000, but leave much unexplained (Borland 1999: 193–8).

Another explanatory variable, to allow directly for the impact of institutional determinants of pay, would be the award or agreement rate of pay applicable to the worker. Unfortunately, the available data do not permit this extension of the analysis. The history of arbitral policy over the last quarter of the century, however, offers little to explain the process demonstrated in Figure 4.10. Commission decisions in general wage cases led to a mix of percentage and flat-rate wage increases. Their net effect would have been a *compression* of the award wage structure.[45] It may be that the wage explosion of the early 1980s favoured the better-paid and therefore stretched the pay structure. Enterprise bargaining in the 1990s might similarly have favoured high-wage workers. Such speculations must, however, be seen in the context of the actual movement of pay dispersion. The clear impression given by Figure 4.10 is that the movement towards less equal pay has been a long-term phenomenon. The inference must be that the dominant explanations for the process lie outside the domain of institutional wage-setting. This, incidentally, should reinforce our caution in ascribing to arbitration the relative position of Australia in the international 'league table' of wage inequality.

Among the factors *likely* to affect the degree of inequality between workers are the occupational and industrial structures of the labour force. For example, a diminution in the number of middle-level jobs relative to high-paid and low-paid jobs will increase the overall dispersion of pay. Over the course of the twentieth century, the industrial structure of employment changed dramatically. The proportion of workers employed in agriculture fell from 25 per cent in 1901 to 15 per cent in 1950 and 5 per cent in 1998. The respective shares in mining were 7 per cent, 2 per cent and 1 per cent; in manufacturing, 15 per cent, 28 per cent and 13 per cent; and in services, 52 per cent, 55 per cent and 81 per cent (Meredith and Dyster 1999: 329). Likewise, the proportions of workers in different occupations evolved to reflect both the changing content of demand and the changing skill content of the labour force. It would be surprising if these changes did not affect the structure of earnings. Structural change might, for example, contribute to the growth of inequality shown in Figure 4.10. Equally, differences of economic structure would affect international comparisons such as those illustrated in Figure 4.9. The industrial relations system would have minimal, and only indirect, effects on the *relative numbers* of people working in different occupations and industries.

A line of research in Australia that is relevant to the growth in pay inequality over the last quarter of the century relates to the alleged 'disappearing middle' (King et al. 1992; Gregory 1993; Belchamber 1996; Borland 1999). For example, if manufacturing is typically an area of concentration of middle-level jobs, its long-term relative decline might have caused an increase in the relative importance of high-paid and low-paid jobs and, hence, an increase in overall inequality. The effects of structural change on measured inequality can, to some extent, be neutralised by focusing on the differences of pay between industries and between occupations. Studies by Hughes (1973), Norris (1980, 1986) and Rowe (1982) focused on the inter-industry pay structure, comparing particularly Australia and the United Kingdom. The concentration on inter-industry pay differences reflected the availability of data. These studies conveyed the impression that there was little difference between the two countries. Norris (1986: 198), however, said in his later study that 'virtually every difference identified (admittedly some of them small) pointed in the same direction, that relativities are narrower in Australia'; and although the seemingly more equal distribution that prevailed in Australia could not conclusively be ascribed to arbitration, 'it would be churlish to deny that it might be'. This view is consistent with the stronger conclusions of Borland and Woodbridge (1999) that the arbitration system has compressed wage differentials, even if modestly. Of equal importance is their conclusion that some of the most vulnerable types of workers – women generally and particularly low-skilled and part-time women, immigrants and young people – have all enjoyed significant protection from very low wages as a result of the operations of the Commission.

The question of whether arbitration affected pay inequality can also be approached from the perspective of tribunal decisions and policies. The clearest example of their affecting actual pay differences is the 'equal pay' decisions of 1969 and 1972. Those decisions caused a marked decrease in gender-related pay differences (Gregory and Duncan 1983; Hancock 1985, vol. 3: 20–7). With few exceptions, however, the tribunals did not attempt systematically to alter the degree of inequality in pay. Their attitude to relativities was tacitly conservative. The only instances known to us of their articulating opinions about the degree of dispersion were occasions when they supported increases in margins to restore earlier relativities and recent comments about the effects of flat-rate safety net increases on the relative rewards of more-skilled workers.

CONCLUSION

The existence of a conciliation and arbitration system recognised public interests in the operation of the labour market. An obvious public interest was in the prevention and settlement of disputes. That, however, was never a goal to be achieved at all costs. If it were, attention might have been given to draconian measures such as the prohibition of trade unions or leaving the labour market to be 'regulated' solely by common law. Rather, the public interest lay in the *reconciliation* of an effective voice for employees with avoidance of damaging clashes between workers and employers.

Another public interest was in achieving fair labour market outcomes. In particular, there was a concern that the individual employee, 'trading' in the labour market on his or her own behalf, might be forced to accept terms of employment that offended widely held conceptions of humanity, fairness and dignity.[46] There were several ways in which better outcomes might be pursued. Trade unions could change the relative bargaining capacities of employers and employees. Regulation (such as minimum wages in the United States and the United Kingdom and the award system in Australia) is another mode of modifying market outcomes. These methods are not exclusive. Australian arbitration came into being to complement rather than to displace trade unionism. It recognised both a potential for public detriment in collective bargaining and a need to supplement the protections that unions afforded to workers. A further public interest was in avoiding economic harm from the operation of a labour market subject to these interferences.

Because the 'public interest' had multiple, but interrelated, dimensions, judging success or failure is not straightforward. For example, the question whether the Australian system of industrial regulations increased or reduced the rate of inflation might be answered differently according to the assumed alternative. Does the alternative involve a labour force devoid of protections or one represented by powerful trade unions? Arbitration may have performed worse, in respect of inflation, than the former, but better than the latter. Much the same might be said with respect to unemployment. Thus, there can be no simple verdict on the Australian experiment. Some historical generalisations are possible, however.

The principal arbitration authority was never in full control of the terms of employment. In a strictly legal sense, this is obvious. Its awards covered a minority of employees; and they fixed only the minimum standards that employers must observe. The concept of 'control' clearly implies *de facto* influence going well beyond *de jure* authority. The nature of the gap between the *de jure* and the *de facto* was defined by the preparedness of State tribunals to apply within their own jurisdictions the decisions made by the federal tribunal; the readiness of trade unions to abide by tribunal decisions and their capacity to extract additional benefits from employers; and the modification of terms of employment by market forces. As we have seen, the tribunal from time to time found it necessary to adapt its policies to the limitations of its *de facto* power.

In the earlier decades of arbitration – roughly until the Second World War – the ethos of arbitration was of a contest between the granting of benefits that wage-earners might not otherwise enjoy and limiting them to the capacity of employers to provide them. This contest was progressively and perhaps unwittingly redefined so as to shift the notion of capacity away from a focus on particular employers and industries and towards the consideration of macroeconomic criteria such as unemployment and the ability of the economy to generate the means of paying for imports. There is little sign of any expectation of long-term growth in real wages.

The quarter-century after the Second World War stands in stark contrast. There was an underlying presumption in the tribunal's policies that real wages (and other employee benefits) would and should rise. But acting on this presumption was not a simple exercise. Short-term economic constraints, especially the threat of inflation, frequently restricted the wage increases that the Court and the Commission felt able to impose. Accentuating these immediate restraints was the longer-term reality of earnings drift, which limited the achievable growth in the real value of award wages.

Between the late 1960s and 1990, there was a repeated sequence of rapid wage growth, achieved by the exercise of trade union power, and subsequent restraint overseen by the Commission. In the breakout periods, the Commission could contribute little or nothing to the avoidance of inflation; in the periods of restraint, the goals of wage policy included a gradual reining-in of wage increases with a view to both reducing the rate of inflation and avoiding a wage-related increase in unemployment. Although the link between wage behaviour and unemployment is contentious and complex, unemployment intensified the sense of crisis engendered by the wage explosions and contributed to the acceptance of the wage policies administered by the Commission. Trade union acceptance was precarious in the 1970s. It ran deeper in the years 1983–90, but wage policy eventually disintegrated through the collision of the industrial parties' desire to move to enterprise bargaining with the Commission's forebodings about its consequences. The Commission's fears of further wage breakouts have not been realised; but its concerns about the emergence of a disadvantaged class of wage-earners – those dependent on 'safety net' wages and conditions – were well-founded.

At the centenary of the system, there are unresolved questions. These derive from both the decline of arbitration and the dramatic fall in union coverage of the labour force. The scenario that now looks the most probable is that workers in a range of industries, where unions retain a capacity to negotiate with the aid of credible threats of industrial action, will fare well; that some, whose skills are scarce, will prosper through employer competition to secure and retain their services; and that many others will have a hard time or depend increasingly on the protections of social security. Those protections, however generous, cannot replace the tribunals' historic role of enforcing a fair day's pay for a fair day's work.

APPENDIX: THE PRICE AND WAGE SERIES

Our consumer prices series is the result of linking three indices: the 'A Series' Index for the period 1901–14; the 'C Series' Index for 1914–49; and the Consumer Price Index for 1949–2000.[47] This entails using the latest index applicable to the defined period.[48]

Constructing a series for wages is even more problematic than plotting the movement of prices. Various series exist for different periods. They neither cover identical populations nor represent identical aspects of 'wages'. We link the following:[49]

- 1901–12: minimum weekly wage rates of male adults (Vamplew 1987: 155)[50]
- 1912–46: average annual male earnings in manufacturing (Vamplew 1987: 161)
- 1946–72: average weekly earnings (male equivalents) (Vamplew 1987: 157)
- 1972–2000: average adult male weekly earnings.[51]

The principal risk of serious error in the wage data probably lies in the use of data of manufacturing earnings for the period 1912–46. Manufacturing, though constituting a major sector of male employment, may not have been typical of the whole economy; and the calculation of annual rather than weekly earnings creates another discontinuity in the statistics. An alternative was to continue use of the minimum wage data. These are unsatisfactory, however, because they exclude the effects of changes in the composition of the labour force and make no allowance for earnings above the prescribed weekly amounts. But use of manufacturing earnings may lead to wage estimates that are too high. Manufacturing earnings grew more than minimum rates: the cumulative divergence between 1912 and 1946 was about 18 per cent.

5

JUSTICE AND EQUITY: WOMEN AND INDIGENOUS WORKERS

Gillian Whitehouse

Throughout much of its history, the Australian wage-fixing system has been viewed as a significant champion of social justice and equity. At its inception, Alfred Deakin stated that 'no measures ever submitted by any legislature offer greater prospects of the establishment of social justice and of the removal of inequalities than those which are based on the principle of conciliation and arbitration' (*CPD* 30 July 1903: 2883). Much later, reflecting on the period after the Second World War, Kirby (2002: 563) noted that the federal tribunal's role as 'the guardian of industrial equity and the ultimate enforcer of the Australian nation's commitment to a "fair go" in industrial relations' seemed indisputable. In practice, however, justice for all has been an elusive target, and the notions of wage justice pursued have often been conflictual and contested.

Hopes for wage justice in Australia were associated largely with the system's capacity to moderate the power imbalance between employers and employees, with two distinct principles of justice gaining prominence in practice. The first was the notion of a 'fair and reasonable' living wage, elaborated by Higgins in the *Harvester* case in 1907 as a wage adequate for 'a human being living in a

The Commission in 1963. Sir Richard Kirby, President (seated fourth from left) is flanked by his Deputy Presidents. From left to right they are Justices Sweeney, Gallagher, Wright, Ashburner and Moore. His Commissioners stand behind. From left to right they are Commissioners Winter, Apsey, Horan, Chambers, Donovan, Findlay, Senior Commissioner Taylor, Commissioners Portus, Austin, Gough, Hood and Matthews. The dress of this tribunal contrasts with that of Sir Raymond Kelly's Court.

civilized community' (1907 2 CAR 3–4). This reflected an idea of natural justice 'more imperious and ancient than any bargain between man and man, namely, that wages ought not to be insufficient to support a frugal and well-behaved wage earner' (Pope Leo XIII, *Rerum Novarum*, cited in Timbs 1963: 24). 'Wage justice' in this sense is not only 'fair' in the sense of striking a balance between wages and profits, but consistent with basic human dignity and what Marshall (1950) later expressed as the social rights of citizenship. A second notion of wage justice was based on wages commensurate with factors such as effort and skill, and thus a comparative justice with respect to relativities between workers, regardless of location or market demand. Neither of these notions precludes the possibility of 'wage equity' in the sense of equity between men and women or Indigenous and non-Indigenous Australians; in fact, if implemented inclusively they offer the potential to ameliorate gender and race inequality. However, both may be implemented in ways that ignore, or even entrench, such inequities.

The early arbitration system, as part of what Castles (1988) termed a 'historic compromise' involving tariffs and immigration restrictions alongside regulation of wages, delivered a form of industrial citizenship based on economic protectionism. In comparison with more market-reliant approaches, these arrangements enhanced the capacity to introduce norms of social justice into wage fixation. As Eveline notes, however, protectionism can also be 'a recipe for inequity, injustice and exclusion'. White women and Indigenous people, for example, were excluded from direct benefits, and became the objects of other types of 'protection' – as wives and mothers, or as wards of the state – with very different implications for industrial citizenship (Eveline 2001: 144–6).

The story of women under the arbitration system to be told in this chapter is of transition from a system based on notions of wage justice that relegated them to a second class industrial citizenship, to a system in which overt discrimination has been removed but the indirect benefits of earlier notions of wage justice and a centralised institutional framework are being lost. While the earlier arrangements produced forms of wage justice without equity between men and women, 100 years later the risk is that a closer approximation of gender equity will be achieved only alongside an erosion of broader wage justice – in effect through an extension of disadvantage to males. The central theme in the story is thus the tension between these different types of 'wage justice' and between the indirect and direct effects of the wage determination system.

Indigenous workers were also disadvantaged relative to the direct beneficiaries of the protectionist measures underpinning arbitration (white males). In comparison with women, however, for whom separate rates were established in awards, disadvantage under the arbitration system was manifest more in the exclusion of groups such as Indigenous stockmen from award coverage. For these workers, moreover, there was an interweaving of industrial issues with concerns such as land rights. As Aboriginality has not been addressed as directly or as frequently as gender difference in the industrial relations system, the story of Indigenous workers in this chapter is shorter, with the depressed labour market conditions of Indigenous relative to non-Indigenous Australians requiring a broader social analysis beyond the scope of this chapter and its concentration on the wage determination system.

For both Indigenous workers and women, the emphasis here is on selected cases and decisions that have had significant implications for wages and conditions. The chapter is necessarily simplified, and in particular glosses over important differences within the categories of 'women' and 'Indigenous Australians'. The story of women thus concentrates primarily on white women and their situation relative to white men; while the impact of the system on Indigenous Australians is largely the story of its impact on a particular group of Aboriginal men (stockmen).

INDIGENOUS AUSTRALIANS AND THE WAGE DETERMINATION SYSTEM

The engagement of Indigenous Australians in the 'work' that white settlers brought to the country was from the start intermittent and unregulated. In the north, food and tobacco were accepted as wages for assisting European hunters, and informal arrangements developed for work in a number of primary industries, including pearling and prospecting. Dispossessed of land and increasingly dependent on European food, the majority of Aboriginal workers in the north became involved in the cattle industry, which employed around 10000 from 1900 through to the 1960s (Broome 2002: 124–5).

The federal wage-fixing system that was initiated in 1904 did not bring the protection it offered white men; rather, the Indigenous population found itself on the other side of the protective barrier. Alongside the immigration restrictions directed at Asian and Pacific Islander labour that underpinned protection of white men's wages and jobs, legislative means of excluding Aborigines from particular forms of employment were adopted at both State and federal levels. For example, Commonwealth mail contracts were limited to 'white labour', and 'white grown' sugar attracted a bonus and rebate on excise (McCorquodale 1985: 4–5). The fair and reasonable wage adopted in the *Harvester* judgment in 1907, which rested on these protective arrangements, was thus achieved for white men through the explicit exclusion of others.

Protection for the Indigenous population was of a different type – essentially under State and Territory ordinances that cast them as wards. Legislative measures adopted in the late nineteenth and early twentieth centuries required Europeans to obtain permits to employ Aboriginal people, and specified terms and conditions such as the provision of rations, clothing and medical care (Broome 2002: 128). In the Northern Territory, the regulations typically prescribed a small wage supplemented by provision for needs such as food and clothing, with support for a wife and child also provided under ordinance (1967 113 CAR 652). The extent of this protective legislation effectively placed the working conditions of Aboriginal Australians outside the jurisdiction of the wage determination system, and they were explicitly excluded from a number of awards.

In a series of pastoral industry cases beginning in the 1920s, exclusion from federal awards was maintained on the basis that award coverage and rates of pay would mean job losses for Indigenous workers, and that unions' claims for inclusion were disingenuous attempts to achieve this goal. Refusing the application to include Indigenous workers under the award in a 1924 case (*The North Australian Industrial Union v JA Ambrose and Others*), for example, the Court President, Justice Powers, observed, 'I know the union is anxious to reduce the number of aboriginals to be employed in proportion to white men' (1924 20 CAR 507, 511). Similarly, in *North Australian Workers Union v Northern Territory Pastoral Lessees Association* in 1928, the union was accused of seeking 'to exclude aboriginals from employment upon cattle stations so as to make work for white employees' (1928 26 CAR 623). This position was maintained in subsequent applications over the next three decades.[1]

As the following section of the chapter will illustrate, tension between equal pay and access to employment was also frequently evident in the Court's approaches to women, although in their case much greater legitimacy was accorded to the protection of white men's jobs. Equal pay for women, in the few early cases where it was applied, was expressly used as a means to ensure they could not compete for 'male' jobs. White stockmen's jobs were not, however, to be protected in the same way. Women in men's jobs were perhaps perceived as more of a threat, as they were less confined to a narrow industry sector than the stockmen; but it is also apparent that differences of race were seen as justifying a much greater differential in wages and conditions. In a 1944 case, for example, it was observed that 'it would be inadvisable and even cruel to pay [Indigenous workers] for the work they can do at the wage standards found to be appropriate for civilized "whites"' (1944 53 CAR 215).

Both equal pay and access to jobs can be seen as aspects of justice in wage determination, and prioritisation of one over the other necessarily takes place in the context of broader political ideas and policy approaches. Thus, it was in the context of 'assimilation' and rising concerns for Indigenous rights in the 1960s, and with the federal government supporting the case for change, that the Commission reversed its position on the Indigenous stockmen. The application in 1965 to vary *The Cattle Station Industry (Northern Territory) Award 1951* to include Aborigines and thus, in effect, award equal pay was referred to a full bench, and was seen as a test case 'to settle the principle of excluding racial groups from award protection' (Sharp 1966: 158). The decision taken by President Kirby, Justice Moore and Public Service Arbitrator Taylor was delivered in March 1966. It was presented as the only possible decision consistent with the principles of wage justice guiding the wage determination system:

> We consider that overwhelming industrial justice requires us to put aboriginal employees in the Northern Territory on to the same basis as white employees . . . [the pastoralists] have not discharged the heavy burden of persuading us that we should depart from standards and principles which have been part of the Australian arbitration system since its inception. We do not flinch from this decision which we consider is the only proper one to be made at this point in Australia's history. There must be one industrial law, similarly applied, to all Australians, aboriginal or not. (1966 113 CAR 651, 666–9)

Thus, although the Commissioners accepted the pastoralists' evidence that 'aborigines are unable to work as well as whites because of cultural and tribal factors' (1966 113 CAR 658),[2] they nevertheless recognised that industrial justice required a decision for equal pay.[3] The primary concern, for the government as well as the Commission, was that although the decision was consistent with assimilation policy, in that it delivered 'substantive and symbolic equality for Indigenous men in a major northern industry', in the Northern Territory assimilation was in practice dependent on the capacity of pastoral properties to support Aboriginal workers and their dependants in remote areas (Rowse 1998: 128). Large-scale labour-shedding in the pastoral industry would disrupt these arrangements and risk overcrowding in towns, missions and settlements. The Commissioners sought to minimise labour-shedding by delaying implementation of the decision until December 1968, and foreshadowing a simplification of the 'slow worker' clause to facilitate its application to the pastoral industry (1966 113 CAR 651, 668). They also emphasised what they saw as the benefits of retaining Indigenous labour: 'an indigenous labour force resident on the station with cultural and spiritual ties to the land, even if somewhat inefficient, has many advantages over a floating white labour force which has no particular knowledge or feeling for the land in which the station lies' (1966 113 CAR 667).

Nevertheless, significant displacement of labour did occur following the case (Rowse 1998: 128; Bunbury 2002: 107); but the 1966 decision was only one of a series of changes that contributed to this outcome. Additional factors included reduced demand for Aboriginal labour on cattle stations following capital investment over the period from the 1950s and the effects of drought into the 1960s, as well as the Indigenous population's extended access to pensions and unemployment benefits by the early 1970s (Rowse 1993, 1998). Erosion of the interdependence of pastoralists and Aboriginal communities was thus well under way by the 1970s, and it is unlikely that a ruling to continue the exclusion of Indigenous stockmen from award conditions would have stemmed the tide.

For some Indigenous workers, the problem with the Commission's decision in 1966 was not the risk of job loss, but rather the delay in implementation of equal wages and conditions that 'would amount to their being treated as fellow human beings' (Attwood 2000: 9). This fundamental sense of injustice echoed concerns over land rights, and a series of strikes, which began over conditions at Wave Hill, extended to other areas in 1967 and became more inclusive protests (Attwood 2000; Riddett 1997).

Land rights gained an increasing profile alongside the ensuing move away from 'assimilation' towards 'self-determination', and an expanding policy agenda included a focus on economic opportunities beyond mainstream employment and particularly in remote areas. Funding for commercial projects, from the Commonwealth Fund for Aboriginal Enterprises set up in 1969, to various schemes run under the Aboriginal and Torres Strait Islander Commission (ATSIC), has been one of the strategies to extend economic opportunities. Most significantly, the Community Development Employment Projects (CDEP) program, set up in 1977, has been widely adopted. Its aims were to build community, provide employment and develop skills (Spicer 1997: 24), and it contributed to the 'Indigenous sector' of publicly subsidised, representative service and policy organisations that have provided Indigenous employment in the post-assimilation era (Rowse 2002). Rowse (1993) has argued that CDEP was devised partly as an attempt to deal with the surplus population created by the declining capacity of the pastoral industry to support Indigenous people in remote areas. It provides Aboriginal communities with funding equivalent to unemployment benefits for the entire community, and allows local-level decisions about the allocation of work and funds. While debates about its efficacy are beyond the scope of this chapter, what is important here is recognition of the varied 'employment' situations of Indigenous Australians, and the extent to which their working conditions fall outside the scope of the formal wage determination process.

The defining feature of Indigenous employment patterns and conditions in the post-assimilation era remains the significant variation between remote and urban areas. The ongoing movement into urban and near urban areas – only 26 per cent of the Aboriginal population lived in rural areas in 2001,[4] compared with 56 per cent in 1971 (ABS 2001 Census, unpublished data; CBCS 1971b: 1) – has meant the increasing importance of programs to enhance opportunities in mainstream labour markets. The Aboriginal Employment Development policy adopted in 1987 with the aim of employment equity by 2000 significantly boosted spending on employment programs, and equal employment opportunity goals in the public sector have sought to increase the representation of Indigenous Australians in public employment. However, in spite of the spread of both mainstream and Indigenous-specific labour market and training projects in the 1990s, employment growth in mainstream labour markets has been minimal (Taylor and Hunter 1996).

Estimates of the labour market disadvantage of Indigenous people are complicated by substantial regional differences in the type and conditions of employment, as well as by the assumptions inherent in the vocabulary of labour force statistics. As Smith (1991: 23) notes, terms such as 'unemployment' and 'labour force participation' are less meaningful where the formal labour market is seen as partially irrelevant. With these caveats in mind, Figure 5.1 shows the consistently lower levels of labour force participation of Indigenous people compared with all Australians for the period 1971–2001,[5] as well as the considerably higher levels of unemployment experienced. Had CDEP participants been counted as

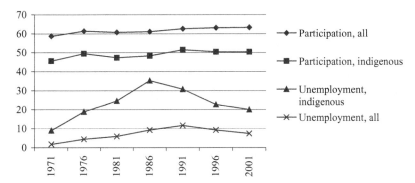

Figure 5.1 Labour force participation and unemployment, 1971–2001 (per cent).
Source: Census data, 1971–2001

'unemployed', the unemployment rate in 2001 would have been 34 per cent rather than the recorded 20 per cent (ABS 2001: table I13).

Underpinning these statistics is a picture of consistent labour market segregation and disadvantage for both male and female Indigenous workers. Aboriginal employees are highly concentrated in two industry sectors (health and community services, and government administration), and substantially over-represented in comparison with non-Indigenous employees in relatively low-paid occupational groups such as Labourers and Related Workers. Private sector employment accounts for a lower proportion of Indigenous than non-Indigenous employment, and even industries such as mining, which often operate in close proximity to remote Aboriginal communities, have provided limited and mainly low-skilled employment opportunities (Cousins and Nieuwenhuysen 1984: 2–3). The median personal income for Indigenous Australians in 2001 was only 72 per cent of that of all Australians, and at this time over 40 per cent of Indigenous employees worked part-time compared with around a quarter of the population as a whole (ABS 2001: table I29), reflecting in part the prevalence of part-time work in CDEP programs.

The capacity of the industrial relations system to assist more equitable outcomes is varied, given the greater proportion of Indigenous compared with non-Indigenous workers located in remote communities and outside the regulated wages system altogether. Lack of award coverage for staff of many Indigenous

organisations is also noted by Altman and Hawke (1993: 8). Even for those
under formal arrangements, the diminishing regulatory scope of the industrial
relations system over the 1990s, in particular through limitations to the scope of
awards and union rights (Hunter 1997: 454), suggests persistent difficulties in
delivering wage justice.

Similar arguments can to some extent be made for (white) women, who – in
comparison with white men – tend to be concentrated in part-time and lower
paid jobs and are thus more vulnerable in a deregulated environment. Historical
parallels with the experiences of women under the arbitration system can also be
seen in the extent to which arguments for equal pay could be driven as much by
the desire to protect white men's jobs as by a concern for social justice. The story
of women under the arbitration system, however, is both more extensive, given
the specific and detailed ways their wages and conditions have been regulated,
and more illustrative of its (often indirect) benefits.

WOMEN AND THE WAGE DETERMINATION SYSTEM

The arbitration system has been only one of a wide range of influences on employment equity for women over the past 100 years, and it has responded, as well as
contributed, to the changing socioeconomic framework over that time. One of
the most marked labour market changes during this period has been the increasing engagement of women in paid employment. As Figure 5.2 shows, following
a relatively static situation in the first half of the twentieth century, women's –
and particularly married women's – labour force participation rates in Australia
have risen dramatically alongside changes in social attitudes, family structures
and the occupational composition of the labour market.

The most significant changes in labour market composition have arisen with
the expansion of the service sector and growth of part-time work in industries
such as retail and hospitality. Much of the increase in participation shown in
Figure 5.2 has been into part-time work (that is, fewer than 35 hours per week),
and by 2001, 45 per cent of female employees, and 47 per cent of married female
employees, worked part-time, whereas only around 15 per cent of male employees
were part-timers (ABS time series data). In contrast, the first collection of data

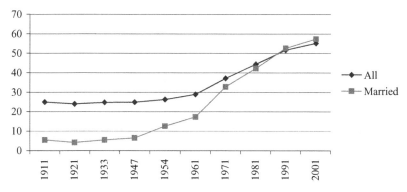

Figure 5.2 Women's labour force participation, 1911–2001 (per cent)
Source: Census data, 1911–86; ABS 6291.0.55.001: table 01

on part-time work in Australia (in the 1933 census) showed that it accounted for around 8 per cent of employment at that time, and that it was more prevalent for males (9 per cent) than for females (5 per cent), reflecting its concentration in the primary production sector, particularly forestry.

Although there have been significant changes in the industry and occupational distribution of women's employment over the period shown in Figure 5.2, sex segregation has remained a defining feature of the labour market. At the beginning of the twentieth century, women's employment was highly concentrated in private domestic service, a poorly remunerated category that accounted for around 30 per cent of female workers. By the 1960s, the proportion of working women engaged in private domestic service had fallen to less than 3 per cent, and women's employment patterns had shifted towards industry sectors such as commerce and public administration.[6] Occupational concentration has remained strong, with sales and clerical jobs accounting for much of women's employment from the 1960s, and teaching and nursing consistently representing a large proportion of women's employment in professional categories.

The arbitration system has reflected rather than directly shaped these ongoing patterns of labour market segregation, but its influence has been somewhat more direct on the issue of gender wage equity. Unlike the situation for Indigenous workers, women's wages have been determined within the wage-fixing system from its inception – with both positive and negative consequences. Figure 5.3 illustrates trends in female–male earnings ratios from the early 1900s, showing

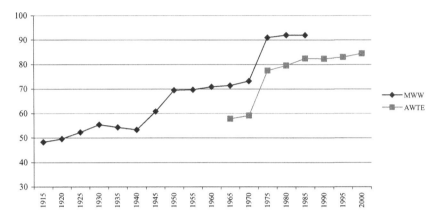

Figure 5.3 Women's earnings as a percentage of men's, 1915–2000 (minimum weekly wage and average weekly total earnings)
Notes: *Minimum weekly wage (MWW) based on average nominal rates of wages payable to adults for a full week's work (weighted by industry), as prescribed in awards, determinations and agreements. Average weekly total earnings (AWTE) based on total weekly earnings of adult, non-managerial, full-time employees.*
Sources: *Commonwealth Bureau of Statistics Labour Reports (ABS 6000.0); Withers et al. 1987: 155–7; ABS 6306.0*

the significant improvements in gender pay equity that have been made, albeit with a substantial gender earnings gap still evident at the beginning of the twenty-first century.

The female–male earnings ratios shown in Figure 5.3 are based on minimum weekly wages (as the most direct indicator of differences attributable to the wage tribunals) and average weekly total earnings (which incorporate differences in payments over and above the minimum) (see Chapter 4). As the graph shows, the two measures exhibit similar trends, with the wider gender pay gap in total earnings reflecting gender inequality in a range of additional payments that have largely fallen outside the scope of pay equity provisions. Trends in the ratios may reflect changes both in women's pay rates relative to men's and in the distribution of women's employment (for example, between and within occupations). However, the changes shown in the 1940s and, most dramatically, in the 1970s are too rapid to be accounted for by distributional changes – rather, their origins lie in specific wage determination decisions that will be elaborated below.

The full story of the impact of the wage determination system on women's working conditions over the past century is beyond the scope of a single chapter. Attention here is on selected highlights: the impact of a 'living' wage in the early 1900s; changes emerging during and following the Second World War; adoption of equal pay principles and their implementation in the 1970s and 1980s; and decentralisation from the 1990s. Decisions taken during these phases illustrate the complex ways in which the wage determination system has affected women, initially with quite explicit forms of exclusion and differential treatment on the one hand, but – often indirect – benefits on the other, reflecting the centralised system's capacity to provide some protection for the industrially weak.

The living wage

When the arbitration system was established, only around 20 per cent of working age women, and around 5 per cent of married women, were in the labour force (see Figure 5.2). Consistent with notions of 'bourgeois philanthropy' (Barrett and McIntosh 1980), the prevailing view was that the engagement of wives and mothers in paid work would risk moral impropriety and degeneration of the family. Ideally, at least for the white middle class, women were 'protected' from both financial and moral risks by their husbands or fathers. In line with the goal of a White Australia (pursued through the *Immigration Restriction Act 1901* and exhortations to 'populate or perish'), their most important role was seen as 'mothers of the white race', or as the domestic servants supporting middle-class women in this task.[7]

The formal establishment of a living wage, and the exclusion of women from the ranks of 'breadwinners' entitled to receive it, were logical outcomes within this social context and under the economic policy framework of new protectionism. Exclusion from breadwinner status formalised women's inferior status in the labour market. The inherent contradictions – the need to pay men as breadwinners even if they had no family to support, and the denial of a breadwinner wage to women who did – were glossed over as anomalies in subsequent cases and not fully resolved until 1974. Occasional deviations from the male breadwinner logic were seen as necessary where lower female wages could risk job loss for men. In the 1912 *Rural Workers Union and United Labourers' Union v Mildura Branch of the Australian Dried Fruits Association and Others* case (1912 6 CAR 61),[8] for example, the threat of cheap female labour underpinned Higgins' decision to award equal pay to female fruit-pickers:

> There has been observed for a long time a tendency to substitute women for men in industries . . . and . . . it is often the result of women being paid lower wages then men. Fortunately for society, however, the greater number of breadwinners are still men. The women are not all dragged from the home to work while the men loaf at home, and in this case the majority even of the fruit-pickers are men. As a result, I come to the conclusion that in the case of the pickers, men and women . . . should be paid on the same level of wages; and the employer will then be at liberty freely to select whichever sex and whichever person he prefers for the work. (1912 6 CAR 61–72)

In 1919, Higgins applied similar logic in ruling that equal margins for skill should be paid in order to assist men in their 'last stand' against the 'gentle invaders' who were displacing them from tailoring jobs (*Federated Clothing Trades of Australia v JA Archer and Others* (1919) 13 CAR 647, 701).[9] In addition, the protection of women's morality occasionally emerged as a justification for equal pay; for example, a 1924 case addressed the issue of equal pay for women involved in the production of 'pernicious rubber goods' such as condoms, in the hope of discouraging employers from hiring women in such work (Patmore 1991: 170).

In the majority of cases, however, the male breadwinner logic implicit in the family wage applied. Women working in male-dominated occupations or women with dependants were seen as exceptions to the rule, and the basic wage was not adjusted for 'exceptional cases' by offering more to a woman having to care for family members, or indeed less to a woman who 'has a legacy from her grandparents, or . . . boards and lodges free with her parents, and merely wants the money for a dress' (1912 6 CAR 62). Women, it seemed, could be quite extravagant on matters such as dress, and while deliberations over a suitable basic wage for women in 1919 did consider clothing along with other necessities, a modest amount was deemed appropriate:

If the girls will have their finery at the sacrifice of other things more
necessary, that is their business; but probably it is not fair to force the
employers to pay for all that a girl may fancy as being necessary for
human requirements. At the same time, we must not forget the important
social function of girls' dress as a bulwark for self-respect . . . (1919 13
CAR 647, 695)

The issue of a female basic wage to reflect the costs of an individual living in
reasonable comfort had been addressed in the 1912 *Rural Workers* case and the
1917 *Theatrical and Amusement* case, with different outcomes: 75 per cent of
the male rate in the former and 54 per cent in the latter (Plowman 1992: 247).
The matter was subsequently considered more comprehensively in the *Clothing
Trades* case of 1919. As in the *Harvester* case, Higgins drew on evidence of living
costs as well as existing rates, particularly a 1918 case in South Australia which
had estimated living costs for females. The result of his deliberations was to affirm
a basic wage for women set at 54 per cent of the male rate; a level subsequently followed in decisions of federal and State tribunals over the following three decades.
Moreover, although the proportions changed over the years, with higher rates
being set in some industries[10] and the federal standard rising to 75 per cent
in 1950, different minimum rates for men and women were retained until the
1970s.

The notion of a living wage that evolved in these early cases has thus been of
considerable significance in establishing conventions for dealing with issues of
women's pay and working conditions over a long period of time. As a form
of 'wage justice', the living wage offered a level of social protection beyond what
might be achieved through bargaining in the marketplace. Although the extent to
which this object was attained has been the subject of much debate, the *Harvester*
decision did establish a standard significantly higher than the existing rate for
'unskilled workers'. Subsequent decisions of the Court provided wage levels and
working conditions (such as sick leave provisions) in regulated employment that
gave some substance to the notion of a 'wage earners' welfare state' (Castles
1985).

For women, however, 'the imposing edifice of a "family wage"' (Ryan and
Conlon 1989: 91) placed a formal barrier in the way of gender wage equality.

It was not the case that the notion of a male breadwinner and its associated female–male wage differentials were peculiarly Australian phenomena, or direct products of the wage-fixing system's institutional structure. In the United Kingdom, for example, the notion of a family wage 'was an important element in late nineteenth century respectability' that underpinned unequal treatment for women in employment (Hinton 1982: 28–9); and pursuit of a family wage in the United States at the beginning of the twentieth century similarly reflected the idea that mothering was 'women's primary life purpose' (Figart et al. 2002: 3–4). Also, the idea that women's wages should be sufficiently low to ensure that motherhood remained an attractive option was voiced in debates over women's wages in both the United Kingdom and the United States (Royal Commission on Equal Pay 1944–46: 189; Figart et al. 2002: 4). By reinforcing existing patterns of sex segregation in efforts to protect men's jobs (Bennett 1984: 34) and entrenching principles of wage determination that outlived their original social context, the institutional framework in Australia nevertheless created particular barriers to change.

At a broader level, though, the regulatory scope of the system, which embodied a form of wage justice through a degree of protection from the market, brought some benefits for women. Bennett (1984: 32–4), for example, notes that in the female-dominated clothing trades in 1919, adoption of a 44-hour week was clearly designed to benefit women rather than simply ensure they were uncompetitive with men. Similarly, examples of significant wage gains suggest that the institutional machinery, at both federal and State levels, delivered benefits that would have been unlikely to accrue through unregulated bargaining. While Reekie (1989: 286) argues that women have been marginalised under an arbitration system that 'bonded male capital and male labour in a validation of men's experiences', her analysis of the *New South Wales Shop Assistants* case of 1907 shows that women gained significant increases on their pre-award rates, and also proportionately more than men. Similarly, Frances' (1993) research on the boot trade shows that the wages and conditions of women working in this industry during the time it remained outside the arbitration system consistently lagged behind those for clothing workers, which had been established in the 1919 *Clothing Trades* case; and that the level of sex segmentation was significantly greater under direct bargaining arrangements than under the federal arbitration system

(Frances 1993: chs 7 and 8). Nevertheless, the primary legacy of these early years was a basic wage set at a little over half that awarded to men, and it was only in the context of labour market shortages generated by the Second World War that this would be effectively challenged.

The Second World War and its aftermath

While there was some variability in the rates established in different awards during the 1920s and 1930s, showing how imprecise estimates of 'male breadwinner' needs were, the basic principles for determination of women's wages remained in place, even in the face of a much greater reliance on notions of 'capacity to pay' throughout the depression in the 1930s. Inconsistencies in the application of a 'family wage', such as its payment to men without families or inadequacy for large families, were dismissed as beyond the Court's jurisdiction, with the latter seen as the province of social welfare policies such as child endowment (1934 33 CAR 149). Although women's employment patterns changed somewhat over the 1920s and 1930s, they were still predominantly concentrated in private domestic service, and overall levels of female participation remained relatively static (see Figure 5.2).

Mobilisation around the issue of equal pay was nevertheless well under way by the end of the 1930s. The formation of the Council of Action for Equal Pay (CAEP) in 1937, for example, brought together unions and women's groups that viewed the wage-fixing system as an important avenue for change (Ranald 1982: 277; D'Aprano 2001: 78–9). The CAEP's approach to equal pay was guided by the ideas of Muriel Heagney (1935), for whom the path to equal pay for the sexes lay in occupational rates established with no reference to the sex of the worker. It was this notion of the 'rate for the job' that underpinned the CAEP's efforts to achieve pay equity, in contrast with the United Associations of Women (UAW), which under Jessie Street's guidance in the late 1930s advocated staged increases in the female rate from 54 to 80 per cent of the male rate. These differences between the organisations caused some tensions, particularly over the UAW's attempt to present its preferred model to the 1940 Basic Wage Case (Ranald 1982: 281–3). At this stage in the history of the arbitration system, however, they were not admitted by the Court.

While attempts to raise women's wages above 54 per cent of men's were refused in the 1930s, establishment of the Women's Employment Board (WEB) in 1942 provided an important stimulus for change. Although the WEB's history was brief, and its decisions resisted, by the end of the 1940s economic and labour market conditions had changed so markedly that a return to the old 54 per cent rule of thumb could not be justified.

The WEB's task was to establish rates for women in those jobs where they were (temporarily) replacing men. Consistent with the government's need to attract women into these jobs, wages could be established within the range of 60–100 per cent of the male rate, based on assessments of women's efficiency and productivity relative to men. Although there was undoubtedly gender bias in the way efficiency and productivity were determined under the WEB (McMurchy et al. 1983: 111–12; Ryan and Conlon 1989: 126–30), the board was not constrained by notions of a family wage, and by 1944 it had awarded rates of up to 100 per cent of the male wage to over 80 000 women. These were seen as radical decisions, as evidenced by the level of resistance from employers and by widespread refusal to pay WEB rates (Beaton 1982: 90, 91).

Additionally, the WEB rates generated dissatisfaction among those women who fell outside its jurisdiction, many of whom were still paid only 54 per cent of the male rate. Within the arbitration system, however, there was little inclination to alter long standing principles of female wage determination. The Court's view was that women covered by WEB rates would be relinquishing their jobs after the war and thus that this was only a temporary aberration in wage determination history (Ryan and Conlon 1989: 133). In a 1943 case seeking a higher rate for munitions workers, existing principles for female wage determination were reiterated:

> so long as the foundational or basic wage for women is assessed
> according to a standard different from that which is the basis of the
> foundational or basic wage – a family wage – for men, the Court will
> not . . . raise the general level of women's minimum wages in occupations
> suitable for women, and in which they do not encounter considerable
> competition from men . . . To do this would at once depress the relative
> standard of living of the family as a group . . . as compared with that of
> the typical single woman wage-earner. (1943 50 CAR 191, 213)

The WEB's short history came to an end in 1944 and, in continuing efforts to attract women into 'vital' industries, the government sought a decision from the arbitration system on the adequacy of women's wages in these areas. Faced with the Court's continued reassertion of its needs-based principles of wage fixation, the government enacted the National Security (Female Minimum Wages) Regulations, which set a 75 per cent minimum rate in all vital industries (Ryan and Rowse 1975: 26; Beaton 1982: 95). In this context, and with the assumption that many women would permanently leave the labour market following the war proving inaccurate (see Figure 5.2), the 1949–50 Basic Wage Case established 75 per cent of the male minimum as the new standard for women. While the Australian Council of Trade Unions' (ACTU) claim for equality in minimum wages was rejected on the rationale that the basic wage was still essentially a 'social wage for a man, his wife and family', and something that married women supported, the majority decision reflected the fact that few women were now paid at the 54 per cent rate, and that industry obviously had the capacity to pay the higher rate. Thus, '[e]conomic forces and not the Court are today largely dictating the wage rates' (1950 68 CAR 698, 816, 818).

Although this decision provided a change in proportions,[11] it retained familiar arguments about needs and family responsibilities in spite of greater deference to economic forces and capacity to pay. Nevertheless, as Figure 5.3 shows, this was an era of rapid change in women's relative pay, and while this reflected a combination of economic, political and social influences, institutional interventions in wage fixation were fundamental in its achievement. Not all these interventions occurred through the arbitration system itself, which resisted the pace of change, but without the framework of awards established under this system the impact of the decisions taken would undoubtedly have been more limited in scope and longevity.

In spite of a subsequent attempt to reduce the female rate to 60 per cent in the 1952–3 Basic Wage inquiry, the new 75 per cent rate was maintained due to the lack of any evidence of adverse economic outcomes. Pressures were building for full equality. Activism on the issue continued to escalate (see, for example, D'Aprano 2001 on the role of Kath Williams and others), with an ACTU conference on equal pay in 1956. Decisions made by the Commission during the 1960s further weakened the notion of a family wage, leaving the way open for a more direct approach to equal pay.

Equal pay cases

Pressure to adopt equal pay provisions increased during the 1960s with the growth of the feminist movement and the continuing escalation of female labour force participation, particularly within the expanding service sector. Married women's participation increased from around 17 per cent in 1961 to 33 per cent in 1971 (see Figure 5.2), a trend clearly involving the widespread engagement of women with children in paid employment and challenging the 'male breadwinner' assumptions that underpinned wage determination principles. In 1966, section 49(2) of the Commonwealth Public Service Act, which decreed that '[e]very female officer shall be deemed to have retired from the Commonwealth service upon her marriage', was belatedly removed,[12] although not without some debate over the extent to which this might reduce the birth rate or produce a generation of neglected children (Sawer 1996).

Rising acceptance of pay equity goals was evident both at an international level, with the adoption of a number of gender equity conventions, particularly the International Labour Organisation's (ILO) Convention 100 on Equal Remuneration in 1951, and in Australia with a series of equal pay initiatives in New South Wales, Tasmania, South Australia and Western Australia. At the federal level, the decision to award equal margins in a 1964 review of the Clothing Trades Award, not on the basis of 'protecting male employees' but 'to prescribe proper margins for work done' (1967 118 CAR 286, 300), and delivery of equal increases to men and women along with the adoption of a 'total wage' in the 1967 National Wage Case, were indicators of receptivity to an equal pay claim.

The ACTU responded in 1969 with a claim to raise women's pay by an amount equivalent to the difference between the former male and female basic wages. Although rejecting concerns that an equal pay decision would have adverse economic consequences, the Commission was not prepared to grant the claim in total, opting instead to establish principles consistent with those in State jurisdictions to guide applications for equal pay, with successful claims to be phased in over a three-year period.

The nine principles adopted placed specific limits on the scope of equal pay claims, which could be made only for adult males and females working under the same determination or award, employed in work normally performed by both

An equal pay demonstration on the steps of the Melbourne Trades Hall: Bob Hawke stands alongside Jack Sparks, the Victorian president of the Australasian Meat Industry Employees Union, and the woman on the right is Zelda D'Aprano.

males and females (expressly excluding work 'essentially or usually performed by females') and of 'the same or a like nature' (1969 127 CAR 1142, 1158–9). These restrictions allowed only a relatively narrow concept of 'equal pay for equal work', and effectively by-passed the majority of women who were employed in female-dominated occupations. As a number of authors have noted (Short 1986: 318; Isaac 1998: 702), this case in effect reiterated the principle adopted in the 1912 *Rural Workers* case, that women should be entitled to equal pay where they worked in 'male' occupations and performed the same work. Estimates of its scope suggest that it affected only around 18 per cent of the female labour force (1972 147 CAR 172, 177); and even where it was applicable, if the male award rate was lower than the minimum wage, women's wages were lifted to the lower rate only (Hutson 1971: 127; Hunter 1988: 159).

Nevertheless, in comparison with equal pay provisions to emerge in other countries, the principles adopted had a number of positive features that reflected

INTERVIEW WITH JUDITH COHEN AND PAULINE GRIFFIN

Judith Cohen was appointed Commissioner in 1975 and was Deputy President from 1980 to 1991. Pauline Griffin was Commissioner from 1975 to 1990. These extracts are taken from an interview conducted by Judy Hughes (a transcript is held in the Sir Richard Kirby Archives):

> Pauline Griffin: In 1975, when we were both appointed, industrial relations generally was very much a male field. I had been a member of the Industrial Relations Society and the Institute of Personnel Management in New South Wales . . . There were some very, very notable pioneer women in both fields, but they were very small, the numbers, in comparison with the men.
>
> I remember in 1962, when I was being interviewed for participation in the Duke of Edinburgh's Commonwealth Study Conference, that the then Secretary of the Department of Labour said, 'I suppose one day we will have to put women like you on the Commission' . . . I remember thinking at the time, oh, wouldn't that have been wonderful, I am ten years too late . . . In fact I wasn't and Judith and I were the first two Commissioners, women Commissioners, appointed . . .
>
> Judith Cohen: It was an act of positive discrimination by the Whitlam government. There wasn't a pool of women with industrial relations experience to appoint to the benches . . . When I happened to mention that I didn't have industrial relations experience, I was told, 'Well, you are a lawyer, aren't you, you know how to read a bloody Act'.
>
> It didn't worry me whether it was a male or female environment, but when I got into the Commission I did wonder what all those Commissioners who had come up from practice in the Industrial Relations Commission were going to think about me, who they knew had not been in the industrial relations area . . . About three or four days after we were appointed, one of them, Len Matthews, who was a very nice man, he was the 'shop steward' of the Commissioners, knocked on my door, came in and sat down and said, 'Judith, do you mind if I have a little talk with you?'

In 1989 Justice Judith Cohen (centre), Jan Marsh, a Deputy President (left), and Pauline Griffin (right), a Commissioner, made history when they constituted the first all-female bench in the history of the tribunal.

And I thought, oh, God, here it comes and he sat down and with a very serious face he said to me, 'We have been talking and the Registry have asked us to ask you – we don't know how you are to be addressed. Downstairs they are putting your name on the list of Commissioners on the board, they are all Mr Commissioner; what are we going to put against yours?' And with a perfectly straight face I said, 'I think if you just drop the prefix it will be all right, Len' . . . And I also said, 'It wouldn't hurt if in due course you dropped your own prefixes as well'.

Pauline Griffin: One case I had was where one of the employers, I think, called me Madam Commissioner and somebody else called me Mrs Commissioner and the other one called Miss Commissioner, and I said, 'When the three of you have sorted out my marital status would you please just let me get on with hearing what you have got to say?'

Judith Cohen: Frankly . . . I was surprised how easily I was accepted, not only within the Commission but by the parties as well . . . And it just astounded me; they really just wanted somebody to pour it all out to, they wanted somebody to resolve the problem. They didn't care whether you were male, female or a ten-headed hydra. They really didn't – it didn't worry them.

Pauline Griffin: But they were delighted when you got a grasp – they didn't always expect that you would – that you got a grasp of something that to them seemed a bit complex. I had a wonderful one once, and I was actually appearing for another Commissioner who was delayed in getting to Sydney due to some air problem, and he had explained to me what he was going to hear and the employers got up and they said their whole piece, and it was quite a complex issue in the middle of the indexation guidelines. Then the union bloke got up and said all his piece, and then the employer got up again and the union bloke said, 'Sit down, you fool, she got it the first time'. I wasn't supposed to hear that and, of course, I did.

There were very few women lawyers in industrial relations. I mean the law firms that used to practise in the industrial relations jurisdiction had very few women at any level. That changed dramatically.

Judith Cohen: Gradually more and more women started popping up at the bar table for both the employers and the unions. When I left in 1991 – when I retired – one of the last cases I presided over was the parental leave case. There were days when the whole bar table was female, and it was a big bar table, all the State governments were represented, all the major interest parties, and mainly by female advocates, and that had changed in the period.

the wage determination system in which they were embedded. For example, although unions were required to bring specific cases before the tribunal with evidence for each classification affected,[13] the process was not reliant on individual grievances, but operated through an award-based system that extended gains from successful cases beyond individuals and single enterprises. The principles adopted were clear that 'consideration should not be restricted to the situation in one establishment, but should extend to the general situation under the determination or award concerned'. Additionally, and in line with historical norms of wage justice, there was clear prohibition against the interpretation of 'value' in purely market terms – 'the expression of "equal value" should not be construed as meaning "of equal value to the employer" but as of equal value . . . from the point of view of wage or salary assessment' (1969 127 CAR 1142, 1159). This reduced the scope for the market defence arguments that have plagued equal pay claims in other countries.

A second Equal Pay Case brought by the ACTU in 1972 (1972 147 CAR 172) overcame some of the limitations of the 1969 principles by broadening the scope from 'equal work' to 'equal value', thus opening the door to claims from female-dominated areas of work. The newly elected Whitlam government supported the case, giving its brief to Mary Gaudron,[14] who argued the case for equal pay for equal value and intimated that, in line with its intention to ratify ILO Convention 100, the government would support extension of the male minimum wage to females (Ryan and Conlon 1989: 169).

In its decision, the Commission noted the 'world wide trend towards equal pay for females', particularly legislation adopted in New Zealand and the United Kingdom, and concluded that the 1969 concept of 'equal pay for equal work' was 'too narrow for today's world'. Its response was to develop a new principle, which again was to be phased in to avoid any adverse economic impact. The new principle sought 'a single rate for an occupational group or classification . . . whether the employee be male or female', an outcome to be delivered through work value comparisons. In order to ensure this process would be more inclusive than the 1969 principles, the decision allowed that, while comparisons should ideally be made within awards, it might be necessary in some cases to compare with male or female classifications across awards (1972 147 CAR 172, 178, 180).

In reality, however, comparisons across awards were rarely undertaken, and there was little qualification of how 'work value' and potential gender bias would be investigated, other than to assert that this would require 'the exercise of the broad judgement that has characterised work value inquiries' (1973 149 CAR 172, 179; Short 1986). Bennett (1988: 535–40) has observed that there are functional advantages for the Commission of vaguely defined work value guidelines, and that comprehensive approaches to the reassessment of work value would be highly labour intensive. Furthermore, it is not clear that alternative methods of job evaluation would necessarily deliver better outcomes, as gender bias is so deeply embedded in these processes (Burton 1988). Nevertheless, the 1972 principles were clearly hampered by an inability to compare effectively dissimilar work and reassess work value in female-dominated areas. Furthermore, the types of strategies unions were adopting in the 1972–75 period of relative decentralisation and high wage growth were not conducive to sustainable equal pay claims, but rather encouraged 'quasi equal pay through consent agreements' (O'Donnell and Golder 1986: 79).

The remaining barrier to formal gender equality in the wage determination system – maintenance of a higher male minimum wage in recognition of men's family responsibilities – was removed in 1974. The achievement of equal minimum rates was of considerable concern to the Whitlam government, which saw it as a necessary step prior to ratification of ILO Convention 100 (Gaudron 1982: 107). The Women's Electoral Lobby (WEL) played a crucial role in this case, with Edna Ryan's use of figures from the Henderson Inquiry into Poverty showing that there were over 130 000 families dependent on the mother's earning power (Sawer 1990: 4–5). WEL also estimated that there were around 300 000 women under federal awards who received less than the male minimum wage (Gaudron and Bosworth 1979: 167). The tribunal finally conceded that the logic embodied in the *Harvester* judgment was no longer applicable, and that it was not after all possible to discriminate between workers on the basis of their family obligations:

> We do not have the information to enable us to discriminate between the
> varying needs of . . . workers. In our awards we do not distinguish
> between the married and the single workers, and we do not vary the

wage in relation to the number of persons dependent on the worker . . .
For the reasons mentioned we believe the family component should be
discarded from the minimum wage concept. (1974 157 CAR 293, 299)

Unlike the 1972 principle, this decision was not dependent on unions bringing
cases, nor did it involve questions of work value. The capacity to deliver such a
change through a system of awards with comprehensive coverage was clearly one
of the advantages of the Australian system in comparison with more decentralised
wage-fixing arrangements. Similarly, in spite of the limitations mentioned, the
design and implementation of the 1969 and 1972 decisions were also enhanced
by aspects of the wages system. Although wage decisions in Australia were clearly
influenced by the market, particularly with increasing reliance on 'capacity to pay',
principles of wage justice and wage-fixing practice could be constructed to avoid
the more market-driven barriers to equal pay experienced elsewhere, such as the
definition of 'equal value' as market value to an employer and the limitation of
cases to single enterprises. Not only was the scope for objections against pay
equity decisions narrowed but benefits could also be delivered more effectively
through the labour market; and the 'comparator' problem (the lack of a suitable male against whom to compare a woman's job) was not so much an issue
in the award-based system, where comparisons were made between job classifications rather than individuals. A more indirect benefit was the comparatively
compressed wage structure of a centralised system.[15] As Gregory, Daly and Ho
(1986) show, the larger impact of equal pay decisions in Australia compared with
the United Kingdom can be partly attributed to the better pay of Australian men
at the lower end of the wage distribution; and a number of cross-national studies
have established the advantage of centralised wage determination for pay equity
outcomes (O'Donnell and Hall 1988; Gregory et al. 1989; Whitehouse 1992).

The effect of the equal pay decisions is illustrated in Figure 5.3, which shows
that women's weekly minimum wages rose from 73 to 93 per cent of men's over
the 1970s, with similar increases in average total earnings over this period.[16] It
is clearly a more dramatic change than could be accounted for by changes in
the human capital attributes of women or their occupational distribution, and
undoubtedly reflects the institutional context of the Australian wage determination system. Figure 5.3 also shows, however, the limited advancement that has

MARY GAUDRON'S INTERVENTION

Following the 1972 'equal pay for work of equal value' award, the 1974 National Wage Case included an application by the ACTU for the same national minimum wage to apply to both male and female adult workers. The application was supported by the Australian government, which was represented by Jim Staples QC and Mary Gaudron.

Late on the morning of 26 March, as Barry Maddern was presenting the employers' submission in the large courtroom at 451 Little Bourke Street, about thirty women burst into the hearing, waving placards and drowning the hearing with a loud-hailer. They were members of a recently formed group known as Women for Equal Minimum Wage.

The President, Sir John Moore, uttered his usual disarming words of welcome and requested them to put down their placards and to follow the proceedings in silence. But when the women responded with loud and persistent abuse, he ordered an adjournment. As the six members of the bench began to file out of the courtroom, the women advanced past the bar table towards the bench calling out, 'Cowards! Cowards!'

The three judges' associates wrestled with the demonstrators but some broke through, and picking up the jugs of water on the table they began to pour water all over the bench. In the middle of this melee, Mary Gaudron went up to them with the advice: 'The feds will be here in a second. You'd better piss off fast.' They took her advice and took to their heels. And the Commission resumed soon after.

(Anonymous witness)

occurred since the 1970s, in spite of legislative initiatives including the *Sex Discrimination Act 1984* and the *Affirmative Action (Equal Opportunity for Women) Act 1986*. While some may view the limited change in the gender pay gap after the 1970s as evidence that wage equity has effectively been achieved, others (for example, Short 1986) argue that issues such as the undervaluation of female-dominated work have not been adequately resolved.

Several attempts were made during the 1980s to address this problem, for although the Commission had initially set a two-and-a-half year time limit on implementation of the 1972 decision, it continued to allow cases to proceed. However, with the advent of the ALP–ACTU Accord, the Commission was also required to adhere to principles of wage restraint; hence, Equal Pay cases that came before it tended to be channelled into anomalies processes that reduced the risk of flow-ons. These tensions are clearly evident in the 1986 test case seeking revaluation of nurses work on the basis of 'comparable worth', through a variation to the Private Hospitals and Doctors' Nurses (ACT) Award (1986 300 CAR 185).[17] The notion of 'comparable worth' was explicitly rejected as inconsistent with the Australian approach to wage fixation, not only because of its capacity for application across any kind of job classification but also because it implied a notion of work value as 'value to an employer'. In combination with the risk of generating flow-ons, it was seen as an approach that 'would strike at the heart of long accepted methods of wage fixation in this country and would be particularly destructive of the present Wage Fixing Principles' (1986 300 CAR 185, 190). The claim failed, in part, because it was presented in a way that ignored the constraints under which the Commission operated (Bennett 1988); yet, as Rafferty (1994: 456) notes, 'rejection of the concept of comparable worth was more apparent than actual', with comparisons of dissimilar types of work undertaken in a number of previous and subsequent cases. The 1985 *Australian Public Service Therapists* case, for example, compared female-dominated therapy jobs with a range of different science-qualified professionals on the basis of qualifications, application of scientific principles and work value factors such as responsibility and complexity; and delivered significant gains for women (Rafferty 1994: 456).

In the 1986 *Nurses* case, use of the anomalies process did produce wage gains, although in this and a number of other cases (for example, the *Dental Therapists Anomalies* case of 1989) there was little evidence of work value assessments in the anomalies process (Rafferty 1994: 455). Overall, then, while there have been means of improving pay in female-dominated work through the system, these have not always been explicitly based on the application of the equal pay principles or direct attempts to assess work value. Further indirect avenues to advance equal pay became available to some extent with the structural efficiency principles adopted towards the end of the 1980s and the associated Minimum Rates Adjustment (MRA) process. Under MRA, for example, comparisons across dissimilar forms of work allowed significant revaluation of some female-dominated occupational groups such as clothing workers (McDermott 1993: 545). The move towards enterprise bargaining in the early 1990s, however, inevitably eroded the capacity for such indirect gains, and at the same time created a new set of difficulties for the prosecution of Equal Pay cases.

Decentralisation

The move towards decentralised wage determination in the 1990s brought a new set of tensions into the relationship between the industrial relations system and gender equity. While risks for women under 'enterprise bargaining' were noted both by outside observers (Bennett 1994b; Hall and Fruin 1994) and within the Commission itself,[18] employment rights such as equal pay and parental leave were given more formal status through inclusion in the *Industrial Relations Reform Act 1993* and subsequently in the *Workplace Relations Act 1996*. These legislative moves were made possible by the ratification of international conventions, including ILO Convention 100 (Equal Remuneration) and ILO Convention 156 (Workers with Family Responsibilities). The question thus raised was whether these formal rights might compensate for anticipated risks associated with decentralisation.

In terms of parental rights, the provisions in the Act ensured equal access for all employees to the entitlements previously established under the ACTU-led Maternity Leave (1979) and Parental Leave (1990) test cases – that is, fifty-two weeks unpaid leave, able to be shared between parents of a newly born or adopted child, and accessible to employees with twelve months continuous service. Further extension of parental rights in the 1990s were attained not through the legislation, but again through ACTU-led test cases. These included the Family Leave test cases of 1994–95, which allowed the use of different forms of leave for family purposes, and the extension of unpaid parental leave to casuals in 2001. This delivery of parental rights through test cases lends some strength to the depiction of Australia as a type of 'wage-earners' welfare state' in which gaps in social provision are filled through the wages system. In adopting this approach, however, the scope for paid maternity and parental leave has been restricted, as in the absence of a national social insurance fund, the costs of an agreement reached in the industrial relations system would fall directly on employers. More-over, although the test case approach has still been accessible under the more decentralised arrangements of the 1990s, the capacity to disseminate benefits evenly is diminished as award coverage narrows and negotiation over details is devolved to workplace level.

There has been a similar tension between new opportunities provided for pay equity by the legislation and the narrowing scope for implementation in a more decentralised context. The difficulties of prosecuting pay equity in the new environment were illustrated most clearly in an application for equal pay lodged by the Automotive, Food, Metals, Engineering, Printing and Kindred Industries Union and the ACTU in December 1995 for some employees of HPM industries (*Automotive, Food, Metals, Engineering, Printing and Kindred Industries Union and HPM Industries, C No 23933 of 1995*). The application sought equal remu-neration between female-dominated groups (process workers and packers) and male-dominated general hands and storepersons. Although the Act's reference to ILO Convention 100 and the term 'equal remuneration' meant that previously excluded aspects of earnings such as over-award payments could be considered, new areas of complexity emerged.

The application was initially referred to conciliation, then to arbitration in 1997, with a decision handed down by Commissioner Simmonds in 1998 (Print P9210, 1998). Complexities included protracted debates over the need to prove discrimination and how it was to be defined, as well as contestation over the proper means of establishing work value. In the course of argument, different pay rates were defended on the basis of market pressures, with turnover rates in the male-dominated jobs cited as necessitating higher pay, and the need for flexibility in over-award payments strongly defended. Additionally, the role of specific comparators became a central issue, with an attempt by the employer to avoid comparison by declaring the male positions redundant (Hunter 2000: 15; Whitehouse et al. 2001: 380). Although the Commission did not allow these moves to invalidate the comparison, neither did it accept the unions' arguments that the competency standards in the award provided an appropriate basis for determining equal value, and after almost three years' negotiation the issues were finally resolved outside the Commission, leaving no guidelines to inform subsequent cases. Moreover, the case's enterprise basis meant that the final agreement affected only a small number of workers; and in the context of the more limited award system and variation in pay rates associated with enterprise bargaining, it would be difficult to prosecute cases at a broader level (Hunter 2000: 15). Thus, the advantages of more formal pay equity rights have proved somewhat elusive within the decentralised environment.[19]

Additional concerns for pay equity in the context of the move to enterprise bargaining are the indirect effects of decentralisation, such as erosion of the wage compression that had previously enhanced efforts for pay equity. Although a trend towards wage dispersion in Australia predates the adoption of enterprise bargaining, the new system is expressly designed to extend wage flexibility. Among the divisions that have emerged within the wages structure over the 1990s is the pay gap between those covered by awards only and those able to access gains through collective or individual agreements. In 2000, average weekly earnings in the 'award only' stream were around 60 per cent of those for employees covered by registered collective agreements, and both women and part-time workers were over-represented in the award-only group. Among those covered by enterprise agreements, concerns that women's lower levels of unionisation and bargaining power would disadvantage them relative to men have been given some credence by evidence from agreements databases of lower average wage increases in female-dominated, compared with male-dominated, agreements (Whitehouse and Frino 2003: 581–2, 586).

These changes have occurred in the context of a continued expansion of part-time employment, reflecting both structural developments in the economy and women's use of part-time work as a means of combining work and family responsibilities. By 2001, 28 per cent of Australian employees (and 45 per cent of female employees) worked part-time, and much of this employment was casual. While part-time work provides the flexibility to assist women (and men) in attaining sustainable work–family balance, a further tension in the system at the beginning of the twenty-first century is between the positive potential of non-standard employment and the reduced capacity to regulate the conditions of such

jobs and limit casualisation under less comprehensive awards and devolution of
negotiation to workplace level.

CONCLUSION

One hundred years after the establishment of a formal system of wage determination at federal level in Australia, notions of wage justice and the capacity to
overcome inequities for groups such as women and Indigenous workers have
undergone considerable change. Early principles of wage justice manifest in a
living wage for male breadwinners and comparative wage justice across different
sections of the labour market have been displaced by wage-fixing principles more
aligned with a perceived need to extend flexibility and market responsiveness. On
the other hand, explicit discrimination against women and Indigenous workers
has been largely eliminated.

These changes have had mixed implications for the pursuit of social equity
in wages. For example, while erosion of a 'family wage' for men was an essential
prerequisite for the pursuit of gender pay equity, what was lost in its elimination
was not only its gender bias, but also a mechanism for a 'fair' wage as a necessary element of industrial citizenship. Although a gender-equitable living wage
is theoretically possible, the problem since the 1990s has been that the types of
wage justice implicit in a social wage and in comparative wage justice across
the labour market are difficult to reconstruct in a decentralised environment.
Thus, while the ACTU has pursued the goal of a (degendered) social wage, for
example in the 1997 Living Wage Case, in an industrial relations system oriented
towards encouragement of enterprise bargaining, there is little scope for substantial increases in award-based wages that would bring them closer to those
settled under enterprise bargaining. Notwithstanding the provision in the present
Workplace Relations Act that the Commission is required to take account of the
Racial, Sex and Disability Discrimination Acts, for both women and Indigenous
workers there remain risks in a system that grants a formal equality in the absence
of broader notions of wage justice. It is thus the combination of different forms of
wage justice, rather than some types at the expense of others, that are necessary
for future advances in justice and equity.

6

EMPLOYERS' ASSOCIATIONS AND COMPULSORY ARBITRATION

David Plowman

This chapter is concerned with the way in which employers have responded to the Commonwealth system of compulsory arbitration. Since employers' associations have played a key role in coordinating their members' response, the chapter concentrates on the activities of the national peak bodies.

Four periods can be identified in the associations' approach to compulsory arbitration. The first was a long period of opposition. This opposition preceded the introduction of the Conciliation and Arbitration Bill of 1903; it was one of the factors leading to the Bruce government's attempts to remove compulsory arbitration in 1928; and was heightened by the depression of the 1930s. It only abated when arbitration provided a mechanism for delaying and reducing union claims as employment recovered. In the second period, from about 1936 to 1950, arbitration became accepted as the 'settled law of the land'. The third period, after the Second World War, was one of full employment. Employers used the arbitration system to retard union claims. Their associations not only accommodated themselves to the needs of the system but also became dependent on it, both in defining their roles and in determining their methods of action. During this period, as national test cases concerning wages, leave entitlements and equal pay came to

require greater resources and more sophisticated submissions, employers' associations developed coordinating mechanisms for such cases. By 1986, the new
political paradigm of deregulation and decentralisation was strongly influencing both product and labour markets. This led to the fourth period, a period of
reassessment on the part of employers' associations. One hundred years after the
introduction of the Arbitration Act, employers' associations are again seeking to
contain and constrain industrial tribunals. The emphasis, here, is on the first and
last periods.

OPPOSITION

Following the strikes of the 1890s, legislatures in Australia and New Zealand
increasingly turned to compulsory arbitration as the mechanism for dealing with
industrial disputes. At the Commonwealth level, industrial legislation was circumscribed by the Constitution to the establishment of tribunals for the prevention
and settlement of industrial disputes extending beyond the boundaries of any one
State by means of conciliation and arbitration. A bill to this effect was introduced
in July 1903.

Employers strenuously opposed compulsory arbitration legislation at both
the federal and State levels.[1] In doing so, they sought both parliamentary representation and to lobby other members. Both the president and secretary of
the Central Council of Employers of Australia (CCEA) were members of the
Victorian Parliament.[2] Indeed, the presidency of this organisation was held by
politicians until 1926. The Legislative Councils of other State parliaments also
included a number of members endorsed by the Employers' Federations. In the
Commonwealth Parliament, there were six members who had been endorsed and
assisted financially by the Employers' Federations or Chambers of Commerce
(Dobson 1979: 149). The Victorian Employers' Federation (VEF) was charged
with spearheading the employers' opposition in the Commonwealth Parliament,
then housed in Melbourne. The VEF prepared lengthy memoranda on the proposed legislation for members of parliament opposed to arbitration. In addition,
it organised a number of petitions and deputations to parliament. With its New
South Wales counterpart, it distributed 30 000 copies of the criticism by Chief
Justice of the Supreme Court of New South Wales of that State's arbitration

Even though Higgins was reluctant to grant preference to union members, the employers argued that this aspect of arbitration locked non-unionists out of work.

legislation. These efforts were only partially successful; they achieved compromise rather than a rejection of the legislation. The *Commonwealth Conciliation and Arbitration Act 1904* was proclaimed in December.

With the passage of this Act, employers followed their New South Wales counterparts in seeking to make the legislation unworkable. They attempted to frustrate the arbitration system by refusing to register their associations (CCEA 1905: 17); by establishing and having registered bogus unions (Spence 1909: 141; Higgins 1922b: 17; Fitzpatrick 1940b: 236; McCarthy 1968: 27); by deliberately lengthening procedures and choking the Court with work (Blake 1929: 9); and by using legal representation to increase costs to unions (Clarke 1905: 113). To reduce the impact of awards, employers installed labour-saving machinery (Clarke 1905: 125; Gollan 1963: 125); replaced males with females (Clarke 1905: 175); and resorted to subcontracting (Clarke 1905: 123).

The employers' most determined bid to reduce the influence of federal arbitration was by way of legal action. So concerted were their actions in this regard, the Solicitor-General RR Garran (1958: 464) noted that, in the first twenty-five years of the Commonwealth, the industrial power came to play 'a greater part in political history and legal controversy than the whole of the rest of the Constitution put together'. Following the passage of the Act, the CCEA brought into being a contingency plan agreed to in March 1904, namely the raising of £5000 to 'test the legality of the Bill in the High Court' (CCEA Minutes 16 October 1924). The rules of the CCEA were amended to provide a distinctly legal role: 'to safeguard the interests of employers by opposing all prejudicial legislation in progress and testing the validity of any Acts which may be against the interests of employers, and to deal with any matters inimical to employers generally' (CCEA Meeting 4 March 1908). This legal approach was highly successful in restricting the scope of federal arbitration until 1913, but less so after that time (Plowman and Smith 1986).

One of the unintended consequences of employers' legal action was the High Court's interpretation in 1910 of consistency between federal and State awards (see Chapter 3). This gave rise to a system in which employers had to satisfy the requirements of both federal and State awards simultaneously in any of their enterprises subject to federal awards. The 1914 Annual Report of the Employers' Federation of New South Wales (EFNSW) reflected on this state of affairs. It reported that, of 3000 builders in New South Wales, only 170 were bound by federal awards, thereby causing 'friction and dissatisfaction all round'. The relevant State award had been made for three years, the federal award for five. Their concurrence involved 'starting and knocking off men at different times, payment of overtime to some and not to others, while others again are out of employment' (EFNSW Annual Report 1914: 9). In 1920, Higgins expressed his concern that tribunals were being used as 'rival shops', but claimed that nothing could be done about it unless there was a change in the Constitution (1920 14 CAR 369).

The constitutional approach sought by Higgins would have enlarged the federal jurisdiction. This was not an approach favoured by employers. Referenda to this effect had been unsuccessful in 1911 and 1913. Nevertheless, employers searched for a method that would harmonise employment conditions.

The first such harmonising initiatives arose from Queensland and New South Wales employers, who complained that the labour costs imposed by their Labor governments put them at a disadvantage with competitors in other States. They pressed for uniformity between the States. Their impractical Anomalies Bill would have required uniform legislation in each State for each industry (EFNSW Annual Report 1914: 9). Though employers in other States gave little support to such a Bill, the problem became more widespread once unions began to make use of dual regulation. A ready solution would have been effected by a transfer of industrial authority to the Commonwealth. Employers opposed this. The economy, and employer organisations, were primarily State-based at this time. Further, employers saw Labor Prime Minister Hughes and Arbitration Court President Higgins as unsuitable architects of a uniform national system. Employers' aversion to Higgins was such that they sought his removal though parliament (where it was even suggested that hanging might be an appropriate penalty for his actions!) (*CPD* 27 September 1917: 2859).

The fragmentation of the Labor government on the issue of conscription and the formation of the National government in 1917 gave employers hope that favourable legislation could at last be expected. They engaged legal counsel to 'prepare the basis for a new arbitration Act defining the limits of State and Federal industrial powers'. They considered only two industries to be 'national', namely shipping and wool production. The National Union Bill, which attempted to allot specific industries to the Arbitration Court and leave the rest to State tribunals, was agreed to by all CCEA affiliates, the affiliates of the Associated Chambers of Manufactures of Australia (ACMA), and twenty-two other associations. The Bill was handed to Prime Minister Hughes in November 1920. Though declaring that he would give it 'careful consideration', Hughes ignored the Bill. Instead, he initiated the *Industrial Peace Act 1920*, which created tribunals to deal with problems in specified industries. Employers feared the flow-ons from these tribunals and saw them as enlarging the federal jurisdiction by stealth (CCEA Conference 1920: 80–98). The Act did not survive Hughes' loss of office as Prime Minister in 1923.

The subsequent Bruce–Page government attempted rationalisation by way of Premiers' Conferences, referendum and legislation. The last, involving the removal of the Commonwealth from the industrial field, brought about Bruce's own downfall.

EMPLOYERS' CONFERENCE 1920

The photograph shows representatives at the Central Council of Employers' Federations' Annual Conference in Perth in 1920. As suggested by its name, the Central Council was constituted by the Employers' Federations of the different States. Western Australia is over-represented at the conference, the result no doubt of its being held in Perth. This involved other delegates travelling to Perth by ship. Two States were not represented. The Tasmanian Employers' Federation dissolved in 1920 and was not reconstituted until nearly forty years later. The Queensland Employers' Federation (QEF) chose not to send delegates, partly because of friction with other delegates who opposed the QEF's stance on centralising industrial relations in the federal jurisdiction, and partly because of the costs involved.

Three of those in the photo were to have long associations with employer associations. Leslie Smith was secretary of the Central Council from 1913 until his death in 1938. GH Boykett was appointed secretary of the South Australian Employers' Federation in 1907, a position he occupied until forced to resign in 1951. TR Ashworth also proved to be controversial. He became president of the Victorian Employers' Federation in 1920 and remained in that position until 1934, despite signs of mental instability and the majority of his executive resigning. Ashworth became president of the Central Council in October 1928 but was forced by affiliates to resign within six months.

The Central Council of Employers' Federations held its Annual Conference in Perth in 1920. L Smith stands on the far right of the second row; GH Boykett stands beside him with a flower in his lapel; TR Ashworth sits second from the left in front row with papers in his hands.

A complete revision of the arbitration system is being urged.—News Item.

CAPITALISM: "Good boy, Billy! That's the way to deal with it!"

The labour movement saw Hughes' post-war amendments to the arbitration system as favouring employers, here represented by the figure of 'Mr Fat'.

As early as 1917, Premiers' Conferences sought a political solution to the problem of dual awards. Since neither the States nor the Commonwealth would cede any of their industrial powers, the solution sought was to assign specified industries to the Commonwealth and leave all others to the States. In 1918, New South Wales Attorney-General Beeby proposed assigning shipping, wool production, coal-mining, coal lumping, sugar production and stevedoring to the Commonwealth. The States would have jurisdiction over all other industries. However, the Commonwealth sought an expansion of this list and the Conference concluded without any outcome.

In 1923, the CCEA submitted to the Premiers' Conference the need to 'take prompt legislative action to amend the existing system of industrial arbitration with the object of relieving the industries of the Commonwealth of the intolerable conditions brought by the overlapping of conflicting awards'. It added that it was essential that 'the jurisdiction of the Federal Arbitration Court be strictly confined to industries which are purely federal in character like shearing and shipping' (CCEA Minutes 1 March 1923). The Premiers' proposed solution was not to the CCEA's liking. This involved amendments to the Constitution that would enable the States, by agreement, to decide upon a list of industries to be deemed federal. The list would be revised at intervals 'of no less than five years'.

Though seeking a solution to dual arbitration, the CCEA considered that these proposals would offer relief in the 'wrong direction', namely by an expansion of the federal jurisdiction. It created an Industrial Arbitration Propaganda Committee in order to conduct 'a rigorous publicity campaign through the daily papers in each State respecting overlapping of State and Federal industrial arbitration and the necessity of a clear line of demarcation being drawn between such legislation as intended by the Constitution' (CCEA Minutes 1 March 1923). The committee spent over £1000 in commissioning articles for publication in the major papers in each capital city. Through the CCEA President, Senator Drake-Brockman, CCEA members met with Bruce and indicated their proposals. Bruce noted that without the support of the Premiers he could do little to bring about the demarcation sought by employers (Plowman 1986: 165).

At the 1925 Premiers' Conference, Bruce was confronted by four new ministries and five State Labor governments. Unable to make any headway, he decided to seek increased Commonwealth industrial powers. A referendum to this effect was conducted in May 1926. Employers in Queensland and New South Wales actively supported the constitutional proposals. Though a majority of voters in these two States voted in favour, the referendum was lost.

From 1926 on, the High Court provided some measure of relief from dual awards for those employers prepared to accept federal jurisdiction. In the *Cowburn* case, the Court held that, if it was the intent of the federal award to cover the field, then it was inconsistent for State regulation also to be invoked (1926 37 CLR 466). In 1928, the Commonwealth Act was amended to give federal awards exclusive coverage over matters in their awards. Thus, the *Cowburn* case removed an important problem associated with dual awards. Employers expressed little joy at this landmark decision. They saw the decision as offering relief in the wrong direction. Further, the decision did not remove the problem of flow-ons from jurisdictions, nor the coexistence of State and federal award employees in many enterprises.

From the beginning of 1929, recession and strikes added to the government's industrial relations problems. The government's earlier election policy included a 'legislative programme of taming the unions' (Hagan 1981: 41). The Crimes Act was amended and its provisions extended to industrial disputes. The Immigration Act was also amended to provide for the deportation of those 'convicted of offences under federal commerce and arbitration laws'. However, when the government sought the deportation of striking seamen, the High Court prevented such action. The Transport Workers Act attempted 'to deal with industrial unrest and associated political or revolutionary activities . . . by the widest delegation of legislative power to the Governor General which had so far been attempted in peace time' (Sawer 1956: 265). A system of licensing was introduced for waterside workers in an attempt to discipline them. Despite this, and the strengthening of the penal provisions of the Act, strikes increased.

The government increasingly came to consider economic deterioration as the product of worsening industrial relations. This view was supported by the British Economic Mission. It recommended a number of major changes to tariff and wage regulation. It also claimed 'a change in the method prevalent in Australia in dealing with industrial disputes appears to us to be essential' (*CPD* 14 March 1929: 1248). The Mission's views, according to ex-Prime Minister Hughes

(1941: 255), were suspiciously close to the submissions of the Employers' Federations.

At the 1929 Premiers' Conference, Bruce requested that the States surrender their industrial powers to the Commonwealth. When none of the States agreed to this course of action, the Prime Minister acted to divest the Commonwealth of arbitration by introducing the Maritime Industries Bill. This provided for the repeal of the Act and for the regulation of the stevedoring and maritime industries under the Trade and Commerce powers of the Constitution by way of round-table conferences of employer and employee representatives. In September, the second reading of the bill was carried by only four votes. The next day, the government lost a motion of confidence by one vote. The ensuing election centred on compulsory arbitration, an issue on which employers themselves were divided. In some industries, such as textiles and pastoralism, employers sought to preserve the Court. The State-based Chambers and Federations, as well as employers in many industries, supported the abandonment of Commonwealth arbitration. Bruce lost not only government but also his seat of Flinders.

The Labor government, under Scullin, was sworn in on 22 October 1929, the day following the Wall Street stock-market crash. Economic deterioration brought renewed calls for the abandonment of arbitration. The EFNSW considered that arbitration 'was a greater curse than droughts, prickly-pear or any other curse in Australia [and had] done nothing else but cripple industry' (*Employers' Review* 30 August 1930). The ACMA expressed the view that arbitration was a burden that could only be supported during periods of prosperity and whose abandonment was inevitable during a major recession. It concluded that the 'obvious and increasing defects of arbitration . . . have at last reached a stage when failure of this industrial experiment is gaining general recognition. The restrictions and conditions imposed by the courts represent a burden which it is imperative to remove'. The ACMA's New South Wales affiliate was more direct: 'The evil which now obstructs our path to better conditions is without doubt compulsory arbitration. This must be suspended for it has completely failed us' (Hall 1971: 402, 445). The Metal Trades Employers' Association agreed: 'Away with it, and let us get back to the clear, open, economic ring' (Carboch 1958: 192). Even the Pastoralist Associations, which until June 1929 had defended federal arbitration against the Bruce initiatives, now began to call for its abolition (*Sydney Morning Herald* 25 June 1929: 10).

Despite the combined associations' success in having the 'sacrosanct and irreducible' basic wage reduced by 10 per cent in 1931, employers persisted in their calls for the abolition of arbitration. They were unlikely to make legislative headway during a Labor administration and warmly welcomed the election of a non-Labor government in December 1931. However, the United Australia government's inactivity on the industrial relations front soon became the subject of employer criticism.

By 1932, employers' federations in Queensland, New South Wales and Victoria had agreed to uniform federal regulation. The South Australian and Western Australian federations also agreed with uniform regulation, but in their case directed by State tribunals (CCEA Conference 27 June 1932). The VEF president, Thomas Ashworth, indicated that his federation's support for federal regulation resulted from its belief, somewhat paradoxically, that this would be the best way to eliminate compulsory arbitration altogether. Ashworth advocated 'the Federal authority' because he regarded it 'as the first essential step to put an end of the evils of compulsory arbitration' (CCEA Conference 27 June 1932).

But times were again changing. The 10 per cent wage reduction was, in large measure, restored in 1934, and in 1937 unions sought an increase in the real basic wage on account of economic prosperity. As the economy was increasingly placed on a war footing, and as levels of employment surpassed historical norms, unions sought to exploit their new-found opportunities. Under these circumstances, rather than seek a return to the 'clear, open, economic ring', employers used compulsory arbitration to reduce union gains. In doing so, they came to accept and champion the institution they had so long derided.

ACCEPTANCE AND ACCOMMODATION

Economic recovery was accompanied by a remarkable policy transformation on the part of employers. Initially, they gave a reluctant acceptance 'that the arbitration tree is rooted in the community' (CCEA Conference 1932); then qualified support for uniform industrial standards regulated by the federal tribunal; and finally championed arbitration as the appropriate mechanism for dispute handling. In a period of increased collective bargaining, prominent communist union leadership, imminent war and increased government regulation, employers saw arbitration in a different light. The EFNSW, which had previously sought the abolition of arbitration, now claimed:

> We Australians, employers and employees alike, are a type – we should know how to work together, and if differences do arrive, we have an Arbitration Court to settle them. In our arbitration system we have machinery for settling disputes. This machinery has been built up over the past 30 years. It has stood the test of the Great War and the Great Depression. It has become a part of the life of our democratic country . . . If employers cannot get on without having strikes, they should question the ability of their managers. If employees cannot get on without strikes they should change their leaders. Disputes should always be settled by Arbitration. (*Employers' Review* 31 December 1938)

The EFNSW was supported by other associations. The Metal Trades Employers' Association now claimed that 'as far as Arbitration is concerned . . . the Association's view was that the Arbitration system was a sound one and that it would be a permanent feature of the Australian system' (*Metal Trades Journal* 23 April 1937).

Economic buoyancy and the shift in bargaining power was a major cause of this transformation. 'What this country needs', the EFNSW claimed, 'is not a job for every man, but a man for every job' (*Employers' Review* 30 October 1937). Associations now sought to have their members hold the line against union attempts to exploit changed circumstances. Typical of many resolutions passed by associations at this time was that of the Victorian Chamber of Manufactures (VCM). This resolved 'that no individual, firm, company or section of the Chamber should voluntarily promise or make any change in working hours, nor comply with demands of unions or groups of workers as to wages or conditions laid down by the Arbitration Court and/or Wages Boards' (VCM Minutes 27 April 1936). Its South Australian counterpart urged 'that in view of the very complete system operating in Australia to regulate wages and conditions of employment in industry, this Chamber considers the growing movement by representatives of employees to secure by direct action wages and working conditions which are in excess of Arbitration Awards should be resisted' (quoted in VCM Minutes 28 September 1937).

War was declared on 3 September 1939. It was to be accompanied by the greatest centralising of industrial regulation ever exercised in Australia. The fact that, after 1941, such executive action came from a Labor government only served to make the arbitration system, so long condemned, more attractive to employers. The *National Security Act 1939* effectively authorised full military and industrial conscription of persons and property (Hall 1971: 569). In time, the Act came to regulate most aspects of economic activity. Thus, limits (of 4 per cent) were placed on private profits; wages and prices were frozen; training requirements of tradesmen were 'diluted'; recruitment was channelled through the Department of Labour and National Service; female labour was attracted into occupations previously reserved for males; ceilings were placed upon hours of work; employers' dismissal powers were curbed; new lines of manufacturing were encouraged and existing ones limited or prohibited; the Arbitration Court's scope was expanded; and special tribunals were established to regulate specific areas of employment and dispute-prone industries.

Employers initially accepted this system of regulation with neither great debate nor strong objection. Developments on the political front soon led to employers taking a less cooperative approach. The elections of September 1940 led to a hung parliament. Labor refused to support Menzies' attempt to form a National War Government and itself took office two months later with the support of two independents. Thereafter, employers became increasingly apprehensive. 'Under the National Security Act', the New South Wales Chamber of Manufactures reported, 'the government can take sufficient powers to almost socialise Australia and made us a totalitarian State' (NSWCM Annual Report 1940: 3). It further claimed that the emergency powers were being used to 'introduce socialism by stealth and regulation' (Hall 1971: 592).

Employers' opposition to the Women's Employment Board (WEB) serves to illustrate the state of relations between the government and employer bodies at this time. The WEB grew out of the government's desire to attract females into the munitions and armaments industries. When the regulations for this board were gazetted, they provided that female wage rates were to be set between 60 per cent and 100 per cent of the appropriate male rate. At the time, female rates were 54 per cent of the male rate (VCM 1944: 8). Concerned about anomalies and flow-ons, employers opposed the creation of the WEB. They claimed that 'not only is the Arbitration Court quite capable of handling this question, but is the proper authority to do so and that any separate tribunal would be subversive to the principle upon which the Commonwealth Arbitration System is founded' (VCM 1942: 9). Employers refused the minister's request to nominate an employers' representative on the board because the WEB 'cuts diametrically across the functions of the Arbitration Court as the recognised wage-fixing tribunal' (VCM 1943: 6).

Until the WEB's functions were absorbed by the Arbitration Court in 1944, employers continued to oppose and obstruct it. Reverting to form, they mounted five High Court challenges against the WEB, only one of which was successful (VCM 1943–45). Employers greeted the government's announcement of the dissolution of the WEB as a vindication of their position (VCM 1945: 7). Their expectations of untrammelled Arbitration Court regulation of female rates, however, were unfounded. The government overturned the Arbitration Court's ruling in relation to minimum rates for females. By way of the National Security (Female Minimum Rates) Regulations, the government provided for rates of 'not less than 75 per cent of the corresponding male rate'.

Employers also fell out with the government over the formation of the Industrial Relations Council. The gazetted regulations establishing this council noted its purpose was 'to assist the Government in its objective, that of achieving the continuous production at the highest possible level in all branches of industry throughout Australia for the duration of the war'. It was to be composed of eight employer representatives, eight union representatives, a chairman and a deputy chairman (*Manufacturers' Bulletin* 1 January 1942). Employers considered this council to be an advisory forum, but soon claimed that it was proposed 'to invest it with executive powers comparable with those of the Arbitration Courts, and that the decision of the Chairman would prevail'. This, and the matters raised in the first meeting (equal pay and preference for unionists), resulted in employer representatives withdrawing from the council and led to its abolition (*Employers' Review* 30 November 1942; Hall 1971: 639–41).

Executive action took place alongside a Court that had additional powers conferred on it by the National Security (Industrial Peace) Regulations. It was empowered to declare a common rule for any industry or calling; its jurisdiction was not limited to the matters in dispute; it was empowered to settle intra-state disputes and 'non-industrial' disputes; and its orders could not be challenged because it had not engaged in 'conciliation and arbitration'. This resulted in Court dominance over State awards and the removal of many of the difficulties arising out of the dual tribunal system. Employers complained that the elimination of this dualism had been replaced by a different form of dualism: the Court, and executive action by the government. Employers condemned government interference and registered their support for the Court. Under the heading 'Arbitration – Not Regulation', the *Employers' Review* (31 October 1940) voiced employers' concerns about the extension of such regulation into the area of industrial relations. It instanced the case of regulations prescribing wage rates for those in the munitions industry, even though the matter was under review by the Court. 'Such actions', the *Review* claimed, 'must result in impairing the efficiency and destroying the confidence in which [the Court] is held'.

By 1940, employers, though stating their commitment to work within the arbitral system, nevertheless found cause for complaint. The EFNSW claimed that 'conciliation was starved and arbitration fed until it grew out of its industrial disputes clothes and came to dominate all industry . . . [and this] has encouraged the attitude of agreeing to nothing and "passing the buck" on to the Court to make a decision' (*Employers' Review* 31 July 1940: 1). In 1943, the same organ claimed that conciliation 'was very much in the background' and that the 'technicalities and difficulties inherent in arbitration are such that only union officials have any hope of mastering them' (*Employers' Review* 30 September 1943: 1).

Labor's efforts to remove some of these weaknesses soon had employers backtracking. Employers were particularly hostile to the appointment of lay members to the Court in October 1947. The judges' industrial role was limited to full bench matters in relation to standard hours of work, the basic wage, paid leave, and minimum rates for females, while the Commissioners took charge of other award matters. The EFNSW claimed that eleven new Commissioners had been appointed and that 'with one exception, all were Union Officials or known adherents of the Labor Party' (*Employers' Review* 31 October 1947: 21).

In 1948 the Western Australian Employers' Federation hosted a luncheon for ODA Oberg, the immediate past president of the Australian Council of Employers 'Federation'. Oberg was an influential and long-serving member of both the Australian Council of Employers' Federations and the Associated Chamber of Manufactures of Australia.

With the election of the Menzies government in December 1949, employers sought changes to the Labor reforms. They were not successful in having lay Commissioners removed, but the appeals and referencing systems that were introduced (and the subsequent panel system) went a long way to removing a major employer concern, that of a lack of uniformity or consistency in approach by different members of the tribunal.

EMPLOYER COORDINATION

By 1950, the structure and functions of employers' associations had come to reflect the needs of operating within the arbitration system. By then, too, the system of test cases had evolved to a point where it was necessary to effect some coordinating mechanisms for these cases. As the scope of such cases increased, so too did the need for coordinating mechanisms. These mechanisms attempted to maintain the independence sought by associations while also providing for combined action. As test cases became more and more elaborate, sophisticated

and expensive, the nature of the mechanisms changed from ad hoc and informal structures to a permanent organisation constituted by the Confederation of
Australian Industry (CAI).

The test cases arose from the economy-wide significance, particularly of basic
wage and standard hours claims. The basic wage determined by Higgins in 1907
became the foundation wage for all federal awards. Thus, variations in this foundation wage affected all federal awards and, indirectly, also State tribunal awards.
Until 1921, the need for coordinating machinery was not apparent since awards
could not be varied during their currency. As a result, it was not possible to
vary all awards simultaneously. The Court adopted the practice of inserting the
appropriately adjusted basic wage into new awards, and varying the basic wage
of existing awards when these came up for renewal. In 1921, the Act was varied
to allow for awards to be varied during their currency. This made it possible
for all awards to be varied in line with the Court's determination of the appropriate basic wage. Inevitably, this led to joint applications. Indeed, at the 1921
Basic Wage Case, Higgins directed that all union applications should be joined
together and that one advocate should present the unions' case. Similarly, he
directed that all employers should be represented by one advocate (1921 15 CAR
840). In 1923, unions formed the Commonwealth Council of Federated Unions,
which was charged with the handling of Basic Wage Case submissions (Donn
and Dunkley 1977). This was a forerunner to the Australian Council of Trade
Unions (ACTU).

For their part, employers formed the Committee of Control re Basic Wage
and Standard Hours in 1924. This was initially constituted by the CCEA, the
Graziers' Federal Council of Australia (GFCA), the Australian Mines and Metals
Association, the Timber Merchants' Association, a number of national companies
and the State-based Chambers of Manufactures and the Employers' Federations.
The two Victorian-based organisations, the VCM and the VEF, undertook much
of the preparation of submissions. They also briefed counsel, a method of case
presentation that continued until the late 1970s. A major reason for using outside
representation was to remove any hint of 'control' by any one organisation. The
costs of cases were met by a levy on those associations and companies prepared
to be a part of the Committee of Control. By the time the committee had taken

charge of the 1926–27 Main Hours Case, there were twenty-four organisations subscribing to its work. This case cost employers over $16 000 (CCEA Meeting 21 March 1927).

This loose-knit form of coordination, though undergoing a number of name changes, persisted until 1961. Four major organisations – the Australian Council of Employers' Federations (ACEF), the ACMA, the Metal Trades Industry Association (MTIA), and the GFCA – came to control both the policy and the operations committees. The number of subscribing associations increased.

A difficulty with employer coordination was that the only way in which to reach some form of agreement was by agreeing to the lowest common denominator of assent for any improvements in working conditions, a policy described as 'no increase, no way, no how!' This approach met with criticism from the Commission. More importantly, it led to diminishing returns. In 1959, the ACTU was successful in winning a 5.7 per cent increase in the basic wage as well as a 28 per cent increase in the margins awarded to metal industry tradesmen. Adjustments to the metal margins traditionally led to flow-ons to other industries, and this case proved no exception. In these circumstances, most associations supported the ACEF's move to reconstitute the coordinating machinery so as to provide for a more flexible and positive approach to general cases. By now, the ACEF had come under the sway of George Polites. He was to be an important shaper of national employer policy for the next two decades. In this, he was assisted by the cleavages within the ACMA's ranks, and in particular by the MTIA's successful capture of most Victorian metal industry employers from the ranks of the VCM.

In 1961, three new bodies were established. The first was the National Employers' Association (NEA). This body, consisting of forty national organisations, was to meet at least annually 'for the purpose of considering generally policy in connection with actual or pending national industrial proceedings and overall questions of finance relating thereto' (NEA Meeting 7 February 1961). In addition, there was to be the National Employers' Policy Committee (NEPC), consisting of a representative of the four key associations that were associated with the Basic Wage Working Party. It had the general supervision of cases, was responsible for the raising of funds for these cases, and convened the general meetings of the NEA. The third body was the National Employers' Industrial

GEORGE POLITES

George Polites was the executive director of the Australian Council of Employers' Federations from 1959 to 1978 and in this capacity he developed a far more professional approach to the employers' participation in National Wage cases. He subsequently became director-general of the Confederation of Australian Industry, and from 1978 to 1983 was a member of the Committee of Review into Australian Industrial Relations Law and Systems, chaired by Keith Hancock.

In this interview with Steven Kates he begins by describing the way the employers had conducted wage cases in the 1950s and the new approach in the 1960s:

> George Polites: They [the various employer bodies] were, generally speaking, able to agree, for instance, on Basic Wage cases. They were able to agree to say no. And on the basis of saying no to everything, there was no problem of getting agreement. There would be arguments amongst us about who should do it and what you might say. But even then not too much about what you might say but how vehemently you said it.

> In the sixties we sought to change that a bit and indeed we did change it. On one occasion we made an application for a wage increase which was the first time that had ever been done. It was a remarkable turn of events because up until that point any suggestion that you would even concede that there might be half a case for some change was just unacceptable.

> Steven Kates: What was it like dealing with the ACTU leadership?

> George Polites: At the head of the ACTU in my time, I never found anybody who would act in any way other than absolutely with honesty and purpose.

> Steven Kates: 'Honesty and purpose.' That's an interesting phrase. What does that mean?

> George Polites: Well, it means that he's got his own job to do and he acts honestly towards it. He can understand you and he won't use anything against you. He believes in what he is doing and he will pursue it to the best of his ability.

George Polites was Director-General of the Confederation of Australian Industry from 1978 to 1983, and a leading figure in employers' associations for over forty years.

Steven Kates: There is the famous fact that there was you, Bob Hawke, who was then ACTU president and the then head of the Commission, Sir John Moore. What was it called? The Industrial Relations Club?

George Polites: No, but if there was a club, I was a member. I don't believe there was a club. I think that was pure nonsense, invented by people who were trying to denigrate the system. If you mean, did we talk to each other, Yes we did. We talked about the issues which faced the Commission but not in a way which compromised the Commission or any party during a Commission hearing. In all the discussions in which I was involved no one ever sought to denigrate the other; the discussions were about ensuring that there was full understanding of the position of each of us. The Commission treated the discussions as useful and in confidence. I was never party to any fix. There was never ever a fix in my time.

Committee (NEICe). This consisted of 'one officer with industrial experience nominated by each member of the Policy Committee'. The NEICe was charged with the 'detailed conduct of national industrial proceedings' as well as the research needed for such cases (NEA Meeting 7 February 1961). These bodies had no permanent secretariat. It was assumed that the four organisations constituting the Policy and Industrial committees would provide secretarial and support services.

Though these bodies achieved a high degree of coordination, they were also subject to divisions. This was particularly so during the 1969 Equal Pay Case. Though a constituent member of both the Policy and Industrial committees, the MTIA sought separate representation and submitted views that were contrary to those agreed to by other members of the NEA (Plowman 1986: 422–30). There was a degree of criticism and hostility at the controlling influence exercised by the 'big four'. There were a number of calls for the creation of a Confederation of Employers that would be less dependent on them. Paradoxically, the ACEF, which for over forty years had been active in seeking support for a confederation, now used its influence to oppose such a development. In response to pressures, the National Employers' Consultative Committee (NECCe) was formed to act as an advisory body to the NEPC. The NECCe comprised the four members of the NEPC and five others elected at NEA meetings.

By the 1970s, a number of national industry associations were challenging the ACEF and the ACMA as the employers' voice. In particular, strong associations had emerged in the metal and printing industries. Since 1904, the two national umbrella organisations had been divided over the issue of tariffs. This was no longer an issue, as all political parties had espoused support for the protectionist system. The ACEF and the ACMA moved closer together. In 1972, the two organisations merged their industrial relations departments. George Polites was appointed Director of the resultant Central Industrial Secretariat (CIS). This was the beginning of the total merger between the two national organisations.

The NEA was very active during the first half of the 1970s. Indeed, though only required to hold twice-yearly meetings, by 1974 monthly meetings were being called. This was partly because of the advent of a Labor government, partly because of the degree of industrial action being undertaken by unions, and partly because of the government's submissions to the Commission for the introduction of wage indexation. The NEA's budget for 1974–75 was $36 000. A year later, it was fixed at $100 000 and within five years it had mushroomed to nearly $555 000. Despite these increases, the demands of the centralised wages system ensured that expenditure continued to outstrip income. During the indexation period (April 1974 to July 1981), employers were confronted with 22 National Wage cases and seven Wage Fixing Principles conferences. In addition, at the behest of the NEA, in the first five months of indexation the NEPC intervened in cases involving the metal, building, oil, wool-selling, maritime, banking, municipal, vehicle-building, coal, printing, and insurance industries. These 'policing' interventions were augmented by the requirements of the indexation guidelines. Thus, until the end of 1978, the guidelines provided for 'community catch-up'. The NEPC was active in opposing claims under this provision, as it was under the work value principle and the Commission's 'anomalies' conferences for 'special and extra-ordinary' problems. By February 1980, some 130 cases had been brought before anomalies conferences.

The indexation system not only created logistical and resource problems for the NEA, but also confronted it with policy problems. Both the ACEF and the ACMA argued strongly against support for indexation. The MTIA supported indexation. Thus, there was a rift between the CIS and the MTIA on the NEICe, NEPC and NECC. Indexation was introduced without CIS support. Once introduced, more associations came to support the MTIA view. Nevertheless, the majority of associations sided with the CIS. The NEA came to adopt a negative and reactive stance towards indexation.

Meanwhile the ACEF–ACMA linkages strengthened. Since the ACEF had the dominant influence in formulating CIS policy, and since the CIS had a dominant influence in the NEA's Policy and Industrial committees, it followed that the ACEF was the dominant, national policy-initiating organisation. Most NEA policies of the period 'can be traced by way of a Polites-ACEF-CIS-NEICe-NEPC-NEA linkage' (Plowman 1986: 465). In 1974, the ACEF and the ACMA began discussions about a complete merger. This was accomplished in December 1977 with the formation of the Confederation of Australian Industry (CAI).

Though formed by the merger of the ACEF and the ACMA, in many ways the CAI preserved the approach to industrial relations issues developed under the NEA. The CAI had two wings; a trade wing located in Canberra and an industrial relations wing. The latter, called the National Employers' Industrial Council (NEICl), was headed by Polites and located in Melbourne. The NEICl effectively subsumed the NEA, but, unlike the latter, had its own full-time secretariat. Twenty-three national employer associations, as well as the State-based Employers' Federations and Chambers of Manufactures, were members of the NEICl when Prime Minister Fraser launched the CAI on 19 June 1978. By 1980, CAI membership stood at thirty-six. It had brought about a degree of formal national coordination not previously experienced by employer groups. However, by the mid-1980s, the drive towards deregulation and increased emphasis on 'enterprise bargaining' revived historical divisions between manufacturers and other employers. The developments resulted in changes in the membership, operations and structures of associations and their coordinating mechanisms.

REASSESSMENT

The emergence of the CAI coincided with the emergence of a highly centralised wages system. Indexation was briefly abandoned in 1981 but it was reintroduced in 1983 as part of the newly elected Labor government's Prices and Incomes Accord. This Accord, and its accompanying indexation, brought about a rift between employers' associations. The CAI was highly critical of an incomes policy determined jointly by unions and the government. It refused to give the Accord the appearance of a tripartite process since it had little confidence that it could influence outcomes. The Accord gave the ACTU unprecedented influence in economic policy formation notwithstanding a general decline in union membership at this time. The Accord also challenged the traditional influence over policy-making exercised directly or indirectly by business. For many employers, the 'consensus approach' claimed by the Accord rang hollow. In effect, they were 'bypassed and excluded on the issue of appropriate pay increases argued by the Government and the ACTU for submissions to the Commission' (Isaac 1994: 92).

The MTIA, which had dissented from NEA and CAI policies on previous occasions, again did so at this time. A supporter of centralism and regulated and predictable wage outcomes, the MTIA saw benefits in both the wage restraint induced by the Accord and the wage outcomes of indexation. Its support was rewarded. The government afforded the MTIA the tripartite representation normally afforded peak employer bodies such as the CAI. This drove a wedge between the MTIA and other employer groups.

Though the Accord continued in modified form until Labor's loss of government in 1995, indexation was abandoned in March 1987. At this time the Commission adopted the 'restructuring and efficiency' principle and awarded a two-tiered wage rise. The first tier was a general wage increase of $10 per week. The second tier provided for wage increases, of up to 4 per cent, for those sectors implementing measures 'to improve efficiency'. This was the beginning of 'managed decentralism', one in which National Wage cases provided ceilings and conditions for wage increases on an award-by-award basis, rather than the generalised wage increases of previous years. This approach was extended by the structural efficiency principle adopted in August 1988, and then by the enterprise bargaining principle adopted in October 1991. By this last date, many of the parties to National Wage cases were claiming the need for a workplace, rather than an award, focus. Developments on the national wage front were complemented and augmented by legislative changes. In 1993, the Act provided for a system of enterprise agreements. In 1996, the Coalition replaced the *Industrial Relations Act* with one having a distinctive workplace emphasis: the *Workplace Relations Act 1996*. This Act reduced the award-making role of the Commission, introduced a system of Australian Workplace Agreements, and reduced the content of federal awards to twenty 'allowable matters'. By then, national test cases no longer acted as a mechanism for generalised wage increases or to afford benchmarks for enterprise wage agreements. Instead, these cases came to ensure the preservation of a 'safety net' of minimum employment conditions.

By the time wage indexation was abandoned, a number of developments had been set in train that were to fracture the symbiotic relationship between employers' associations and the arbitration system. The deregulatory regime now openly espoused by both sides of politics, and support for 'globalisation' rather than protection, put pressure on the accommodative arrangements that had developed during the 1970s. By the late 1980s, a number of associations were reassessing their traditional role and adjusting to the new environment. In addition, a number of new employer bodies came to champion deregulation. Referred to as the 'New Right', these were critical of the established employers' associations that they considered to be a part of the 'Industrial Relations Club'. To these new groups, the established associations were a part of the problem of, rather than the solution to, economic malaise. With funding assistance from the National Farmers' Federation (the successor of the GFCA), the New Right was successful in prosecuting a number of unions in civil courts.

One such body was the Australian Federation of Employers (AFE). This aimed to oust the CAI as the employers' peak body. Though it was able to attract a number of small employer organisations to affiliate, it was unable to entice any of the mainstream associations. The AFE did not have a long existence. Its major role was to articulate an alternative paradigm to the existing arbitral system. In this, it was assisted by the HR Nicholls Society, which provided the intellectual foundations for the New Right. The Society's formation in 1986 was seen by one of its members as 'the beginnings of attempts to destroy the arbitration system. It is an attempt to burn down Nauru House [the Commission's headquarters] and everything the Arbitration Commission stands for' (Plowman 1987). The New Right's openly confrontational approach may have reduced its appeal. This made it easier for more moderate organisations, such as the Business Council of Australia (BCA), to influence the debate.

The BCA was a by-product of the formation of the CAI. An important influence on the development of the confederation was the pressure exerted by the 'Big 50', or what became known as the 'Companies Group'. This group had sought a confederation that would include both national associations and large employers, and offered to pay half the expenses of running the confederation. However, this was not the model adopted and, in order to fit in with the CAI's membership requirements, a number of companies, such as BHP, CSR and Qantas, formed 'industry' associations under their control (Plowman 1987). This left the Companies Group, which became the BCA in 1983, to take an independent line from the CAI (Plowman 1986: 466–80). This was to have significant consequences for both industrial relations and employers' associations.

In July 1989, the BCA published *Enterprise-Based Bargaining Units: A Better Way of Working*, the report of the Industrial Relations Study Commission that it had appointed. This report shaped the industrial relations debate for the next decade. By the time the BCA had shifted its attention to other policy areas in 1992, it had created a wave that was to change the contours of Australian industrial relations. The BCA's approach 'found ultimate political confirmation with the new federal Coalition government's December 1996 Workplace Relations Act' (Sheldon and Thornthwaite 1999a: 48).

Enterprise bargaining was to make headway, not only because the BCA had come to dominate the intellectual debate and the New Right had brought civil court action to bear on industrial relations, but also because large companies came to take responsibility for their own industrial relations. In many instances, this included disaffiliation from employers' associations, resulting in a significant loss of membership fees (Plowman and Rimmer 1991: 50–8). The enterprise bargaining debate increased award fragmentation, a development that had slowly gathered pace from about 1974. This can be illustrated by the metal industry. The Metal Trades Award was determined in 1954. In 1972, at the behest of private employers, the Metal Industry Award was carved out of the parent award. The former became the domain of public employers who were less prepared to negotiate settlements in favour of arbitrated outcomes. Other industries, confronted by external pressures, sought to remove themselves from this conglomerate award. In 1974, the automotive manufacturing industry and the aluminium industry split from the Metal Industry Award and formed their own industry awards. These two industry awards have since been further fragmented into company-specific awards. In addition, the aluminium company awards have been further splintered into site-specific awards. In 1989, in recognition of the problems arising from flow-ons from the building and construction industry into the metal industry parent award, the MTIA sought to insulate the latter by the creation of the Metal Industry (Building and Construction) Award.

The forces leading to award fragmentation also led to the development of a large number of single-employer awards. In 1975, there were about 340 federal awards, of which only about 30 were single-employer awards. By 1987, there were over 1200 awards, 740 of which were single-employer awards. By 2000, the number of awards had grown to 2300 and the number of single-employer award to about 1700. At this time, there were 500 multi-employer awards and a number of public sector awards.

The gradual fragmenting of multi-employer awards into single-employer awards was neither recognised at the time nor, if recognised, would have satisfied those seeking faster and more extensive changes. Employers' associations were increasingly drawn into the BCA's enterprise bargaining policy wake. A number of mainstream associations, such as the Australian Mines and Metals Association, were to the fore in championing enterprise bargaining. Some accepted it reluctantly; others had it thrust upon them. The Meat and Allied Trades Federation of Australia (MATFA) and the Australian Road Transport Federation (ARTF) are illustrative of those associations which were forced into the new arrangements. The MTIA and CAI exemplify the reluctants.

Historically, the meat industry had a highly centralised approach to award determination. However, the development of Australian Meat Holdings (AMH) from the 1980s had a significant impact on industrial relations in the industry. This company became the industry's largest employer and openly confronted the MATFA's centralist policies. In 1986, it took on unions in Queensland's most militant plant at Rockhampton. It summarily dismissed slaughtermen engaged in a stop-work meeting. It subsequently dismissed the entire workforce for engaging in a sympathy strike. When the plant became operational four months later, seventy 'black-listed' workers were not re-employed. Others were re-employed under reduced conditions.

Two years later, AMH took the battle to Victoria where the industry's union was most militant. In May 1988, determined to cut labour costs, it retrenched about 550 employees at its Portland plant. The plant was kept closed until September when it was re-opened 'but under radically worsened wages and conditions' (O'Leary 1999: 150). O'Leary notes that 'the resulting dispute radically changed industrial relations in the Victorian meat industry, although no one could predict this at the time. The Portland dispute was the first attempt by an employer to break away from the much-manipulated Victorian Meat Industry Award'. Within a short period the Victorian meat industry came to be regulated by thirty-seven enterprise agreements. The role of the MATFA was, and remains, marginalised in Victoria. In Queensland, most employers signed enterprise agreements following the lead of the AMH in 1996. The newly named employer association (the National Meat Association of Australia) has since encouraged its members to take an enterprise approach (O'Leary 1999: 150, 154).

The meat industry's experience testifies to the capacity of large employers to fragment industry awards, particularly in a period characterised by the acceptance of enterprise bargaining, unions' inability to hold the line, and the Commission's inability, or lack of will, to maintain relativities across multi-employer awards. The road transport industry also illustrates this role of large employers. In this industry, 'the process of industrial relations change initiated in the mid-1980s presented the ARTF with the greatest challenge in its history' (Bowden 1999: 94). Between 1990 and 1992, even though the ARTF had resolved to remain within the centralised wage-fixing system, the three largest employers in the industry, Brambles, TNT and Mayne Nickless, withdrew from the association in order to pursue a more independent industrial relations approach. This resulted in the demise of the ARTF and an increased capacity for other New Right organisations within the industry (such as the National Transport Forum) to exert greater influence in the direction of decentralisation. The latter succeeded in splitting the Long Distance Drivers Award from the Transport Workers' Award and in providing for enterprise agreements to be set for each trip, something the union had historically opposed. The ARTF's fortunes potentially changed for the better when, in 1996, Linfox, TNT, Brambles and Mayne Nickless determined that an award system, rather than enterprise bargaining, best suited their interests. However, the Commission thwarted this attempt to re-institute awards and claimed that 'the statutory scheme is to encourage enterprise bargaining' (Bowden 1999: 94).

As noted, the MTIA was at odds with other employer groups for much of the post-1960 period. Initially, this resulted from the benchmarking and pace-setting role of the Metal Trades Award. Flow-ons from this award were recognised as a fact of life, with the Commission recognising Metal Trades cases as 'economic reviews in miniature'. In the MTIA's view, this situation militated against its capacity to negotiate agreements, something that was common in many other industries. Such negotiations were constrained by the large number of interveners fearing flow-ons. Inevitably, Commission decisions were determined with regard to national, rather than industry, considerations. To escape this situation, the MTIA sought to establish a system of 'collective negotiations' outside the realm of the Commission and where other parties could not intervene. Other associations saw this as a naïve approach; one that hardened into further opposition as unions in other industries used the negotiated settlements in the metal industry as benchmarks for their own awards.

The MTIA also found itself out of step with other employer groups in the Equal Pay Case of 1969. In the early 1970s, and in the context of spiralling labour costs, the MTIA's search for some control mechanisms against union demands again put it at odds with other employers organisations. Unlike the latter, it supported the introduction of wage indexation, since this had the potential to place a ceiling on union demands. The demise of indexation was followed by major concessions to metal unions in 1981. When the agreement expired in 1982, the MTIA sought help from the government by way of a wages freeze. Again, in opposition to a number of other employer groups, it sought recentralisation (including wage indexation) in 1983 and, as noted earlier, was not averse to the Accord. Further, its approach to award restructuring was accepted at National Wage cases despite opposition from other employer groups.

For a number of years the MTIA and the Amalgamated Metal Workers' Union entered into constructive dialogue to modernise an industry that had lost nearly half of its employees in the early 1980s. This relationship led to changes in training systems, the development of broadbanding and career paths, and to appropriate adjustment in the industry award. In 1988, the MTIA opposed the introduction of enterprise-based bargaining, claiming that 'enterprise agreements could not achieve the requisite broad institutional changes to the industry's training system and award structures' (Sheldon and Thornthwaite 1999a: 79). The study mission to Sweden and West Germany which it undertook that year with metal unions only served to confirm its corporatist approach.

By the 1990s, the MTIA had to confront the enterprise bargaining tide. It attempted to do so by defining its own system: one in which awards would be permissive of 'envelope' or supplementary bargaining, and one in which the Commission would safeguard against flow-ons. The association remained fearful that enterprise bargaining would result in the stagflationary situation that had resulted from its previous sortie into 'collective negotiations'. By mid-1991, the MTIA was claiming that 'the deregulationists are simply fooling themselves if they believe that you can achieve rapid change by throwing the entire responsibility back to individual enterprises and in the process deliberately provoke a confrontation with the unions' (MTIA 1991). At the National Wage Case of September 1991, it again argued for an industry framework.

In this case, and unlike the situation in April 1991, the Commission accepted the arguments in favour of enterprise bargaining. To the MTIA's chagrin, the enterprise bargaining principles did not include any ceiling on wages, and thus, in the association's view, did not have any mechanism for controlling wages. This anxiety was heightened the following year when changes to the Act removed the

Commission's role in monitoring enterprise agreements for their impact on the level of wages generally, or on enterprise productivity. More was to follow. In 1993, just prior to Labor retaining office, the Accord Mark VII proposed the removal of any controls on wage limits, a reduction in the role of the Commission, and a greater emphasis on enterprise-determined wage outcomes (Green 1993). A further impediment to the MTIA's position was that the metal unions initiated an industrial campaign in which they sought wage increases of 6 per cent with no productivity trade-offs. This campaign did much to undermine MTIA's confidence that it could achieve industry modernisation and

Justice Barry James Maddern, third President of the Commission (1985–1994)

competitiveness through its dialogue with unions. In addition, the larger firms indicated a lack of commitment to industry bargaining, though this remained the preferred position of smaller companies.

Facing altering external conditions and changed impulses from within its ranks, the MTIA's policy began shifting more dramatically. It now supported calls for a widening of the coverage of enterprise bargaining. In particular, faced with restlessness among its large and influential membership and a union campaign that undermined its ability to deliver industrial peace and contain wage costs, the association took a dramatic step away from its long-held commitment to an industry framework agreement (Sheldon and Thornthwaite 1999a: 85).

Naturally, the policy debate and enterprise trends affected the CAI. The trend towards increasing deregulation revived historical animosities between protectionist and free market associations. The cumulative weight of the changes was the disaffiliation of a great number of members. These included a number of

dominant players, such as the MTIA and the NFF. It also included the disaffiliation of two foundation members, the New South Wales Chamber of Manufactures
(now called Business Australia Ltd) and the VCM (renamed the ACM). Between
1980 and 1988, the CAI experienced sixteen disaffiliations. By then, the number of affiliations had dropped to thirty-six. The MTIA merged with the ACM
to form the Australian Industry Group in 1998. For its part, the CAI merged
with the Australian Chamber of Commerce to form the Australian Chamber of
Commerce and Industry (ACCI) in 1991.

The CAI had consistently argued for a centralised wages system, claiming
that collective negotiations usually resulted in larger companies paying above-
average wages that were then transmitted through institutional mechanisms to
other employers. It rejected the New Right rhetoric and considered that the
'notion that industrial relations should be a matter for the individual employer
and individual employee [to be] so far removed from reality that it is a dangerous
distraction' (Kelly 1992: 263). The CAI remained a staunch defender of the
arbitration system until 1991, by which time indexation had been abolished and
the trend towards enterprise bargaining had been established through the national
wage principles.

Despite its public advocacy of a centralised system, a vigorous policy debate
and transformation had been taking place within the CAI. This, in part, was a
logical outcome of the removal of much of the protectionist environment that had
previously made a centralised system more benign and which had reduced the
competitive impact of wage rounds. The policy transformation was made public
in mid-1991, a move that was probably accelerated by the ACTU's vehement and
coarse rejection of the Commission's decision at the April 1991 Enterprise Bargaining Case. At its July council meeting, the CAI adopted a new policy entitled
'A new system for industrial relations in Australia'. In this, it called for complete decentralisation of wage-fixing, the dismantling of industrial tribunals, the
abolition of National Wage cases and other test cases, voluntary unionism, and
more effective enforcement mechanisms. The new policy sought a rationalisation
of federal and State tribunals, something it had rejected in the 1985 Hancock
inquiry. The CAI contended that it had not resigned from the Industrial Relations
Club: union and government actions had burnt the clubhouse down (*Industrial
Review* July 1991).

By the federal election of 1996, the CAI (by now ACCI) was well placed to take a proactive role in influencing Coalition legislation, including convening an employers' summit on the legislative contents of the proposed new Act. The ACCI was also proactive in seeking the implementation of legislative changes, including its initiation of the Award Simplification Test Case of February 1997 (ACCI 1997). This has been accompanied by its traditional reactive and negative role at Safety Net, Living Wage, Reasonable Hours and other cases, and strident criticism of the Coalition's inertia on 'the second wave'.

The role of the ACCI (and other employers' groups) in such test cases testifies to the hybrid arbitration system that has evolved to date. As described, at one level there has been a trend towards devolution to the enterprise. There are legislative limitations placed on the number of award matters that can be covered by awards, including multi-employer awards. This has necessitated enterprise-level agreements in the area of 'non-allowable matters'. However, the 'safety net' system, which has evolved to ensure that minimum employment standards are maintained, has resulted in the continuation of national test cases. These continue to require a coordinated employer response.

As adaptive organisations, employers' associations have come to operate in this dual system, notwithstanding their statements about continued devolution. The inability of the Coalition government to push through further legislative changes because of Senate opposition means that the present situation is likely to persist into the near future. The current system is likely to survive future Labor governments. Though these may increase the Commission's role, the more open nature of the Australian economy would restrict moves to recentralise industrial relations. In any event, employers' associations can be expected to react in two ways to any future changes: to voice disapproval, and then to adapt to the new requirements.

CONCLUSION

This chapter has explored the relationship between employers' associations and the compulsory arbitration systems that assisted in bringing them into being and which determined, for the most part, their methods of operation. The approach of associations to arbitration has gone through four stages: a period of opposition;

a period of acceptance; a period of dependency; and a period of reassessment. Of importance was the first period, the period in which the foundations of the system were laid. Employers' associations' negative approach of 'legislation and litigation' was counterproductive, and enabled unions to determine the award structure that developed. This structure, with its parent awards and high degree of flow-ons, was ill-suited when Australia jettisoned its protectionist approach to economic regulation. This has led to significant policy shifts and realignments on the part of associations. Associations, which, by the 1930s, had come to an accommodation with arbitration if not a dependency upon it, came to challenge existing employment relations that put their members at a competitive disadvantage in the global market. Though much decentralisation has taken place, the safety net provisions of the Act result in some standards being determined on a national test case basis. Associations have accommodated to these conditions. In a hybrid system that is not fully centralised nor yet fully decentralised, associations can be expected to act in both reactive and adaptive ways to future changes.

7

UNIONS AND ARBITRATION

Malcolm Rimmer

Australian unions have chosen throughout the past 100 years to do most of their industrial relations work within the compulsory arbitration system, resulting in 'formal government intervention on a massive scale, in the collective bargaining process' (Martin 1989: 202). The longevity and strength of this preference remains a puzzle to some overseas commentators unaccustomed to such a high level of state intervention in union affairs. One British observer, Henry Phelps Brown (1983: 252), found it strange that Australian unions agreed to compulsory arbitration in the first place, given their shared legacy with British unions: 'For the British worker there has seemed to be an overt opposition between compulsory arbitration and democratic freedom: to be obliged to accept whatever the award may be is to be compelled to work on terms that may be repugnant'. There are few other countries in the world where unions freely have allowed state agencies such power to direct them. How can the Australian case be explained? Two theories deal with this question. First is the argument that, in a notional sense, 'union principles have captured the arbitration tribunals' (Scherer 1985: 94). Second, the 'dependency' theory claims that Australian unions became abnormally reliant on the state (Howard 1977).

This chapter will refer to the first of these arguments as the 'capture' theory, noting that it differs from a similarly titled theory of regulation. When applied to the Commission, the capture theory rests on the following points. First, the creation by unions of the Australian Labor Party (ALP) after 1890 eased union fears of oppressive labour courts and planted the expectation that state arbitrators would help unions advance their claims (Markey 1989: 167). Second, arbitration conferred advantages on unions by guaranteeing legal rights to recognition, award enforcement, exclusive jurisdiction, and preference in employment. Third, when arbitration courts were established their major decisions were based on social justice rather than economic criteria and so conformed to the natural expectation of workers or, in Phelps Brown's (1983: 277) words, 'worked with the grain of labour'. Fourth was the emergence of an accommodative style of arbitration in which, as Eggleston (cited in Perlman 1954: viii) put it, tribunal decisions were 'modified by the realisation that the effectiveness of the Court's operations depends to a large extent on persuading the parties that the long term advantages of arbitration outweigh the immediate disadvantages of an unfavourable decision'. Fifth, unions with sufficient strength found they could supplement compulsory arbitration with its notional alternative, collective bargaining supported by strike action, and enjoy the best of both worlds (Martin 1975: 110). The capture theory concludes from these points that arbitral tribunals came to embrace union interests (Dabscheck 1980: 430), acting 'not to protect the public from irresponsible unions but to protect workers from a greedy public' (Scherer 1985: 94).

The second explanation for union acceptance of the Commission is that the unions became dependent on its support. According to the dependency theory, reliance on the arbitration system shaped both the methods of unions and their ultimate purpose. 'If the system required unions to exist, the operation of the system did not require a wide and conventional range of industrial relations activity from the unions' (Howard 1977: 266). Australian unions did not need the strength to press their demands on employers. Since this capability was not required, it atrophied. Shop-floor organisation became weak and unions did not collect the high contributions needed to finance lengthy trials of strength with employers (Gahan 1996). Evolving to perform as 'cogs in a bureaucratic machine' of the arbitration system, this became their main purpose. Their role, claimed Howard (1977), became to 'provide comfort, security and peace of mind, not to unionists alone, but to society'. Unions existed as much to facilitate the workings of the arbitration system as to service their members' needs.

The capture and dependency theories outlined here present plausible explanations of the durability of the relationship between unions and arbitration tribunals. But to what extent do they faithfully represent that relationship over time?

FORMATIVE YEARS: 1890–1921

The origins of union support for compulsory arbitration are sometimes traced to the failure of collective bargaining in the decade following the 1890 Maritime Strike. Accounts of this period emphasise four main points. First, negotiation and conciliation between unions and employers began to develop before 1890 in unionised industries such as engineering, printing, coal-mining, and boot and shoe manufacture (Patmore 1991: 60). Second, collective bargaining broke down after the 1890s strikes in the pastoral, maritime and mining industries, mainly because of 'the refusal of employers to recognise unions and to negotiate with them' (Markey 1989: 156). Third, in response to industrial defeat, unions formed the Labor Party and overcame their distrust of the state, agreeing to compulsory arbitration in order to guarantee recognition and security. Fourth, acting in conjunction with protectionists and social reformers in the State and federal parliaments, the newly formed Labor Party succeeded in obtaining workable compulsory arbitration legislation (Macintyre 1989: 189–93).

Ironically, one factor contributing to the failure to develop collective bargaining was its rejection by unions as well as employers in the lead-up to the Maritime Strike. Instead, the newly organised unions of labourers such as shearers and waterside workers attempted to impose on employers standard wage rates, hours and working conditions, fixed unilaterally in their 'working rules' or 'by-laws' (Rimmer and Sheldon 1989: 276). This method raised the ire of employers because it challenged fundamental beliefs about the rights of property. FJ Thomas, manager of the HRN Steam Navigation Company, conveyed this dislike in his account of dealings with the Seamen's Union:

> The seamen made their own rules, and sent the shipowners a copy of
> them, with a notification that such and such alterations had been made,
> and we had to adopt them or do without their services. It would be much

better if they were made mutually, instead of being presented to you, and your being told these were the rules. (Royal Commission on Strikes 1891: 192)

It is curious that Australian labourers' unions attempted to use this method. A similar approach, labelled by the Webbs (1902: 152) the 'method of mutual insurance', was common among those British and Australian craft unions able to both restrict scarce labour supply and support their members through extensive friendly benefits. Where such resources were available to what Turner (1962) called 'closed unions' they could force employers and members alike to observe their working rules. However, no such sanctions were available to the 'open' or inclusive unions that organised Australian labourers. Instead, they made an adventurous attempt to spread the 'religion of unionism' to all workers by enforcing the closed shop and refusing to touch 'blacked' or 'non-union' goods – demands that were backed by inter-union alliances committed to mutual support. In response, the organisations of pastoral and shipping employers demanded (and won in the Maritime Strike) 'freedom of contract', an equally uncompromising counter-assertion of the employers' absolute right to hire non-union labour and set employment conditions without union interference.

As far as is known, this method was unique to labourers' unions in Australia. It proved short-lived and was abandoned after the Maritime Strike as unions accepted the need to compromise through collective bargaining, conciliation and arbitration. What did not change after 1890 was the commitment of the labour movement to 'open' or inclusive unionism that aimed (through the closed shop if necessary) to enrol all workers and extend to them the protection of standard employment conditions.

Vigorous recruitment led to the recovery of inclusive unionism (Cooper 1996), the number of unionists swelling from an estimated 97 000 in 1901 (6.1 per cent of employees) to 703 000 in 1921 (51.6 per cent of employees). As union membership and bargaining power expanded, employers were increasingly willing to accept collective bargaining. One motive for doing so was to keep out of the newly formed arbitration tribunals. Yet, despite the employers' willingness to negotiate, unions still took their claims to the tribunals. A reason for this was the willingness of tribunals to award conditions that the employers would not voluntarily concede, especially union preference (to encourage membership and prevent employers blacklisting union activists) and the common rule (which made an award applicable to all employees in a particular industry or occupation, thus preventing employers from undercutting standard wages).

The Sydney Trolley and Draymen's Union illustrates this point. After being crushed in the Maritime Strike, the union was re-established in 1901 and immediately negotiated with the Master Carriers a collective agreement fixing standard wages and hours (Bray and Rimmer 1987: 34). However, the employers' association would not agree to union demands for compulsory unionism and could not prevent either member or non-member firms from undercutting the agreed wage rates. The agreement expired after a year and was not renewed. The union then claimed from the newly formed New South Wales Arbitration Court what the employers refused, finally winning in 1907 an award that included both union preference and common rule clauses. In this case, the Trolley and Draymen's Union chose compulsory arbitration not because it was unable to win from the employers the right to negotiate, but because arbitration offered better results.

This union was not alone in exploring the advantages of arbitration. William Pember Reeves (1902b: 326), the architect of New Zealand compulsory arbitration, remarked how the 'Arbitration Court in Sydney is besieged with applications for hearings, and the President has had to protest against an ugly rush of cases'. Some other unions, mainly socialist-led or craft organisations, resisted arbitration because it undermined self-reliance (Markey 1989: 174). But the temptation for unions to try compulsory arbitration was powerful when it appeared better able than collective bargaining to permit the rapid and peaceful establishment of an inclusive award system strengthened by union preference and the common rule. Such pragmatic reasoning attracted unions to both the State tribunals and, after it was established in 1905, the Commonwealth Court of Conciliation and Arbitration. In practice, their confidence in the federal tribunal had yet to be justified by experience. One test came when employers provoked disputes with the same destructive potential as the Maritime Strike, instilling fears that the Court would be powerless to protect union rights.

An example of this was the dispute in 1908–09 when the Broken Hill Proprietary Company (BHP) locked out its miners and smelter workers for four months to enforce a wage cut. Falling metal prices had forced the abandonment of wage rates agreed in 1906 (Osborne 1973: 30). The Court heard the dispute and Justice Higgins made an award to restore the 1906 wage rates, but non-unionists had taken many unionists' jobs and the BHP mines remained shut until prices recovered. However, the dispute did not spread as the Maritime Strike had done. Peter Bowling, the leader of the Amalgamated Miners' Association, pressed the New South Wales Trade Union Congress for a 'general strike' to release imprisoned strikers, but was defeated by the vote of craft unionists who argued that only the return of a Labor government could help.

A second example was the 1912 Brisbane general strike that began when tram employees were dismissed for wearing union badges. This stoppage spread to railwaymen, miners, and other workers from Brisbane to North Queensland. Higgins again showed sympathy for the union cause, ordering that unionists be allowed to wear badges, but once more the employer defied his decision by retaining non-unionists in their jobs. The strike ended after five weeks and the union proceeded to obtain a binding award over the employer.

Both disputes could have led militant unions to reject the peaceful methods of political action and arbitration, but they did not do so. Compare this with the situation in New Zealand, where union claims could be heard through compulsory arbitration but the moderating influence of a Labor Party had yet to be established. Faced with the use of penalties against strikers in the 1908 'Blackball strike', militant elements in New Zealand unionism rejected compulsory arbitration as a matter of principle and formed the New Zealand Federation of Labour (the 'Red Feds'). This socialist union federation mobilised unskilled workers in a wave of strikes climaxing in the 1913 New Zealand general strike (Olssen 1988). Some Australian unions were sympathetic to the Red Feds, especially those associated with the Industrial Workers of the World (IWW), which supported the syndicalist method of the general strike (Turner 1979: 55–67). However, the spirit of compromise proved stronger in Australia.

Two unions illustrate why Australian unionism took a different path from their New Zealand counterparts. First was the Australian Workers' Union (AWU). When the Commonwealth Arbitration Court began operating in 1905, the AWU applied quickly for an award. Its reasons for doing so included frustration with collective bargaining, competition from the 'scab' Machine Shearers' Union (MSU), and the influence of leaders such as WG Spence who had been elected to parliament and favoured political action and compulsory arbitration. By 1907, the AWU had gained federal registration (blocking the MSU from doing so), won a shearers' award, and was a firm convert to compulsory arbitration (Merritt 1986).

Second was the Waterside Workers' Federation (WWF). This union was also led by an ALP leader – WM (Billy) Hughes, who in 1909 negotiated an agreement with the Commonwealth Steamship Owners. Despite the agreement, waterfront strikes broke out in 1911, and in 1913 Hughes' control of the union was threatened by militants proposing to join the New Zealand general strike. Nevertheless, Hughes (by this time, both president of the WWF and Commonwealth Attorney-General) finally triumphed in 1914 when a federal award was made for waterside workers. The award was a generous one. Higgins fixed high hourly rates to compensate for the irregularity of casual work. These two cases are similar and revealing. They show how two unions whose forerunners were prominent in the 1890s strikes had, by 1914, been converted to peaceful methods by their parliamentary leaders and their successes in arbitration.

One factor winning union support for federal arbitration was the personal popularity of Higgins, who presided over the Court from 1907 to 1921. His standing among unionists was conveyed by Tom Mann, a militant leader of the 1909 Broken Hill strike, who described him as 'sympathetic and fair minded' and 'a judge as good as they could get in Australia' (Rickard 1984: 180). Higgins laid down wage-fixing principles that embraced union standards and policies. Early in his term of office, he established social 'needs' rather than economic criteria as the foundation for award wages. Thus, the *Harvester* judgment in 1907 established a living wage to meet the normal needs of a labourer with a family. Consistent with this, in *Barrier Branch of the Amalgamated Miners' Association v BHP* (1909) he opposed reducing wages below this level because of the employer's incapacity to pay; 'if a man cannot maintain his enterprise without cutting down the wages which are proper to be paid to his employees, it would be better he should abandon the enterprise' (1909 3 CAR 32). Such decisions, in Phelps Brown's (1983: 277) words, 'placed the claims of humanity above the workings of the market'.

Commonwealth arbitration also appealed to unions because it secured basic union organisational rights. An original object of the Act (deleted in 1996) was 'to encourage the organisation of representative bodies of employers and employees and their registration under this Act'. Registered organisations were guaranteed the rights to compel employers to attend hearings, to observe awards, and for unionists to have preference in employment. Despite the disappointment of the *Whybrow* case in 1910, where the High Court determined that the common rule was outside the Court's powers, unions found the benefits of registration attractive. However, they were also motivated by the fear that competing unions registering in their place would steal a legal monopoly over their jurisdiction and take their members. This caused a race for unions to register and lay first claim to jurisdictional territory. By 1914, eighty-four unions with 60 per cent of total union membership had federal registration, and by 1917 this had risen to 90 per cent (CBCS 1918:16).

The rush to federal registration far outstripped the spread of federal awards. Between 1905 and 1914, the Court made only twenty awards covering the pastoral and maritime industries, journalists, theatre workers, builders' labourers, meat workers, and boot and shoemakers. It also registered 217 agreements, mostly covering members of the Federated Engine Drivers and Firemen's Association (FEDFA). Major industries such as coal mining, railways, the metal trades, the building crafts, textiles and clothing, and many service industries remained largely untouched.

Several factors explain the slow spread of federal awards. First, the Court was prohibited from regulating State government employees such as railwaymen. Second, award-making was slow because it relied on a single judge obliged to conduct lengthy hearings. For example, the hearings for the Builders' Labourers' Award were held in three States and took forty-three days, and the 1914 *Waterside Workers* case was heard over twenty-three days in two States. Third, many employers impeded award hearings by contesting legal principles in the High Court. Higgins' frustration spilled out in *Australian Boot Trade Employees' Federation v Whybrow & Co.* (1910 4 CAR 3) when he complained 'everything is disputed – even the fact that there is a dispute'.

To avoid these problems, unions turned to the State arbitration tribunals, several of which used wages boards to expedite the heavy labour of drafting awards and offered the added advantage that they could order a common rule. By 1914, 579 State awards existed. Approximate estimates of State award coverage in Queensland, South Australia and Victoria suggest they covered a majority of the workforce at this time, as was likely in the other States (CBCS 1914: 62). The creation between 1901 and 1914 of an inclusive award system regulating a majority of employees was the handiwork of the State tribunals rather than federal arbitration.

The war years saw some expansion in federal award coverage. Notable additions were the coal and metal mining industries so that the federal tribunal gained jurisdiction over Australia's two major trouble spots – the mining and maritime industries. Together, these two industry groups accounted for three-quarters of all industrial disputes throughout the First World War. At the same time, moderate union leaders in these industries were losing their grip over the unions. By 1916, several miners' leaders were IWW members, and in the same year Hughes was expelled by the WWF over his support for conscription. As wartime dislocation and price rises fed rank-and-file grievances, strikes broke out in coal and metal mining and the maritime and shearing industries. The IWW portrayed these strikes as a struggle between 'direct action' and compulsory arbitration. For once, Higgins was on the opposing side to the unions, refusing to arbitrate in disputes while a union was on strike. When Billy Hughes became Prime Minister in 1916, he gave precedence to getting strikers back to work, even if this meant undermining Higgins' principle that arbitration should not be performed under duress. In that year, he arranged a special tribunal to concede the demands of striking coal-miners, an act described by Higgins as 'a most baleful precedent' (Turner 1962: 90).

The end of hostilities brought no return to normality. Returned servicemen flooded the labour market, the union movement was gripped with 'Bolshevik' ideas, and prices skyrocketed. Pent-up union demands spilled over in 1919, the year of strikes, as Australia suffered the greatest recorded strike wave in its history. Yet Higgins refused to hear disputes under pressure from strikers. In 1919, the seamen led by Tom Walsh, a militant socialist, struck work in support of an overdue wage claim. The crisis affected movements of coal stocks, bringing transport and manufacturing to a standstill, and was made worse by the gaoling of Walsh. Since Higgins would not arbitrate, the government was left to find a solution, which it did by interceding with the employers to grant the union's claims. The following year, Hughes' government passed the *Industrial Peace Act 1920* giving the government power to create special tribunals to resolve emergency disputes of this kind. This was unacceptable to Higgins because it undermined the authority of the Court and sabotaged the possibility of disinterested arbitration. He continued in office so he could hear the *Timber Workers'* 44-hour case and then resigned in June 1921.

Unions benefited greatly from federal arbitration under Higgins. But the more powerful unions were not tamed by it. Finding that Higgins would not deal with disputes while a strike was in progress, the government chose to bypass him and establish alternative tribunals that were more open to political direction. Through the Industrial Peace Act, Hughes – a champion of the Court in its early years – presented the greatest threat yet to its independence and authority.

RESTORING THE COURT'S AUTHORITY: 1921–1931

The immediate post-war years saw union power at a pinnacle. Between 1918 and 1920, there was a short, sharp economic boom in which retail prices rose more than 30 per cent and unemployment fell as low as 5 per cent. Union membership peaked in 1920 at 53.3 per cent of the workforce. There was also a movement to consolidate union power by merging existing unions into industrial unions. Compulsory arbitration was associated with a fragmented union structure, despite some mergers by single-State organisations seeking federal awards. In 1921, there were still 382 unions of which 281, organised in a single State, held less than one-third of total membership. This reality was a far cry from the 'industrial union' ideal popularised by the IWW. Between 1918 and 1923, the union movement attempted to implement this ideal in the form of the 'One Big Union' (OBU) (Bedford 1963: 5–46).

Plans for the OBU finally dissolved in a crossfire of rival schemes and sectional claims between the AWU (which planned to become the OBU after absorbing unions of railway, building, and rural workers), the industrial unions of miners, railwaymen and meatworkers (who considered themselves spokes in the wheel of industrial unionism), and the urban craft unions (who jealously guarded their sectional identity). Several things came out of the movement. First, there were some union mergers, although the process had become bogged down since any associated change in eligibility rules provoked an avalanche of objections from rival unions claiming that members could 'conveniently belong' to them. Second, in 1927 a watered-down version of the OBU came into existence: the Australasian (later Australian) Council of Trade Unions (ACTU), which retained in its Constitution the soon-to-be-forgotten object of establishing industrial unionism. Unlike the OBU schemes, the ACTU required no mergers or redistribution of membership; it was simply a parliament for unions in their existing form.

The post-war boom ended abruptly in 1921 as retail prices fell and unemployment jumped to more than 11 per cent of the workforce. Union membership dropped slightly and unions turned away from 'direct action' towards the peaceful methods of arbitration and pressure group politics. Two developments signified this change in union methods: automatic adjustments to the basic wage, and the tactic of seeking reduced hours of work from State Labor governments.

Justice Powers, Higgins' successor, introduced automatic, quarterly cost-of-living adjustments to the basic wage in 1921. Controversy had arisen when the Piddington inquiry concluded that the *Harvester* basic wage had been eroded by inflation. Powers' award of 3 shillings defused past union 'catch-up' claims. Automatic cost-of-living adjustments to the basic wage were intended to prevent the problem recurring. One significant outcome of this decision was that it eliminated the need for unions to seek increases. Before 1921, adjustments to the basic wage were made on an award-by-award basis as their term expired. Each union had to take care of its own members. Automatic indexation ended all that. As Powers noted in the 1922 Basic Wage Case, 'The new method will avoid the necessity for either party to come to this court for variation of the award because of the increased or decreased cost of living' (1922 16 CAR 833). Once the responsibility for basic wage adjustments was taken out of union officers' workloads, they became less directly involved in protecting their members' employment conditions.

A similar change overtook adjustments to standard hours. Until the 1920s, these were determined solely in tribunal awards. In 1913, Higgins declared 48 hours to be a standard in the *Builders' Labourers* case. However, he was careful to confine that standard to 'average or normal' industries, allowing different hours to be determined on a case-by-case basis. In the 1920 *Timber Workers* case, he established general principles to allow a reduction to a 44-hour week. The government acted promptly to limit the damage. It amended the Act to reserve

The union campaign in the 1920s to secure the forty-four hour week was accompanied by demonstrations and direct action: the banner suggests these alternatives to arbitration.

the power to vary standard hours to the Full Court rather than a single member. In 1922, the Full Court (Justice Powers and Deputy Presidents Webb and Quick) re-heard the standard hours issue and reverted to a 48-hour week because of depressed economic conditions. In the past, unions might have resorted to direct action to win their claim. Instead they turned to State Labor governments. In 1924, Queensland legislated for a 44-hour week, followed in 1925 by New South Wales. These statutes applied generally in those States irrespective of whether workers were covered by federal or State awards. In 1926, the federal tribunal revisited working hours and reverted to the 44-hour standard. However, the unions had won the hours reduction primarily through State legislation, once again dispensing with the duty to press claims on an award-by-award basis.

By 1925, the choice, as most unions saw it, no longer lay between 'direct action' or compulsory arbitration but between federal or State arbitration, with the further option of political action. Indeed, where possible, unions liked to play different tribunals off against each other. The Federated Moulders' Union offers an interesting illustration. In 1925, the federal tribunal fined the union for an illegal strike. The union balloted its members and found 1211 still favoured arbitration, compared with only 429 supporting 'other methods'. However, 1067 preferred the State courts or boards to 761 favouring the federal tribunal (Hargreaves 1958: 70). Acting on these preferences, the union tried to withdraw from its federal award but was blocked by the employers. Although the union bid was unsuccessful, it illustrates how unions firmly understood the value of shopping between jurisdictions.

Yet the dominant trend in the 1920s remained the further extension of federal award coverage into industries previously unregulated or covered by State awards only. First, the *Public Service Arbitration Act 1920* established a public service arbitrator (Attlee A Hunt) to deal with federal public employees. Unionism and awards were already well established in the postal and telegraph services, and quickly spread through the remainder of the Commonwealth Public Service. Second, in 1920, the High Court ruled in the *Engineers* case that the Court could make awards for employees of State instrumentalities. This opened the door for Australia's 100 000 railway employees (5 per cent of the workforce) who were previously covered by unsatisfactory determinations of the State tribunals and Railway Classification Boards. Because their wages accounted for a quarter of total state expenditure, the State governments and Railway Commissioners were reluctant to cede control to the federal tribunal. Nevertheless, in 1924 the Court made an interim federal award for railway workers in all States other than Queensland and Western Australia. The Court also extended its awards into manufacturing. A federal award was made for metal industry tradesmen in May 1921. This was Higgins last award and it restored to a 3 to 7 ratio the value of the tradesmen's 'margin' for skill in relation to the basic wage, making it a benchmark for future federal margins cases in other industries.

Throughout the 1920s, the federal tribunal secured its coverage over the major industries in the Australian economy. Federal awards applied to all the main primary industries (pastoral, timber, and mining), transport (maritime, rail, road, and tram), communications (postal and telegraph), much of manufacturing (notably metalworking), and the Commonwealth Public Service. Despite this growth in federal award coverage, State awards probably still covered a larger number of workers. Unions of clerks, shop assistants, building tradesmen, and other workers dispersed in small businesses preferred State awards because (unlike federal awards) they could be enforced through common rule provisions. Also, the High Court's decision in 1929 in the *State School Teachers* case blocked, until 1983, many white-collar and State employees from seeking a federal award on the grounds that they did not work 'industrially'. Yet, despite the greater award coverage of State tribunals, leadership lay with the Federal Court.

In 1926, the Bruce–Page federal government appointed new judges to the Court. Dethridge replaced Powers as Chief Judge and Justices Beeby and Lukin were added to the bench. In June 1928, changes to the Conciliation and Arbitration Act instructed the Court, when making awards, to 'take account of economic realities' and armed it with tougher penalties against striking unions. After twenty years in which the Court had delivered many favourable decisions, unions began to suffer defeat after defeat.

The new Court was the instrument for many of these reversals. In July 1927, Beeby made an award for the metal industry allowing employers to introduce payments by results, a practice long opposed by metalworking unions (Sheridan 1975: 102). In this case, a strike was narrowly averted. In August 1928, Beeby amended the Waterside Workers' Award to provide for two labour pick-ups a day and to remove the scope for port branches to negotiate local issues. Beeby's judgment in *Commonwealth Steamship Owners' Association v Waterside Workers' Federation of Australia* took the employers' side in blaming the WWF for the local disputes that grew out of port negotiations: 'The union advocate contended that most of the disputes of recent years were the results of "pin pricks" by foremen . . . There is not a scintilla of evidence that the bullying ganger of the old days is now tolerated on the waterfront' (1928 26 CAR 867).

Perhaps so, but the bad old days were soon to return. The WWF struck work on 10 September 1928. Fines were imposed on the union and its preference clauses withdrawn from the award. Moves for a general strike were resisted by the newly formed ACTU (Hagan 1981: 91), and the strike failed as a 'scab' union took WWF members' jobs. The WWF was broken by the dispute and employer despotism was reinstated on the wharves.

In January 1929, Justice Lukin handed down a new award for timber workers that returned standard hours to forty-eight a week. Victorian and New South Wales unionists rejected these conditions and were locked out in a dispute which failed after a ten month test of strength during which the Timber Workers' Union

Two unlikely friends: Herbert Brookes, the president of the Employers' Federation, is sheltering alongside Jock Garden, the fiery secretary of the New South Wales Labor Council. Both men criticised arbitration but the cartoonist suggests that both took advantage of the tattered protection it offered.

was fined, much of the award was suspended and several union leaders were imprisoned. Worse was to follow. In March 1929, the Hunter Valley coalfields stopped work to prevent a proposed wage cut caused by plummeting coal prices. This lockout lasted fifteen months, ending only when the miners returned on the employer's terms. The coal industry had been regulated since 1920 by special tribunals created under the Industrial Peace Act, and so the Court played no direct part in it. However, the Court did order wage cuts in other industries. In 1930, it ordered a reduction in shearing rates (for example, from 41 shillings to 32 shillings and 6 pence per 100 sheep in New South Wales). Stoppages delayed shearing in three States, but for less than a month. In August 1930, the Railway Commissioners of New South Wales and Victoria applied to cut the basic wage for railwaymen by abolishing the 'Powers three shillings' and altering the price index. This application began as yet another attempt by the Railway Commissioners to undermine the federal award in that industry. However, the Court converted it into a test case to consider a general reduction of the basic wage. In January 1931, a 10 per cent cut in the basic wage was ordered in all federal awards.

For militant unions this looked like the last straw. The New South Wales Labor Council referred a motion for a general strike to the ACTU. But in the depressed economic conditions of the time the futility of strike action was clear and moderates defeated the move. Union strength was at its weakest since the early years of the century. The strongholds of union power – miners, waterside workers, railwaymen, and the like – had been defeated in one dispute after another. They had no power to do other than accept the awards of a seemingly hostile Court.

Unlike 1921, when the Court's independence was under simultaneous threat from militant unions and interfering politicians, in 1931 the Court held firm control. Its awards covered Australia's major industries and union independence had been subdued by the Depression and the Court's exercise of judicial authority. Yet, although the relationship between the Court and a disappointed union movement had soured, there was no alternative forum for union claims. One option, of course, was to reform the Court. In 1930, the Scullin Labor government removed the Court's power to fine striking unions. However, the fall of this government put on hold until 1947 more adventurous plans to reduce legalism and add more 'lay' Commissioners.

THE CRISES OF DEPRESSION AND WAR:
1931–1945

The Great Depression greatly weakened unionism. Unemployment rose to over 28 per cent of the workforce in 1932, sapping union bargaining power. Union membership also fell, although official records understate the extent of the decline. Membership returns from union secretaries show a reduction in numbers from the inter-war high of 911 500 members (57.2 per cent of the workforce) in 1928 to 762 600 members (42.6 per cent of the workforce) in 1933. However, the latter figure is probably exaggerated by the practice of retaining unemployed and 'non-financial' members on the books. For example, the New South Wales Transport Workers' Union claimed 4000 members in 1934 but only 1088 were financial (Bray and Rimmer 1987: 284). On paper, the union was as strong as in the late 1920s. In reality, it was bankrupt and had to discharge most of its organisers, thus losing the means to recruit and collect dues.

Most accounts of unionism during the 1930s emphasise the 10 per cent cut to the federal basic wage in 1931. The case was significant in several ways. First, it introduced 'capacity to pay' as a criterion for basic wage adjustment, confirming the use of economic criteria as well as 'social justice' factors in the Court's deliberations. Second, the ACTU assumed leadership in Basic Wage hearings, reaffirming the growing centralisation of union organisation and the declining need for individual unions to take action on behalf of their own members. Third, the 1931 basic wage cut symbolised worker hardship, at least until relief came from the 1934 hearing and the 1937 'prosperity loading' case. In fact, the true extent of worker hardship may have been much greater than official unemployment and wage data suggest due to the high incidence of 'short-time' working and the failure of established methods for enforcing awards. Such factors may have contributed to the finding in the 1933 census that only one in three male breadwinners earned more in a week than the federal basic wage.

Unions were powerless to help. Almost without exception, they had no bargaining power, little capacity to sway arbitration tribunals, and (outside Queensland) no recourse to ALP governments. Once these established methods failed, many union officials became demoralised and inactive (Louis 1968: 146). These moribund union leaders faced electoral challenges by candidates from the Communist Party of Australia (CPA). Successful left-wing candidates included Charlie Nelson and Bill Orr (miners), Jim Healy (WWF), Lloyd Ross (railways), Tom Wright (sheet metal workers), and many others. In the case of the AWU, the deeply entrenched conservative leadership was challenged by the formation of a rival union, the Pastoral Workers' Industrial Union. At the grassroots level, communist influence also spread through the shop committee movement. Beginning in the early 1930s, a network of 'inter-union' shop committees was formed in the industrial heartlands of Australia's major cities. Shop committees were elected in the railway workshops, power stations, and dockyards of Sydney, Melbourne, and other major cities. Communist influence over these organisations was unmistakable. The Eveleigh Carriage Works shop committee in Sydney was headquartered in an abandoned carriage known as the 'Kremlin'. From these training grounds came a second generation of communist union officials such as 'Red' Ted Rowe (engineers) and JJ Brown (railways). But the industrial role of most shop committees remained limited. Union officials excluded them from award matters such as wages, confining them to factory welfare problems like safety and amenities (Sutcliffe and Rimmer 1981: 231). They contributed to union radicalisation but not to the restoration of industrial conditions.

The private sector metal trades were an exception. Economic recovery in this industry created scope for bargaining. In 1935, a Foundry Workers' Joint Management Committee was established in Sydney made up of officials of the Federated Moulders, the Federated Ironworkers, and the FEDFA. This body encouraged the formation of shop committees throughout Sydney's larger private metal-working factories – Metters, Clyde Engineering, Hadfields, and the like. In 1936, the foundry shop committees went on strike and won an over-award payment of 3 shillings for tradesmen and 2 shillings for labourers. Responding to these 'market pressures', in February 1937 Beeby incorporated these rates in the award. This decision led to several stoppages. First, the metal unions struck in Sydney to resist absorption of the over-award (Hargreaves 1958: 78). This led to a six-week lockout of New South Wales foundry employees that ended on the union's terms. More difficult was the dispute at Cockatoo and Mort's Docks in Sydney where Beeby refused to extend the 3-shilling award payment to some members of the Amalgamated Engineering Union (AEU).

The AEU gave strike pay to its members during the ensuing stoppage. Beeby interpreted this as a challenge to the integrity of the Act and deregistered the union in 1938 (Sheridan 1975: 135). Initially, the AEU accepted this decision, prepared to rely on collective bargaining in place of compulsory arbitration. But then it changed its mind. Informally, it heard that Chief Judge Dethridge believed that Beeby had erred by choosing to hear that the AEU was paying strike benefits, thus placing himself in a position where he had to order deregistration. Dethridge was prepared to accept, if the union re-registered, that it could have the best of both worlds, combining over-award bargaining with awards of the court (Perlman 1954: 108). And so was established the archetypal metal unions' campaign for the next half-century: a combination of force applied in the 'hot shops', followed up by across-the-board award adjustment to help the weaker members catch up.

As the 1930s came to an end, economic recovery brought union membership back to its pre-Depression level and led to new wage claims. In 1939, the ACTU applied for a basic wage increase. Although prepared to concede that general prosperity justified an increase, war conditions and the prospect of Commonwealth child endowment decided the Court against it. Indeed, wartime conditions came to dominate union affairs. The establishment of the Curtin ALP government in October 1941 put the ACTU in a position to form a partnership with the government, and the entry of Japan into the war in December 1941 meant that partnership had to confront a crisis. In December 1941, the ACTU executive established a four-point wartime policy that would give it control over disputes, provide real wage maintenance, and make unions partners in production (Hagan 1981: 179). In fact, it was government rather than ACTU control that prevailed. As total war enveloped the Australian economy, emergency regulations blocked any prospect of unions acting to improve conditions. The 'wage-pegging' regulations of February 1942 held award rates steady, while manpower regulations restricted the movement of labour to capitalise on market scarcity (CBCS 1947: 55).

Unions did become partners in improving factory productivity. The German attack on the Soviet Union in June 1941 proved critical in bringing communist union officials behind the war effort. Declaring the war a 'war of machines', the communist secretary of the Federated Ironworkers, Ernie Thornton (1942: 19), announced a 'campaign for increased production'. In an extended military metaphor, he proclaimed the need to 'tighten union discipline over sick leave and absenteeism' while fighting 'the employers, who are in the position of snipers' because they were more concerned about profits than production.

From the end of 1941 till the 1945 ceasefire, Australian unions, whether conservative or communist, displayed an unusual degree of consensus among themselves, with the government, with the federal tribunal, and with most employers. In Howard's (1977) terminology, their role had become to 'provide comfort, security and peace of mind . . . to society'. But this was the product of wartime conditions and could not last.

THE POST-WAR BOOM: 1945-1974

Union membership stood at 54.2 per cent of the workforce in 1945 and totalled 1.2 million members, almost 60 per cent more than the number in 1934. Returning servicemen caused membership as a proportion of the workforce to drop in the following year, but by 1950 it had climbed to 58 per cent and it reached an all-time high of 63 per cent in 1953. There was much less post-war dislocation in 1945 than in 1919. There was, however, another strike wave. Working days lost almost doubled, from an annual average of over 860 000 (1939–44) to 1.6 million (1945–50).

Unlike in 1919, most major post-1945 stoppages were defensive, prompted by the initiatives of naïve employers or governments. The 1945 steel strike in New South Wales and the Queensland meat workers' strike both arose from attempts by employers to revert to pre-war conditions (Sheridan 1989: 89). The 1946 Victorian rail strike grew out of frustration with the continuation of wartime wage-pegging, and the ten-day waterfront strike in 1946 opposed continuation of a wartime emergency work practice. Similarly, the 1946–47 Victorian metal trades dispute and its 1948 sequel in the Queensland railways arose because the Chifley ALP government refused to lift wage-pegging regulations to allow claims to be heard for restoration of the value of the metal industry margin for skill, fixed in 1921. In late 1946, AEU members banned overtime and the employers locked them out. On 20 January 1947, the lockout ended, but the AEU stayed out, extending the dispute progressively to new sectors of the workforce. By this time, the union was pitted against the employers, the Chifley government, and the ACTU (whose president, P W Clarey, was also Chifley's Minister for Labour). It was also, once again, deregistered. In May, the Chief Judge, Drake-Brockman, finally broke the deadlock by arranging a hearing that conceded the union's claim. Accommodative arbitration (where the tribunal reconciles powerful unions and employers) helped the union out of a normally un-winnable confrontation with the combined forces of the employers and the government.

By contrast, the 1949 coal strike represented a major defeat in which a judicial approach to arbitration (where the tribunal imposes its own principles irrespective of the parties' wishes and power) played a significant part. Although the strike is conventionally seen as a struggle between Chifley's ALP government and communist troublemakers in the Miners' Federation, the origins of the dispute really lay in rank-and-file frustrations, bred by dreadful working conditions, and the rigid insistence of both the employers and Justice Gallagher (who chaired the Coal Industry Tribunal) that miners must tolerate them. Chifley's determination to tackle the strikers 'boots and all' was supported by an equally inflexible Gallagher. When the miners returned after a seven-week stoppage, they had gained none of their log of claims and had seen draconian anti-union legislation enacted, union and Communist Party officials fined and gaoled, and 13 000 troops working the coalfields.

While the post-war strike wave was in progress, the unions campaigned on two fronts: first for changes to the personnel and procedures of the Court and, second, for long-awaited increases to the basic wage and reductions in standard hours. Demands to reform the Court had grown throughout the war. They led to the 1947 amendments to the Act. These amendments, according to Perlman (1954: 31–40), were intended to free the Court from legalism and 'make it easier for unions to get what they wanted from arbitration'. Union hopes of an accommodative approach to dispute settlement were vested in the seventeen Commissioners appointed in 1947, a majority of whom were drawn from unions or a Labor background (Sheridan 1989: 155).

Despite some teething troubles about their coordination and integration, there is little doubt that the appointment of lay Commissioners was a step in the right direction and did much to cement an enduring role for the Court in settling disputes involving powerful unions. However, some judicial members of the tribunal were less able to come to grips with the realities of post-war union power.

The 1949–50 Basic Wage Case, like the 1953 case to follow, was complicated by several factors. The use of 'capacity to pay' as a criterion opened the door for the introduction of economic arguments and data that reduced the Court's capacity to communicate clear decisions; there were divisions between members of the bench; and union industrial action was a reminder of the shift in market power. The 1950 Basic Wage decision found the new Chief Judge (Kelly) in a minority when the Court approved the large sum of £1. The 1953 decision was more in keeping with the Court's leanings towards economic responsibility and awarded no increase while abolishing, during a period of inflation, automatic quarterly cost-of-living adjustments.

These decisions, and the equally cautious metal industry margins decisions of 1952 and 1954, were imposed in a climate where unions were simultaneously negotiating their claims in the field. Unwilling to depend solely on the Court, unions had developed the tactic of applying pressure in several places to win their claims at the point of least resistance. The 40-hour week was won first through direct negotiation and State legislation before it was granted in the 1947 Standard Hours Inquiry (1947 59 CAR 581). Similarly, the metal unions adopted the practice of negotiating basic wage and margins adjustments directly with employers before or during test cases such as the 1949–50 Basic Wage Inquiry. The long duration of this hearing caused the frustrated metal unions to apply overtime bans and bargain directly with employers. At the request of the Metal Trades Employers' Association, Kelly excluded the major metal trades unions from the hearing, spoke ominously about the risk of deregistration, and fined five unions for refusing to lift bans.

Kelly was Chief Judge of the Court from 1949 to 1956. Throughout this period, tensions grew between him and the unions. He would not accommodate powerful unions, and used fines and deregistration to deal with them. After 1950, the Court's major decisions were conservative, encouraging unions to use over-award bargaining instead. Isaac (1967: 118) has dated concerted over-award bargaining to 1954 when union action was sparked by the caution of the Court. According to Dabscheck (1983: 156), Kelly's approach to arbitration also lost him the support of the government. In 1956, the High Court decision in the *Boilermakers* case provided the government with an opportunity to push him upstairs. The case arose from a dispute in the Sydney dockyards that led to fines being imposed on two metal trades unions. In hearing an appeal by the Boilermakers' Society, the High Court ruled that the Court had exceeded its constitutional authority by exercising judicial powers. To resolve the problem, the government vested judicial functions in a new Industrial Court (under Kelly as Chief Judge) and reserved arbitral functions for the Commission (under Sir Richard Kirby as President). Kirby's appointment ushered in a more pragmatic approach to dispute settlement by the Commission (d'Alpuget 1977).

However, the issue of penalising strikers was not finally resolved. The metal trades employers had adopted the practice of seeking the insertion in awards of 'bans clauses' forbidding stoppages. This procedure was widely invoked after the lengthy Metal Trades Work Value Case in 1967–68. A majority decision by the Commission adjusted margins but allowed employers paying over-awards to absorb those work-value increases (Hutson 1971: 196–202). A rash of strikes broke out which, despite fines, did not end until the Commission amended the first decision. Once again, tension between unions and the Commission was at a peak. The ACTU president described the second decision as 'a really pathetic industrial exercise' (Hutson 1971: 203). But it was sufficient to hose down a difficult case.

In 1969, penal sanctions were applied again when the secretary of the Victorian tramways' union, Clarrie O'Shea, was imprisoned for non-payment of a fine; he was subsequently released when the fine was paid by an anonymous well-wisher. After this case, the major employers chose to make less use of penal sanctions and the government amended the Act to give the Commission more scope to resolve disputes by other means. As the long post-war boom came towards its end, the Commission found there was less call for it to participate in punishing striking unions, a role that had periodically poisoned its relations with them.

UNIONS AND INCOMES POLICIES: 1975–1991

Three major changes affected unionism in the early 1970s. First was the growth of white-collar unionism, which restored union membership from 49 per cent of the workforce in 1970 to 56 per cent in 1975. Some of this growth came from compulsory unionism agreements such as the 1969 retail agreement negotiated

ALBERT ERNEST MONK

Albert Monk promoted the ACTU as the accepted voice of the Australian trade union movement. He emigrated with his parents from England in 1910 at the age of 10 and was associated with the trade union movement and the Australian Labor Party all his working life. From 1924 he worked for the Melbourne Trades Hall Council. His connection with the ACTU began in 1927 when his skill as a shorthand writer earned him the position of minute secretary of the All-Australian Trade Union Congress that gave birth to the ACTU. He was the ACTU's first full-time secretary (1943–49) and president (1949–69).

Monk served on the governing body of the International Labour Organisation through most of the post-war years, becoming vice-president of the International Labour Conference in 1969. He was also a long-time member of the governing body of the World Federation of Trade Unions. From the late 1940s, he was an active member of the Immigration Advisory Council. He has been described as 'cautious, phlegmatic, somewhat retiring in manner, and a poor public speaker. He was also a most exceptional behind-the-scenes negotiator, with a flair for sensing and formulating acceptable lines of compromise, and for knowing when to stand firm' (Martin 1975: 21). When the federal government agreed to establish child endowment in 1942, Monk is credited with persuading the government to pay it to mothers instead of fathers (d'Alpuget 1977: 238).

Bob Hawke (1994: 45–6), who Monk appointed as an ACTU industrial officer in 1959 and who would succeed him as president in 1969, has this to say of him:

> To my mind he made two outstanding contributions which have served as a permanent monument to him within the trade union movement and the nation as a whole. First, he kept the ACTU as the one central trade union organisation against successive threats from the Left and Right to establish rival bodies. This is a tribute to his quiet, patient negotiating skills in times of crisis. Second, he gave strong and courageous support to the Labor Government's massive postwar immigration program against initial opposition of many sections of the trade union movement.

George Polites, Hawke's counterpart in the employers associations for many years, made this personal recollection:

During the Great Depression and its aftermath, the Arbitration Court made decisions which reflected the stringent economic circumstances of the time and which were the subject of considerable debate and industrial disruption. During this period Albert Monk, then a trade union official, was active in championing the cause of the unemployed. He led marches in Melbourne and displayed a strong militant approach to the problem. The advent of World War II and the implementation of the National Security Regulations put an end to much of this activity. Throughout this period, Albert Monk, as Secretary and later as President of the ACTU, stood firm in his belief that the Court should be maintained and retain independent powers. This was not a shared view among his constituents but Monk held it firmly and worked to ensure it prevailed within the trade union movement. He was a strong and determined advocate for causes in which he believed but accepted that compromise was better than all-out conformation. He frequently intervened in disputes, seeking to bring reason to bear in their resolution, generally by the use of the Court and later the Commission as the vehicle. Albert Monk made a significant contribution to maintaining community acceptance of the Court/Commission as an institution with a proper role to play in industrial relations and the maintenance of community standards.

'ARRESTED – AS HE SITS IN COURTROOM'

'In these circumstances, Clarence Lyell O'Shea, I have no alternative but to order you to be committed to prison, there to be detained until you make to the satisfaction of the court proper answers on your oral examination or until the court otherwise orders.'

With these words Mr Justice Kerr sentenced Tramways Union secretary Clarence O'Shea in the Commonwealth Industrial Court.

The hearing opened at exactly 10.30.

Mr Justice Kerr asked the court crier, Mr Keith Page, to call O'Shea's name.

The court crier called the name three times outside the court and then announced: 'No appearance, Your Honour'.

As Mr RL Gilbert, who appeared for the Industrial Registrar, was outlining the proceedings, O'Shea walked into the court at 10.32 and sat at the bar table.

Mr Justice Kerr said: 'You are a little late, but it is close enough to 10.30'.

The judge said O'Shea had been called for examination and to produce the books.

Mr Gilbert asked that O'Shea go into the witness box for examination.

O'Shea, from the bar table, said he did not wish to be examined. He challenged the authority of the court to deal with the matter and said he was merely defending the funds of the union.

Mr Justice Kerr told him he did not want to hear any speeches from him. He merely wanted him to enter the witness box for examination and produce the books.

When he entered the witness box, O'Shea refused to take the oath or make an affirmation.

(Melbourne *Herald*, 15 May 1969)

These dramatic court proceedings were reported by Bede Healy.

Clarrie O'Shea is led from the Industrial Court.

A union campaign against penal powers came to a head with the gaoling of Clarrie O'Shea in 1969. His union, the Victorian branch of the Australian Tramways and Motor Omnibus Employees Federation, had been conducting a series of one-day stoppages of Melbourne's tram services, and the Industrial Court had imposed fines totalling $8000.

Part of this amount had been obtained by the Registrar using garnishee proceedings on the union's bank account, and the purpose of this court proceeding was to identify further union funds.

O'Shea, the secretary of the Victorian branch, left the witness box after refusing to cooperate. He was arrested while sitting in the public area, fined $5000 and sentenced to imprisonment for contempt.

'Throughout the proceedings', reported Bede Healy, 'cheering from unionists outside the building could be heard inside the court on the first floor'. Several thousand unionists had marched with O'Shea down to the Court in Little Bourke Street. In the next days, a million more participated in stop-work protests in every mainland capital.

O'Shea, who was in poor health, remained adamant he would not comply with the court orders. With the ACTU executive urging all of its affiliates to refuse payment of any outstanding fines, the government lost its nerve. An anonymous 'benefactor' paid O'Shea's fine (Hagan 1981: 226).

Even though O'Shea had technically not purged his contempt, John Kerr ordered his release just six days after he went to prison. The government agreed to amend the Conciliation and Arbitration Act so that proceedings against a union for breach of bans clauses could not be taken until the Commission had issued a certificate for the matter to proceed to the Industrial (later Federal) Court following failure to resolve the matter by conciliation.

by ACTU secretary Harold Souter. The attitudes of white-collar workers were also changing to favour unionism. A second development was signalled by Bob Hawke's election as ACTU president in 1969. Educated and economically literate union leaders were becoming more numerous and powerful, while the long-running ideological struggle between Catholic and communist union factions was subsiding. Third, ACTU power was growing. Hawke's negotiation skills settled a series of oil industry strikes and gave the ACTU a role brokering settlements of major disputes. In the late 1970s, the ACTU's power to speak for all unions was increased by absorption of the major white-collar union federations. Finally, in the mid-1980s, the new ACTU leadership of Simon Crean and Bill Kelty oversaw a revolution in the internal organisation of the ACTU, employing a large professional secretariat and transforming the ACTU from a factional battleground into a political machine where every major union had a place on the executive, and Congress 'educated' delegates to support the Accord.

Growing ACTU power had much to do with increasing demands placed on it by national incomes policies. Before 1975 there was little interest by government and no agreement between unions and employers on the need for an incomes policy. These attitudes changed in 1973–74 when inflation rose to double digits (13 per cent in 1974) and unemployment rose from 1.3 per cent in 1974 to 4 per cent in 1975. The long post-war boom was over and an incomes policy was needed to restrain wage increases, thus allowing federal governments to reduce unemployment through expansionary fiscal and monetary policies.

The inflation of the early 1970s was fanned and sustained by a disorderly wage-fixing system. After the 1967–68 Metal Trades Work Value Case, an uncoordinated 'three-tier' bargaining system evolved in which National Wage Case increases were supplemented by industry award variations (often made by consent) and workplace over-award bargaining (Plowman 1981:6). Central control over wage determination was restored in April 1975 when the Commission, with the agreement of the government, the ACTU and the employers, adopted wage indexation. This system provided for award wages to be adjusted across the board to compensate for changes in prices and productivity, while all other forms of wage adjustment were restricted. National Wage cases took centre stage, giving the ACTU a key role both to advocate union wage claims (initially every three months and, after 1978, every six months) and also to persuade affiliates to observe restrictions on collective bargaining.

Between 1975 and 1977, unions accepted the principles of indexation because they considered them fair. They conformed with what Isaac (1977: 16–24) called the 'three conventional norms of the Australian labour market', that wages should be adjusted: to preserve workers' living standards; to allow them to share in growing national wealth; and to compensate particular groups for changes in work value. Developments in 1977 persuaded unions that indexation was no longer equitable, causing the system to break down. In 1976, the newly elected Fraser Coalition government inserted section 39(2) into the Act formally requiring the Commission to take account of the effect of its decisions on inflation and unemployment, as had been its practice before. Influenced by this explicit constraint, the Commission took the middle ground between union submissions seeking full indexation and government submissions seeking zero indexation. As full indexation was abandoned, unions looked for other ways to obtain wage increases. Throughout 1978 a contrived 'work value' wage round spread across the workforce, and in June 1979 the Commission threatened to end the system, claiming of unions and employers that 'one wants indexation without restraints and the other wants restraints without indexation' (ACAC 1979).

Wage indexation struggled on for a further two years, finally ending in July 1981 after a resources boom prompted a rash of pay claims and a campaign in the metal trades sought to reduce standard weekly hours from 40 to 35. The 'case-by-case' system that followed climaxed in the second wage explosion in less than a decade which, combined with drought and a world recession, dragged the economy into a deep trough. At the government's request, an emergency wage freeze was imposed for the last half of 1982. Shortly after, the Fraser government fell.

The Hawke ALP government elected in March 1983 negotiated an Accord with the ACTU that promised to restore wage indexation as part of a broad economic and social policy package. While the wage-fixing principles adopted by the Commission in September 1983 closely resembled the old 1975 principles, there was a new policy environment to win union support. Most important was the government's commitment to maintaining the 'social wage' through supportive social and taxation policies. Persuaded by this, and bound by their own undertakings to the Commission of 'no further claims', unions accepted wage indexation, which succeeded between 1983 and 1986 in holding down wage inflation and reducing unemployment (Chapman and Gruen 1990). After 1985, pressure upon the dollar and declining commodity prices forced the government and the ACTU to explore creative alternatives to indexation. Innovations in wage policy can be traced through five National Wage Case decisions between 1986 and 1989. In these, the Commission first diverted wage increases into future consumption through superannuation (in May 1986); then took a series of steps on the path towards enterprise productivity bargaining (March 1987, August 1988 and August 1989); and finally, in February 1989, adopted part of the ACTU's 'blueprint' to restructure the award wages system around a framework of minimum rates (linking key rates in the building, metalworking, transport, storemen, and clerical awards), supplementary payments, and paid rates awards.

The 'two-tier' and award-restructuring decisions between 1987 and 1989 constituted a revolutionary departure for Australian wage policy. Until 1987, industry and workplace bargaining were viewed with distrust by governments, the ACTU and employers alike as the cause of the wage breakouts in 1973–74 and 1981–82 (Hancock 1985). However, these lessons from history were discarded in the late 1980s. First, the ACTU and the government embraced decentralised bargaining as a means to re-skill Australia and deliver improved workplace productivity and worker incomes (ACTU/TDC 1987). Second, the Business Council of Australia (1989) promoted enterprise-based bargaining units as the key to improved business competitiveness.

As decentralised bargaining developed, the relationship between the ACTU and the Commission deteriorated. Much of this was due to the strain encountered by the ACTU, sandwiched between the government (committed to productivity bargaining for economic reasons) and its affiliates (who found these policies difficult to administer, frustratingly slow, and often unacceptable). While the government and employers treated second-tier negotiations as vital microeconomic reform, unions condemned the cost offsets as 'negative cost-cutting' and attacked the slow spread of wage increases. Union criticism intensified again in August 1989 when the Commission adopted the employers' 'page 10' agenda to remove from awards such prescriptive terms as part-time and casual ratios and loadings, and penalty rates. Unions saw this as an attack on hard-won award conditions.

BOB HAWKE AS INDUSTRIAL ADVOCATE

In 1952, the young Bob Hawke went to Oxford as a Rhodes scholar. While he began a degree in philosophy, politics and economics, he felt he was going over the ground already covered in his studies at the University of Western Australia and he switched to a postgraduate study of the Australian arbitration system.

Having completed it in 1956, he returned to doctoral studies in law at the Australian National University. The Dean, Geoffrey Sawer, encouraged him to pursue practical research. He therefore attended the Special Congress of the ACTU called in 1956 to consider the unions' approach to a basic wage case in that year. After assisting the preparation of this and subsequent cases, Hawke became the ACTU's research officer and was entrusted with the presentation of its submission in the 1959 Basic Wage Case hearing. In his memoirs, he recalls his early experiences as a union advocate (1994: 38–40):

> . . . as I began my preparation for the 1959 Basic Wage Case, there was still plenty of scepticism about me in various quarters. Tom Dougherty, General Secretary of the Australian Workers' Union (at that stage unaffiliated with the ACTU) ran a headline in *The Worker*: 'From Eggleston to Egghead'; while Judge Foster, sitting on his first basic wage Bench since 1950, got a backdoor message to Albert Monk complaining that he deserved to have the services of senior counsel, not some whippersnapper just out of university . . .

> In the event I was able to destroy the legal and economic underpinning of the 1953 decision which had abolished the automatic adjustments of the basic wage. It was a particular pleasure to demolish in the process the employers' witness, who had been trotted out year after year to give a thoroughly misleading story about company profits and whose evidence up to this point had been uncritically endorsed by the court . . .

> Some of the cases had their rough, tough and tense passages. Justice Frank Gallagher, who became a dear friend, boiled over with annoyance on one occasion, calling me a 'Domain Demosthenes and Hyde Park Cicero' – a flourish of rhetoric which later often gave us reason for a good laugh together. As an advocate I favoured none of the niceties and euphemisms beloved by lawyers when gently suggesting an alternative interpretation, or even the

At the fiftieth anniversary dinner of the ACTU in 1977, Bob Hawke joined hands with representatives of the employers, the unions and the Commission. Gough Whitlam watches from behind.

possibility of error, to the Bench. I was enraged by the enormous injustice done to Australian workers by the 1953 decision, and as the representative of the workers, I did not feel it in me in those early days to go beyond the necessary formalities of respect. The Arbitration Court had been manipulated at the workers' expense to give effect to an absurd and covert agenda. Its President, Dick Kirby, was innocent of this agenda, but his initial sensitivity to my harsh and uncompromising advocacy changed to a feeling of horror at what had been done. He and his colleagues seemed to sense the cause of my uncompromising passion, and became prepared to listen and, as they openly conceded, to learn. The arbitration judges were, with some exceptions, good men.

Tension also grew from the Commission's insistence on wage restraint while the slow process of award restructuring meandered on. Continued wage restraint was undermined by several circumstances in 1989 – a strong economy, falling unemployment, and huge executive salary increases – that aroused union pressures for a wages breakout. The ACTU distanced itself from one such claim by airline pilots, leaving the union to be destroyed by the airlines, the government and the Commission. But it could not separate itself from the groundswell of pay demands coming from major blue-collar affiliates.

Union discontent flared up during the September 1990 National Wage Case hearings. Bill Kelty spelt out to the Commission the ACTU's continuing commitment to the Accord Mark VI aggregate wage target of 7 per cent for 1990 and agreed with the need to make award restructuring succeed. He then attacked the Commission for making inconsistent decisions. The ACTU 'blueprint' was meant to end inter-union bickering and inflationary leapfrogging claims. Kelty claimed this framework was undermined by the Commission, concluding that 'an industrial tribunal with that characteristic [inconsistency] cannot survive' (AIRC 1990: 47–72). The decisions of individual Commissioners were singled out for condemnation, and a list presented. One example was the vehicle industry, where the production workers (under a paid rates award) had gained much more from award restructuring than the maintenance trades (under a minimum rates award).

Having proclaimed the importance of uniform treatment for all workers, Kelty then criticised the flow-on to the Commission itself of a 36 per cent salary increase awarded by the Remuneration Tribunal to Federal Court judges. If the wages principles prevented award workers getting pay increases on the basis of an historical nexus, how could the Commission that administered those principles receive such an increase? Kelty's forceful views prompted a quarrel with the bench about whether the Commission could deal with the ACTU without the cloud of 'bias' hanging over those proceedings, and whether unions would accept that the Commission was acting 'in equity and good conscience'. The working relationship between unions and the Commission was at breaking point.

The 1990 case ended with the ACTU withdrawing its 'no extra claims' commitment (the bedrock on which Accord wages discipline was built), indicating it would win the promised Accord wages outcome in the field. Indeed, an over-award campaign was already under way in the metal trades, stirring fears of the next wages explosion (Briggs 2001: 35). Ironically, the 1990 metal trades wages campaign came to nothing since many metal industry workplace militants had been rendered impotent by falling tariffs, lean production methods and, by late 1990, economic downturn.

Next year, the breach between the ACTU and the Commission widened. In March, the Gleeson Committee recommended to the government that the pay nexus between the Commission and the Federal Court should be severed. Some members of the Commission blamed the ACTU for this apparent threat to judicial status and independence. In April, the Commission rejected the ACTU's claim (backed by the government and most employers other than the Metal Trades Industry Association) for an enterprise bargaining system. The report of the first Australian Workplace Industrial Relations Survey showed that Australian workplaces were poorly equipped to handle workplace bargaining (Callus et al. 1991) and the Commission concurred, questioning the 'maturity' of the parties to conduct enterprise bargaining. Kelty's response was a stinging one: 'It is a sickening decision but there is no reason for the trade union movement to eat the vomit' (*Australian* 2 May 1991). Although the Commission reversed its position and adopted enterprise bargaining in October 1991, the relationship between the Commission and the ACTU lay in tatters.

MUTUAL DECLINE: 1991–2004

The tensions between the ACTU and the Commission eased throughout the 1990s. In part this was because the conditions that bred conflict no longer existed. Disciplined incomes policies gave way to the 'de-institutionalisation' of industrial relations, a term that refers to the decline of the collective institutions of industrial relations. In Australia this had four features relevant to the themes of this paper: falling union membership and power; the alteration of tribunal powers; the dominance of microeconomic criteria over social equity criteria in fixing wages and employment conditions; and shrinkage of the previously inclusive award system.

First was the declining proportion of employees belonging to unions. As early as 1987, the ACTU warned that Australian unionism was at risk from the

*Justice Deirdre Frances O'Connor, fourth
President of the Commission (1994–1997).*

employer attacks and falling membership already suffered by unions in Britain and the United States. At Congress that year, a plan was adopted (Future Strategies for the Union Movement) which recommended reorganising a still-fragmented union structure into twenty more-effective 'super unions'. With assistance from the government, this plan was largely accomplished; between 1987 and 1996 the number of unions was cut from 316 to 132. Another measure to be tried was Organising Works, which hired young officials to recruit young employees. Despite all this, membership continued to plummet. When the ALP lost office in 1996 to a coalition government hostile to unions, membership stood at 31.1 per cent of the workforce. By the end of the century, it had fallen below 25 per cent.

Second was the amendment of tribunal powers to obstruct unionism. The *Workplace Relations Act 1996* proclaimed 'freedom of association' for non-unionists, instead of the long-standing provision encouraging the organisation of trade unions. It abolished union preference, and allowed for non-union agreements and for 'enterprise unions' to break away from existing organisations. It restricted union organisers' rights of access to workplaces and strengthened prohibitions on industrial action. It circumscribed the Commission's powers to arbitrate, and it created a narrow list of 'allowable matters' that could be included in tribunal awards. One review of these changes concluded that 'unions are facing their most difficult challenges for at least 60 and possibly 100 years' (Lee and Peetz 1998: 19).

Third was the adoption of microeconomic factors in place of social equity principles in fixing wages and employment conditions. The wages system adopted in October 1991 led to a 'two-track' method of adjusting pay. Those unions strong enough for enterprise bargaining secured substantial wage increases, while those who were not so well organised received much smaller Safety Net adjustments; this allowed a union–non-union wage differential to grow (Wooden 2000: 143). Furthermore, within both the enterprise bargaining and the award sectors 'concession bargaining' progressively deregulated working time, further reducing earnings (ACIRRT 1999; Underhill et al. 2003: 155). A comparison of the 1990s with the period 1975–90 shows that pay and conditions have become more exposed to competitive market forces.

Fourth is contraction of the award system. In 1990, awards were estimated to apply to about 80 per cent of Australian wage and salary earners, many of whom topped up their pay through over-awards. Throughout the 1990s, the forms of employment regulation separated into three principal types: awards, registered collective agreements (federal and State), and individual contracts (registered and unregistered). Although award conditions may form a safety net under the other types of regulation, their practical significance in fixing actual employment conditions is more restricted. For example, estimates of methods of pay adjustment in 2000 found that 40.0 per cent of employees relied on individual contracts (38.2 per cent unregistered), 36.7 per cent on collective agreements (35.2 per cent registered), and only 23.2 per cent on awards (White et al. 2003: 71).

Since 1991, unions and tribunals have become weaker and market forces have assumed greater importance in determining pay and employment conditions. This process of de-institutionalisation can be largely explained by factors exogenous to industrial relations, such as structural change in the economy, increased product market competition, changing workforce demographics and the transmission of free-market ideologies. Yet the severity of the impact of de-institutionalisation on unions might have been due to the character of those institutions, especially excessive union reliance on industrial tribunals. According to Peetz (1998), the withdrawal of state support left unions without protection to combat growing employer anti-unionism. Legislation in the 1990s by the federal government and several States guaranteed freedom of association and outlawed union preference. Although employee sympathy for unions remained high, the collapse of compulsion caused membership to fall because unions were poorly equipped to organise. In addition, unions lacked the shop-floor strength

CENTENARY REFLECTIONS

The Commission conducted a ceremonial sitting on 5 June 2001 to mark the Centenary of Federation. Representatives of unions, employers and government reflected on the past and future of arbitration (AIRC 2001b: 93–4).

Sharan Burrow, the president of the ACTU, said that unions 'are passionate in their defence of this great institution'. She went on to consider two aspects of its operation:

Unions recognise that there is a tension between the right to free collective bargaining and the existence of compulsory arbitration, but in the interests of some equity for working Australians – particularly those without bargaining power – an appropriate balance between the two must be found. This balance would marry the best of the Australian vision of 1904 with the international standards of 2004. So within the walls of this institution, rich industrial and social history has been made.

In regard to equal pay for women, we take great pride in the success of women workers. I might add that some things have not changed all that much in a hundred years. There are a few more of you up there, but only one sister on this Bench. I am sure that will change in the twenty-first century, and the 50 per cent rule that the unions championed would not be a bad idea for all such major Australian institutions (AIRC 2001b: 31, 37).

Bob Herbert, the chief executive of the Australian Industry Group, thought further improvements were needed:

Australia should strive for a system which is far less adversarial. The emphasis must be to encourage agreed outcomes in the workplace. In my experience, employers do not want to sue their employees to force compliance; rather, the process to resolve genuine disputes must be simple, trusted, inexpensive and easily accessible. We certainly do not want six or eight competing systems in a country with a working population of just over eight million people to deliver such outcomes . . .

A hundred years of Federation have come and will soon go. Throughout the past century the Commission has played a significant role which we in the Australian Industry Group, as a major customer, are only too pleased to recognise. It has demonstrated a resilience and an adaptability, and has quite adequately protected the public interest. It is to the future that we must now direct our attention.

As we start the twenty-first century the circumstances of Australia are starkly different from what they were at the beginning of the twentieth century. When another hundred years pass, one can only hope that whatever kind of industrial relations system we have, whatever kind of tribunals then exist, there is mutuality of interests and we treat ourselves to a fair go all round (AIRC 2001b: 73, 75).

Peter Shergold, then the secretary of the Department of Employment, Workplace Relations and Small Business, and now the secretary of the Department of Prime Minister and Cabinet, offered a more historical perspective. Prior to his career in the public service, he had been an economic historian:

It seems to me that certain distinctively Australian values are as powerful today as in 1904. I speak here not of the more obvious characteristics of a fair go and mateship, for these terms – whether normative or positive – remain as ambiguous as they are powerful. Rather, I emphasise the notion of a safety net, of most Australians' continuing support for the shield of institutional government to protect those most in need . . .

There can be little doubt that there will continue to be strong arguments about the rules of engagement, about the objectives of the game, even – to dangerously extend the metaphor – about which code is being played. Hopefully there will be harmonisation of industrial relations systems and agreement on a single level playing-field.

But the attraction of an umpire able to make judgement and to exert authority remains strong in popular sentiment. If the past century tells us anything, it is that the Commission will continue to evolve this role, adapting itself to an ever-changing environment and, through its words or actions, playing a key role in the discourse that articulates public policy.

needed to resist employer attacks directly, making membership unattractive to many employees. These factors, allied with persistent unemployment and work-force changes favouring poorly unionised jobs, made the 1990s difficult years for unions.

CONCLUSION

Two arguments – the 'capture' and 'dependency' theories – were introduced in this chapter to explain the longevity and strength of the relationship between unions and the Commission. Both theories are helpful up to 1990. The capture theory throws light on several periods during the last century. For example, during Higgins' presidency the Court 'protected workers from a greedy public' (Scherer 1985: 94) by encouraging unionism, extending awards and developing egalitarian wage principles to protect the working class as a whole. The tribunal's willingness after 1945 to adopt an accommodative style, and to allow collective bargaining to supplement arbitral wage adjustments, gives further support for this theory. Second, the dependency theory fits with developments such as those in the 1920s when automatic basic wage adjustments and standard hours test cases relieved unions of much responsibility for industrial campaigns.

It is equally clear that both theories have their limitations. The capture theory goes too far. Episodes such as the 1919 seamen's strike and the disagreements in 1990–91 show there has been too much conflict between unions and the Commission to pretend that union principles 'captured' the Commission. Rather, the history of the Commission reveals a precarious balance between union princi-ples, the claims of employers, and the public interest. At times, unions have been disappointed because the balance tipped against them.

The dependency theory also overstates the case. The record of the past century suggests three limitations. First, the extent of union reliance on the arbitration system has varied over time depending on economic and political conditions. Second, union strategy reveals their reluctance to place 'all their eggs in one bas-ket', be it arbitration (federal or State), political action or collective bargaining. Rather, unions perfected the combination of these approaches. Third, the degree of reliance on arbitration varies between unions. Writing in 1952, JDB Miller (1952: 2) remarked how 'even today, some people say they can see a difference between "court-made unions" and those which had their beginnings before arbitration'. Unions of miners, transport workers, builders, and metalworkers have sustained traditions of militancy and self-reliance never present among many organisations of white-collar workers.

The age of incomes policies saw the relationship between unions and the Commission at its closest (when consensus on ideals prevailed) and also at its most distant (when adverse political or economic conditions made incomes policy unsustainable). At one such crisis point in 1990–91, the ACTU came close to rejecting the federal tribunal, a position not contemplated by Australian unions since the 10 per cent basic wage cut in 1931. Before the breach could be repaired, Australian industrial relations took the path of 'de-institutionalisation' pioneered in Britain, the United States and New Zealand. In the process, some of the century-old foundations of the arbitration system central to the capture and dependency theories were demolished. The capture theory reflects contemporary reality poorly since union legal rights have been stripped back, egalitarian wage-fixing principles diluted, union membership almost halved, and award coverage greatly reduced. Unions can no longer rely on state protection from competition in either product or labour markets. Similarly, the dependency theory is less apt after a decade in which unions have been thrown back on their own resources to protect their organisations and negotiate enterprise agreements. The capture and dependency theories never expressed exactly the relationship between unions and the Commission. Since 1991, the conditions that gave rise to those theories have changed and they have become even less relevant.

Also of decreasing applicability is the century-old commitment of Australian unions to 'inclusive' unionism. Since the late 1880s, the aim of the union movement was to represent and regulate the whole workforce. Falling membership and enterprise bargaining threaten the notion that Australian unions can still support such principles effectively without the restoration of state support.

8

MANAGING INDUSTRIAL CONFLICT

Bill Harley

The object of the measure is to prevent strikes

Alfred Deakin[1]

Arbitration was introduced primarily as a means to manage conflict in the wake of the 'big strikes' of the 1890s (Macintyre and Mitchell 1989: 16; Plowman 1989b: 135; Drago et al. 1992: 10–11).[2] The need for an institution to regulate conflict within a capitalist economy is summarised neatly by Higgins (1922a: 1):

> The war between the profit-maker and the wage-earner is always with us; and although not so dramatic or catastrophic as the present war in Europe,[3] it probably produces in the long run as much loss and suffering, not only to the actual combatants, but also to the public.

Inherent in the system from early in its life were two features that were intended to contribute to industrial peace. First, the role of the Court in providing working people with a living wage must be seen as being partly aimed at fostering peace. Higgins (1922a: 6) argued that 'One cannot conceive of industrial peace unless the employee has secured to him wages sufficient for the essentials of human existence' (see also Rickard 1984: 174–5). And further: 'the object of the Federal

Court is to preserve or restore industrial peace. The Federal Court . . . prescribes wages, etc., merely as incidental to the prevention or settlement of disputes' (Higgins 1922a: 31).

Second, the provision of a right for unions to represent workers, though not exclusively based on a concern with conflict management, was designed to overcome a major issue in dispute in the great strikes of the 1890s. Macintyre and Mitchell have argued that in these strikes the right of unions to represent workers was called into question by employers who insisted on freedom of contract. Accordingly, they contend, it was necessary to provide unions with a legitimate role in industrial relations, via registration, as a means to remove the potential for strikes over union recognition (Macintyre and Mitchell 1989: 15–16; see also Higgins 1922a: 15).

At the very heart of the system's procedure are the twin principles of conciliation – the process of bringing the parties to a dispute together and encouraging agreement – and arbitration – the imposition of a settlement on the parties. It has been a constant feature of the system that it should attempt first to conciliate and, should that fail, to arbitrate.[4] In a statement when he resigned from the vice-presidency of the Court in 1920, Powers noted that 'the Court is a Court of Conciliation as well as an Arbitration Court; and that that branch of the Court's work has been successfully used to the fullest extent possible' (1920 14 CAR vii).

It is sometimes asserted that conciliation has been largely ineffective and that arbitration has been the dominant means of dealing with disputes (Watson 1966). Unfortunately, there are no statistics available to allow an assessment of the relative importance of conciliation and arbitration. The Australian Bureau of Statistics collects data on industrial disputes, including the method of settlement, but these data do not distinguish between conciliation and arbitration. Even so, the claim that conciliation has been unimportant is highly questionable. It seems clear that those who designed the system meant conciliation to be the primary means by which disputes would be prevented and settled (Ross 2001: 17), and equally clear that conciliation has remained of central importance for most of the twentieth century (see Hancock 1985: 533–46).

Inherent in the concept of the 'new province for law and order' was that 'strikes and lockouts were seen as quasi-criminal acts . . . They should be prevented and where they could not be prevented they should be suppressed by the common

Norman Lindsay suggests that the ostensible purpose of the Court, to create a new province for law and order in place of strikes and lockouts, was negated by Higgins' willingness to allow striking workers to come before his tribunal.

criminal penalty of heavy fines' (Rawson 1986: 276). The 'law and order' philosophy behind this view was that, since conciliation and arbitration provided avenues for settlement in an orderly way, there was no need to use coercive pressure by means of strikes or lockouts (Fox et al. 1995: 98).

A further power available to the tribunal to deal with recalcitrant parties has been the power to deregister unions or employer associations (although all cases of deregistration have applied to unions). The *Commonwealth Conciliation and Arbitration Act 1904* included provision for deregistration and subsequent Acts have, with minor modifications, maintained this sanction. As noted above, the registration of industrial organisations has been a central feature of the arbitration system and especially important for unions because it has given them legal status and the right to represent their members in the system. Accordingly, although there have been cases of unions surviving without registration, deregistration generally poses a significant threat to their power and influence (Creighton, Ford and Mitchell 1993: 843–4).

Finally, although not strictly part of the arbitration system, employers have always had recourse to common law as a means of responding to industrial action. Torts of conspiracy and inducing breach of contract are part of Australian law, which means that in a technical sense virtually all industrial action is potentially illegal under common law (Creighton et al. 1993: 1161). Thus, employers who are targets of industrial action can expect to be able to take legal steps to stop the action (via an injunction) and to seek damages. Up until the 1970s, the common law was virtually never used by employers against unions, presumably because the arbitration system was a cheaper and quicker way of dealing with strikes or because, in industrial relations, it is necessary to maintain a relationship with unions, which could be damaged by common law action (Hancock 1985: 635).[5] More recently, the use of the common law has increased and this will be discussed later in the chapter.

ASSESSING THE PERFORMANCE OF THE ARBITRATION SYSTEM

Any assessment of the success or failure of arbitration in managing conflict must start by establishing criteria. This in turn means that we need to understand the nature of conflict and the role of state institutions in managing it. Conflict over power, authority and resources is a fundamental aspect of all social systems and the central task of government is to manage it, via institutions, rules and sanctions, in the interest of the public (Hobbes 1991). A major and persistent point of contention in liberal democratic societies has been how, and to what extent, the government should intervene to deal with conflict in industry.

The Australian system of conciliation and arbitration has incurred persistent criticism that it has not been the most effective means of dealing with conflict between employers and employees. Such criticism tends to be based on two arguments. The first is that arbitration *causes* conflict by virtue of the fact that it is inherently adversarial – that is, it pits unions and employers against one another in an adversarial legal setting where, inevitably, there will be a winner and a loser – and emphasises conflict at the expense of cooperation (Gutman 1986). This is not a new argument, but it has become increasingly fashionable in recent years. This 'unitarist' view of industrial relations emphasises common interest between individual employers and employees and suggests that 'third parties' – chiefly unions and regulatory agencies – are at best unnecessary and at worst harmful to good industrial relations (Deery et al. 2001: 7–12). It represents a fundamental challenge to the rationale of the arbitration system and has been used at least as a partial justification for the decentralisation of industrial relations in Australia since the late 1980s (BCA 1989).

It is difficult to accept this argument. While there is a good deal of common interest between employers and their employees, they also have conflicting interests (Iremonger et al. 1973: xiii; Ford and Hearn 1987: 7; Brown 1992: 236–7; Blyton and Turnbull 1998: 310–11). This tends to lock them into a relationship of 'structured antagonism' (Edwards 1986: 5–6), in the sense that no matter how harmonious their relations, there is always a latent conflict between them on pay, working conditions and other terms of employment – for such is the essence of the wage bargain. This suggests that some conflict is an inherent feature of the employment relationship and that it is caused by the nature of the relationship rather than by the institutional arrangements regulating it.

The second general criticism of arbitration is that, although conflict is inherent in industry and there is a need to manage it, arbitration is not the most effective way of doing so. This criticism is much more plausible than the first, and provides the basis on which this chapter attempts to evaluate the evidence on the performance of the system.

How then are we to judge the effectiveness of the system? While academics, consultants, practitioners and politicians have engaged in numerous, often acrimonious, debates over this question, it remains very difficult to provide a clear answer. In spite of the volume of literature produced by critics and defenders of the system, little progress has been made in resolving the differences (Mulvey 1986). Difficulties arise in setting criteria for effectiveness and in finding practical ways to measure performance.

Before dealing with these issues, it is important to make clear why the remainder of the chapter focuses on strikes (although it should not be inferred from this emphasis that lockouts have been unimportant).[6] Strikes are the most obvious and easily identifiable indicator of industrial conflict. Almost all the discussion, debate and data collection surrounding industrial disputes in advanced economies are concerned with strikes rather than other forms of conflict. Finally, the arbitration system grew primarily out of a concern with strikes. It is also important to recognise that conflict in the employment relationship can take a number of forms. First, conflict can be covert – that is, there can be conflict between employers and employees which is not actually manifested in any action by either party. Second, conflict can be manifested in ways other than strikes or lockouts, for example sabotage. Third, as noted above, not all disputes involve strikes or lockouts; it is possible for a dispute to exist without either of these forms of action taking place. Nonetheless, the concern of the chapter is with the most common overt manifestation of conflict – strikes – since the concern of the founders of arbitration was with the management of this particular manifestation of conflict. It should also be noted that the ABS figures on disputes do not distinguish between strikes and lockouts, so any such statistics reported in the chapter should be interpreted with this in mind.

Any assessment of the success or failure of arbitration must be made on a realistic basis. Although there has been considerable variation between countries in the incidence and nature of disputes, an enduring feature of the advanced industrialised economies during the twentieth century has been the existence of industrial disputation (Ross et al. 1998). Levels of industrial disputation depend on various economic and social factors that are largely beyond the control of systems of industrial relations regulation; these include unemployment levels, industry structure, rates of unionisation, and so on. Hence, there are very real limitations on the capacity of a tribunal to maintain total 'industrial peace'. Moreover, strikes can have positive outcomes, for example by hastening the resolution of a conflict (Ford and Hearn 1987: 11). The ability to pursue grievances and resolve conflicts of industrial interests through industrial action is also a feature of a healthy democratic political system (Cameron 1982: 1; DEIR 1984: 7). One of the strengths of liberal-democratic systems is their tolerance of conflict and recognition that conflict can be constructive, while a weakness of totalitarian regimes is their refusal to allow conflict (Schlesinger 1962). Probably the best example of a system that maintained 'industrial peace' was Nazi Germany, where organised industrial action was punished by death or incarceration in concentration camps (Neumann 1966: 344).

If we accept that the total suppression of disputes is neither possible nor desirable, how should the effectiveness of the system be judged? A useful starting point is to assess it on the terms used by its founders. In the wake of the economic and social consequences of the big strikes of the 1890s, their concern was 'to avert industrial conflict spilling into ruinous class conflict' (Macintyre and Mitchell 1989: 19). Since Australia has not experienced strikes of such magnitude since Federation, it could be inferred that the system has performed very well indeed.

A number of other features of the Australian strike record provide background for a more informed view of the functioning of the system. Unfortunately, it is not possible to compare patterns of disputation before and after the advent of arbitration, since data were collected only from 1913 onwards (CBCS 1918: 116). It is, however, possible to examine data for most of the life of the system. Although there are fluctuations from year to year, Australian Bureau of Statistics figures show that the trend has been a steady decline in days lost to industrial action per 1000 employees (which is the standard measure) since almost the start of the system (Figure 8.1). The trend is striking, with a decline from a high-point of nearly 2000 person days lost per 1000 workers early in the twentieth century to fewer than 50 person days at the beginning of the twenty-first century.

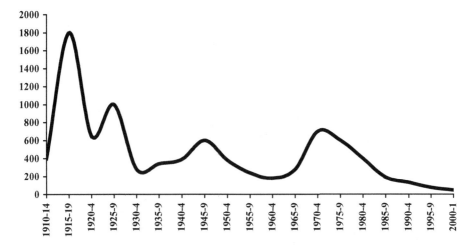

Figure 8.1 Person days lost to industrial action per 1000 employees, 1913–2001 (mean annual rate for five-year periods)
Note: Figure for 2000–01 is annual mean for those two years
Sources: Waters 1982; ABS 1983, 2003

Total days lost or days lost per 1000 workers are a useful measure, but tell only part of the story (Waters 1982). Figure 8.2 presents data on the size of strikes over time, showing that the trend has been towards strikes involving larger numbers of employees. This increase probably simply reflects the fact that, over the life of the system, the average size of firms and unions has increased. The number of disputes between 1913 and 2001 trended upwards till the mid-1970s, followed by a significant reversal in the last two decades of the twentieth century (Figure 8.3). Data on the duration of disputes (the number of person days lost per employee) reveal a substantial downward trend over the period (Figure 8.4).

The general picture which emerges is that the overall reduction in days lost has been associated with a tendency for larger, more frequent and shorter stoppages. There are many reasons for the changes in these different measures of strike activity at different periods, some of which will be considered later in the chapter. The important point to be made at this stage is that, over the life of the system, there has been a dramatic decrease in days lost to industrial action.

Additional useful information can be gleaned from data concerning causes of strikes. Waters (1982: 59), writing in the early 1980s, found that most disputes up until then had been concerned with pay and conditions:

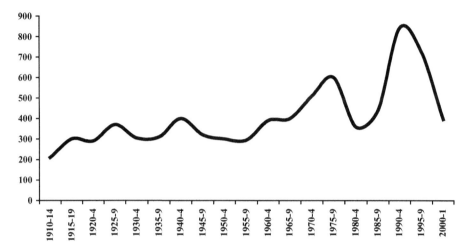

Figure 8.2 Size of disputes, 1913–2001 (employees per strike; mean annual rate for five-year periods)
Note: Figure for 2000–01 is annual mean for those two years
Sources: Waters 1982; ABS 1983, 2003

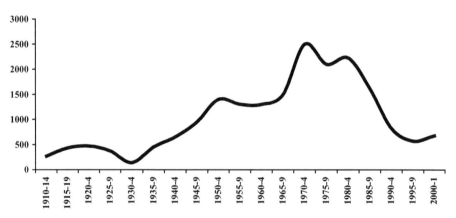

Figure 8.3 Number of disputes, 1913–2001 (mean annual rate for five-year periods)
Note: Figure for 2000–01 is annual mean for those two years
Sources: Waters 1982; ABS 1983, 2003

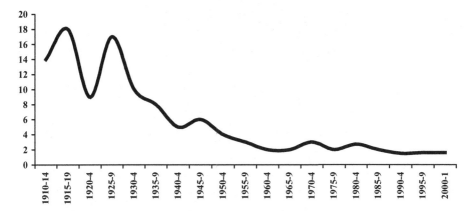

Figure 8.4 Duration of disputes, 1913–2001 (person days lost per employee; mean annual rate for five-year periods)
Note: Figure for 2000–01 is annual mean for those two years
Sources: Waters 1982; ABS 1983, 2003

if 'wage' issues are combined with another material issue, 'physical working conditions', it can be shown that together they never account for less than two-thirds of the time lost in any decade since 1910, and only in the war decades do they account for less than 80 per cent.

Examination of data on reasons for disputes (see Appendix A table), which begin where Waters finished, show that for the past two decades, with the exception of 1992, 'wages', 'physical working conditions' and 'managerial policy' accounted for at least 60 per cent of days lost (and, in a number of years, over 80 per cent). Although the bulk of days lost has been accounted for by these three sources of disputes throughout the life of the arbitration system, their relative importance has fluctuated considerably.

The figures suggest that the majority of days lost have concerned 'bread and butter' issues – pay, conditions and the management of workers – rather than larger social or political issues. It is likely that in many cases the disputes concerned relatively minor grievances about conditions. The plausibility of this suggestion is strengthened by examination of data on methods of settlement of disputes, which show a remarkably consistent picture: the majority of disputes were settled without any intervention by State or Commonwealth conciliation or arbitration, and often indeed without any formal negotiation (CBCS 1914, 1918, 1935, 1955, 1971a; ABS 2003).

The explanatory power of these statistics on reasons for disputes is limited by the broad categories used. Further, it is not possible to make a distinction on the basis of the data between 'interest' disputes – those about the setting of pay and conditions via awards or agreements – and 'rights' disputes – those concerning the rights of a party or parties under an award or agreement, or the interpretation of an award or an agreement.

A further important point is that, for most of the twentieth century, days lost to industrial action were concentrated in a few industries (see Appendix B table). During the twentieth century, mining and stevedoring have accounted for a disproportionate percentage of days lost, although the table also shows the changing importance of different industries, most notably the declining importance of 'blue collar' industries relative to 'white collar' industries. If the 'dispute prone' industries are removed from the equation, it is clear that the majority of Australian industries have experienced negligible levels of disputation. It is tempting to conclude from all this that the system has, in general, achieved effectively what it was intended to do – manage conflict in the public interest.

Another way to put this in perspective is to consider that, across the life of the system, the average loss of productive time to industrial disputes has been considerably less than a day a year for each employee (see Sheridan 1989: 6; ABS 2003). Dabscheck (1986a: 164–5) makes the additional point that if those who regard the system as a failure do so on the basis of lost working time and productivity, they might well look at productivity losses due to industrial accidents, alcohol and drug abuse, worker health, and so on, which he claims are much more costly to industry. Although reliable and comprehensive statistics for days lost to industrial accidents and illness are difficult to find (NOHSC 2000; Bohle and Quinlan 2000: 35–6), the available statistics support Dabscheck's claim. During the period 1992 to 1997 (the only years for which data are available), days lost to occupational injuries in Australia exceeded those lost to industrial action by a considerable margin (ILO 2002). If the effect of industrial disputes on productivity has been of relatively minor significance, then the system might appear to have been a success in keeping the industrial peace.

However, we are still confronted with problems of establishing causal links between arbitration and industrial disputation. Whether or not one regards the levels of industrial disputation in Australia over the life of the system as acceptable, the mere fact that they fall within the period when arbitration operated tells us nothing about whether arbitration has had any impact, positive or negative, on them.

In seeking to assess the system more rigorously, it is necessary to fall back on the principle of comparison, which is a central principle in social scientific research. That is, in asking how well the system has performed, it is necessary to ask 'compared with what?' since there is no widely agreed measure of what constitutes an acceptable level of industrial disputation. One such approach to assessing the performance of the system is to compare Australia's industrial disputes record with those of other countries (Creigh 1986). This approach is informed by a well-established tradition of international and comparative research in a number of areas of public policy (Castles 1991). Its rationale is that since it is not possible to create a counterfactual situation and there is no absolute standard for industrial disputation, the most sensible yardstick is the performance of comparable countries. International comparison at least provides some sort of norm.

There are a number of difficulties with this approach. First, there are problems of direct comparison between countries, since official statistics are gathered in different ways. According to the Department of Employment and Industrial Relations (DEIR) (1984: 151), Australian figures have been collected in ways that are likely to inflate the number of days lost to industrial action. Second, aggregate national-level figures on the magnitude of disputation mask differences in the form of disputes and such things as regional differences and differences in industry structures across countries. For example, since underground coal-mining is an industry that has historically been very strike-prone, countries with large coal industries will almost certainly perform badly in terms of days lost to industrial action regardless of their regulatory system. Oxnam (1965: 161) argues that such cross-national comparisons 'are unlikely to give more than mere first approximations and may even give rise to misleading impressions regarding the incidence of industrial conflict in some countries'.

If we put aside these problems for the moment and regard the various national data as comparable, the finding is that in historical terms Australia has experienced relatively high rates of days lost to industrial action (Creigh 1986; Ross et al. 1998). That is, taken at face value, the statistics suggest that Australia performs badly in international terms. On the basis of these results, some commentators have argued that the system of conciliation and arbitration has been a failure (Drago et al. 1992: 31). But this finding does not tell us anything about *causal* processes and hence cannot inform judgments on the success or failure of arbitration. A further note of caution is sounded by Creigh's (1986) analysis: he compares countries that have systems of collective bargaining with countries that use compulsory arbitration, and finds no statistically significant difference in strike outcomes. While again this tells us nothing about causation, it is consistent with the claim that the presence of arbitration, as opposed to an alternative system of industrial relations, does not determine levels of disputation.

On the basis of the evidence so far, it is clear that the Australian system has been accompanied by levels of disputation that are relatively high in international terms but have fallen far short of the 'ruinous class conflict' that the founders of the system wished to avoid. A fuller assessment of the system requires that the statistical data presented in this section be complemented with more detailed qualitative material as a means to fleshing out the story of arbitration and industrial conflict.

ARBITRATION IN HISTORICAL PERSPECTIVE

The historical account that follows is necessarily selective. Only a few issues and disputes are covered in each period. The emphasis is on change in an attempt to identify the chief developments, although it should be made clear that there has also been a great deal of continuity across the life of the system. The approach and the periodisation draw on the work of Waters (1982), although the periods used here do not exactly match his.

1904–1940: Direct action and sympathy strikes

The very early years of the Court involved it in few disputes (Deery et al. 2001: 131–2), chiefly because there were few disputes falling within its jurisdiction (1920 14 CAR vii). This helps to explain Higgins' (1922a: 35) claim that it had been almost entirely successful in averting conflict.

However, this period was the high-water mark for industrial disputes in Australia, at least in terms of days lost. This can be explained mainly by the fact that, although the number and size of strikes were low by historical standards during this period, their average duration was very high (Waters 1982: 50–5; Sheridan 1989: 6).[7] Mining, stevedoring and transport accounted for a high proportion of days lost (Waters 1982: 90–134; Sheridan 1989: 250–1). Strikes were less frequent than in any other period (as measured by the number of strikes per 100 000 workers) and, in general, smaller than in other periods (as measured by the number of employees involved), but on average the strikes during this period lasted longer than those in later periods.

The strike waves of 1916–20 and of 1927–30 saw more days lost to industrial action than at any other time since statistics have been collected (Gardner and Palmer 1997: 24–5). Turner (1979: 93) describes the 1916–20 period as one characterised by 'working-class revolt against the arbitration system and their political and industrial leaders'. Of particular note were the 1916 waterside workers' strike and mining strike and the New South Wales general strike of 1917.

The particular significance of the waterside workers' strike lies in two closely related features. First, it involved rank-and-file workers acting against the wishes of officials; and, second, there was the involvement of Industrial Workers of the World, or 'Wobblies' (Turner 1979: 83–4). As noted earlier, a key feature of arbitration was that it provided unions with a right to represent workers, precisely as a means to avoid arguments over the legitimacy of unions. This dispute began with men refusing to load flour as a protest against the high price of bread in Melbourne during the First World War. Although there was a federal award covering waterside workers, which included a no-strike agreement consented to by the Waterside Workers' Federation, the men undertook their action independently of the union. They informed a union official that 'he had nothing to do with the matter, that it was not a union affair at all; that there was no strike inasmuch as they "individually" refused' to load the flour (1916 10 CAR 31). Higgins, as President of the Court, ruled that it was indeed a strike, even if the union was not involved, but that he could not impose any penalty because the dispute did not extend beyond Victoria; nor had the men breached the award (1916 10 CAR 4).

The Court was also hampered by legal difficulties in the 1917 mineworkers' strike. It could not proceed to prosecute the Barrier Branch of the Amalgamated

Miners' Association of Broken Hill over strike action by the underground miners because only a section of the membership engaged in the strike, which had no union backing (1916 10 CAR 183). Ultimately, the Court awarded a pay increase and reduced working hours.

The general strike of 1917, which began in the tramways in Sydney, illustrates a slightly different limitation of the Court: the difficulty of dealing with 'sympathy' strikes. Higgins found these 'political' or 'sympathy' strikes – unions going out in support of other unions, while not being in a dispute with their own employers – perplexing (Rickard 1984: 237–8). He considered such action against the public interest in that it was incapable of settlement and detrimental to the principle of arbitration (1917 11 CAR 607). The difficulties posed by sympathy strikes are summed up well by Higgins, here commenting on the 1912 Brisbane tramways strike:

> Perhaps I should say here that I have nothing to do with the conduct of other unions in striking work in sympathy with the . . . men . . . what is called the 'general strike' does not extend beyond any one State; and however fatuous and futile the device of making a quarrel with innocent employers because the . . . men have a quarrel with their employers, or the device of taking on the public as an additional antagonist when you are fighting a powerful company, I cannot use any of the powers of the Court. (1912 6 CAR 41)

Between the strike waves of 1916–20 and 1927–30 there were noteworthy changes to the Act. The *Industrial Peace Act 1920* was passed, providing for the establishment of councils – apparently to conciliate disputes at national and local levels – and the establishment of special tribunals to cover particular industries (Commonwealth of Australia 1920: 60–7). Decisions of the special tribunals overruled those of the Court (Hancock 1985: 31). These developments would have weakened the power of the Court and they contributed to Higgins' resignation in 1921 (see Chapters 1 and 2).

The serious economic deterioration at the end of the 1920s brought rising unemployment, employer demands for reduced pay and conditions, worker discontent and industrial unrest (Foenander 1937: 78–9). There is some disagreement about the role of the Court at this time. For Waters (1982: 125–6), it was undoubtedly acting in the interests of employers by reducing awards to levels that unions could not in conscience accept, while using the penal powers to punish recalcitrant unions. Foenander (1937: 78–9) argues that the effective wage rate had increased during the 1920s and that the Court had also improved the lot of workers by means of reduced working hours, improved hygiene at work and better safety. He considered that the Court was placed in a difficult position by the declining economic situation and the resulting pressure from employers to reduce wage costs (Foenander 1937: 82). Moreover, section 25D, which was added to the Act in 1928, provided that the Court must take into account the probable economic effect on the community in general and the industry or industries concerned (Anderson 1929: 529). The key awards leading to strikes after 1928 involved a reduction of earnings and other losses in the case of the Waterside Workers and Timberworkers, and a lockout for refusal to accept a pay cut in the case of the Miners.

The Court used the penal powers freely. The powers of the Court under the 1904 Act (which included a provision banning strikes and lockouts) to fine unions for strikes and other award breaches had been expanded in the late 1920s (Sheridan 1989: 5; see Chapter 2). After Higgins' resignation, the Court had adopted a generally pro-employer stance and was willing to use the penal powers to punish recalcitrant unions. In 1930, the Scullin government removed many of the penal powers, rendering the arbitration process effectively a voluntary one, at least for unions (Waters 1982: 131; Rawson 1986: 277).

The preceding discussion highlights a number of important issues concerning the operation of the arbitration system during its first thirty-five years. First, direct action by workers, against the wishes of union officials, highlights a problem for a system that depends to a considerable degree on cooperation. While it was a compulsory system and could use sanctions, it still relied for its effectiveness on a willingness by employers and unions to abide by the 'rules of the game' and to come together in pursuit of agreement. This works against the view of those critics who suggest that a tribunal system encourages an adversarial approach. Moreover, as noted earlier, the system was designed to incorporate unions and required for its operation a capacity on the part of unions either to convince or to coerce their membership into acting collectively. In cases when

In this caricature, the judge accuses the worker of mistreating arbitration and unfaithfulness. He pleads in response, 'Yes, y'Honour, but she is so handy. Many's the time, y'Honor, I've got more out of the other lady, simply by threatning to go back to this one.'

union members failed to behave in this way, the system was unable to function as intended.

Second, this period highlights the inability of the system to deal with 'sympathy' or general strikes. Because the system was designed to deal with conflict over pay and conditions, and was based on awards, disputes by actors not directly engaged with each other via employment or award coverage posed major problems. In more recent years, however, this issue has been dealt with by sanctions against such action, which appear to have been a deterrent to sympathy action (see Chapter 3).

Finally, this period highlights the problem of using penal powers. This issue has remained a difficult one for most of the life of the system, with the fundamental problem being that a punitive approach sits uneasily with a system based to some extent on good faith and with an emphasis on cooperation. During this period, the tension was highlighted by the fact that, although penal powers were at times used to break unions and force their members back to work, nonetheless they frequently had the effect of exacerbating disputes rather than helping to resolve them.

1941–1968: Prosperity, economism and the resurgence of penal powers

Apart from the war years, this was a period of relative affluence as Keynesian-influenced economic policy and post-war reconstruction contributed to economic expansion and employment growth. In a growing economy with full employment, the union movement became stronger and more assertive in pursuit of improvements in wages and conditions.[8] Unions were able to take direct action to gain improvements that were beyond what was deemed acceptable by the Court or Government (see Rawson 1978: 125). The union strategy was to use industrial 'muscle' in a favourable environment rather than to rely on arbitration for improvements.

Although there was an increase in the frequency of strikes and while they were not significantly smaller than in the previous period, their duration became very markedly shorter (Waters 1982: 56–7). This probably reflects the fact that they were chiefly over issues of pay and conditions, which could be resolved more easily in a highly protected and expanding economy than the drawn-out defensive actions that were more common in the immediate pre-war years (Gardner and Palmer 1997: 27). The magnitude of disputes during this period was relatively small, with the exception of the second half of the 1940s when levels of disputation were surpassed only by the two strike waves discussed earlier (Sheridan 1989: 1).

During the Second World War, the Court had been assigned considerable additional powers and the effect of this was to make it the dominant tribunal (Deery et al. 2001: 138). In particular, although the Court was constrained by the maximum wage levels set by the *National Security Act 1939*, in 1940 a Regulation was introduced which gave it the power to deal with intra-state disputes and made explicit its ability to deal with industrial unrest before an official dispute was notified (Sheridan 1989: 10).[9] Sheridan (1989: 2–3) claims that the Court was 'cumbersome and conservative' in the early post-war years, and was instrumental in delaying union claims for higher wages as part of a government tactic of keeping wages down to cushion society 'from the full shock of labour's new found bargaining power'.

There were a number of major disputes during this period, but two are particularly noteworthy: the 1946 metal industry strike and the 1949 coal strike. The 1946 strike represents an excellent example of the kind of dispute which Waters (1982: 150) characterises as a 'prototype' of the strikes which followed and were typical of the period. These strikes were about margins, which had effectively been frozen by wartime regulations while the basic wage was adjusted quarterly for cost-of-living changes, thus greatly narrowing the relative gap between different rates. They were well-organised strikes and timed to coincide with labour shortages; and they were mostly successful, in large part because the workers involved in industrial action were skilled and thus valuable to employers.[10]

The second major dispute was the 1949 miners' strike, which lasted seven weeks and resulted in a defeat for the strikers. It was a highly politicised event, partly because the Communist Party of Australia was involved – although its role was almost certainly inflated and distorted by the media and government – and because it pitted the Chifley Labor government against workers (Sheridan 1989). In spite of the existence of the special tribunal for the coal industry, the

Court played an enforcement role in the dispute by fining unions and gaoling their leaders. The Labor government played a highly interventionist role, most notably by bringing in troops to work the coalfields. In addition to the punitive action of the Court and the use of troops, the hostile attitude of many other unions undermined the miners' union's action.

In the wake of the 1949 dispute, there were significant changes to the penal powers. Although many penal provisions were repealed by Scullin in 1930, a High Court decision in 1936 allowed for anti-strike clauses in awards. These anti-strike clauses were not taken up until 1951, when the Commonwealth Parliament began to empower the Court to penalise violations of 'bans clauses' (Waters 1982: 156). Meanwhile, punitive actions had become more prominent during the late 1940s. In 1947, in the *Forty Hours* case, the Court provided in some awards that reasonable overtime should be worked and that bans on overtime would invite a fine of £100 (Cameron 1982: 351). In 1951, the recently elected Liberal–Country Party federal government passed legislation to facilitate the imposition of penalties on striking unions by the Court (Rawson 1978: 126) by the insertion of a bans clause in awards (Cameron 1982: 351), breaches of which, on application by employers party to the award, would be punishable by fines or imprisonment for contempt.

From 1961 onwards, with increased industrial action by unions, the penal provisions were applied more frequently (Isaac 1971: 451). In a context of full employment, high levels of unionisation and high levels of tariff protection, unions were in a strong position to demand award increases and over-award payments. However, in 1968, there was unprecedented imposition of fines (and associated legal costs) on unions, prompted largely by high levels of strike action following the attempt by employers to absorb over-award payments in response to the 1967 work value decision (Isaac 1976: 345). Matters came to a head in 1969 when the ACTU mounted a concerted campaign against the use of penal clauses (ACTU 1969) following the gaoling of Clarrie O'Shea, an official of the Tramways Union, who refused to produce the union's books and to answer questions in connection with the attempts by the Industrial Registrar to collect outstanding fines from the union. Unions in metals and transport struck over the issue for 24 hours, resulting in a significant number of days lost (Rawson 1978: 136). Ultimately, a benefactor paid O'Shea's fine and he was released.

After this case, the penal powers were invoked more sparingly. More importantly, the Act was amended by the Whitlam government to slow the procedure down and provide some discretion in the application of penal sanctions. The bans clause could only be inserted by a presidential member of the Commission on evidence that industrial action was rife or imminent. Further, any orders sought for breaches of the clause also had to be heard by a presidential member, who had to establish that the breach had not ended before certifying that the matter be allowed to proceed to the Industrial Court (later the Federal Court) for any penalty to be considered. This intermediate step provided an opportunity for the presidential member to conciliate with a view to ending the industrial action and any further prosecution of the matter (McCallum et al. 1990: 671–5). The frequent use of legal sanctions might have caused more trouble than it fixed. Certainly, Sir Richard Kirby, who was President of the Commission during the 'high tide' of penal sanctions, argued that this was the case (d'Alpuget 1977: 233).

What are the lessons from this period? First, it again highlights the problem of penal powers, which appear to have exacerbated industrial action during the 1960s. Second, it reminds us again that the arbitration system relied on cooperation between the industrial parties. While direct action was not as prominent as earlier in the century, during this period 'muscular' unions were able to challenge the system and, in many cases, win. This point is further reinforced by the coal dispute. In this case, the Chifley government was willing to utilise the coercive power of the state to beat strong workers, in a situation where the Court acting alone might not have been able to settle the dispute.

1969–1982: The decline of the penal powers

During this period, with the exception of the years 1972–75, Australia was governed at the federal level by Liberal–Country Party (subsequently Liberal–National Party) coalition governments. This fact, the dismissal of the Whitlam government in 1975 and subsequent attempts to dismantle some of its key policies undoubtedly played a role in the growth of 'political' strikes at this time, although they probably also reflected a more general radicalisation of the polity in the late 1960s and early 1970s. A further important feature of the period was the fact

A hostile commentary on the striking timber-workers in 1929: they threaten to bring down the tree that shelters arbitration while the Trades Hall official watches on complacently.

that, like most OECD countries, Australia suffered from rising unemployment and 'stagflation' from the mid-1970s.

In concert with tariff reductions, these economic problems saw a decline in a number of traditional industries, most notably manufacturing, with the result that much of the strike action – at least in the latter half of the period – can be characterised as defensive, with workers and unions in declining sectors of the economy seeking to protect their pay and conditions. Again, during this period the shape of strikes was distinctive, with duration continuing to decline quite markedly, but frequency and size increasing (Waters 1982: 57).

Although political strikes are given prominence here, it is important to remember that most of the strike activity at this time was not politicised (Waters 1982: 172); rather, these political strikes highlight limitations of the system of arbitration. Similarly, the Clarrie O'Shea case has been discussed not because of its magnitude, but because of its bearing on penal sanctions. While the O'Shea case might be characterised as 'political' in the sense that it involved action aimed at changing the practice and legislative basis of a government institution – the arbitration system – a new and much more overtly political form of conflict came to prominence in the 1970s. These were strikes aimed explicitly at protesting government policy, which had no 'industrial' basis at all. A good example of this phenomenon was the 1976 Medibank strike, in which action was taken to protest at changes to the health-care funding arrangements established by the Whitlam government.

A number of relevant changes to the system took place under the Fraser coalition government during the latter part of the 1970s. The Industrial Relations Bureau, an independent agency, was established with the power to invoke the penal provisions independently of the employers concerned (Bennett and Cole 1989: 189).[11] There were also amendments to the Trade Practices Act in 1977, 1978 and 1980, which outlawed secondary and some primary boycotts. In the wake of the O'Shea case and the decline in the use of the penal powers of the Commission, the use of common law actions by employers increased – presumably because, until that time, penal sanctions had provided a speedier and cheaper alternative. Such common law actions decreased again in the late 1970s, quite probably because of the amendments to the Trade Practices Act (Creighton et al. 1993: 1223). In addition, a mechanism was inserted in the

Act to facilitate speedy deregistration of unions if the Commission declared that a particular action was adversely affecting the health, safety or welfare of the community. The power to deregister (and reinstate) unions was held by the Governor-General, thereby reducing the power of the Commission to deal with issues of deregistration (Bennett and Cole 1989: 190).

This period highlights two limitations of the system, neither of which was completely new. First, it was during this period that the extensive use of the Commission's penal powers was abandoned. Second, the limited ability of the system to deal with overtly 'political' disputes was highlighted. Some would suggest that this is a major defect of the system. It is probably asking too much, however, for a system designed to deal with industrial issues to deal also with political ones. As suggested earlier, the desire to impose 'peace' on the polity is problematic and often goes hand in hand with repression. A system of regulation designed to restrict the capacity of citizens to withdraw their labour as a form of protest might well be considered undesirable.

1983–1996: The Accord and the decentralisation of industrial relations

With the election of the Hawke Labor government in 1983, Australian industrial relations entered a period marked by two apparently opposite tendencies – the continued centralisation of wage-setting via the Accord, and then the decentralisation of wage-setting as enterprise bargaining took hold. Both developments had important implications for the arbitration system. This period witnessed a quite remarkable decline in days lost to industrial disputes. Although there has been a trend towards reduced days lost across the OECD during the 1990s, Australia outstripped other countries significantly in this regard, suggesting that something about the industrial arrangements in this country during the period was uniquely effective in managing industrial conflict (Isaac 1998: 707). Industrial action in white-collar industries increased in significance during the period and strikes became increasingly shorter and less frequent, although on average they were relatively large.

The significance of the Accord is chiefly that it represented an unusual experiment in Australian wage-setting, which had as one of its aims the attempt to

TRADE UNION VIEWS

Trade unions have welcomed some decisions of the Court and the Commission and condemned others. They have availed themselves of the opportunity for conciliation and arbitration of disputes, and resented the constraints the system has imposed on them. On first coming before the tribunal many union officials have found its rules, procedures and formal atmosphere to be unfamiliar; they have encountered officials who seem remote from their own background and experience. Over time, however, it is common for an appreciation of the tribunal and its members to develop.

Hence, when the Commission holds ceremonial sessions to farewell retiring members, representatives of the government, employers and the unions express their regard for the retiree. Ralph Willis appeared at the ceremonial session to farewell Sir John Moore on 29 October 1985 in his capacity as Minister for Industrial Relations, but he had previously been the ACTU's research officer and later its advocate. He recalled:

> . . . an event in the late 1970s when the Commission's premises were still at
> 451 Little Bourke Street, a location I recall with some nostalgia. A fire broke
> out in the basement while a National Wage hearing was in progress in the
> courtroom. The fire threatened to assume serious proportions. The fire brigade
> was called and the building was evacuated – except for those involved in the
> National Wage hearing, who were blissfully unaware of the drama being
> enacted outside the courtroom.
>
> The Chief Clerk of the Office of the Industrial Registrar hastily scrawled a note
> to your Honour informing you that the building was on fire and suggesting the
> Court be evacuated. He gave the note to your Honour's associate who handed
> it up to you. He then watched – in absolute consternation – as your Honour
> read it, placed it in your pocket and returned your attention to the no doubt
> fascinating submission an advocate was putting from the bar table. It was not
> until the advocate had completed his submission that your Honour announced
> that this might be a convenient time at which to adjourn the proceedings since
> you understood that the building was on fire.

Bill Kelty was the secretary of the ACTU from 1983 to 2000 and a robust critic of some of the Industrial Relation Commission's decisions. He looks back over a century of work by the Court and Commission thus:

Bill Kelty, the Secretary of the ACTU, and Jan Marsh, its research officer, played a key role in industrial relations during the Accord of the 1980s. In 1989, Marsh became a Deputy President of the Commission.

There is no such thing as a perfect wages system, and no such thing as a perfect institution. Both centralised and decentralised wages systems have advantages and limitations, and the mix changes over time. The best arrangement at one historical juncture will fetter social development at another.

But after 100 years and notwithstanding the great scope still for improvement, we do have an award wages system that, more effectively than in any other country, keeps minimum wages in touch with community standards and affords some comfort to low paid workers. This means that millions of workers' lives have been made better because of the involvement and decisions of the Australian Industrial Relations Commission and its predecessors. This is something in which Australia can take pride.

His successor, Greg Combet, writes that:

All of my practical experience has only reinforced my belief in the Commission as a vital institution in Australia. It has genuinely reconciled unnecessary conflict, it has constructively engaged in economic change, and it has effectively contributed to the living standards of working people. It has made a century of positive contribution to Australian industrial relations.

Martin Ferguson was the general secretary of the Federated Miscellaneous Workers' Union from 1984 to 1990, and president of the ACTU from 1990 to 1996. Here is his appraisal:

In my early years with the union movement it became clear to me that the Industrial Relations Commission never granted employees anything other than their rightful entitlement. To this day, I believe the fundamental duty of the Commission is to reinforce community standards: nothing more, nothing less. While this is justification enough for the existence of this unique Australian institution, the true benefit of the Commission to our society has been to 'humanise' the workplace through its rulings on equal pay, family entitlements, health and safety, rights for disabled workers, and superannuation.

(The views of Bill Kelty, Greg Combet and Martin Ferguson were obtained by Grant Belchamber.)

minimise days lost to industrial action. This aim probably reflected in large part the recognition by Labor politicians that if they were to retain government for any length of time, they must demonstrate their credentials as effective economic and industrial managers, able to avoid the levels of industrial disruption characteristic of the late 1970s and early 1980s, while keeping wage inflation under control.

Until 1987, the Accord involved a return to centralisation based on wage indexation and a set of principles similar to those which applied during 1975–81, but with the addition of undertakings made by unions that there would be no extra claims beyond those allowed under the principles (see Chapter 4). Chapman (1998: 631) argues that the 'no extra claims' arrangements meant that industrial action in pursuit of pay increases above those granted in National Wage cases was considered unacceptable by the Accord partners and that this reduced the levels of disputation. While different econometric studies have estimated different magnitudes of effects, it is fair to conclude that the Accord had a significant positive effect on strike activity and that this positive effect cannot be explained just by changes in factors such as inflation and employment growth that flowed from the Accord (Chapman 1998). Contrary to what one might expect, this positive impact continued even when the system became more decentralised.

Perhaps the outstanding dispute during this period was the 1989 Pilots' Strike. This strike was long and expensive, with one estimate that it cost more than $560 million in lost spending by tourists alone, and a much greater cost to the broader economy (Bray and Wailes 1999: 79). The key feature of the case is that it represented a direct challenge to the Commission and the Accord by a union that sought to gain a massive pay increase, well beyond those settled under the Accord and awarded by the Commission, by going outside the system and dealing directly with the airlines (Norington 1990). The union was comprehensively defeated, but only after very direct intervention by the Hawke government, chiefly in the form of financial assistance to the airlines and the provision of military aircraft to transport civilian passengers.

Although the Commission played a role at various points, it seems likely that without the active involvement of the federal government and the tacit consent of the unions to this government involvement, the Commission would have experienced great difficulty in dealing with the dispute. The dispute highlights the fact that the success of the Accord relied on commitment and consensus (Smith

1990: 250), and that when a union elected not to be bound by the Accord principles, it would fall by the wayside. Much like the 1949 coal strike, it seems that
without the direct intervention of the federal government and the position taken
by the ACTU, the Pilots might well have prevailed.

This period also witnessed perhaps the most important case of deregistration
of a union – that of the Builders Labourers Federation (BLF) in 1986. The BLF
was a long-established union chiefly representing less-skilled workers, with a long
history of militancy and was unpopular with many unions as well as governments
and employers. In its full-bench decision issuing a declaration as part of the
lengthy deregistration process,[12] the Commission stated:

> It has been established beyond question that the Builders Labourers
> Federation has rejected the standards of behaviour accepted by most
> trade unions in Australia. The Federation has no standards as that word
> is commonly understood but reacts to events according to the view taken
> at the time by the Federal Management Committee instead of a rational
> policy designed to advance the interests of the members. (cited in
> Stackpool 1986: 96)

As a sanction against unions that do not abide by the rules of the system,
deregistration is something of a two-edged sword. Should a large, strong and
militant union be deregistered, it is then free to use direct action and bargaining
outside the system to get what it wants. This means that deregistration is only
likely to be effective if there is another union or unions waiting to 'poach' members
of the deregistered union (Creighton et al. 1993: 844). In the case of the BLF,
there were other unions waiting in the wings and the majority of members went to
the Building Workers' Industrial Union (Gardner 1987: 109). Had this condition
not applied, it is doubtful that deregistration would have been an effective means
of destroying the union. It is noteworthy that of all the unions which have been
deregistered for industrial misconduct, the only one not to be re-registered in
due course was the BLF (Creighton et al. 1993: 844).

During this period a number of changes to the system had a bearing on the
Commission's capacity to manage conflict. The most significant change involved
the *Industrial Relations Reform Act 1993*, which was passed by the Keating

government and which formalised the operation of enterprise bargaining, with the right to strike in pursuit of workplace agreements. In a general sense, this legislation reduced the role of the Commission by shifting the centre of gravity of the system to the workplace level, but more specifically it reduced the powers of the Commission to refuse certification of collective agreements on the basis of the public interest test. Ludeke (1993: 328) argues that 'the federal industrial tribunal has been moved to the periphery of the new environment' created by the Act.

The passing of the Reform Act and the emphasis it placed on workplace bargaining led to renewed prominence for conciliation as a means to encourage the parties in workplace bargaining to reach agreement. The Act also granted limited immunity from the common law for industrial action, by introducing a 'cooling off' period to facilitate the settlement of disputes by conciliation (Macdermott 1997: 65). There was, however, also an increase in the use of common law action after 1993. Common law actions by employers had increased during the 1970s following the Clarrie O'Shea case, dropped off following changes to the Trade Practices Act in the late 1970s, and then started to increase again in the late 1980s in part because of the influence of 'New Right' groups such as the HR Nicholls Society (Williams 1988; Creighton et al. 1993: 1223). After 1993, its use increased further, perhaps reflecting the fact that the use of common law became increasingly legitimate in circumstances where it was, for the first time, lawful to take industrial action.[13]

The Accord represented a significant departure from previous approaches to managing conflict. While the arbitration system went on dealing with individual disputes, the Accord framework provided a 'macro' mechanism that appears to have functioned successfully in reducing overt conflict. This highlights the contribution to industrial peace derived from a quasi-corporatist institutional framework, in concert with the traditional arbitral system. Moreover, it suggests that the greater the extent to which cooperation can be institutionalised in this way, the greater the potential for the system to manage conflict.

A second issue highlighted by this period, and discussed earlier in the chapter, is the extent to which cooperative approaches to conflict management rely on the goodwill of the parties involved. In the case of the pilots' dispute, a single union was able to mount a major challenge to the system which, had it been

REDUCING INCONSISTENCY

The coexistence of federal and State industrial tribunals, and the inconsistency of outcomes, have been recurrent issues over the past 100 years. Here, Justice Giudice (2001), the President of the Australian Industrial Relations Commission, reflects on the reduction of inconsistency:

> The uncertainty generated by the mixture of laws which impact on employment relationships in this country constitutes an erosion of our freedoms and impacts on the quality of our society. Laws at State and federal level which ostensibly have the same purpose are often quite different in their effect. One only has to consider again the laws dealing with termination of employment. The conditions for access differ, the remedies differ both between States and federally, and there are other differences of significance. Treatment of costs is one example. The same general subject matter in some legislative schemes may be dealt with by a court, in others by an industrial commission and in others again by a specialist tribunal. The potential for different outcomes in similar factual situations is widespread. To the extent that the potential for inconsistent treatment is avoidable the situation is quite simply unfair . . .

> What can be done about these matters? The answer is obvious. Our industrial laws must be rationalised, as must the number of courts and tribunals exercising jurisdiction. By rationalisation I do not mean to suggest that there should only be one tribunal and one statute. But so far as possible, overlap between jurisdictions should be avoided. One way of reducing overlap is by drawing boundaries more clearly. Another way is to give each court or tribunal exclusive jurisdiction in the matters with which it is concerned. Only where overlap cannot be avoided should consideration be given to merging jurisdictions.

> Some progress has been made, however, and its significance should not be undervalued. By a cooperative approach between the federal and State industrial commissions much has been done in recent years to reduce inconsistency of treatment. This has been achieved through increased consultation, harmonisation of registry services and dual appointments.

Justice Geoffrey Michael Giudice, fifth President of the Commission (1997–)

For example, members of a number of State tribunals who are also members of the federal tribunal now sit regularly in the federal jurisdiction and exercise federal powers. There are also a number of respects in which the differences in the legislative frameworks have been reduced. While much remains to be done, for example there are still significant differences in the nature of the remedies available in relation to termination of employment, there may be some useful indications in what has occurred so far for the rationalisation of industrial relations laws and processes more generally.

The means by which rationalisation is to be achieved are far from obvious. Change is difficult because of the competing interests – ideological, commercial and political – which always lie just beneath the surface of industrial relations only to erupt into the open at the first mention of reform.

successful, would have done serious damage to the Accord. In much the same way as metalworkers in previous decades, the pilots attempted to use force to gain pay increases beyond the norms of the system.

1997–2003: Continued decentralisation

Following its election in 1996, the Howard government wasted little time in introducing a bill, which was passed as the *Workplace Relations and Other Legislation Amendment Act 1996* with some of the more radical provisions in the bill deleted, largely due to pressure in the Senate from the Australian Democrats. Nonetheless, the Act took up where the 1993 Reform Act had left off and continued a policy trajectory of decentralisation and a further reduced role for arbitration (Macdermott 1997: 61).

Protected industrial action in pursuit of agreements (interest disputes), which had been introduced under the Reform Act (Naughton 1994: 6), continued under the Workplace Relations Act (Macdermott 1997: 60).[14] Designed specifically to contribute to reduced levels of disputation, industrial action during the currency of a certified agreement or an Australian Workplace Agreement (rights disputes) was prohibited (Macdermott 1997: 65). The Commission has the power to order that such industrial action cease (section 127) and the aggrieved party may seek an injunction from the Federal Court. To avoid industrial action, certified agreements are required to include dispute resolution clauses that allow dispute resolution to be facilitated by the Commission conciliating.[15]

The nature of changes to the system can best be illustrated by considering a dispute in which the Commission had virtually no involvement: the 1998 waterfront dispute. It is noteworthy that, in spite of being widely recognised as a momentous dispute, in a technical sense it was not a dispute at all and the days lost during it do not appear in official statistics (Ellem 1999: 134–6). The story of the waterfront dispute is an extraordinary one, with the labyrinthine strategies of Patrick Stevedores and the extensive though often covert involvement of the Howard government (Wiseman 1998; Glasbeek 1998; Dabscheck 1998). Like the Maritime Strike of the 1890s, which played a role in spawning arbitration, this dispute was about unionism. More particularly, it was about an attempt by an employer (with government support) to exclude the Maritime Union of Australia

(MUA) and to move to a non-union workforce covered by individual employment contracts (Griffin and Svensen 1998). To that extent it represented a challenge to key aspects of the arbitration system.

It would be incorrect to say that the Commission had no role in the dispute – notably, it issued an order instructing the MUA to cease stoppages and bans – but this case was largely fought out in the courts. Under the terms of the Workplace Relations Act, the Commission did not have the power to intervene and impose a settlement on the parties (Frazer 1999: 80). Instead, the case was dealt with in the Victorian Supreme Court and the Federal Court. Griffin and Svensen (1998: 204) maintain that:

> From an industrial relations perspective, one of the most striking features of the case was the involvement of a variety of state and federal courts, with their plethora of injunctions, that, in a sense, filled the breach created by the erosion of the powers of the AIRC to resolve disputes. This winding back of the powers of the AIRC was supposed to produce settlements at the workplace; instead it appears likely that increasing use will be made of state and federal civil and criminal courts.

A further feature of the dispute was the lack of action by other unions. Sheldon and Thornthwaite (1999b: 157) argue that the waterfront dispute demonstrated the effectiveness of the secondary boycott provisions of the Act. They suggest that in the past it would have been expected that there would have been sympathetic action by other unions, but that the secondary boycott arrangements discouraged such action. The waterfront dispute highlights the massive changes that have taken place in the industrial relations system since the 1990s and the very real limits placed on arbitration by the legislative reforms begun by the Reform Act and continued with the Workplace Relations Act.

A noteworthy feature of this post-Accord period is that, even as the system was radically decentralised, the trend towards reduced levels of disputation was maintained, suggesting that it was not simply the centralisation of wage-fixing that had reduced days lost during the life of the Accord. It is not entirely clear why there has continued to be such a marked decline in days lost even after the institutional arrangements of the Accord era have been dismantled. Chapman

(1998) suggests that it might reflect a legacy of cultural change in the sphere of industrial relations, while Isaac (1998) is sceptical of this claim and gives a greater role to economic changes since Labor lost office. It is noteworthy that the decline in days lost is not a uniquely Australian phenomenon and that the same pattern is observed across many of the OECD countries, suggesting that the causes go beyond national-level regulatory mechanisms. One plausible explanation is that shifts in the industry and occupational structures of most advanced economies – towards services and away from industrial production – have played a role by reducing the significance of industries and occupations traditionally associated with industrial militancy.

The Accord produced substantial growth in the economy and in employment, with industrial disputation restrained to an extent by the institutional arrangements. Since then, however, the reduction in disputation largely reflects the weakened position of labour. Union density has continued to decline and although unemployment has fallen, it remains high while employment prospects for large numbers of workers are less secure because of global competition and the spread of new employment practices such as outsourcing, downsizing, casualisation, and labour hire arrangements.

CONCLUSION

How are we to assess the success or failure of the arbitration system in managing conflict? Clearly it has not been possible to test the success of the system in a conclusive way, but equally clearly a measured assessment of the history of arbitration leads to the conclusion that it has been an effective means of managing conflict. Has it been the best possible mechanism? This remains a question that cannot be answered, but during the life of the system industrial conflict has never posed a threat to the economic or political stability of the nation. To that extent, the system must be judged a success.

The strength of the system has been that, despite the arguments made by some critics, it encourages cooperation. To say this is not to gloss over the fact that the tribunal is a site of conflict and that, in many cases, employers and unions have been engaged in bitter struggles within it. Rather, it is to argue that, like many institutions in liberal democracies, the arbitration system has encouraged (and admittedly sometimes forced) representatives of capital and labour to come together in an orderly manner in pursuit of agreement. It has provided an arena in which class conflict is channelled into orderly processing of issues, rather than exploding into industrial warfare. There have been occasions when major conflicts have erupted that the tribunal has been unable to resolve without the direct intervention of the government, but in its normal operations this has not been the case.

The major limitations of the system relate chiefly to situations where its broadly cooperative nature has been challenged, either by the excessive use of punitive measures by the tribunal or because parties have elected not to 'play by the rules' and have gone outside the system, sometimes to their grief. The system has by no means done away with overt displays of conflict and it is possible that some other institutional arrangement might have been more effective in realising total 'peace'. It is difficult to imagine, however, that this would have taken place without the very heavy use of coercion and repression. For the most part, this has been avoided in the Australian context and this is something to be applauded rather than regretted.

A further sign of the strength of the Australian arbitration system is that it has shown itself to be adaptable and flexible over time. Both supporters and critics have tended to present the more recent changes to the system as a process of decline or 'crumbling' (Gardner and Palmer 1997: 37). It is undeniable that these changes have involved quite different approaches from the past, but there has also been continuity. While it is easy during a period of historically low levels of disputation to downplay the role of arbitration in managing conflict, it is important to recognise that in the future this conflict management role may well come to the fore once more (Giudice 2003: 15).

Although arbitration was introduced as a means to avert major industrial conflict, it is important to remember that at the time the system began to operate the context was one of significant high unemployment and union weakness; the emphasis in the initial operation of the Court was on protecting workers who were in a position of weakness (Isaac 1976: 325–6). Its jurisdiction has been narrowed and currently its role emphasises the protection of the weak via 'safety net' adjustments and the application of the 'no disadvantage' test. To this extent, it is similar to Higgins' Court early in the twentieth century.

It would be a mistake, however, to assume that this means that arbitration's role as a manager of conflict is in terminal decline. It is entirely possible, should economic conditions change, that labour will become more assertive and levels of industrial disputation could well rise. Should that happen, the role of the arbitration system will no doubt change to meet the changing circumstances. Clearly, the institutional arrangements regulating conflict in Australia will continue to change, but it is unlikely that a time will come in the foreseeable future when they will no longer be needed. The force of long history on institutional arrangements should not be discounted.

Appendix A. *Days lost to industrial disputes, by reason for dispute, 1983–2002*

	Wages	Leave, pensions, compensation	Managerial policy	Physical working conditions	Trade unionism	Hours of work	Other causes	TOTAL
1983	207,200 (12%)	NA	735,100 (43%)	532,200 (31%)	55,300 (3%)	84,600 (5%)	77,600 (5%)	1,691,900 (100%)
1984	308,400 (25%)	NA	406,900 (32%)	202,900 (16%)	109,500 (9%)	73,400 (6%)	151,000 (12%)	1,252,200 (100%)
1985	301,700 (23%)	41,500 (3%)	323,500 (25%)	193,500 (15%)	215,600 (17%)	49,500 (4%)	178,600 (14%)	1,303,900 (100%)
1986	546,300 (40%)	148,000 (11%)	486,000 (35%)	93,700 (7%)	45,700 (3%)	13,200 (1%)	33,300 (2%)	1,366,200 (100%)
1987	519,700 (42%)	195,000 (16%)	330,900 (27%)	88,700 (7%)	36,800 (3%)	20,300 (2%)	18,100 (1%)	1,209,500 (100%)
1988	507,900 (30%)	50,000 (3%)	897,600 (52%)	158,100 (9%)	34,000 (2%)	31,500 (2%)	34,600 (2%)	1,713,700 (100%)
1989	169,600 (14%)	145,800 (12%)	639,300 (52%)	61,900 (5%)	73,300 (6%)	5,600 (<1%)	124,200 (10%)	1,219,800 (100%)
1990	154,500 (11%)	20,500 (1%)	1,060,300 (75%)	99,300 (7%)	52,400 (4%)	4,300 (<1%)	29,000 (2%)	1,420,300 (100%)
1991	37,800 (2%)	22,600 (1%)	869,400 (54%)	60,800 (4%)	31,200 (2%)	3,900 (<1%)	597,400 (37%)	1,623,100 (100%)
1992	23,200 (2%)	15,000 (2%)	224,000 (24%)	27,200 (3%)	47,200 (5%)	300 (<1%)	606,100 (64%)	943,000 (100%)
1993	137,000 (23%)	12,300 (2%)	271,200 (46%)	18,900 (3%)	10,500 (2%)	3,500 (1%)	134,100 (23%)	587,300 (100%)
1994	140,600 (27%)	19,000 (4%)	158,900 (31%)	17,600 (3%)	7,800 (2%)	5,400 (1%)	165,600 (32%)	514,800 (100%)
1995	155,700 (28%)	16,400 (3%)	207,300 (37%)	24,600 (4%)	22,800 (4%)	2,700 (<1%)	127,300 (23%)	556,700 (100%)
1996	247,100 (27%)	0 (0%)	426,500 (46%)	19,600 (2%)	46,600 (5%)	8,300 (1%)	183,300 (20%)	931,400 (100%)
1997	108,700 (24%)	4,300 (1%)	234,400 (53%)	14,900 (3%)	7,200 (%)	4,000 (1%)	71,900 (16%)	445,300 (100%)
1998	37,300 (6%)	3,600 (1%)	378,500 (62%)	41,600 (7%)	13,300 (2%)	100 (<1%)	138,400 (23%)	612,900 (100%)
1999	42,800 (7%)	38,200 (6%)	387,700 (60%)	33,600 (5%)	7,000 (1%)	700 (<1%)	135,800 (21%)	645,700 (100%)
2000	77,300 (17%)	11,300 (2%)	280,400 (61%)	27,100 (6%)	6,400 (1%)	1,400 (<1%)	56,100 (12%)	460,000 (100%)
2001	14,500 (4%)	15,800 (4%)	224,300 (59%)	38,000 (10%)	11,000 (3%)	3,100 (1%)	74,700 (20%)	381,500 (100%)
2002	9,700 (4%)	3,900 (2%)	176,000 (71%)	30,000 (12%)	13,000 (5%)	1,900 (1%)	13,300 (5%)	247,800 (100%)

Notes: Available data prior to 1985 do not contain the category 'Leave, pensions, compensation'. 'Managerial policy' and 'Physical working conditions' cover disciplinary action, the promotion of employers, the employment of particular individuals, personal disagreements between employees, and supervisory staff, and disputes arising from the computation of wages, leave, etc., in individual cases. 'Trade unionism' covers stoppages over employment of non-unionists, inter-union and intra-union disputes, disputes about recognition of union activities, and sympathy stoppages in support of employees in another industry. 'Other causes' include political matters and where the cause of the stoppage is not officially made known to management.

Sources: ABS 1985, 2003

Appendix B. Days lost to industrial disputes, number of disputes and duration of disputes, by industry, selected years and industries, 1913–93

	1913			1933			1953			1973			1993		
	Days lost	No. of disputes	Duration	Days lost	No. of disputes	Duration	Days lost	No. of disputes	Duration	Days lost	No. of disputes	Duration	Days lost	No. of disputes	Duration
Mining	383,335 (61%)	103 (50%)	11	75,513 (67%)	58 (64%)	3	397,671 (38%)	950	3	242,800 (9%)	340	3	93,000 (15%)	190	2
Rail/tramways	70,887 (11%)	16 (8%)	11	100 (1%)	1 (1%)	2	32,659 (3%)	27	1	32,500 (1%)	57	1	*	*	*
Shipping/ stevedoring	37,108 (6%)	18 (9%)	16	*	*	*	177,030 (17%)	280	1	49,500 (2%)	275	1	*	*	*
Manufacturing	74,328 (12%)	33 (16%)	15	31,505 (28%)	15 (17%)	6	351,672 (33%)	142	2	1,462,200 (55%)	1,151	5	238,100 (37%)	170	1
Building/ Construction	2,303 (<1%)	10 (5%)	10	*	*	*	67,506 (6%)	41	8	439,300 (17%)	276	3	13,100 (2%)	27	1
Education/ Health/ Community Services	*	*	*	*	*	*	*	*	*	*	*	*	147,500 (23%)	49	1
All Industries	623,528	208	12	111,956	90	4	1,050,830	1,459	2	2,634,700	2,538	3	635,800	610	1

Notes: These figures are for the whole of Australia and include strikes and lockouts which took place within single states and territories as well as interstate disputes; * indicates that no figures are provided for a particular industry in a given year; industry classifications have changed over time and the labels in the left-hand column are generic. 'Duration' is the number of days lost per worker involved (days lost divided by number of people involved). For some years separate figures are reported for workers directly involved (i.e. on strike or locked out) and indirectly involved (i.e. thrown out of work due to the dispute), while for others only a total figure is given. For the sake of accurate comparison, the total figure is used for all years.

Sources: CBCS 1914, 1935, 1955; ABS 1974, 1994, 2003

APPENDIX I
MAIN TRIBUNAL
CHANGES

1905 Commonwealth Court of Conciliation and Arbitration; appointment of President, Industrial Registrar and five Deputy Registrars

1911 Federal public servants brought within jurisdiction of the Court

1913 Addition of two Deputy Presidents, appointed for seven years

1920 Public servants removed from jurisdiction of the Court and a Public Service Arbitrator created

1926 Status of President and Deputy Presidents changed to Chief Judge and Judges, appointed for life; provision for Conciliation Commissioners

1947 Restriction of powers of Judges, Conciliation Commissioners to deal with other matters

1956 Separation of Conciliation and Arbitration Commission and Industrial Court

1973 Commission renamed Australian Conciliation and Arbitration Commission

1977 Court becomes Industrial Division of the new Federal Court of Australia

1988 Commission renamed Australian Industrial Relations Commission

1990 Dual appointees: members whose primary appointment continues to be with State industrial tribunals

1992 Office of Vice President and Senior Deputy President created

1993 Court's functions assumed by the Industrial Relations Court of Australia

1997 Court's functions returned to the Federal Court

APPENDIX II
MEMBERSHIP

COMMONWEALTH COURT OF CONCILIATION AND ARBITRATION 1905–1956

Presidents

O'Connor, Justice Richard Edward, 1905–07
Higgins, Justice Henry Bournes, 1907–21
Powers, Sir Charles, KCMG, 1921–26

Deputy Presidents

Powers, Sir Charles, KCMG, 1913–21
Isaacs, Sir Isaac Alfred, PC, GCB, GCMG, 1917
Starke, Sir Hayden Erskine, KCMG, 1920–21
Gavan Duffy, Sir Frank, PC, KCMG, 1921–22
Rich, Sir George Edward, PC, KCMG, 1921–22
Quick, Sir John, 1922–30
Webb, Noel Augustin, 1922–27

Chief Judges

Dethridge, George James, 1926–38
Beeby, Sir George Stephenson, KBE, 1939–41

Piper, Harold Bayard, 1941–47
Drake-Brockman, Edmund Alfred, CB, CMG, DSO, 1947–49
Kelly, Sir William Raymond, KBE, 1949–56

Judges

Lukin, Lionel Oscar, 1926–43
Beeby, Sir George Stephenson, KBE, 1926–39
Drake-Brockman, Edmund Alfred, CB, CMG, DSO, 1927–47
Piper, Harold Bayard, 1938–41
O'Mara, Thomas, 1939–46
Kelly, Sir William Raymond, KBE, 1941–49
Foster, Alfred William, 1944–56
Sugerman, Bernard, 1946–47
Kirby, Sir Richard Clarence, AC, 1947–56
Dunphy, Edward Arthur, 1949–56[1]
Wright, Sydney Charles Grenville, 1951–56
McIntyre, Malcolm William Donald, 1952–53
Morgan, Sir Edward James Ranembe, 1952–56[2]
Ashburner, Richard, 1954–56

Conciliation Commissioners

Chief Conciliation Commissioners

Mooney, George Austin, 1947–54
Galvin, John Michael, CBE, 1954–56

Conciliation Commissioners

Stewart, Alexander Murdoch, 1927–29
Coneybeer, Edmund Harold, 1930–34
Stewart, Murray Milne, OBE, 1940–53
Morrison, Donald Vincent, 1940–52
Middlemiss, Anthony Ronald, 1941–45
Mooney, George Austin, 1941–47
Rowlands, Edgar Harrold, 1942–47

Blakeley, Arthur, 1941–52
Portus, John Hereford, OBE, DFC, 1944–56
Willis, Albert Charles, 1944–46
Craig, Henry John, 1944–45
Findlay, George Andrew, 1944–56
Austin, Leslie Paul, 1947–56
Blackburn, Arthur Seaforth, VC, CMG, CBE, 1947–55
Buckland, George Henry, 1947–54
Donovan, John Rawdon, 1947–56
Dwyer, John Vincent, 1947–53
Kelly, Francis Daniel, 1947–56
Wallis, Alfred Russell, 1947–53
Galvin, John Michael, CBE, 1947–54
Knight, Hamilton, 1947–53
Hewitt, Joseph Martin, OBE, 1947–56
Hall, Vivian Gerald, 1949–53
Tonkin, Eric William, 1949–56
Chambers, Edward Alfred Charles, CBE, 1954–56
Webb, Frederick John, 1954–56

COMMONWEALTH CONCILIATION AND ARBITRATION COMMISSION 1956–1973

AUSTRALIAN CONCILIATION AND ARBITRATION COMMISSION 1973–1988

AUSTRALIAN INDUSTRIAL RELATIONS COMMISSION 1988–

Presidents

Kirby, Sir Richard Clarence, AC, 1956–73
Moore, Sir John Cochrane, AC, 1973–85
Maddern, Justice Barry James, AC, 1985–94
O'Connor, Justice Deirdre Frances, 1994–97
Giudice, Justice Geoffrey Michael, 1997–

Vice Presidents

Moore, Michael Francis, 1992–94

Ross, Iain James Kerr, 1994–

McIntyre, Anthony William Donald, 1994–2002

Lawler, Michael Joseph, 2002–

Senior Deputy Presidents[3] and Deputy Presidents

Foster, Justice Alfred William, 1956–62

Wright, Justice Sydney Charles Grenville, 1956–70

Ashburner, Justice Richard, 1956–63

Gallagher, Justice Francis Heath, CMG, 1957–71

Moore, Sir John Cochrane, AC, 1959–73

Sweeney, Justice Charles Augustine, 1963–69

Nimmo, Sir John Angus, CBE, 1964–69

Williams, Justice Lindsay Hale, 1968–91

Franki, Justice Robert James Anning, 1969–72

Aird, Justice Andrew Paton, 1970–74

Robinson, Justice James, 1970–86

Coldham, Justice Peter Abernethy, DFC, 1971–89

Ludeke, Justice John Terrence, 1972–91

Watson, Frederick Vernon, 1972–73

Chambers, Edward Alfred Charles, CBE, 1972–75

Evatt, Justice Elizabeth Andreas, AC, Deputy President 1973–92, Senior Deputy
     President 1992–94

Sweeney, John Bernard, AO, 1973

Williams, Rees David, 1973–75

Isaac, Joseph Ezra, AO, 1974–87

Gaudron, Justice Mary Genevieve, 1974–80

Kirby, Justice Michael Donald, AC, CMG, 1975–83

Staples, Justice James Frederick, 1975–89

Sharp, Justice Ian Gordon, AO, 1975–78

Alley, Justice Stephen George, 1977–87

Taylor, James Edward, CBE, 1978–79

McKenzie, Keith Colin, CMG, 1979–86

Marks, Justice Keith David, 1980–86

Maddern, Justice Barry James, AC, 1980–85

Cohen, Justice Judith Jacqueline, AO, 1980–91

Keogh, Michael Brendan, Deputy President 1982–92, Senior Deputy President 1992–95

Boulton, Justice Alan James, AO, Deputy President 1986–92, Senior Deputy President 1992–[4]

Riordan, Joseph Martin, AO, Deputy President 1986–92, Senior Deputy President 1992–95

Munro, Justice Paul Robert, Deputy President 1986–92, Senior Deputy President 1992–2004

Hancock, Keith Jackson, AO, Deputy President 1987–92, Senior Deputy President 1992–97

Peterson, Justice Russell John, 1987–92

Marsh, Jeanette Isabel, Deputy President 1988–93, Senior Deputy President 1993–

MacBean, John William, AM, Deputy President 1989–94, Senior Deputy President 1994–2000

Moore, Michael Francis, 1989–92

Polites, Colin George, Deputy President 1989–94, Senior Deputy President 1994–2003

Watson, Ian Robert, Deputy President 1991–97, Senior Deputy President 1997–

Harrison, Anne Marie, Deputy President 1991–97, Senior Deputy President 1997–

Williams, Simon John, Deputy President 1991–97, Senior Deputy President 1997–

Maher, John Michael, 1992–98

Acton, Jennifer Mary, Deputy President 1992–99, Senior Deputy President 1999–

Hall, David Ross, 1992–93

Drake, Lea Ellen Cecelia, Deputy President 1994–99, Senior Deputy President 1999–

Bryant, John Kenneth, 1995–98

Duncan, David Anthony, Deputy President 1995–2000, Senior Deputy President 2000–

Lacy, Brian James, Senior Deputy President 2001–

O'Callaghan, Matthew Gerrard, Senior Deputy President 2001–

Cartwright, Robert Neale, Senior Deputy President 2001–

Kaufman, Leslie, Senior Deputy President 2001–

Leary, Patricia Lilian, 2001–[5]

Ives, Kenneth Bruce, 2001–

Hamilton, Reginald Sydney, 2001–

McCarthy, Brendan Patrick, 2001–

Blain, Alexander Nicholas John, 2001–

Commissioners

Portus, John Hereford, OBE, DFC, 1956–78

Findlay, George Andrew, 1956–67

Austin, Leslie Paul, 1956–65

Donovan, John Rawdon, 1956–67

Kelly, Francis Daniel, 1956–58

Hewitt, Joseph Martin, OBE, 1956–62

Tonkin, Eric William, 1956–58

Chambers, Edward Alfred Charles, CBE, Senior Commissioner 1956–61[6]

Webb, Frederick John, 1956–63

Horan, John Patrick, OBE, 1957–70

Apsey, Douglas Gerard, 1959–63

Hood, Norman John, CBE, 1961–72

Taylor, James Edward, CBE, Senior Commissioner 1961–72,[7] Commissioner 1972–78[8]

Gough, John Lewis, 1962–84

Matthews, Leonard George, CBE, 1963–80

Winter, Terence Cecil, OBE, 1963–71

McCreadie, John James, 1964–68

Clarkson, Eric John, 1965–82

Neil, Harold Gibson, MBE, 1965–79

Holmes, John Bede, 1967–80

Watson, Richard Hugh Caiger, 1968–82[9]

O'Reilly, Oscar Owen, 1968–73

Brack, Thomas James, 1968–84

Deverall, Edward George, 1968–80

Wilson, Walter Bazeley, 1968–73

Lyttleton, Maurice Francis, 1970–73

Stanton, Jack, 1971–82

McCloghry, Thomas William Sydney, 1972–75

Mansini, Norman James, AM, 1972–89

Allsop, Paul Darley, 1972–76

Taylor, Norman Aubrey, 1972–84

Vosti, Allan Raymond, AM, 1972–80

Booth, Lyndon Harold, 1972–84

Brown, Frederick William John, 1972–90

Heagney, Matthew Edward, AM, 1972–85

Paine, Alan Sidney, 1972–90

Heffernan, John Edward, OAM, 1973–81

Cohen, Judith Jacqueline, AO, 1975–80

Walker, Graham Lytton, 1975–87

Griffin, Pauline Marcus, AM, 1975–90

Coleman, James William, 1975–87

Sweeney, Rupert George, 1976–94

Connell, Vincent Joseph, 1977–92

Barnes, Pauline St. George, 1978–85

Turbet, Kenneth Charles, 1978–92

Neyland, Francis James, 1979–91

Merriman, Robert Frederick, AM, 1980–2000

McKenzie, Ian Thomas, 1980–90

McLagan, Alexander, 1980–84

Bennett, Edward Charles, 1980–89

Johnson, Bevan Ross, 1980–93

Bain, Leslie Nelson, 1982–89

Hastings, Selby Gordon, 1982–85

Sheather, James Walter, 1982–92

Cross, John William, 1982–94

Cox, Philip Alfred, 1982–95

Lear, James Francis, 1983–92

Maher, John Michael, 1983–92

Baird, James Albert, 1984–89

Donaldson, Edward Malcolm, 1984–91

Nolan, Peter Ian, 1984–97

Palmer, Frank Edwin, 1984–98

Grimshaw, Geoffrey Allan, 1984–98

Leary, Patricia Lilian, 1984–2001

Caesar, Joseph Gerard, 1985–91

Peterson, Frederick Eugene, OAM, 1987–98

Laing, Robert Samuel, 1987–2001

Smith, Gregory Robert, 1987–

Fogarty, Adrian Daniel, 1987–94

Lewin, John Charles William, 1987–

McMahon, John Denis, 1989–90

Frawley, Bernard John, 1989–99

Oldmeadow, Justine, 1989–97

Harrison, Gregory James, 1989–

Simmonds, James William Leslie, 1989–

Lawson, Peter Ashby, 1990–

Gay, Michael Arthur George, 1990–

Hoffman, David Anthony, 1990–

McDonald, Kenneth John, 1990–98

Hodder, Errol Raymond, 1991–2003

Bacon, Kenneth John, 1991–

O'Shea, James Patrick, 1992–98

Foggo, Dianne Blair, 1992–

Jones, Ronald Stewart, 1992–2003

Holmes, John Graham, 1993–

Blair, Wayne Douglas, 1993–

Bryant, John Kenneth, 1993–95

Mahon, Keith William, 1994–98
Hingley, Leonard Norton, AM, 1994–
Cribb, Anna Lee Margaret Bridson, 1994–
Eames, Brendan John, 1994–
Redmond, Robert Arthur, 1994–
Cargill, Helen Margaret, 1994–
Larkin, Annette Patricia, 1994–
O'Connor, John Joseph, 1995–2003
Tolley, John Raymond George, 1995–
Dight, Rosalind Diana, 1995–97
Whelan, Dominica Mary, 1995–
Wilks, Eric Anthony, 1995–2001
Deegan, Barbara, 1996–
Raffaelli, Frank Julian, 1996–
Grainger, Gareth Simon Graham, 2001–
Spencer, Paula Judith, 2001–
Roberts, Michael Gordon, 2001–
Richards, Peter John, 2002–
Mansfield, William Clements, 2002–
Thatcher, Colin William, 2003–

Dual Appointees

Members of the Commission whose primary appointment was to a State industrial authority.

Deputy Presidents

Stanley, Justice Brian Charles, AM, 1990–94[10]
Fisher, Justice William Kenneth, AO, 1990–98[11]
Ledlie, Lionel Norman, AM, 1990–93[12]
Westwood, Frederick David, 1990–2000[13]
Coleman, William Stewart, AM, 1990–[14]
Marsh, Peter Ronald, 1991–93

Cawthorne, Judge Franklyn King, 1991–
McCusker, Judge James Peter, 1991–
Garlick, Robert John, AM, 1992–93
Parsons, Judge Helen Webster, 1992–
Hall, David Ross, 1993–[15]
Jennings, Senior Judge William David, 1996–[16]
Stevens, Gregory Munson, 1996–2000
Hampton, Peter John, 1996–
Fielding, Gavin Leonard, 1998–2001
Wright, Justice Frederick Lance, 1998–[17]
Cahill, Justice John Joseph, 1998
Peterson, Justice Russell John, 1998–
Marks, Justice Francis, 1998–
Schmidt, Justice Monika, 1998–
Harrison, Rodney William, 1998–
Gilchrist, Judge Brian Patrick, 2000–
Linnane, Dianne Margaret, 2001–

Commissioners

Halliwell, Gary George, 1990–96
Gregor, John Francis, 1990–
Lane, Gerald Calton, 1991–93
Stevens, Gregory Munson, 1991–96
Perry, Michael Graham Rhodes, AM, 1991–94
Fairweather, Robert Weir, 1991–2000
McCutcheon, Michael Guy Geoffrey, 1991–2003
Ashwood, Graham Matthew, 1991–93
Edwards, Kevin Leonard, 1991–
Bougoure, Robert William, 1991–98
Fisher, Glenys Kay, 1991–
Dempsey, Henry, 1991–97
Bechly, Robin Edward, 1991–
Swan, Deirdre Anne, 1991–

Pimm, William Charles, 1992–93
Williams, Kenneth, 1992–93
Nutter, Barry John, 1992–99
Bussell, Sue-Ellen, 1992–93
Campbell, Neil, 1992–93
Bloomfield, Adrian Leslie, 1993–
Huxter, Richard John, 1996–2000
Baldwin, Diane Beth, 1998–2000
Blades, Brian James, 1998–
Lesses, John Kosmas, AM, 2000–
Dangerfield, Adrian John, 2000–
Bartel, Karen Marilyn, 2000–
Asbury, Ingrid Catherine, 2001–
Brown, Donald Keith, 2001–
Thompson, John Murray, 2001–

Industrial Registrars

Castle, Gordon Harwood, OBE, 1905–07
Stewart, Alexander Murdoch, 1907–29
Stewart, Murray Milne, OBE, 1930–47
Taylor, James Edward, CBE, 1947–61
O'Brien, Albert Edgar, ISO, 1961–66
Sharp, Ian Gordon, AO, 1966–72
Marshall, Keith Douglas, AM, 1973–81
McMahon, John Denis, 1981–89
O'Shea, James Patrick, 1989–92
Deegan, Barbara, 1992–93
Kelly, Michael Desmond, 1994–99
Richards, Peter John, 1999–2002
Wilson, Nicholas Paul, 2002–

APPENDIX III
THE OBJECTS OF
THE ACT

The objects of the Act have been revised from time to time to give effect to differences in political and industrial attitudes on the operation of the industrial relations system. The brief annotations below refer to the main changes in the objects of the Act over the century.

The original *Commonwealth Conciliation and Arbitration Act 1904* listed as its 'chief objects':

i. To prevent lock-outs and strikes in relation to industrial disputes;

ii. To constitute a Commonwealth Court of Conciliation and Arbitration having jurisdiction for the prevention and settlement of industrial disputes;

iii. To provide for the exercise of the jurisdiction of the Court by conciliation with a view to amicable agreement between the parties;

iv. In default of amicable agreement between the parties, to provide for the exercise of the jurisdiction of the Court by equitable award;

v. To enable States to refer industrial disputes to the Court, and to permit the working of the Court and of State Industrial Authorities in aid of each other;

vi. To facilitate and encourage the organization of representative bodies of employers and of employees and the submission of industrial disputes to the Court by organizations, and to permit representative bodies of employers and of employees to be declared organizations for the purposes of this Act;

vii. To provide for the making and enforcement of industrial agreements between employers and employees in relation to industrial disputes.

Following the election of the Scullin (Labor) government, the 1930 Act altered the first object to:

To promote goodwill in industry by conciliation and arbitration;

Under pressure from the trade union movement, the Chifley (Labor) government amended the Act to increase the number of (lay) Commissioners, to give them a greater role in wage determination and to strengthen conciliation processes. Accordingly, the 1947 Act listed as the chief objects:

(a) to establish an expeditious system for preventing and settling industrial disputes by the methods of conciliation and arbitration;

(b) to promote good will in industry and to encourage the continued and amicable operation of orders and awards made in settlement of industrial disputes;

(c) to provide for the appointment of Conciliation Commissioners having power to prevent and settle industrial disputes by conciliation and arbitration;

(d) to provide means whereby a Conciliation Commissioner may promptly and effectively, whether of his own motion or otherwise, prevent and settle threatened, impending, probable or existing industrial disputes;

(e) to provide for observance and enforcement of such orders and awards;

(f) to constitute a Commonwealth Court of Conciliation and Arbitration having exclusive appellate jurisdiction in matters of law arising under this Act and limited jurisdiction in relation to industrial disputes; and

(g) to encourage the organization of representative bodies of employers and of employees and their registration under this Act.

Following the *Boilermakers* case and the establishment of the Commonwealth Conciliation and Arbitration Commission, the chief objects of the 1956 Act reverted substantially to those of the 1930 Act but with the addition of 'maximum of expedition and the minimum of legal form and technicality' in the settlement of disputes:

(a) to promote goodwill in industry;

(b) to encourage conciliation with a view to amicable agreement, thereby preventing and settling industrial disputes;

(c) to provide means for preventing and settling industrial disputes not resolved by amicable agreement, including threatened, impending and probable industrial disputes, with the maximum of expedition and the minimum of legal form and technicality;

(d) to provide for the observance and enforcement of agreements and awards made in settlement of industrial disputes; and

(e) to encourage the organization of representative bodies of employers and employees and their registration under this Act.

Under the influence of Clyde Cameron, the new (Labor) Minister for Labour and National Service, the 1973 Act made some minor amendments to these objects and added:

(f) to encourage the democratic control of organizations so registered and the full participation by members of such an organization in the affairs of the organization.

In the context of the Accord, the objects of the *Industrial Relations Act 1988* gave special emphasis to the 'interests (including the economic interests) of the Australian community as a whole' and the 'efficient management of organisations':

(a) to promote industrial harmony and co-operation among the parties involved in industrial relations in Australia;

(b) to provide a framework for the prevention and settlement of industrial disputes by conciliation and arbitration in a manner that minimises the disruptive effects of industrial disputes on the community;

(c) to ensure that, in the prevention and settlement of industrial disputes, proper regard is had to the interests of the parties immediately concerned and to the interests (including the economic interests) of the Australian community as a whole;

(d) to facilitate the prevention and prompt settlement of industrial disputes in a fair manner, and with the minimum of legal form and technicality;

(e) to provide for the observance and enforcement of agreements and awards made for the prevention or settlement of industrial disputes;

(f) to encourage the organisation of representative bodies of employers and employees and their registration under this Act;

(g) to encourage the democratic control of organisations, and the participation by their members in the affairs of organisations; and

(h) to encourage the efficient management of organisations.

The *Industrial Relations Reform Act 1993* marked the most significant change in the legislative framework of the industrial relations system since 1904. This is reflected in the objects of the 1993 Act in favour of decentralisation of wage determination through collective bargaining and agreements, particularly at the enterprise level, while those relying on awards are to be protected by a 'safety net'. The objects make reference for the first time to reducing the number of unions in line with the new policy of the ACTU (clause f) and, in conformity with ILO Conventions, to anti-discrimination (clause g):

> The principal object of this Act is to provide a framework for the prevention and settlement of industrial disputes which promotes the economic prosperity and welfare of the people of Australia by:
>
> (a) encouraging and facilitating the making of agreements, between the parties involved in industrial relations, to determine matters pertaining to the relationship between employers and employees, particularly at the workplace or enterprise level; and
>
> (b) providing the means for:
>   (i) establishing and maintaining an effective framework for protecting wages and conditions of employment through awards; and
>   (ii) ensuring that labour standards meet Australia's international obligations; and
>
> (c) providing a framework of rights and responsibilities for the parties involved in industrial relations which encourages fair and effective bargaining and ensures that those parties abide by agreements between them; and
>
> (d) enabling the Commission to prevent and settle industrial disputes:
>   (i) so far as possible, by conciliation; and
>   (ii) where necessary, by arbitration; and
>
> (e) encouraging the organisation of representative bodies of employers and employees and their registration under this Act; and
>
> (f) encouraging and facilitating the development of organisations, particularly by reducing the number of organisations in an industry or enterprise; and

(g) helping to prevent and eliminate discrimination on the basis of race,
     colour, sex, sexual preference, age, physical or mental disability,
     marital status, family responsibilities, pregnancy, religion, political
     opinion, national extraction or social origin.

The 1996 Act gives greater emphasis to workplace relations specifically
between employers and employees and extends the scope of bargaining of the
1993 Act to individual bargaining, while the object of 'encouraging and facilitating the development of organisations', which had been in substance among the
objects of all the Acts since 1904, has been changed to a more neutral object of
'ensuring freedom of association':

The principal object of this Act is to provide a framework for cooperative
workplace relations which promotes the economic prosperity and welfare
of the people of Australia by:
(a) encouraging the pursuit of high employment, improved living
     standards, low inflation and international competitiveness through
     higher productivity and a flexible and fair labour market; and
(aa) protecting the competitive position of young people in the labour
     market, promoting youth employment, youth skills and community
     standards and assisting in reducing youth unemployment;
     and
(b) ensuring that the primary responsibility for determining matters
     affecting the relationship between employers and employees rests
     with the employer and employees at the workplace or enterprise
     level; and
(c) enabling employers and employees to choose the most appropriate
     form of agreement for their particular circumstances, whether or not
     that form is provided for by this Act; and
(d) providing the means:
     (i) for wages and conditions of employment to be determined as far
          as possible by the agreement of employers and employees at the
          workplace or enterprise level, upon a foundation of minimum
          standards; and

(ii) to ensure the maintenance of an effective award safety net of fair and enforceable minimum wages and conditions of employment; and

(e) providing a framework of rights and responsibilities for employers and employees, and their organisations, which supports fair and effective agreement-making and ensures that they abide by awards and agreements applying to them; and

(f) ensuring freedom of association, including the rights of employees and employers to join an organisation or association of their choice, or not to join an organisation or association; and

(g) ensuring that employee and employer organisations registered under this Act are representative of and accountable to their members, and are able to operate effectively; and [Repealed by No. 105 of 2002]

(h) enabling the Commission to prevent and settle industrial disputes as far as possible by conciliation and, where appropriate and within specified limits, by arbitration; and

(i) assisting employees to balance their work and family responsibilities effectively through the development of mutually beneficial work practices with employers; and

(j) respecting and valuing the diversity of the work force by helping to prevent and eliminate discrimination on the basis of race, colour, sex, sexual preference, age, physical or mental disability, marital status, family responsibilities, pregnancy, religion, political opinion, national extraction or social origin; and

(k) assisting in giving effect to Australia's international obligations in relation to labour standards.

NOTES

1 ELUSIVE MIDDLE GROUND

1. Trenwith referred here to a dispute that arose in Victoria in July 1888 when a shipping company employed non-union labour, but the threatened strike did not proceed (Coghlan 1918: 1492).
2. *R v Commonwealth Court etc, Ex parte GP Jones* (1914) 18 CLR 224.
3. Isaac notes that he completed this paper by August 1991, revising it 'somewhat' in March 1993.

2 ARBITRATION IN ACTION

1. I acknowledge the research assistance provided by Ian Davidoff and the advice given by Helen Coulson and Richard Mitchell.

3 THE LAW OF CONCILIATION AND ARBITRATION

1. See further Plowman and Smith (1986: 206–9). On the origins of section 51 (xxxv), see Fitzpatrick (1940b), Macintyre and Mitchell (1989), Patmore (1991, ch. 5), Bennett (1994a), and Plowman and Rowse in this volume.
2. *Amalgamated Society of Engineers v Adelaide Steamship Co Ltd* (1920) 28 CLR 129.
3. *Theophanous v Herald & Weekly Times Ltd* (1994) 182 CLR 104, 171, 174 per Deane J quoting Clark (1901); cf. *R v Commonwealth Conciliation and Arbitration Commission; Ex parte Professional Engineers Association* (1959) 107 CLR 208, 267; *Victoria v The Commonwealth* (1971) 122 CLR 353, 396 per Windeyer J.
4. *Re Wakim, Ex parte McNally* (1999) 198 CLR 511, 551–4 [40]–[49]; 599–600 [186]; *Grain Pool of Western Australia v The Commonwealth* (2000) 202 CLR 479, 511–13 [76]–[80], 522–30 [110]–[129]; *Eastman v The Queen* (2000) 203 CLR 1, 41–51 [134]–[158]; 79–81 [240]–[245]; *Brownlee v The Queen* (2001) 207 CLR 278, 285 [8], 297 [52], 300–1 [59]–[64], 320–7 [122]–[128].
5. See Craven (1990), Dawson (1990), Goldsworthy (1997), Kirk (1999), Bagaric (2000), Goldsworthy (2000), Kirby (2000), and Meagher (2002a, 2002b).
6. See further Higgins (1915, 1919 and 1920).
7. *The Australian Boot Trade Employees Federation v Whybrow & Co* (1910) 11 CLR 311.
8. (1910) 10 CLR 267.
9. This proposition has played an important role in determining the relationship between federal awards and State laws (and awards and agreements). It has the effect that employees who are covered by both State and federal provision on a given topic may obtain the benefit of both sets of provisions, so long as it is possible to comply with both of them in a manner that is not inconsistent with the federal provision – cf. *Blakeley v Devondale Cream (Victoria) Pty Ltd* (1968) 117 CLR 253.
10. (1910) 11 CLR 1.
11. *Federated Sawmill, Timberyard and General Woodworkers Employees' Association of Australasia v James Moore & Son Pty Ltd* (1909) 8 CLR 465, 468.
12. (1910) 11 CLR 311, 317–18.

13. (1910) 11 CLR 311, 336 (Isaacs J), 342 (Higgins J). See further McCallum and Smith (1986: 68–9).

14. The legislation has for many years contained provision for the making of common rule awards in the Territories. These provisions depend for the constitutionality upon the Territories' power in section 122 of the Constitution. See now *Workplace Relations Act 1996*, sections 141–2.

15. *R v Commonwealth Court of Conciliation and Arbitration; Ex parte Ozone Theatres (Aust) Ltd* (1949) 78 CLR 389, 401. See also *R v Kelly; Ex parte State of Victoria* (1950) 81 CLR 64. The provision that was at issue in *Ozone Theatres* was an attempt to extend the operation of a common rule measure that had been put in place during the Second World War in reliance upon the defence power in section 51(vi).

16. See further Ford (1984: 65–78) – but cf. *R v Turbet; Ex parte Australian Building Construction Employees and Builders Labourers Federation* (1980) 144 CLR 335, 353–6 (per Murphy J); *Re Federated Storemen and Packers Union of Australia; Ex parte Wooldumpers (Victoria) Ltd* (1989) 166 CLR 311, 320–1 (per Mason CJ), 327–8 (per Deane J). Partly in response to the observations in *Wooldumpers*, the legislation was amended in 1993 by the insertion of provision intended to prevent 'industrial situations' developing into 'disputes' – see *Workplace Relations Act 1996*, section 4(1).

17. *Amalgamated Society of Engineers v Adelaide Steamship Co Ltd* (1920) 28 CLR 129.

18. *Burwood Cinema Limited v The Australian Theatrical and Amusement Employees' Association* (1925) 35 CLR 528.

19. *The Metal Trades Employers Association v The Amalgamated Engineering Union* (1935) 54 CLR 387.

20. On the origins of paper disputes, see *R v Commonwealth Court of Conciliation and Arbitration; Ex parte GP Jones* (1914) 18 CLR 224.

21. In deciding this case, the Court overruled its earlier decision in *Amalgamated Engineering Union v Alderdice Pty Ltd, In Re Metropolitan Gas Co* (1928) 41 CLR 402, in which the Court had decided that the Commonwealth Court of Conciliation and Arbitration did not have power to make awards 'prescribing the duties of employers to employees who are neither parties to the industrial dispute before the Court nor members of nor represented by an organisation which is a party to that dispute' (per Knox CJ, 411). Interestingly, only one member of the Court (Isaacs J, 419) made even passing reference to the decision in *Burwood Cinema*. In *Re Finance Sector Union of Australia; Ex parte Financial Clinic (Vic) Pty Ltd* (1993) 178 CLR 352, by a 4:3 majority the Court determined that the Australian Industrial Relations Commission could not include provision in an award to the effect that employers in the insurance industry make superannuation contributions in respect of all employees, irrespective of union membership, into a named superannuation fund. In reaching this decision, Mason CJ, Deane, Toohey and Gaudron JJ (at 361) suggested that the *Metal Trades* principle extended only to claims relating to wages and conditions of non-members, and not to claims that relate to matters beyond that. This decision is not without difficulty. On one view, any claim that falls within the jurisdiction of the Commission in relation to employees who are union members ought logically also to pertain to the terms and conditions of non-members. Unfortunately, their Honours did not provide any guidance as to how the distinction between member and non-member claims was to be drawn, and subsequent decisions provide little indication as to the extent, if any, to which the *Metal Trades* principle has been compromised.

22. See *Re Media, Entertainment and Arts Alliance; Ex parte Arnel* (1994) 179 CLR 84; *Re National Tertiary Education Industry Union; Ex parte Quickenden* (1996) 71 ALJR 75; *Attorney-General (Queensland) v Riordan* (1998) 192 CLR 1, 39–48 (per Kirby J).

23. See now *Workplace Relations Act 1996*, section 149(1)(f).

24. This logic caused some employer organisations to devise a form of 'associate' or 'non-industrial' membership, which carried most (if not all) of the benefits of membership, but did not carry the burden of award coverage. The efficacy of this technique has been thrown into some doubt by the decision of the AIRC in *Carpenter v Corona Manufacturing Pty Ltd*, Whelan C, 30 October 2002, PR924136.

25. Section 111AAA of the *Workplace Relations Act 1996* is intended to help preserve the integrity of State systems of conciliation and arbitration by requiring the AIRC to cease dealing with a dispute involving employees whose terms and conditions are regulated by a State award or agreement, unless satisfied that it would not be in the public interest for it to cease dealing with the dispute. This provision was introduced in 1996 and appears to have had the effect of reducing the use of roping-in awards, although it certainly has not eliminated the practice.

26. *George Hudson Limited v Australian Timber Workers' Union* (1923) 32 CLR 413.

27. See *Shaw v United Felt Hat Pty Ltd* (1927) 39 CLR 533. More recently, see *North Western Health Care Network v Health Services Union of Australia* (1999) 92 FCR 477; *PP Consultants Pty Ltd v Finance Sector Union* (2000) 201 CLR 648. For comment, see Creighton (1998), Ginters (1999), and McCallum (2001).

28. *Jumbunna Coal Mine NL v Victorian Coal Miners' Association* (1908) 6 CLR 309.

29. *Ibid.*, 358–9. See also Griffith CJ at 334; Barton J at 345; and Isaacs J at 377–8.

30. Plowman and Smith (1986: 213) suggest that the decision may be attributed to the fact that the members of the Court may not have fully considered the implications of the decision; that they may 'have been carried away by the sense of occasion', given that this was the first time they had been called upon to examine the scope of the conciliation and arbitration power; and that 'having excluded the majority of employees of State governments' (*sic*) and State instrumentalities from the jurisdiction of the Arbitration Court [in *Federated Amalgamated Government Railway and Tramway Service Association v New South Wales Railway Traffic Employees Association* (1906) 4 CLR 488] the Judges were more prepared to give the Arbitration court a free reign [*sic*]'.

31. *Amalgamated Society of Engineers v Adelaide Steamship Co Ltd* (1920) 28 CLR 129.

32. (1908) 6 CLR 309, 365. See also Griffith CJ at 333, and Isaacs J at 370. Barton J did not make any direct reference to this issue, but nor did he disagree with his colleagues on this point.

33. *Federated Municipal and Shire Council Employees' Union of Australia v City of Melbourne* (1919) 26 CLR 508.

34. *Ibid.*, 575.

35. *Ibid.*, 584. It is perhaps worth mentioning in this context that Gavan Duffy J was counsel for the employers in *Jumbunna*.

36. *Australian Insurance Staffs' Federation v Accident Underwriters' Association* and *Bank Officials Association v Bank of Australasia* (1923) 33 CLR 517. The two cases were heard together.

37. See Rich and Isaacs JJ, *ibid.*, 527. See also *Proprietors of Daily News Limited v Australian Journalists Association* (1920) 27 CLR 532, where the High Court unanimously rejected the proposition that journalists were incapable of being involved in an industrial dispute.

38. *Federated State School Teachers Association of Australia v Victoria* (1929) 41 CLR 569. Prior to the decision in the *Engineers* case (above), the majority could have achieved the same result in reliance upon either or both of the reserved State powers and implied governmental immunities doctrines.

39. *The Queen v The President etc of the Commonwealth Conciliation and Arbitration Commission; Ex parte Association of Professional Engineers, Australia* (1959) 107 CLR 155.

40. *The Queen v Marshall; Ex parte Federated Clerks Union of Australia* (1975) 132 CLR 595.

41. *R v Cohen; Ex parte Motor Accidents Insurance Board* (1979) 141 CLR 577.

42. *R v Holmes and Federated Clerks Union of Australia; Ex parte Manchester Unity Independent Order of Oddfellows in Victoria* (1980) 147 CLR 65.

43. *The King v Commonwealth Court of Conciliation and Arbitration; Ex parte Victoria* (1942) 66 CLR 488.

44. *R v Holmes, Ex parte Public Service Association of New South Wales* (1978) 140 CLR 63.

45. *Pitfield v Franki* (1970) 123 CLR 448.

46. *R v McMahon, Ex parte Darvall* (1982) 151 CLR 57.

47. For more detailed consideration of the industry requirement see Creighton, Ford & Mitchell (1993: ch. 17) and Williams (1998: 68–78).

48. *Clancy v Butchers' Shop Employees Union* (1904) 1 CLR 181.

49. *Australian Tramway Employees' Association v Prahran & Malvern Tramways Trust* (1913) 17 CLR 680, 702. In this case, the majority of the Court determined that a dispute about whether union members could wear a union badge on their watchchains while on duty was a dispute as to an industrial matter. Note also the expansive approach adopted by the majority in *Federated Clothing Trades v Archer* (1919) 27 CLR 207 (a demand that all garments made by respondent employers should carry a label identifying the actual manufacturer of the garment was found to be 'industrial' in character).

50. *The Queen v Commonwealth Conciliation and Arbitration Commission; Ex parte Melbourne and Metropolitan Tramways Board* (1966) 115 CLR 443, 451. To the same effect, see also his Honour's observations in *R v Flight Crew Officers' Industrial Tribunal; Ex parte Australian Federation of Air Pilots* (1971) 127 CLR 11, 20.

51. *R v Commonwealth Conciliation and Arbitration Commission; Ex parte Melbourne & Metropolitan Tramways Board* (1965) 113 CLR 228 (*Tramways No 1*).

52. *Melbourne & Metropolitan Tramways Board v Horan* (1967) 117 CLR 78 (*Tramways No 3*). For a critical analysis of the *Tramways* decisions, see Maher and Sexton (1972: 111–14).

53. *The Queen v Gallagher; Ex parte Commonwealth Steamship Owners' Association* (1968) 121 CLR 330, 335. The Court comprised Kitto, Taylor, Menzies, Windeyer and Owen JJ. Of these, two (Kitto and Owen JJ) had dissented in *Tramways No 1*, while two (Taylor and Menzies JJ) had been in the majority in that case. Taylor, Menzies and Owen JJ had been members of the Court in *Tramways No 2*. Menzies and Owen JJ had been part of the majority in *Tramways No 3*, while Taylor J had dissented in that case.

54. In addition to *Clancy*, see *R v Kelly; Ex parte State of Victoria* (1950) 81 CLR 64.

55. See *Tramways No 1, Tramways No 2*, and *Australian Federation of Air Pilots v Flightcrew Officers Industrial Tribunal* (1968) 119 CLR 16. The logic of the position adopted by Barwick CJ in this latter case would have the effect that occupational health and safety of employees might not constitute an industrial matter.

56. *R v Wallis; Ex parte Employers' Association of Wool Selling Brokers* (1949) 78 CLR 529; *R v Findlay; Ex parte Victorian Chamber of Manufactures* (1950) 81 CLR 537 – cf. *R v Gaudron; Ex parte Uniroyal Pty Ltd* (1978) 141 CLR 204. For comment on these decisions, see Mitchell (1986, 1987, 1988) and Weeks (1995).

57. *R v Hamilton Knight; Ex parte Commonwealth Steamship Owners' Association* (1952) 86 CLR 283. Although the decision is commonly cited as authority for the proposition that occupational superannuation could not constitute an 'industrial matter', this may be to overstate the matter. This is because only two members of the Court (McTiernan and Williams JJ) expressly based their decision on the proposition that occupational superannuation could not constitute an 'industrial matter'. Two (Webb and Kitto JJ) determined that it could constitute an industrial matter, while two (Dixon CJ and Fullagar J) based their decision on the fact that, as the legislation then stood, awards could not operate for a period of more than five years. This would have meant that in many instances the award which created an entitlement to

a superannuation payment would no longer be operative by the time the benefit became payable.

58. *R v Judges of the Commonwealth Industrial Court; Ex parte Cocks* (1968) 121 CLR 313 – cf. *R v Moore; Ex parte Federated Miscellaneous Workers' Union of Australia* (1978) 140 CLR 470, 477 (per Jacobs J).

59. *R v Gough; Ex parte Meat and Allied Trades Federation (Australia)* (1969) 122 CLR 237; *R v Flight Crew Officers' Industrial Tribunal, Ex parte Australian Federation of Air Pilots* (1971) 127 CLR 11; *R v Portus; Ex parte City of Perth* (1973) 129 CLR 312.

60. *R v Flight Crew Officers' Industrial Tribunal; Ex parte Australian Federation of Air Pilots* (1971) 127 CLR 11 – cf. *R v Coldham; Ex parte Fitzsimons* (1976) 137 CLR 153.

61. *R v Portus; Ex parte ANZ Group* (1972) 127 CLR 353 – cf. *Re Alcan Australia Ltd, Ex parte Federation of Industrial, Manufacturing and Engineering Employees* (1994) 181 CLR 96, discussed below.

62. See, for example, *R v Commonwealth Conciliation and Arbitration Commission; Ex parte Transport Workers' Union of Australia* (1969) 119 CLR 529 (demarcation disputes); *R v Coldham; Ex parte Fitzsimons* (1976) 137 CLR 153 (establishment and maintenance of a seniority list for airline pilots and its application in relation to promotion and redundancy); *R v Moore; Ex parte Federated Miscellaneous Workers' Union of Australia* (1978) 140 CLR 470, 477 (per Jacobs J) (terms upon which contractors might be engaged on a mine construction site); and *R v Gaudron; Ex parte Uniroyal Pty Ltd* (1978) 141 CLR 204 (preference in employment for union members).

63. For more detailed studies of the industrial matter concept, see Creighton, Ford & Mitchell (1993: ch. 18) and Pittard & Noughton (2003: 458–86).

64. This colourful metaphor was employed by Higgins J (in the Commonwealth Court of Conciliation and Arbitration) in the aftermath of the decision in the second *Whybrow* case – see *Australian Boot Trade Employees Federation v Whybrow & Co* (1910) 4 CAR 1 42 – cf. *Attorney-General (Queensland) v Riordan* (1998) 192 CLR 1 39–48 (per Kirby J).

65. *The Queen v McMahon; Ex parte Darvall* (1982) 151 CLR 57.

66. *Ibid.*, 60–1 (per Gibbs CJ), 65–6 (per Mason J), 73–4 (per Murphy J) and 74–5 (per Brennan J).

67. *The Queen v Coldham; Ex parte Australian Social Welfare Union* (1983) 153 CLR 297. The Court comprised Gibbs CJ, Mason, Murphy, Wilson, Brennan, Deane and Dawson JJ.

68. *State School Teachers' Association of Australia v Victoria* (1929) 41 CLR 569.

69. *Federated Municipal and Shire Council Employees' Union of Australia v Melbourne Corporation* (1919) 26 CLR 508, 572.

70. *Australian Insurance Staffs' Association v Accident Underwriters' Association* (1923) 33 CLR 517, 528–9.

71. (1947) 74 CLR 31.

72. (1971) 122 CLR 353.

73. *Re Lee; Ex parte Harper* (1986) 160 CLR 430.

74. *Ibid.*, 453 (per Mason, Brennan and Deane JJ).

75. *Re State Public Services Federation; Ex parte Attorney-General (WA)* (1993) 178 CLR 249.

76. This case arose out of some rather vague and highly inflated claims in a log of claims served upon the governments of Western Australia and a number of other States. The case was decided on the basis that the union's demands constituted a claim for pay increases as determined by the AIRC, and that, as such, they were not capable of giving rise to a genuine interstate dispute between the parties.

77. *Re Australian Education Union; Ex parte State of Victoria* (1995) 184 CLR 188.

78. A majority, composed of Mason CJ, Brennan, Deane, Toohey, Gaudron and McHugh JJ, delivered joint reasons. Dawson J dissented, essentially on the ground that he did not consider that an industrial dispute between a State and its employees could possess the necessary element of interstatedness to fall within the jurisdiction of the tribunal.

79. *R v Coldham; Ex parte Australian Social Welfare Union* (1983) 153 CLR 297, 312.

80. *Federated Clerks Union of Australia v Victorian Employers Federation* (1984) 154 CLR 472.

81. *Ibid.*, 514 (per Wilson J).

82. *Re Ranger Uranium Mines Pty Ltd; Ex parte Federated Miscellaneous Workers' Union of Australia* (1987) 163 CLR 656.

83. *Re Federated Storemen and Packers Union of Australia; Ex parte Wooldumpers (Victoria) Ltd* (1989) 166 CLR 311. See also *Re Boyne Smelters Ltd; Ex parte Federation of Industrial Manufacturing and Engineering Employees of Australia* (1993) 177 CLR 446; *Re Printing and Kindred Industries Union; Ex parte Vista Paper Products Pty Ltd* (1993) 67 ALJR 604.

84. *Re Manufacturing Grocers' Employees Federation (Australia); Ex parte Australian Chamber of Manufactures* (1986) 160 CLR 341. It should be noted that the demands in this instance were rather less ambitious than in *R v Hamilton Knight; Ex parte Commonwealth Steamship Owners' Association* (1952) 86 CLR 283, which is discussed at note 56, above. In *Re Amalgamated Metal Workers Union of Australia; Ex parte Shell Co of Australia Ltd* (1992) 174 CLR 345, the High Court determined that the identity and form of superannuation schemes into which superannuation payments should be made was a matter that pertained to the employment relationship in the relevant sense. On the other hand, as noted earlier, the Court in *Re Finance Sector Union of Australia; Ex parte Financial Clinic (Vic) Pty Ltd* (1993) 178 CLR 352 adopted a restrictive view of the capacity to make award provision in respect of superannuation contributions on behalf of non-union members.

85. *Re Cram; Ex parte New South Wales Colliery Proprietors' Association Ltd* (1987) 163 CLR 117.

86. *Re Alcan Australia Ltd; Ex parte Federation of Industrial, Manufacturing and Engineering Employees* (1994) 181 CLR 96.

87. The Court did not express any decided view as to whether deductions which had not been authorised by the employee fell within the scope of section 51(xxxv), but clearly had some doubts on the matter – *ibid.*, 104.

88. *The Queen v Portus; Ex parte ANZ Banking Group Ltd* (1972) 127 CLR 353.

89. For an unsuccessful challenge to the validity of the removal of provisions dealing with non-allowable matters from existing awards, see *Re Pacific Coal Pty Limited; Ex parte Construction, Forestry, Mining & Energy Union; Construction, Forestry, Mining & Energy Union v Commonwealth* (2000) 203 CLR 346.

90. *R v Kirby; Ex parte Boilermakers' Society of Australia* (1956) 94 CLR 254 (HC) and *Attorney-General (Commonwealth) v The Queen* (1957) 95 CLR 529 (PC).

91. *Waterside Workers' Federation of Australia v JW Alexander Ltd* (1918) 25 CLR 434.

92. (1956) 94 CLR 254, 289 (per Dixon CJ, McTiernan, Fullagar and Kitto JJ). The dissentients were Williams, Webb and Taylor JJ.

93. *The Queen v Joske; Ex parte Australian Building Construction Employees' and Builders Labourers' Federation* (1974) 130 CLR 87, 90. See too Mason J, 102. See also *R v Joske; Ex parte Shop Distributive and Allied Employees Association* (1976) 135 CLR 194. For comment, see Lane (1981).

94. See, for example, *Harris v Caladine* (1991) 172 CLR 84; *Brandy v Human Rights and Equal Opportunity Commission* (1995) 183 CLR 245; *Wilson v Minister for Aboriginal and Torres Strait Islander Affairs* (1997) 189 CLR 1; *Re Wakin; Ex parte McNally* (1999) 198 CLR 511.

95. See, for example, *Re Cram; Ex parte Newcastle Wallsend Coal Co Pty Ltd* (1987) 143 CLR 140.

96. For comment on this phase in the history of the judicial power, see McCallum (1992).

97. This apparently innocuous change generated significant controversy in consequence of the decision of the government of the day not to appoint one of the members of the Australian Conciliation and Arbitration Commission, Justice Staples, to the new tribunal. See Kirby (1989, 1990).

98. Perhaps the best-known attempt to describe the judicial function is to be found in the judgment of Griffith CJ in *Huddart Parker & Co Pty Ltd v Moorehead* (1909) 8 CLR 330, 357. See also more recent decisions such as *R v Trade Practices Tribunal; Ex parte Tasmanian Breweries Pty Ltd* (1970) 123 CLR 361, 378 (per Kitto J); *Attorney-General (Commonwealth) v Breckler* 197 CLR 83 at 111 [42–7] (per Gleeson CJ, Gaudron, McHugh, Hayne, and Callinan JJ), 124–31 [78–95] (per Kirby J).

99. For detailed accounts of the O'Shea incident, see Sykes and Glasbeek (1972: 551–2), d'Alpuget (1977: 232–5), Hutson (1983: 264–80) and Hancock (1985: 59–61). On the 'paradox' this incident created for the federal system, see Creighton (1991).

100. There were attempts at such reform in 1911, 1913, 1919, 1926, 1944, 1946 and 1973. For further discussion of these endeavours, see Frazer (2001).

101. *Jumbunna Coal Mine No Liability v Victorian Coal Miners' Association* (1908) 6 CLR 309.

102. See, for example, *Amalgamated Society of Engineers v Adelaide Steamship Co Ltd* (1920) 28 CLR 129.

103. See, for example, *Burwood Cinema Ltd v Australian Theatrical and Amusement Employees' Association* (1925) 35 CLR 528; *Metal Trades Employers' Association v Amalgamated Engineering Union* (1935) 54 CLR 387.

104. See further Creighton, Ford & Mitchell (1993): 858–62; Creighton (2003) – cf. Isaac (1958); Laffer (1958); Niland (1978).

105. This shift of emphasis is neatly encapsulated in the Principal Object of the current version of the federal legislation, as set out in section 3 of the 1996 Act.

106. For a brief summary of the legislative changes of the 1990s concerning enterprise bargaining, see Creighton and Stewart (2000: 20–2, 148–50). For more detailed analysis, see McCallum (1993), Naughton (1994), Pittard (1997) and McCarry (1998). On protected industrial action, see McCarry (1994, 1997). On the constitutional validity of these provisions, see *Victoria v Commonwealth* (1996) 187 CLR 416. For international perspectives, see McCallum (1994), Creighton (1997) and Kirby (2002).

107. *Workplace Relations Act 1996*, Part VID. For comment, see Coulthard (1997, 1999), Stewart (1999) and Creighton and Stewart (2000: 174–87). See also Roan et al. (2001), Fetter (2002) and Mitchell and Fetter (2002).

108. See *Workplace Relations Act 1996*, Part VIB, Division 3.

109. For comment on the Victorian referral, see Kollmorgen (1997).

110. See *Workplace Relations Act 1996*, sections 170LT(2), 170VPB, 170VPC, 170X–170XF.

111. See, for example, *Reasonable Hours* case, AIRC, 23 July 2002, PR 072002; *Living Wage Case 2002*, AIRC, 9 May 2002, PR 002002.

112. For overviews and assessments of the traditional system, and the continuing role of conciliation and arbitration, see Creighton (1999: 645–56, and 2000) and Kirby (2001a). For (premature) obituaries, see Mitchell and Rimmer (1990), Vranken (1994) and Dabscheck (2001).

4 ECONOMIC AND SOCIAL EFFECTS

1. *R. v Kelly, Ex Parte ARU* (1953) 89 CLR 474.

2. The contents of this chapter take account of those of other chapters. In particular, it gives less emphasis to gender issues than would be appropriate if there were not a separate chapter dealing with them.

3. The construction of the series, which are inevitably approximate, is described in an appendix.

4. We have constructed a series of working hours based on various data that are available for the years from 1914 onward. These are inexact estimates. Details of the series are available on request to the authors. For the years 1901–14, we have assumed that working hours were constant.

5. The data sources are: for the first three series, Vamplew (1987: 155–61); for AWE (FT), Reserve Bank of Australia (1996: table 4.18); for AWOTE, ABS cat. 6291.0; and for the May survey, data supplied by the Department of Employment, Workplace Relations and Small Business and ABS cat. 6305.0. The May series data used are the median earnings of full-time non-managerial employees.

6. The 1907 value is the *Harvester* 42 shillings. That amount is retained until 1912, whereafter the Court took account of the price index. For the years 1913–21, there was not a single basic wage, as the amount fixed in any award remained unaltered for the duration of the award. The line must be regarded as an approximation of *the* basic wage. This caveat does not apply to the observations from 1922 onward.

7. At this time, the Piddington inquiry (discussed below) took place.

8. Awarded by Justice Powers in 1921.

9. This sub-section draws upon a more extended discussion in Hancock (1998).

10. See also Evans (1996).

11. Brigden said that a paper by Copland had led to the appointment of the Commission and that Copland would have been a member of it had he been able to spare the time (University of Tasmania 1925: 40).

12. This is the skeleton of a rather complicated proposal. Higgins discussed it at some length and critically in 1926 (Higgins 1926: 184–6).

13. Beeby's doubts about the benefits of the reduction were stronger: 'I am convinced from our past three years' experience that in times of economic panic and uncertainty [the transfer of real income away from wage-earners] is not conducive to recovery unless it be part of a planned scheme of reorganization which guarantees that the transferred amount is either immediately spent on commodities or re-invested in labour-employing concerns' (1934 33 CAR 169).

14. Reddaway was then a Research Fellow at the University of Melbourne.

15. Ritchie was Professor of Economic Research in the University of Melbourne.

16. Russell's proviso about the constancy of employment is met by expressing both wage and non-wage income as amounts *per worker*.

17. Russell discussed some qualifications to this rule. For example, it would not apply if a rise in prices was due to higher indirect taxes.

18. This model was advanced, with various qualifications, by Hancock (1960), Karmel (1960), Downing and Isaac (1961), Cockburn and Whitehead (1962), Whitehead and Cockburn (1963), the Committee of Economic Enquiry (the Vernon Committee) (1965) and Isaac (1967). For contemporary criticisms, see Russell (1965) and Pitchford (1971). Whitehead (1966) is a reply to Russell.

19. Kirby and Ashburner constituted a majority against the restoration of automatic adjustments. The decision about a basic wage increase was complicated. The three members of the bench supported different amounts, but to achieve a majority outcome Foster concurred with Kirby.

20. Female wages grew even faster because of the Equal Pay decisions of 1969 and 1972.

21. The government could reinforce the restraining influence of indexation by influencing the behaviour of prices and through tax–wage trade-offs. In November 1974, the Prime Minister said: 'Changes in the rates of income tax should be regarded by the Commission as compensation for the increase in the cost of living which is expected for the December quarter 1974 . . . We will be making it clear wherever possible that money wage restraint is essential' (McGavin 1985: 18).

22. See Carr (1980: 98) for an account of a 1979 union 'rebellion' against a suggestion of wage restraint.

23. Mulvey (1983: 70) says of the Commission's refusal to revert to a centralised system: 'In part this was because the Commonwealth opposed such a system, preferring instead a system of decentralised collective bargaining conducted within an appropriate monetary policy, but it was also clear that the Commission wished to let the current wage round run its course before adopting a public stance on the issue'.

24. There was a precursor in a discussion paper published before the 1980 election (Wright 1981: 112).

25. In the event, the Commission, in February 1988, granted a further flat-rate increase of $6. The delay was related to the share-market collapse of October 1987 and uncertainty about its economic effects.

26. See Hancock (1998).

27. These calculations take account of the diminished proportion of the labour force that is subject to awards. In 2002, the Commission said that safety net increases directly apply to the wages of around 23 per cent of the employed workforce (AIRC 2002: 58).

28. 'Despite our decision that safety net adjustments in excess of $10 per week should not be granted, we repeat our concern about the size and continued growth of the gap between wages emerging under workplace bargaining and award rates. Achievement of a fairer outcome may require a reduction in the average level of negotiated increases' (AIRC 1997: 75).

29. Further increases granted by Beeby in 1937 were not generally followed.

30. The emergency reduction of 1931 did not alter proportional relativities. In 1934, however, the 'new start' for the basic wage resulted in a lesser increase than would have occurred if the Court had simply cancelled the 10 per cent reduction. As the cancellation applied fully to margins, vertical relativities were further stretched.

31. The White Australia policy has also been depicted as part of the settlement.

32. See, for example, Kelly (1992: 668): 'Protection's abolition . . . will smash the reliance upon a centralised wages system embodied in the Industrial Relations Commission: a free market for goods and services must be linked with a relatively free market for labour'.

33. Hancock discusses the purposes of regulation in chapter 2 of Richardson (2000).

34. For example, the Committee of Review into Australian Industrial Relations Law and Systems (Hancock 1985, vol. 2: 229) said that wage policy was 'no panacea for economic ills'. The authority administering it had limited room to manoeuvre. Nevertheless, 'a decision to relinquish an instrument of macro-economic policy should be taken only if there are clear and available offsetting benefits'.

35. The figure is derived from the same data as Figure 4.1. The first time interval, 1901–10, is nine years.

36. The value of r^2 is 0.74.

37. Sources of data used for Figure 4.6: for the Butlin estimates (made by the late Professor NG Butlin), Vamplew (1987); for registered unemployed and survey (RBA), the Reserve Bank of Australia (1996); for the authors' survey series, ABS spreadsheets (ABS cat. 6291.0.40.001); and for the census data, Professor Graeme Hugo. Professor Hugo prepared the census data for use in a special article in the *Commonwealth Yearbook* for 2001, and we thank him for making them available to us.

38. There is considerable short-term variance in the rankings. For example, Australia's rank in 1994 was 12th.

39. The standard deviations were 34 and 14 percentage units in 1900 and 1998, respectively.

40. Over the last quarter-century, much has been said and written about the causes of Australia's inferior performance. See, for example, the essays of Hugh Stretton and Gordon Jackson in Graubard (1985). To Stretton, the main culprits are incompetent and conservative owners and managers. Jackson discerns a number of impediments to performance, including the isolation of the wage structure from 'the discipline of the market place'. Neither questions the assumption that something has to be explained.

41. ABS spreadsheet, cat. 5204.0.

42. If all wage-earners are ranked from top to bottom in terms of their earnings, the tenth percentile corresponds to the amount earned by the person who receives more than 90 per cent of workers but less than the top 10 per cent. The ninetieth percentile wage is that of the person who receives less than 90 per cent of workers but more than 10 per cent. The data are for both sexes combined.

43. The data were collected annually or biennially from employers (ABS cat. 6305.0). (Early data were kindly supplied to us by the Department of Employment, Workplace Relations and Small Business.)

44. Borland (1999) provides a helpful survey.

45. In its submission to the 2001 Safety Net Case, the ACTU demonstrated this compression in the Metal Industry Award over the period 1991–2000. The lowest classification (C14) rate was 78.0 per cent of the tradesman (C10) rate in 1991 and 81.3 per cent in 2000. The maximum (C1b) rate fell from 210 to 192 per cent. We thank Grant Belchamber for this information.

46. Hancock (in Richardson 2000: ch. 2) discusses the view, advanced especially by FA Hayek, that labour market outcomes should not be subjected to tests of fairness.

47. The source for the first two indices is Vamplew (1987: 213). CPI data are taken from a spreadsheet on the ABS website, cat 6401.0.

48. The 'C Series' index is available from 1914 and the CPI from 1949.

49. Some adaptation of the data is required to achieve consistency of time periods. This introduces an additional, but small, scope for error in the data.

50. Minimum weekly wage rates represent amounts prescribed in legal instruments, namely, tribunal awards and determinations and registered agreements.

51. For 1972–84, Reserve Bank of Australia (1996: table 4.18); for 1984–2000, ABS spreadsheet, cat. 6302.0.

5 JUSTICE AND EQUITY

1. See, for example, (1932) 31 CAR 710, (1938) 39 CAR 632, (1944) 53 CAR 212, (1951) 71 CAR 319.

2. Research work prior to the case did not fully endorse this position, with claims that Indigenous stockmen were more productive in some tasks than their white counterparts (see Rowley 1971: 318–19).

3. As Stackpool-Moore (1990: 279) notes, this was a more direct approach than that subsequently taken in the equal pay cases for women in 1969 and 1972, which required equal value to be established under prescribed principles.

4. In the Northern Territory, however, the figure was 60 per cent (ABS 2001 Census, unpublished data).

5. Census data for the Aboriginal population are not available prior to this time.

6. Information is based on census data from various years. Precise comparisons over the whole time period addressed here are not possible due to frequent changes in industry and occupational classifications.

7. The need to look after 'the typical mother of the white race' and ensure her access to affordable domestic help were voiced explicitly by the President of the South Australian Industrial Court, William Jethro Brown, in the 1919 *Women's Living Wage (Cardboard Box Makers)* case (3 SAIR 11, 23). The influence of this type of racism on early Australian wage fixation is elaborated in Dabscheck (1986b).

8. Referred to hereafter as the *Rural Workers* case.

9. Referred to hereafter as the *Clothing Trades* case.

10. In banking, for example, women were awarded 66 per cent of the male basic wage in 1923 (Ryan and Conlon 1989: 116).

11. Although proportionally only to the same level that had been set by Higgins in the 1912 *Rural Workers* case.

12. Similar restrictions had been lifted in 1946 in the United Kingdom (Sawer 1996: 1).

13. A process that significantly limited the scope of the 1969 *AMIEU v Meat and Allied Trades Federation* case (129 CAR 743), as in some classifications women were judged not to be performing the same 'range' of work as men, and in others the work was predominantly performed by women (Hutson 1971: 127).

14. Later to be appointed a Deputy President of the Commission, where she served from 1974 to 1980. The first woman appointed to the Commission was Elizabeth Evatt in 1973.

15. Blau and Kahn's (1992) analysis demonstrates how gender labour market inequality is moderated by overall wage compression.

16. The different ratios for minimum weekly wages and average weekly total wage illustrate that women's pay disadvantage is not simply the result of being paid different minimum amounts, but also reflects the additional benefits that accrue to men through over-award, overtime and other bonus payments.

17. Referred to hereafter as the *Nurses* case.

18. In the context of the National Wage Case of April 1991, it was observed that enterprise bargaining would place 'those sections of the labour force where women predominate' at a relative disadvantage (AIRC 1991: 56).

19. In both New South Wales and Queensland, however, pay equity inquiries have led to the establishment of equal remuneration principles that avoid many of the problems encountered in the HPM case – for example, removing the need for a comparator or proof of discrimination, and allowing investigation to proceed on the basis of criteria that could predispose towards the undervaluation of women's work (NSWIRC 1998; Queensland Industrial Relations Commission 2001).

6 EMPLOYERS' ASSOCIATIONS AND COMPULSORY ARBITRATION

1. Compulsory arbitration legislation was introduced in South Australia in 1892, Western Australia in 1898, Victoria in 1900 and New South Wales in 1901.

2. The CCEA was the national organisation of the State Employers' Federations.

8 MANAGING INDUSTRIAL CONFLICT

1. Cited in Foenander (1937: 4).
2. I am indebted to Breen Creighton for advice on legal issues and to the staff of the AIRC Library for assistance.
3. Although his *New Province for Law and Order* was published in 1922, it comprised articles written earlier. This quote is drawn from a paper written in 1915, during the First World War.
4. The *Commonwealth Conciliation and Arbitration Act 1904* stipulated that the Court had a broad duty to attempt to 'reconcile the parties' to industrial disputes (section 16) and that 'the Court or Conciliation Commissioner shall make all such suggestions and do all such things as appear to it or him to be right and proper for reconciling the parties and for inducing the settlement of the dispute by amicable agreement' (section 23), with arbitration kept as a course of last resort (McGrath and O'Sullivan 1932: 398–408).
5. See Creighton et al. (1993: 1222) for discussion of additional reasons for employers not favouring the use of common law.
6. Rimmer's chapter discusses some noteworthy cases of lockouts.
7. As official statistics on industrial disputes were collected only from 1913 onwards, there are no reliable data available for the period 1904–12.
8. See Sheridan (1989) and Turner (1979) for discussion of the changes in union strategy corresponding with changes in the economic environment.
9. On the issue of the Court dealing with disputes before notification, it should be made clear that this power has always been available, since the Constitution refers to '*prevention* and settlement' of disputes (emphasis added). Thus, the Regulation merely made explicit this power.
10. Keith Hancock and Sue Richardson discuss the issue of margins in more detail in their chapter.
11. It was abolished by the Hawke government in 1983.
12. The deregistration did not simply take place under the Conciliation and Arbitration Act, but involved the Commonwealth Parliament making the *Building Industry Act 1985*, which allowed the Commission to make a 'declaration' concerning certain conduct of the BLF. This was followed in 1986 by the Commission declaring that the union had a history of engaging in industrial action in breach of agreements with various parties and had engaged in conduct contrary to the objects of the Conciliation and Arbitration Act. The parliament then passed the *Builders Labourers (Cancellation of Registration) Act 1986*, which provided for cancellation of registration. The BLF took action in the High Court, which ruled the Act constitutional and the BLF was duly deregistered (Harbord 1986: 72).
13. I am indebted to Breen Creighton for advice concerning the use of common law and the factors influencing its use at different times.
14. It is possible for the Commission to terminate a bargaining period if it is satisfied of the existence of one of a number of specific circumstances, including that action being taken in support of bargaining is damaging to the Australian economy or a significant part of it (see Coulthard 2000: 47–8 for further discussion of this feature of the 1996 Act).
15. Anecdotal evidence suggests that this is a common practice. See Frazer (1998: 83–4) for discussion of the Commission's role in dispute resolution during the life of a certified agreement.

APPENDIX II: MEMBERSHIP

1. Appointed to the Commonwealth Industrial Court in 1956.
2. Appointed to the Commonwealth Industrial Court in 1956.

3. Office introduced in 1992.
4. President of the Industrial Relations Commission of Victoria 1989–93.
5. President of the Tasmanian Industrial Commission 2001–.
6. Position of Senior Commissioner abolished in 1972.
7. Position of Senior Commissioner abolished in 1972.
8. Public Service Arbitrator 1972–78.
9. Public Service Arbitrator 1981–82.
10. President of the Industrial Relations Commission of South Australia 1984–94.
11. President of the Industrial Relations Commission of New South Wales 1981–98.
12. Chief Commissioner of the Queensland Industrial Relations Commission 1990–93.
13. President of the Tasmanian Industrial Commission 1990–2000.
14. Chief Commissioner of the Western Australian Industrial Relations Commission 1987–.
15. Chief Commissioner of the Queensland Industrial Relations Commission 1993–99; President of the Queensland Industrial Relations Commission 1999–.
16. President of the Industrial Relations Commission of South Australia 1994–.
17. President of the Industrial Relations Commission of New South Wales 1998–.

REFERENCES

'Advocatus' 1966, 'Legislation and decisions affecting industrial relations', *Journal of Industrial Relations* 8, 298–304.

Altman, J. and Hawke, A. 1993, 'Indigenous Australians and the labour market: Issues for the union movement', Discussion Paper No. 45, Centre for Aboriginal Economic Policy Research, Australian National University, Canberra.

Anderson, G. 1929, *Fixation of Wages in Australia*, Melbourne: Macmillan and Melbourne University Press.

Attwood, B. 2000, 'The articulation of "land rights" in Australia: The case of Wave Hill', *Social Analysis* 44, 3–39.

Australasian Convention 1897, Official Report of the National Australasian Convention Debates, Adelaide, 22 March–5 May 1897.

1898, Official Record of the Debates of the Australasian Federal Convention, Third Session, Melbourne, 20 January–17 March 1898.

Australian Bureau of Statistics (ABS), Time series data, Labour Force Australia, Detailed, Electronic Delivery, 6291.0.55.001, <http://www.abs.gov.au> (accessed May 2003).

ABS, various years, *Employee Earnings and Hours*, 6306.0, Canberra: ABS.

1974, *Labour Report, No. 53, 1973*, Canberra: ABS.

1983, *Labour Statistics Australia 1982*, 6101.0, Canberra: ABS.

1985, *Labour Statistics Australia 1984*, Canberra: ABS.

1990, *Award Coverage Australia, May 1990*, 6315.0, Canberra: ABS.

1994, *Industrial Disputes Australia*, 6322.0, Canberra: ABS.

2001, Indigenous Profile, 2001 Population of Census and Housing, on-line publication, <http://www.abs.gov.au> (accessed August 2003).

2003, Industrial Disputes Australia, 6321.0, Time Series Spreadsheet 1982–2002, Canberra: ABS.

Australian Centre for Industrial Relations Research and Training (ACIRRT) 1999, *Australia at Work*, Sydney: Prentice Hall.

Australian Chamber of Commerce and Industry (ACCI) 1997, ACCI Review, October.

Australian Conciliation and Arbitration Commission (ACAC) 1979, National Wage Case, Reasons for Decision, Print E267.

1985, Transcript of the 'Ceremonial Session of the Australian Conciliation and Arbitration Commission to farewell Sir John Moore, Sydney, 29 October 1985', Sir Richard Kirby Archives of the Commission.

Australian Council of Trade Unions (ACTU) 1969, 'The end of penal provisions', ACTU Executive Minutes, 21 May, in Hagan, J. (ed.), *Australian Trade Unionism in Documents*, Melbourne: Longman Cheshire.

Australian Council of Trade Unions/Trade Development Commission (ACTU/TDC) 1987, *Australia Reconstructed*, Canberra: AGPS.

Australian Industrial Registry (AIR) 1999, *Australian Industrial Relations Commission – General Information*, August, Melbourne: AIR.

Australian Industrial Relations Commission (AIRC) various years, *Annual Report of the President of the Australian Industrial Relations Commission*, Canberra: AGPS.

1988, National Wage Case, August 1988, Print H4000.

1989a, February 1989 Review, Print H8200.

1989b, National Wage Case, August 1989, Print H9100.

1990, National Wage Case, Transcript of Proceedings, 13 September, Melbourne.

1991, National Wage Case, April 1991, Print J7400.

1997, Safety Net Review – Wages, Print P1997.

2000, Safety Net Review – Wages, Print S5000.

2001a, Safety Net Review – Wages, PR002001.

2001b, Ceremonial Sitting of Australian Industrial Relations Commission to Mark the Centenary of Federation, Sydney, 5 June 2001.

2002, Safety Net Review – Wages, PR002002.

2003, Safety Net Review – Wages, PR002003.

Bagaric, M. 2000, 'Originalism: Why some things should never change – or at least not too quickly', *University of Tasmania Law Review* 19, 173–204.

Barrett, M and McIntosh, M 1980, 'The "family wage": Some problems for socialists and feminists', *Capital and Class* 11, 51–72.

Beaton, L. 1982, 'The importance of women's paid labour: Women at work in World War II', in Bevege, M., James, M. and Shute, C. (eds), *Worth Her Salt: Women at Work in Australia*, Sydney: Hale & Iremonger, 84–98.

Bedford, I. 1963, 'The one big union, 1918–1923', in Bedford, I. and Curnow, R. (eds), *Initiative and Organisation*, Sydney: Cheshire, 5–43.

Belchamber, G. 1996, 'Disappearing middle or vanishing bottom: A comment on Gregory', *Economic Record* 72, 287–93.

Bennett, B. and Cole, K. 1989, 'Industrial relations', in Head, B. and Patience, A. (eds), *From Fraser to Hawke: Australian Public Policy in the 1980s*, Melbourne: Longman Cheshire, 177–212.

Bennett, L. 1984, 'Legal intervention and the female workforce: The Australian Conciliation and Arbitration Court 1907–1921', *International Journal of the Sociology of Law* 12, 23–36.

1988, 'Equal pay and comparable worth and the Australian Conciliation and Arbitration Commission', *Journal of Industrial Relations* 30, 533–45.

1994a, *Making Labour Law in Australia: Industrial Relations, Politics and Law*, Sydney: Law Book Co.

1994b, 'Women and enterprise bargaining: The legal and institutional framework', *Journal of Industrial Relations* 36, 191–212.

Blain, N. 1984, *Industrial Relations in the Air: Australian Airline Pilots*, St Lucia: University of Queensland Press.

Blake, G. 1929, *Arbitration's Chequered Career from 1901–1927*, Sydney: privately published.

Blandy, R. and Richardson, S. (eds) 1982, *How Labour Markets Work*, Melbourne: Longman Cheshire.

Blau, F. D. and Kahn, L. M. 1992, 'The gender earnings gap: Learning from international comparisons', *American Economic Review, Papers and Proceedings*, May, 533–8.

Blyton, P. and Turnbull, P. 1998, *The Dynamics of Employee Relations*, London: Macmillan.

Bohle, P. and Quinlan, M. 2000, *Managing Occupational Health and Safety*, Melbourne: Macmillan.

Bolton, G. 2000, *Edmund Barton*, Sydney: Allen & Unwin.

Borland, J. 1999, 'Earnings inequality in Australia: Changes, causes and consequences', *Economic Record* 75, 177–202.

Borland, J. and Woodbridge, G. 1999, 'Wage regulation, low-wage workers, and employment', in Richardson, *Reshaping the Labour Market*, 122–58.

Bowden, B. 1999, 'Employer associations in road transport', in Sheldon and Thornthwaite, *Employer Associations and Industrial Relations Change*, 94–114.

Bray, M. 1994, 'The unions, the Accord and economic restructuring', in Brett, J., Gillespie, J. and Goot, M. (eds), *Developments in Australian Politics*, Melbourne: Macmillan, 259–76.

Bray, M. and Rimmer, M. 1987, *Delivering the Goods: A History of the NSW Transport Workers' Union, 1888–1996*, Sydney: Allen & Unwin.

1989, 'Voluntarism or compulsion? Public inquiries into industrial relations in New South Wales and Great Britain, 1890–94', in Macintyre and Mitchell, *Foundations of Arbitration*, 50–73.

Bray, M. and Wailes, N. 1999, 'Reinterpreting the 1989 pilots' dispute: The role of managerial control and labour productivity', *Labour and Industry* 10, 79–106.

Brereton, D. 1989, 'Institutions in the wage determination process: The Australian Conciliation and Arbitration Commission, 1904–70', PhD thesis, Stanford University.

Brigden, J. B., Copland, D. B., Dyason, E. C., Giblin, L. F. and Wickens, C. H. 1929, *The Australian Tariff: An Economic Enquiry*, Melbourne University Press in association with Macmillan.

Briggs, C. 2001, 'Australian exceptionalism: The role of trade unions in the emergence of enterprise bargaining', *Journal of Industrial Relations* 43, 27–43.

Broome, R. 2002, *Aboriginal Australians: Black Responses to White Dominance 1788–2001*, 3rd edn, Sydney: Allen & Unwin.

Brown, R. 1992, *Understanding Industrial Organizations: Theoretical Perspectives in Industrial Sociology*, London: Routledge.

Bunbury, B. 2002, *It's Not the Money It's the Land: Aboriginal Stockmen and the Equal Wages Case*, Fremantle Arts Centre Press.

Burton, C. 1988, *Gender Bias in Job Evaluation*, Monograph No. 3, Canberra: Affirmative Action Agency.

Business Council of Australia (BCA) 1989, *Enterprise-Based Bargaining Units: A Better Way of Working*, Report to the Business Council of Australia by the Industrial Relations Study Commission, Melbourne: BCA.

Callus, R., Morehead, A., Cully, M. and Buchanan, J. 1991, *Industrial Relations at Work: The Australian Workplace Industrial Relations Survey*, Canberra: AGPS.

Cameron, C. 1982, *Unions in Crisis*, Melbourne: Hill of Content.

1990, *The Cameron Diaries*, North Sydney: Susan Haynes and Allen & Unwin.

Campbell, D. A. 1996, 'The evolution of enterprise bargaining policy in Australian employer organisations: 1982 to 1992', PhD thesis, Monash University.

Campbell, G. 1999, 'Wages, the Accord and the new working week', in Carman, M. and Rogers, I. (eds), *Out of the Rut: Making Labor a Genuine Alternative*, Sydney: Allen & Unwin, 49–69.

Carboch, D. 1958, 'The fall of the Bruce–Page government', in Wildavsky, A. and Carboch, D., *Studies in Australian Politics*, Melbourne: Cheshire, 121–275.

Carr, B. 1977, 'Australian trade unionism in 1976', *Journal of Industrial Relations* 19, 80–6.

1980, 'Australian trade unionism in 1979', *Journal of Industrial Relations* 22, 98–103.

Castles, F. G. 1985, *Working Class and Welfare: Reflections on the Political Development of the Welfare State in Australia and New Zealand, 1890–1980*, Sydney: Allen & Unwin in association with Port Nicholson Press.

1988, *Australian Public Policy and Economic Vulnerability*, Sydney: Allen & Unwin.

(ed.) 1991, *Australia Compared: People, Policies and Politics*, Sydney: Allen & Unwin.

1994, 'The wage earners' welfare state revisited: Refurbishing the established model of Australian social protection, 1983–93', *Australian Journal of Social Issues* 29, 120–45.

Central Council of Employers of Australia (CCEA), various dates, Minutes of Meetings and Conference Proceedings.

Chapman, B. J. 1998, 'The Accord: background changes and aggregate outcomes', *Journal of Industrial Relations* 40, 624–42.

Chapman, B. J. and Gruen, F. 1990, 'An analysis of the Australian consensual incomes policy: The prices and incomes Accord', Discussion Paper No. 221, Centre for Economic Policy Research, Australian National University, Canberra.

Clark, A. I. 1901, *Studies in Australian Constitutional Law*, Melbourne: Charles F. Maxwell.

Clarke, V. S. 1905, 'Labor conditions in Australia', *Bulletin of the Bureau of Labor*, vol. X, Washington: Government Printer.

Cockburn, M. and Whitehead, D. 1962, 'Wages in Australia: practices and prescriptions', *Oxford University Institute of Statistics Bulletin* 24, May, 235–56.

Cockfield, S. 1993, 'Arbitration, mass production and workplace relations: Metal industry developments in the 1920s', *Journal of Industrial Relations* 35, 19–38.

Coghlan, T. A. 1918, *Labour and Industry in Australia*, London: Oxford University Press.

Committee of Economic Enquiry 1965, *Report of the Committee of Economic Enquiry* (Dr J. Vernon, Chairman), Canberra: Commonwealth of Australia.

Commonwealth Arbitration Reports (CAR) 1905–, Melbourne: Government Printer.

Commonwealth Bureau of Census and Statistics (CBCS) 1914, *Prices, Cost of Living, Wages, Trade Unions, Unemployment and General Industrial Conditions, 1913–14*, Labour and Industrial Branch Report No. 5, Melbourne: CBCS.

1918, *Prices, Purchasing-Power of Money, Wages, Trade Unions, Unemployment and General Industrial Conditions, 1917*, Labour and Industrial Branch Report No. 8, Melbourne: CBCS.

1935, *Labour Report No. 23*, Canberra: CBCS.

1947, *Labour Report No. 36*, Canberra: CBCS.

1955, *Labour Report No. 42*, Canberra: CBCS.

1971a, *Labour Report No. 55*, Canberra: CBCS.

1971b, *The Aboriginal Population: Characteristics of the Aboriginal and Torres Strait Islander Population*, Bulletin 9, 1971 Census of Population and Housing.

Commonwealth Conciliation and Arbitration Commission (CCAC) 1958, *Second Annual Report of the President of the Commonwealth Conciliation and Arbitration Commission, 14 August 1957–13 August 1958*, Canberra.

1960, *Fourth Annual Report of the President of the Commonwealth Conciliation and Arbitration Commission, 14 August 1959–13 August 1960*, Canberra.

Commonwealth Court of Conciliation and Arbitration (CCCA) 1951, *Fourth Annual Report of the Commonwealth Court of Conciliation and Arbitration, 8 October 1950–7 October 1951*, Canberra.

1952, *Fifth Annual Report of the Commonwealth Court of Conciliation and Arbitration, 8 October 1951–7 October 1952*, Canberra.

Commonwealth Law Reports (CLR) 1903–, Sydney: Law Book Company.

Commonwealth of Australia 1920, *The Acts of the Parliament of the Commonwealth of Australia Passed during the Year 1920*, Melbourne: Government Printer.

Commonwealth Parliamentary Debates (CPD) 1901–, AGPS.

Commonwealth Parliamentary Papers (CPP) 1905, 'President of the Conciliation and Arbitration Court, (Papers Relating to the Appointment of His Honour Mr Justice O'Connor)', vol. 2, 209–13.

1914–17, 'Conciliation and Arbitration. Report of Proceedings', vol. 2, 102.

1929, 'Report of the British Economic Mission to Australia', vol. 2, 1231–72.

1951–53, 'Fifth Annual Report of the Chief Judge of the Commonwealth Court of Conciliation and Arbitration, 31 October 1952', vol. 2, 1207.

Commonwealth Submission 2002, Safety Net Review – Wages, 2001–2002, Commonwealth Department of Employment and Workplace Relations.

Commonwealth Treasury 1976, Budget Paper No. 2.

1979, Budget Paper No. 2.

1980, Budget Paper No. 2.

1988, Budget Paper No. 2.

1990, Budget Paper No. 2.

Confederation of Australian Industry 1991, Industrial Review, July.

Cooper, R. 1996, *Making the NSW Union Movement? A Study of the Organising and Recruitment Activities of the NSW Labor Council, 1900–1910*, Monograph No. 39, Industrial Relations Research Centre, University of New South Wales, Sydney.

Copland, D. B. 1923, 'The trade depression in Australia in relation to economic thought', Report of the Sixteenth Meeting of the Australian and New Zealand Association for the Advancement of Science.

Copland, D. B. 1934, *Australia in the World Crisis*, Cambridge University Press.

Coulthard, A. 1997, 'The individualisation of Australian labour law', *International Journal of Comparative Labour Law and Industrial Relations* 13, 95–112.

1999, 'The decollectivisation of Australian industrial relations: Trade union exclusion under the Workplace Relations Act 1996 (Commonwealth)', in Deery, S. and Mitchell, R. (eds), *Employment Relations: Individualisation and Union Exclusion*, Sydney: Federation Press, 48–68.

2000, 'Major tribunal decisions in 1999', *Journal of Industrial Relations* 42, 41–58.

Cousins, D. and Nieuwenhuysen, J. 1984, *Aboriginals and the Mining Industry: Case Studies of the Australian Experience*, Sydney: Committee for Economic Development of Australia/George Allen & Unwin.

Craven, G. 1990, 'Original intent and the Australian Constitution – coming soon to a court near you?', *Public Law Review* 1, 166–85.

Creigh, S. 1986, 'Australia's strike record: The international perspective', in Blandy, R. and Niland, J. (eds), *Alternatives to Arbitration*, Sydney: Allen & Unwin, 29–51.

Creighton, W. B. 1991, 'Enforcement in the federal industrial relations system: An Australian paradox', *Australian Journal of Labour Law* 4, 197–225.

1997, 'The Workplace Relations Act in international perspective', *Australian Journal of Labour Law* 10, 31–49.

1998, 'Transmission of all or part of a business: A neglected issue in Australian industrial and employment law', *Australian Business Law Review* 26, 162–83.

1999, 'Transformation of labor and future of labor law in Europe: An Australian perspective', *Comparative Labor Law and Policy Journal* 20, 635–80.

2000, 'One hundred years of the conciliation and arbitration power: A province lost?', *Melbourne University Law Review* 24, 839–65.

2003, 'Modernising Australian labour law: Individualisation and the shift from "compulsory" conciliation and arbitration to enterprise bargaining', in Blanpain, R. and Weiss, M. (eds), *Industrial Relations: Liber Amicorum dedicated to the memory of Professor Marco Biagi*, Deventer: Kluwer, 93–112.

Creighton, W. B., Ford, W. J. and Mitchell, R. J. 1993, *Labour Law: Text and Materials*, 2nd edn, Sydney: Law Book Company.

Creighton, W. B. and Stewart, A. 2000, *Labour Law: An Introduction*, 3rd edn, Sydney: Federation Press.

Crisp, L. F. 1990, *Federation Fathers*, Melbourne University Press.

Dabscheck, B. 1975, 'The 1975 national wage case: Now we have an incomes policy', *Journal of Industrial Relations* 17, 298–309.

1977, 'National wage case decisions 1976: The golden age of indexation', *Journal of Industrial Relations* 19, 65–82.

1980, 'Theories of regulation and Australian industrial relations', *Journal of Industrial Relations* 22, 196–218.

1983, *Arbitrator at Work: Sir William Raymond Kelly and the Regulation of Australian Industrial Relations*, Sydney: George Allen & Unwin.

1986a, 'In search of the holy grail: proposals for the reform of Australian industrial relations', in Blandy, R. and Niland, J. (eds), *Alternatives to Arbitration*, Sydney: Allen & Unwin, 163–82.

1986b, 'The "typical mother of the white race" and the origins of female wage determination', *Hecate* 12, 147–52.

1989, *Australian Industrial Relations in the 1980s*, Melbourne: Oxford University Press.

1994, 'The arbitration system since 1967', in Bell, S. and Head, B. (eds), *State, Economy and Public Policy in Australia*, Melbourne: Oxford University Press, 142–68.

1995, *The Struggle for Australian Industrial Relations*, Melbourne: Oxford University Press.

1998, 'The waterfront dispute: Of vendetta and the Australian way', *Economic and Labour Relations Review* 9, 155–84.

2001, 'The slow and agonising death of the Australian experiment with conciliation and arbitration', *Journal of Industrial Relations* 43, 277–93.

d'Alpuget, B. 1977, *Mediator: A Biography of Sir Richard Kirby*, Melbourne University Press.

D'Aprano, Z. 2001, *Kath Williams: The Unions and the Fight for Equal Pay*, North Melbourne: Spinifex Press.

Davies, P. 1983, 'Gregory, Henry', in *1860–1940 Australian Dictionary of Biography*, vol. 9, Melbourne University Press, 98–9.

Dawkins, P. and Kelly, P. 2003, *Hard Heads, Soft Hearts: A New Reform Agenda for Australia*, Sydney: Allen & Unwin.

Dawson, D. 1990, 'Intention and the Constitution – whose intent?', *Australian Bar Review* 6, 93–102.

Deery, S., Plowman, D. and Walsh, J. 1997, *Industrial Relations: A Contemporary Analysis*, Sydney: McGraw-Hill.

Deery, S., Plowman, D., Walsh, J. and Brown, M. 2001, *Industrial Relations: A Contemporary Analysis*, 2nd edn, Sydney: McGraw-Hill.

Department of Employment and Industrial Relations (DEIR) 1984, *Submission to the Committee of Review into Australian Industrial Relations Law and Systems*, Canberra: AGPS.

2002, Commonwealth Submission, Safety Net Review – Wages, 2001–2002.

Dixson, M. 1963, 'The timber strike of 1929', *Historical Studies Australia and New Zealand* 10, 479–92.

Dobson, W. T. 1979, 'The Associated Chamber of Manufactures of Australia 1904–1977', MA thesis, University of Melbourne.

Donn, C. B. and Dunkley, G. 1977, 'The founding of the ACTU: The origins of a central trade union federation', *Journal of Industrial Relations* 19, 404–23.

Downing, R. I. 1956, 'Wage determination and some controlling factors in the Australian economy', in Walker, K. F. (ed.), *Unions, Management and the Public*, Perth: University of Western Australia Press, 49–61.

Downing, R. I. and Isaac, J. E. 1961, 'The 1961 basic wage judgment and wage policy', *Economic Record* 37, 480–94.

Drago, R., Wooden, M. and Sloan, J. 1992, *Productive Relations? Australian Industrial Relations and Workplace Performance*, Sydney: Allen & Unwin.

Edwards, J. 1996, *Keating: The Inside Story*, Ringwood: Viking.

Edwards, P. 1986, *Conflict at Work: A Materialist Analysis of Workplace Relations*, Oxford: Blackwell.

Eldridge, J. E. T. 1968, *Industrial Disputes: Essays in the Sociology of Industrial Relations*, London: Routledge and Kegan Paul.

Ellem, B. 1999, 'Trade unionism in 1998', *Journal of Industrial Relations* 41, 127–52.

Employers' Federation of New South Wales (EFNSW), various dates, Minutes, Annual Reports, *Employers' Review*.

Evans, T. 1996, 'Addressing Australia's unemployment problem', in Commonwealth Treasury, *Economic Roundup*, Spring, 25–38.

Eveline, J. 2001 'Feminism, racism and citizenship in twentieth century Australia', in Crawford, P. and Maddern, P. (eds), *Women as Australian Citizens: Underlying Theories*, Melbourne University Press, 141–77.

Fetter, J. 2002, 'The strategic use of individual employment agreements: Three case studies', Working Paper No. 26, Centre for Employment and Labour Relations Law, University of Melbourne.

Figart, D., Mutari, E. and Power, M. 2002, *Living Wages, Equal Wages: Gender and Labor Market Policies in the United States*, New York: Routledge.

Fisher, C. 1983, *Innovation and Australian Industrial Relations*, Sydney: Croom Helm.

Fitzhardinge, L. F. 1979, *The Little Digger 1914–1952: William Morris Hughes, a Political Biography*, vol. 2, Sydney: Angus & Robertson.

Fitzpatrick, B. 1940a, *A Short History of the Australian Labor Movement*, Melbourne: Rawson's Bookshop.

1940b, *The British Empire in Australia 1834–1939*, Melbourne: Macmillan.

1949, *The British Empire in Australia: An Economic History 1834–1939*, 2nd edn, Melbourne University Press.

Foenander, O. 1928, 'The forty-four hours case in Australia, 1926–1927', *Quarterly Journal of Economics* 42, 307–27.

1937, *Towards Industrial Peace in Australia: A Series of Essays in the History of the Commonwealth Court of Conciliation and Arbitration*, Melbourne University Press.

1941, *Solving Labour Problems in Australia*, Melbourne University Press.

1952, *Studies in Australian Labour Law and Relations*, Melbourne University Press.

Ford, G. and Hearn, J. 1987, 'Conflict and industrial relations', in Ford, G., Hearn, J. and Lansbury, R. (eds), *Australian Labour Relations: Readings*, 4th edn, Melbourne: Macmillan, 2–19.

Ford, W. J. 1984, 'The federal industrial disputes power: Comments on some constitutional considerations', in Rawson, D. and Fisher, C. (eds), *Changing Industrial Law*, Sydney: Croom Helm, 46–83.

Forsyth, A. 2001, 'Re-regulatory tendencies in Australian and New Zealand labour law', Working Paper No. 21, Centre for Employment and Labour Relations Law, University of Melbourne.

Fox, C., Howard, W. and Pittard, M. 1995, *Industrial Relations in Australia: Development, Law and Operation*, Melbourne: Longman.

Frances, R. 1993, *The Politics of Work: Gender and Labour in Victoria, 1880–1939*, Cambridge University Press.

Frazer, A. 1998, 'Major tribunal decisions in 1997', *Journal of Industrial Relations* 40, 71–87.

1999, 'Major tribunal decisions in 1998', *Journal of Industrial Relations* 41, 80–102.

2001, 'Parliament and the industrial power', in Lindell, G. and Bennett, R. (eds), *Parliament: The Vision and the Hindsight*, Sydney: Federation Press, 93–148.

Fricke, G. 2001, 'Charles Powers', in Blackshield, T., Coper, M. and Williams, G. (eds), *The Oxford Companion to the High Court*, Melbourne: Oxford University Press, 548–50.

Gahan, P. 1996, 'Did arbitration make for dependent unionism? Evidence from historical case studies', *Journal of Industrial Relations* 39, 533–56.

Gardner, M. 1987, 'Australian trade unionism in 1986', *Journal of Industrial Relations* 29, 102–10.

Gardner, M. and Palmer, G. 1997, *Employment Relations: Industrial Relations and Human Resource Management in Australia*, 2nd edn, Melbourne: Macmillan.

Garran, R. R. 1958, *Prosper the Commonwealth*, Sydney: Angus & Robertson.

Gaudron, M. 1982, 'Women in the workforce and the elimination of discrimination: Whose responsibility?', *Labour History* 42, 106–11.

2001, Speech for the Australian Industrial Relations Commission's Dinner to Mark the Centenary of Federation, Sydney, June 2001, Sir Richard Kirby Archives.

Gaudron, M. and Bosworth, M. 1979, 'Equal pay?', in Macinolty, J. and Radi, H. (eds), *In Pursuit of Justice: Australian Women and the Law 1788–1979*, Sydney: Hale & Iremonger, 161–9.

Ginters, P. 1999, 'The transmission of business provisions in the Workplace Relations Act 1996 (Commonwealth): Reaffirming the primacy of the "substantial identity" test', *Australian Journal of Labour Law* 12, 211–16.

Giudice, G. 2001, Keynote address to Bar Association of Queensland Industrial and Employment Law Conference, 20 April, <http://www.airc.gov.au/research/speeches/speeches/Giudice0401.htm> (accessed August 2003).

2002, 'Our industrial relations system: what makes it unique?', Paper presented to the Sydney Institute, <http://www.airc.gov.au> (accessed August 2003).

2003, 'Dispute resolution in the last decade of the twentieth century', Address to the Association of Industrial Relations Academics of Australia and New Zealand, Melbourne, 6 February.

Glasbeek, H. 1998, 'The MUA affair: The role of law vs. the rule of law', *Economic and Labour Relations Review* 9, 188–220.

Goldsworthy, J. 1997, 'Originalism in constitutional interpretation', *Federal Law Review* 25, 1–50.

2000, 'Interpreting the Constitution in its second century', *Melbourne University Law Review* 24, 677–710.

Gollan, R. 1963, *The Coalminers of New South Wales: A History of the Union 1860–1960*, Melbourne University Press.

Graubard, S. R. (ed.) 1985, *Australia: The Daedalus Symposium*, Sydney: Angus & Robertson.

Green, R. 1993, 'Wages policy and wage determination in 1992', *Journal of Industrial Relations* 35, 141–55.

Gregory R. G. 1993, 'Aspects of Australian and U.S. living standards: The disappointing decades 1970–1990', *Economic Record* 69, 61–76.

Gregory, R. G., Daly, A., Anstie, R. and Ho, V. 1989, 'Women's pay in Australia, Great Britain and the United States: The role of laws regulation and human capital', in Michael, R., Hartmann, H. and O'Farrell, B. (eds), *Pay Equity: Empirical Inquiries*, Washington DC: National Academy Press, 222–42.

Gregory, R. G., Daly, A. and Ho, V. 1986, 'A tale of two countries: Equal pay for women in Australia and Britain', Discussion Paper No. 147, Centre for Economic Policy Research, Australian National University, Canberra.

Gregory, R. G. and Duncan, R. C. 1981, 'Employment, unemployment and income effects of relative wage changes', in Hancock, K. J. (ed.), *Incomes Policy in Australia*, Sydney: Harcourt Brace Jovanovich, 297–318.

1983, 'Equal pay for women: A reply (segmented labour market theories and the Australian experience of equal pay for women)', *Australian Economic Papers* 22, 60–4.

Gregory, R. G., Ho, V. and McDermott, L. 1988, 'Sharing the burden: The Australian labour market during the 1930s', in Gregory, R. G. and Butlin, N. G. (eds), *Recovery from the Depression: Australia and the World Economy in the 1930s*, Cambridge University Press, 217–44.

Griffin, G. and Scarcebrook, V. 1990, 'The dependency theory of trade unionism and the role of the Industrial Registrar', *Australian Bulletin of Labour* 16, 21–31.

Griffin, G. and Svensen, S. 1998, 'Industrial relations implications of the Australian water-side dispute', *Australian Bulletin of Labour* 24, 194–206.

Gutman, G. 1986, 'The Hancock report: A last hurrah for the system', in *Arbitration in Contempt*, the Proceedings of the Inaugural Seminar of the HR Nicholls Society, Melbourne, 28 February–2 March, Melbourne: HR Nicholls Society.

Guy, B. 1999, *A Life on the Left: A Biography of Clyde Cameron*, Kent Town, SA: Wakefield Press.

Hagan, J. 1981, *The History of the ACTU*, Melbourne: Longman Cheshire.

Hall, C. R. 1971, *The Manufacturers: Australian Manufacturing Achievements to 1960*, Sydney: Angus & Robertson.

Hall, P. and Fruin, D. 1994, 'Gender aspects of enterprise bargaining: The good, the bad and the ugly', in Morgan, D. E. (ed.), *Dimensions of Enterprise Bargaining and Organisational Relations*, Monograph No. 36, UNSW Studies in Australian Industrial Relations, Kensington: Industrial Relations Research Centre.

Hampson, I. 1996, 'The Accord: A post-mortem', *Labour and Industry* 7, 55–77.

Hancock, J. and Smith, J. 2001, *Financing the Federation*, Adelaide: South Australian Centre for Economic Studies, Adelaide and Flinders Universities.

Hancock, K. J. 1960, 'Wage policy in Australia', *Economic Journal* 70, 543–60.

1964, 'Wages policy in Australia, 1964', *Journal of Industrial Relations* 6, 256–62.

1966, 'Earnings drift in Australia', *Journal of Industrial Relations* 8, 128–57.

1969, 'The wages of the workers', *Journal of Industrial Relations* 11, 17–38.

1979, 'The first half century of Australian wage policy – part 2', *Journal of Industrial Relations* 21, 129–60.

1985, *Australian Industrial Relations Law and Systems*, Committee of Review into Australian Industrial Relations Law and Systems, Report, Canberra: AGPS.

1998, 'The needs of the low paid', *Journal of Industrial Relations* 40, 42–62.

Hancock, K. J. and Moore, K. 1972, 'The occupational wage structure in Australia since 1914', *British Journal of Industrial Relations* 10, 107–22.

Hancock, K. J. and Rawson, D. 1993, 'The metamorphosis of Australian industrial relations', *British Journal of Industrial Relations* 31, 489–513.

Harbord, G. 1986, 'Major tribunal decisions in 1986', *Journal of Industrial Relations* 29, 66–74.

Hargreaves, W. J. 1958, *History of the Federated Moulders' Metals Union of Australia 1858–1958*, Sydney: The Worker Print.

Hastings, S. 2001, letter to Geoffrey Guidice, Sir Richard Kirby Archives of the AIRC.

Hawke, R. 1993, 'Industrial relations in Australia: A turbulent past, and uncertain future', *Journal of Industrial Relations* 35, 475–85.

Hawke, R. J. L. 1994, *The Hawke Memoirs*, Port Melbourne: Reed Books.

Hayden, B. 1992, 'Review of Paul Kelly's *The End of Certainty*', *Australian Quarterly* 644, 451–61.

Heagney, M. 1935, *Are Women Taking Men's Jobs? A Survey of Women's Work in Victoria with Special Regard to Equal Status, Equal Pay, and Equality of Opportunity*, Melbourne: Hilton and Veitch.

Higgins, B. 1950, Submission to the Commonwealth Court of Conciliation and Arbitration, Basic Wage Case 1949–50, (mimeo).

Higgins, H. B. 1915, 'A new province for law and order – part I', *Harvard Law Review* 29, 13–39.

1919, 'A new province for law and order – part II', *Harvard Law Review* 32, 189–212.

1920, 'A new province for law and order – part III', *Harvard Law Review* 34, 105–36.

1922a, *A New Province for Law and Order*, Sydney: Constable and Company; reissue, London: Dawson, 1968.

1922b, 'The future of industrial tribunals', *The New Outlook*, April, 8–9.

1924, *The (Australian) Commonwealth Court of Conciliation and Arbitration: An Address Delivered at Oxford before Members of the University Association for Philosophy, Politics and Economics on 14 June 1924*, Canberra: Federal Capital Press.

1926, 'Industrial arbitration', reprinted in *Australian Bulletin of Labour* 27, 2001, 177–91.

Higgins, W. 1994, 'Industry policy', in Brett, J., Gillespie, J. and Goot, M. (eds), *Developments in Australian Politics*, Melbourne: Macmillan, 234–58.

Hinton, J. 1982, 'The rise of a mass labour movement: Growth and limits', in Wrigley, C. (ed.), *A History of British Industrial Relations 1875–1914*, Brighton: Harvester Press, 20–46.

Hobbes, T. 1991, *Leviathan*, Cambridge University Press.

Holt, J. 1986, *Compulsory Arbitration in New Zealand: The First Forty Years*, Auckland University Press.

Horn, R. V. 1970, 'Wages drift and salary trends (male employees, Australia, 1954–1969)', *Journal of Industrial Relations* 11, 89–98.

Howard, J. 1990, 'The Liberal-National Parties' industrial relations policy: Deregulation by providing an enterprise focus', *Economic and Labour Relations Review* 12, 34–47.

Howard, W. A. 1977, 'Australian trade unions in the context of union theory', *Journal of Industrial Relations* 20, 255–73.

HR Nicholls Society 1986, 'Arbitration in contempt', *Proceedings of the Inaugural Seminar of the HR Nicholls Society, Melbourne 28 February–2 March 1986*, Melbourne: HR Nicholls Society.

Hughes, B. 1970, 'The national wage case', *Journal of Industrial Relations* 12, 72–80.

1973, 'The wages of the strong and the weak', *Journal of Industrial Relations* 15, 1–24.

Hughes, C. A. 1980, 'Government action and the judicial model', in Tay, A. E.-S. and Kamenka, E. (eds), *Law-Making in Australia*, Port Melbourne: Edward Arnold.

Hughes, W. M. 1941, 'The tribute of a contemporary', in Groom, J. (ed.), *Nation Building in Australia: The Life and Work of Sir Littleton Ernest Groom*, Sydney: Angus & Robertson.

Hunter, B. 1997, 'An Indigenous workers' guide to the Workplace Relations Act', *Journal of Industrial Relations* 39, 439–56.

Hunter, R. 1988, 'Women workers and industrial law: From Harvester to comparable worth', *Australian Journal of Labour Law* 1, 147–72.

2000, *The Beauty Therapist, the Mechanic, the Geoscientist and the Librarian: Addressing Undervaluation of Women's Work*, Sydney: Australian Technology Network. Women's Executive Development Program.

Hutson, J. H. 1966, *Penal Colony to Penal Powers*, Surry Hills: Amalgamated Engineering Union.

1971, *Six Wage Concepts*, Surry Hills: Amalgamated Engineering Union.

1983, *Penal Colony to Penal Powers*, rev. edn, Sydney: Amalgamated Metal Workers and Shipwrights Union.

International Labour Organisation (ILO) 2002, *Yearbook of Labour Statistics*, Geneva: ILO.

Iremonger, J., Merritt, J. and Osborne, G. 1973, 'Introduction', in Iremonger, J., Merritt, J. and Osborne, G. (eds), *Strikes: Studies in Twentieth Century Australian Social History*, Sydney: Angus & Robertson.

Isaac, J. E. 1954, 'The basic wage and standard inquiry in Australia, 1952–53', *International Labour Review* 69, May, 570–93.

1958, 'The prospects for collective bargaining in Australia', *Economic Record* 34, 69, December, 347–61.

1965, 'The federal basic wage-margins case, 1965', *Journal of Industrial Relations* 7, 225–49.

1967, *Wages and Productivity*, Melbourne: Cheshire.

1971, 'Penal provisions under Commonwealth arbitration', in Isaac, J. and Ford, G. (eds), *Australian Labour Relations: Readings*, 2nd edn, Melbourne: Sun Books.

1973, 'Incomes policy: Unnecessary? undesirable/impracticable?', *Journal of Industrial Relations* 15, 237–58.

1976, 'Lawyers and industrial relations', in Hambly, A. and Goldring, J. (eds), *Australian Lawyers and Social Change*, Sydney: Law Book Company, 321–49.

1977, 'Wage determination and economic policy', *Australian Economic Review*, Third Quarter, 16–24.

1989, 'The Arbitration Commission: Prime mover or facilitator', *Journal of Industrial Relations* 31, 407–27.

1994, 'Australia', in Trebilcock, A. (ed.), *Towards Social Dialogue*, Geneva: ILO, 67–100.

1998, 'Australian labour market issues: An historical perspective', *Journal of Industrial Relations* 40, 690–715.

Karmel, P. H. 1960, 'A wages policy for Australia', in Wage Determination and Economic Stability, Economic Papers, Economic Society of Australia and New Zealand, NSW Branch.

Kelly, P. 1992, *The End of Certainty*, Sydney: Allen & Unwin.

Kelty, B. 1984, 'An income and prices policy for Australia', in Aldred, J. (ed.), *Industrial Confrontation*, Sydney: George Allen & Unwin, 42–8.

Kerr, J. R. 1961, 'Procedures in general wage cases in the Commonwealth Arbitration Commission', *Journal of Industrial Relations* 3, 81–93.

King, J. E., Rimmer, R. J. and Rimmer, S. M. 1992, 'The law of the shrinking middle: Inequality of earnings in Australia 1975–1989', *Scottish Journal of Political Economy* 39, 391–412.

Kirby, M. D. 1989, 'The removal of Justice Staples and the silent forces of industrial relations', *Journal of Industrial Relations* 31, 334–71.

1990, 'Judicial independence in Australia reaches a moment of truth', *University of New South Wales Law Journal* 13, 187–211.

2000, 'Constitutional interpretation and original intent: A form of ancestor worship?', *Melbourne University Law Review* 24, 1–14.

2001a, 'Industrial relations law – call off the funeral', *Deakin Law Review* 6, 256–60.

2001b, 'Sir Richard Kirby and a century of industrial arbitration', Sir Richard Kirby Lecture, University of Wollongong, 16 October 2001.

2002, 'Human rights and industrial relations', *Journal of Industrial Relations* 44, 562–78.

Kirby, R. 1970, 'Conciliation and arbitration in Australia – where the emphasis?', *Federal Law Review* 4, 1–29.

1973, Farewell Speech, transcript held by Sir Richard Kirby Archives of the Commission.

Kirk, J. 1999, 'Constitutional interpretation and a theory of evolutionary originalism', *Federal Law Review* 27, 323–66.

Kollmorgen, S. 1997, 'Towards a unitary national system of industrial relations?', *Australian Journal of Labour Law* 10, 158–69.

Laffer, K. 1958, 'Problems of compulsory arbitration in Australia', *International Labour Review* 77, 417–33.

La Nauze, J. 1965, *Alfred Deakin: A Biography*, Melbourne: Angus & Robertson.

1972, *The Making of the Australian Constitution*, Melbourne University Press.

Lane, P. H. 1981, 'The decline of the boilermakers separation of powers doctrine', *Australian Law Journal* 55, 6–14.

Larmour, C. 1985, *Labor Judge: The Life and Times of Judge Alfred William Foster*, Sydney: Hale & Iremonger.

Lee, M. and Peetz, D. 1998, 'Trade unions and the Workplace Relations Act', *Labour and Industry* 9, 5–19.

Lloyd, C. 1985, *Profession: Journalist. A History of the Australian Journalists' Association*, Sydney: Hale & Iremonger.

Louis, L. J. 1968, *Trade Unions and the Depression: A Study of Victoria 1930–1932*, Canberra: Australian National University Press.

Loundes, J., Tseng, Y.-P., and Wooden, M. 2003, 'Enterprise bargaining and productivity in Australia: What do we know?', *Economic Record* 79, 245–58.

Ludeke, J. T. 1992, 'The public interest and the Australian Industrial Relations Commission', *Journal of Industrial Relations* 34, 593–604.

1993, 'The Government's new charter for industrial relations in Australia 1993–1996', *Journal of Industrial Relations* 35, 316–28.

Lydall, H. F. 1965, 'The dispersion of employment incomes in Australia', *Economic Record* 41, 549–69.

1968, *The Structure of Earnings*, Oxford University Press.

Lynch, P. 1971, 'Industrial relations in the community – with particular reference to the role of government', *Journal of Industrial Relations* 13, 241–50.

McCallum, R. C. 1992, '"A modern renaissance" – industrial law and relations under federal wigs 1977–1992', *Sydney Law Review* 14, 401–31.

1993, 'Enhancing federal enterprise bargaining: The Industrial Relations Legislation Amendment Act 1992 (Commonwealth)', *Australian Journal of Labour Law* 6, 63–8.

1994, 'The internationalisation of Australian labour law: The Industrial Relations Reform Act 1993', *Sydney Law Review* 16, 122–34.

2001, 'Labour outsourcing and the High Court', *Australian Journal of Labour Law* 14, 97–103.

McCallum, R. C., Pittard, M. and Smith, G. 1990, *Australian Labour Law: Cases and Materials*, 2nd edn, Sydney: Butterworths.

McCallum, R. C. and Smith, G. F. 1986, 'Opting out from within: industrial agreements under the Conciliation and Arbitration Act 1904', *Journal of Industrial Relations* 28, 57–85.

McCarry, G. J. 1994, 'Sanctions and industrial action: The impact of the Industrial Relations Reform Act', *Australian Journal of Labour Law* 7, 198–226.

1997, 'Industrial action under the Workplace Relations Act 1996 (Commonwealth)', *Australian Journal of Labour Law* 10, 133–57.

1998, 'From industry to enterprise, from award to agreement: Federal laws and work-place change in Australia', in Nolan, D. R. (ed.), *The Australasian Labour Law Reforms: Australia and New Zealand at the End of the Twentieth Century*, Sydney: Federation Press, 52–71.

McCarthy, P. G. 1968, 'Wage determination in New South Wales 1890–1921', *Journal of Industrial Relations* 10, 189–205.

McClelland, J. 1988, *Stirring the Possum*, Ringwood: Penguin.

McCorquodale, J. 1985, 'The myth of mateship: Aborigines and employment', *Journal of Industrial Relations* 27, 3–16.

McDermott, K. 1993, 'Women's productivity: Productivity bargaining and service work-ers', *Journal of Industrial Relations* 35, 538–53.

Macdermott, T. 1997, 'Industrial legislation in 1996: The reform agenda', *Journal of Industrial Relations* 39, 52–76.

Macdonald, C. 1972, 'Sir Thomas Naghten Fitzgerald', in Pike, D. (ed.), *Australian Dictionary of Biography*, vol. 4, 180–1.

McGavin, P. A. 1985, 'The introduction of wage indexation under the Whitlam Govern-ment', *Journal of Industrial Relations* 27, 17–37.

McGrath, B. and O'Sullivan, G. 1932, *The Laws of the Commonwealth of Australia 1901–1931*, Sydney: Law Book Company.

McGuinness, P. P. 1985, *The Case against the Arbitration Commission*, Sydney: Centre for Independent Studies.

Macintyre, S. 1986, *The Oxford History of Australia, Volume 4: The Succeeding Age*, Melbourne: Oxford University Press.

1989, 'Neither capital nor labour: The politics of the establishment of arbitration', in Macintyre and Mitchell, *Foundations of Arbitration*, 178–200.

Macintyre, S. and Mitchell, R. (eds) 1989, *Foundations of Arbitration: The Origins and Effect of State Compulsory Education 1890–1914*, Melbourne: Oxford University Press.

McMurchy, M., Oliver, M. and Thornley, J. 1983, *For Love or Money: A Pictorial History of Women and Work in Australia*, Ringwood: Penguin.

Maddison, A. 1995, *Monitoring the World Economy 1820–1992*, Paris: OECD Publications.

2001, *The World Economy: A Millennial Perspective*, Paris: OECD Publications.

Maher, L. W. and Sexton, M. G. 1972, 'The High Court and industrial relations', *Australian Law Journal* 46, 109–23.

Markey, R. 1989, 'Trade unions, the Labor Party and the introduction of arbitration in New South Wales and the Commonwealth', in Macintyre and Mitchell, *Foundations of Arbitration*, 156–77.

Marshall, T. H. 1950, *Citizenship and Social Class and Other Essays*, Cambridge University Press.

Martin, R. 1975, *Trade Unions in Australia*, Ringwood: Penguin.

1989, *Trade Unionism, Purposes and Forms*, Oxford: Clarendon Press.

Meagher, D. 2002a, 'New day rising? Non-originalism, Justice Kirby and s. 80 of the Constitution', *Sydney Law Review* 24, 141–88.

2002b, 'Guided by voices? – constitutional interpretation on the Gleeson Court', *Deakin Law Review* 7, 261–93.

Meredith, D. and Dyster, B. 1999, *Australia in the Global Economy*, Cambridge University Press.

Merritt, J. 1986, *The Making of the AWU*, Melbourne: Oxford University Press.

Metal Trades Industry Association (MTIA) 1923, Metal Trades Journal, April.

1991, *Deregulation of the Labour Market: A Risky Business*, Sydney: MTIA.

Miller, J.D.B. 1952, 'History of Australian trade unionism', in Miller, J.D.B. (ed.), Australian Trade Unionism; Addresses Delivered at Australia's First Trade Union School at Newport, (mimeo).

Mills, C. P. 1968, 'Legislation and decisions affecting industrial relations', *Journal of Industrial Relations* 10, 54–63 and 154–64.

Mitchell, R. J. 1986, 'The High Court and the preference power: Wallis and Findlay in the context of the 1947 amendments', *University of Western Australia Law Review* 16, 338–60.

1987, 'The preference power and the practice of the Federal Industrial Tribunal, 1904–1970', *Journal of Industrial Relations* 29, 3–24.

1988, 'The rise and fall of the preference power: The practice of the Federal Commission, 1970–1987', *Australian Journal of Labour Law* 1, 224–46.

1989, 'State systems of conciliation and arbitration: The legal origins of the Australasian model', in Macintyre and Mitchell, *Foundations of Arbitration*, 74–103.

Mitchell, R. J. and Fetter, J. 2002, 'Human resource management and the individualisation of Australian relations', Working Paper No. 25, Centre for Employment and Labour Relations Law, University of Melbourne.

2003, 'Human resource management and individualisation in Australian labour law', *Journal of Industrial Relations* 45, 292–325.

Mitchell, R. J. and Naughton, R. 1993, 'Australian compulsory arbitration: Will it survive into the twenty-first century?', *Osgoode Hall Law Journal* 31, 265–95.

Mitchell, R. J. and Rimmer, M. 1990, 'Labour law, deregulation, and flexibility in Australian industrial relations', *Comparative Labor Law Journal* 12, 1–34.

Mitchell, W. F. 1992, 'Wages policy and wage determination in 1991', *Journal of Industrial Relations* 34, 153–61.

Mulvey, C. 1983, 'Wage policy and wage determination in 1982', *Journal of Industrial Relations* 25, 68–74.

1984, 'Wage policy and wage determination in 1983', *Journal of Industrial Relations* 26, 112–19.

1986, 'Alternatives to arbitration: Overview of the debate', in Blandy, R. and Niland, J. (eds), *Alternatives to Arbitration*, Sydney: Allen & Unwin, 11–28.

National Archives of Australia (NAA), Memorandum re: Administration: A432 1929/ 2656; Appointment of Deputy Industrial Registrar: A432 1929/3456, part 1; Arrangements with the States . . . with respect to District Registries: A432 1929/3456, part 2; Appointment of Industrial Registrar: A432 1929/3456, part 3; Deputy Registrar . . . Sydney Registry: A432 1929/3456, part 8; Sydney – Resignation of Officers: A432 1929/3456, part 20; Memorial from the Judges: M1505/27.

National Occupational Health and Safety Commission (NOHSC) 2000, *Data on OHS in Australia: The Overall Scene*, Sydney: NOHSC.

Naughton, A. 1994, 'The Industrial Relations Reform Act 1993', Working Paper No. 2, Centre for Employment and Labour Relations Law, University of Melbourne.

Naughton, R. B. 1994, 'The new bargaining regime', *Australian Journal of Labour Law* 7, 147–69.

Neumann, F. 1966, *Behemoth: The Structure and Practice of National Socialism, 1933– 1944*, New York: Harper.

New South Wales Chamber of Manufactures (NSWCM), Manufacturing Bulletin, various dates.

New South Wales Industrial Relations Commission (NSWIRC) 1998, Pay Equity Inquiry, Report to the Minister, Sydney: NSWIRC.

Nieuwenhuysen, J. 1973, 'The national wage case 1972–73', *Journal of Industrial Relations* 15, 324–30.

1974, 'The national wage case, 1974', *Journal of Industrial Relations* 16, 284–90.

Niland, J. 1978, *Collective Bargaining and Compulsory Arbitration in Australia*, Sydney: University of New South Wales Press.

Norington, B. 1998, *Jennie George*, Sydney: Allen & Unwin.

1990, *Sky Pirates: The Pilots' Strike that Grounded Australia*, Sydney: ABC Enterprises.

Norris, K. 1980, 'Compulsory arbitration and the wage structure in Australia', *Journal of Industrial Relations* 22, 249–63.

1986, 'The wages structure: Does arbitration make any difference?', in Niland, J. (ed.), *Wage Fixation in Australia*, Sydney: Allen & Unwin, 183–202.

O'Charley, L. 1978, *Anatomy of a Strike: An Australian Novel*, Sydney: Jack de Lissa.

O'Donnell, C. and Golder, N. 1986, 'A comparative analysis of equal pay: The United States, Britain and Australia', *Australian Feminist Studies* 3, 59–90.

O'Donnell, C. and Hall, P. 1988, *Getting Equal: Labour Market Regulation and Women's Work*, Sydney: Allen & Unwin.

O'Leary, P. 1999, 'The National Meat Association of Australia', in Sheldon and Thornthwaite, *Employer Associations and Industrial Relations Change*, 138–58.

Olssen, E. 1988, *The Red Feds, Revolutionary Industrial Unionism and the New Zealand Federation of Labour, 1908–1913*, Auckland: Oxford University Press.

Organisation for Economic Cooperation and Development (OECD) 1996, *Employment Outlook*, July, Paris: OECD Publications.

Osborne, G. 1973, 'Town and company: The Broken Hill industrial dispute of 1908–09', in Iremonger et al., *Strikes*, 26–50.

Oxnam, D. 1965, 'International comparisons of industrial conflict: an appraisal', *Journal of Industrial Relations* 7, 149–63.

Parker, R. S. 1965, 'Power in Australia', *Australia and New Zealand Journal of Sociology* 1, 85–96.

Patmore, G. 1991, *Australian Labour History*, Melbourne: Longman Cheshire.

Peetz, D. 1998, *Unions in a Contrary World: The Future of the Australian Union Movement*, Cambridge University Press.

Perlman, M. 1954, *Judges in Industry*, Melbourne University Press.

Petridis, A. 1986, 'Wages policy and wage determination in 1985', *Journal of Industrial Relations* 28, 124–32.

   1987, 'Wage policy and wage determination 1986', *Journal of Industrial Relations* 29, 75–83.

Phelps Brown, H. 1969, 'Balancing external payments by adjusting domestic income', reprinted in Anderson, K. (ed.) 2001, *Australia's Economy in its International Context: The Joseph Fisher Lectures*, vol. 2, Adelaide University, 213–22.

   1983, *The Origins of Trade Union Power*, Oxford: Clarendon Press.

Pitchford, J. D. 1971, 'The usefulness of the average-productivity wage adjustment rule', *Economic Record* 47, 255–61.

Pittard, M. J. 1997, 'Collective employment relationships: Reforms to arbitrated awards and certified agreements', *Australian Journal of Labour Law* 10, 62–88.

Pittard, M. J. and Naughton, R. B., 2003, *Australian Labour Law: Cases and Materials*, 4th edn, Sydney: Butterworths.

Plowman, D. H. 1980, 'National wage determination 1979', *Journal of Industrial Relations* 22, 79–89.

   1981, *Wage Indexation: A Study of Australian Wage Issues, 1975–1980*, Sydney: George Allen & Unwin.

   1986, 'Compulsory arbitration and national employer co-ordination 1890–1980', PhD thesis, Flinders University.

1987, 'Economic forces and the New Right: Employer matters in 1986', *Journal of Industrial Relations* 28, 84–91.

1989a, *Holding the Line: Compulsory Arbitration and National Employer Co-ordination in Australia*, Cambridge University Press.

1989b, 'Forced march: The employers and arbitration', in Macintyre and Mitchell, *Foundations of Arbitration*, 135–55.

1992, *Australian Wage Determination: Select Documents*, Industrial Relations Resource Series No. 9, Industrial Relations Research Centre, University of New South Wales.

Plowman, D. H. and Rimmer, M. 1992, 'Bargaining structure, award respondency and employer associations', Working Paper No. 33, UNSW Studies in Australian Industrial Relations, Sydney: Industrial Relations Research Centre, University of New South Wales.

Plowman, D. H. and Smith, G. F. 1986, 'Moulding federal arbitration: The employers and the High Court 1903–1935', *Australian Journal of Management* 11, 203–29.

Polites, C. G. 1984, 'Major tribunal decisions in 1983', *Journal of Industrial Relations* 26, 105–11.

Powers, C. 1926, 'The work and history for twenty-one years of the Commonwealth Court of Conciliation and Arbitration', *Queensland Industrial Gazette* 11, 252–6.

Queensland Industrial Relations Commission 2001, *Valuing Worth: A Report of the Pay Equity Inquiry*, Brisbane: Queensland Industrial Relations Commission.

Rafferty, F. 1994, 'Equal pay: The evolutionary process 1984–1994', *Journal of Industrial Relations* 36, 451–67.

Ranald, P. 1982, 'Feminism and class: The United Associations of Women and the Council of Action for Equal Pay in the Depression', in Bevege, M., James, M. and Shute, C. (eds), *Worth Her Salt: Women at Work in Australia*, Sydney: Hale & Iremonger, 270–85.

Rawson, D. 1978, *Unions and Unionists in Australia*, Sydney: George Allen & Unwin.

1984, 'Comment', in Rawson, D. and Fisher, C. (eds), *Changing Industrial Law*, Sydney: Croom Helm, 36–45.

1986, 'Industrial relations and the art of the possible', in Blandy, R. and Niland, J. (eds), *Alternatives to Arbitration*, Sydney: Allen & Unwin, 273–97.

Reddaway, W. B. 1937, transcript of evidence in the Commonwealth Court of Conciliation and Arbitration, 14 May.

Reekie, G. 1989, 'The Shop Assistants' Case of 1907 and industrial relations in Sydney's retail industry', in Macintyre and Mitchell, *Foundations of Arbitration*, 269–90.

Reeves, W. P. 1902a, *State Experiments in Australia and New Zealand*, London: Grant Richards; reissue, Melbourne: Macmillan, 1969.

1902b, 'Mr. Wise's Industrial Arbitration Act', *Economic Journal* 12, 320–6.

Reserve Bank of Australia (RBA) 1996, 'Australian economic statistics 1949–50 to 1994–95', Occasional Paper No. 8, report R. A. Foster, RBA.

Richardson, S. (ed.) 1999, *Reshaping the Labour Market: Regulation, Efficiency and Equality in Australia*, Cambridge University Press.

Richardson, S. 2000, 'Society's investment in children', Working Paper Series No. 15, National Institute of Labour Studies, Flinders University, Adelaide.

Rickard, J. 1984, *H. B. Higgins: The Rebel as Judge*, Sydney: George Allen & Unwin.

Riddett, L. 1997, 'The strike that became a land rights movement: A southern "do-gooder" reflects on Wattie Creek 1966–74', *Labour History* 72, 50–65.

Rimmer, M. and Sheldon, P. 1989, '"Union control" against management power: labourers' unions in New South Wales before the Maritime Strike', *Australian Historical Studies* 23, 274–92.

Roan, A., Bramble, T. and Lafferty, G. 2001, 'Australian workplace agreements in practice: The "hard" and "soft" dimensions', *Journal of Industrial Relations* 43, 387–401.

Ross, I. 2001, 'The impact of legal architecture, conciliator style and other factors on the settlement of unfair dismissal claims', PhD thesis, University of Sydney.

Ross, P., Bamber, G. and Whitehouse, G. 1998, 'Employment, economics and industrial relations: Comparative statistics', in Bamber, G. and Lansbury, R. (eds), *International and Comparative Employment Relations: A Study of Industrialised Market Economies*, 3rd edn, Sydney: Allen & Unwin, 328–66.

Rowe, L. 1982, 'Reason, force or compromise: Egalitarian wage structures under bargaining and arbitration', *Journal of Industrial Relations* 24, 245–65.

Rowley, C. 1971, *The Remote Aborigines: Aboriginal Policy and Practice*, vol. III, Canberra: Australian National University Press.

Rowse, T. 1993, 'Rethinking Aboriginal "resistance": The Community Development Employment Program', *Oceania* 63, 268–86.

1998, *White Flour, White Power: From Rations to Citizenship in Central Australia*, Cambridge University Press.

2002, *Indigenous Futures: Choice and Development for Aboriginal and Islander Australia*, Sydney: University of New South Wales Press.

Royal Commission on Equal Pay 1944–46, Report, London: HMSO.

Royal Commission on Strikes 1891, Report, Sydney: New South Wales Government Printer.

Russell, E. A. 1959, statement of evidence in the 1959 Basic Wage Case.

1965, 'Wages policy in Australia', *Australian Economic Papers* 4, 1–26.

Ryan, E. and Conlon, A. 1989, *Gentle Invaders: Australian Women at Work*, Ringwood: Penguin.

Ryan, P. and Rowse, T. 1975, 'Women, arbitration and the family', in Curthoys, A., Eade, S. and Sperritt, P. (eds), *Women at Work*, Canberra: Australian Society for the Study of Labour History, 15–30.

Sawer, G. 1956, *Australian Federal Politics and Law 1901–29*, Melbourne University Press.

1963, *Australian Federal Politics and Law 1929–49*, Melbourne University Press.

Sawer, M. 1990, *Sisters in Suits: Women and Public Policy in Australia*, Sydney: Allen & Unwin.

(ed.) 1996, *Removal of the Commonwealth Marriage Bar: A Documentary History*, Centre for Research in Public Sector Management, University of Canberra.

Scalia, A. 1995, 'The role of a constitutional court in a democratic society', *The Judicial Review* 2, 141–51.

Schedvin, C. B. 1970, *Australia and the Great Depression*, Sydney University Press.

Scherer, P. 1985, 'State syndicalism', in Hyde, J. and Nurick, J. (eds), *Wages Wasteland*, Sydney: Hale & Iremonger, 75–94.

Schlesinger, A. 1962, *The Vital Center: The Politics of Freedom*, Boston: Houghton Mifflin.

Sharp, I. 1966, 'Report on the present position of Aborigines in the Northern Territory and the States', in Sharp, I. and Tatz, C. (eds), *Aborigines in the Economy: Employment, Wages and Training*, Brisbane: Jacaranda Press, 145–73.

Sheldon, P. and Thornthwaite, L. (eds) 1999a, *Employer Associations and Industrial Relations Change*, Sydney: Allen & Unwin.

1999b, 'Employer matters in 1998', *Journal of Industrial Relations* 41, 152–69.

Sheridan, T. 1975, *Mindful Militants: The Amalgamated Engineering Union in Australia 1920–1972*, Cambridge University Press.

1989, *Division of Labour: Industrial Relations in the Chifley Years, 1945–49*, Melbourne: Oxford University Press.

Short, C. 1986, 'Equal pay – what happened?', *Journal of Industrial Relations* 28, 315–35.

Silverman, S. 1971, 'Political strikes in Australia', in Isaac, J. and Ford, G. (eds), *Australian Labour Relations: Readings*, 2nd edn, Melbourne: Sun Books, 79–89.

Singleton, G. 1990, *The Accord and the Australian Labour Movement*, Melbourne University Press.

1997, 'Industrial relations: Pragmatic change', in Prasser, S. and Starr, G. (eds), *Policy and Change: The Howard Mandate*, Sydney: Hale & Iremonger, 192–207.

Smith, D. 1991, 'Aboriginal employment statistics: Policy implications of the divergence between official and case study data', Discussion Paper No. 13, Centre for Aboriginal Economic Policy Research, Australian National University, Canberra.

Smith, G. 1990, 'From consensus to coercion: The Australian air pilots dispute', *Journal of Industrial Relations* 32, 238–53.

South Australian Industrial Reports (SAIR) 1916–, Adelaide: Government Printer.

South Australian Industrial Reports (SAIR) 1919–, Adelaide: Government Printer.

Spence, W. G. 1909, *Australia's Awakening: Thirty Years in the Life of an Australian Agitator*, Sydney: Workers' Trustees.

Spicer, I. 1997, *Independent Review of the Community Development Employment Projects CDEP Scheme*, Canberra: Office of Public Affairs, ATSIC.

Stackpool, J. E. 1986, 'Industrial relations in 1986', *Journal of Industrial Relations* 29, 92–101.

Stackpool-Moore, J. 1990, 'From equal pay to equal value in Australia: Myth or reality?', *Comparative Labour Law Journal* 11, 273–94.

Stewart, A. 1999, 'The legal framework for individual employment agreements in Australia', in Deery, S. and Mitchell, R. J. (eds), *Employment Relations: Individualisation and Union Exclusion*, Sydney: Federation Press, 18–47.

Stilwell, F. 1986, *The Accord . . . and Beyond: The Political Economy of the Labor Government*, Sydney: Pluto Press.

Sutcliffe, J. T., Mills, R. C. and Brigden, J. B. 1925, *Report of the Economic Commission on the Queensland Basic Wage*, Queensland: Government Printer.

Sutcliffe, P. and Rimmer, M. 1981, 'The origins of Australian workshop organisation, 1918 to 1950', *Journal of Industrial Relations* 24, 216–39.

Sykes, E. I. and Glasbeek, H. J. 1972, *Labour Law in Australia*, Sydney: Butterworths.

Taylor, J. and Hunter, B. 1996, 'Indigenous participation in labour market training programs', Discussion Paper No. 108, Centre for Aboriginal Economic Policy Research, Australian National University, Canberra.

Thornton, E. 1942, *Trade Unions and the War*, Sydney: Federated Ironworkers' Association.

Timbs, J. 1963, *Towards Wage Justice by Judicial Regulation: An Appreciation of Australia's Experience under Compulsory Arbitration*, Louvain: Institut de Recherches Économiques, Sociales et Politiques.

Turner, H. A. 1962, *Trade Union Growth, Structure and Policy*, London: George Allen & Unwin.

Turner, I. 1965, *Industrial Labour and Politics: The Labour Movement in Eastern Australia 1900–1921*, Canberra: ANU Press.

1979, *Industrial Labour and Politics: The Dynamics of the Labour Movement in Eastern Australia 1900–1921*, Sydney: Hale & Iremonger.

Underhill, E., Bertone, S. and Doughney, J. 2003, 'Workplace "bargaining" and the wages/working time nexus: Counting the cost of decentralisation', in Burgess, J. and McDonald, D. (eds), *Developments in Enterprise Bargaining in Australia*, Melbourne: Tertiary Press, 141–57.

University of Tasmania 1925, *Employment Relations and the Basic Wage: Lectures and Papers Published in Connection with the Pitt Cobbett Foundation*, Hobart: University of Tasmania.

Vamplew, W. (ed.) 1987, *Australians: Historical Statistics*, Broadway: Fairfax, Syme and Weldon Associates.

Victorian Chamber of Manufactures, various dates, Annual Reports.

Victorian Employers' Federation, various dates, Minutes of Meetings.

Vranken, M. 1994, 'Demise of the Australasian model of labour law in the 1990s', *Comparative Labor Law Journal* 16, 1–25.

Walker, K. F. 1970, *Australian Industrial Relations Systems*, Cambridge, MA: Harvard University Press.

Waters, M. 1982, *Strikes in Australia: A Sociological Analysis of Industrial Conflict*, Sydney: George Allen & Unwin.

Watson, D. 2002, *Recollections of a Bleeding Heart*, Milsons Point: Knopf.

Watson, V. 1966, 'Possibilities and limitations of conciliation procedures', *Journal of Industrial Relations* 8, 25–35.

Webb, S. and Webb, B. 1898, *Industrial Democracy*, London: Private.

1902, *Industrial Democracy*, London: Longman.

Weeks, P. 1995, *Trade Union Security Law: A Study of Preference and Compulsory Unionism*, Federation Press: Sydney.

White, L., Steel, M., and Haddrick, S. 2003, 'A decade of formal collective agreement making in the federal jurisdiction', in Burgess, J. and McDonald, D. (eds), *Developments in Enterprise Bargaining in Australia*, Melbourne: Tertiary Press, 69–96.

Whitehead, D. 1966, 'Professor Russell on wages policy: A comment', *Australian Economic Papers* 5, 224–9.

Whitehead, D. and Cockburn, M. 1963, 'Shares of national income: Some neglected implications', *Journal of Industrial Relations* 5, 134–5.

Whitehouse, G. 1992, 'Legislation and labour market gender inequality: An analysis of OECD countries', *Work, Employment and Society* 6, 65–86.

Whitehouse, G. and Frino, B. 2003, 'Women, wages and industrial agreements', *Australian Journal of Labour Economics*, 6, 4, 579–96.

Whitehouse, G., Zetlin, D. and Earnshaw, J. 2001, 'Prosecuting pay equity: Evolving strategies in Britain and Australia', *Gender, Work and Organization* 8, 365–86.

Wildavsky, A. 1958, 'The 1926 referendum', in Wildavsky, A. and Carboch, D. (eds), *Studies in Australian Politics*, Melbourne: Cheshire, 3–118.

Williams, G. 1998, *Labour Law and the Constitution*, Sydney: Federation Press.

Williams, P. 1988, 'Dollar Sweets case wasn't a precedent', *Australian Financial Review*, 14 April, 10.

Wiseman, J. 1998, 'Here to stay? The 1997–1998 Australian waterfront dispute and its implications', *Labour and Industry* 9, 1–16.

Withers, G., Endres, A. and Perry, L. 1987, 'Labour', in Vamplew, *Australians*, 145–64.

Wood, C. 1979, 'Establishment and operations of the Industrial Relations Bureau', in Australian Conciliation and Arbitration after 75 Years, One-day Seminar at the Faculty of Law, Monash University, Melbourne, 14 July.

Wooden, M. 2000, *The Transformation of Australian Industrial Relations*, Sydney: Federation Press.

Woodward, A. E. 1968, 'A review of developments in industrial relations 1967/68', *Journal of Industrial Relations* 10, 104–15.

1970, 'Industrial relations in the 70s', *Journal of Industrial Relations* 12, 115–29.

Wootten, J. H. 1970, 'The role of tribunals', *Journal of Industrial Relations* 12, 130–44.

Worland, D. 1972, 'Variations in award rates of pay and the absorption of over-award payments', *Journal of Industrial Relations* 14, 396–412.

Wright, M. 1981, 'Wage policy and wage determination in 1980', *Journal of Industrial Relations* 23, 102–13.

1982, 'Wage policy and wage determination in 1981', *Journal of Industrial Relations* 24, 69–76.

Yerbury, D. 1981, 'The Government, the Arbitration Commission and wages policy: The role of the "supporting mechanisms" under the Whitlam government', in Hancock, K. J. (ed.), *Incomes Policy in Australia*, Sydney/Melbourne: Harcourt Brace Jovanovich, 195–234.

Yerbury, D. and Isaac, J. E. 1971, 'Recent trends in collective bargaining in Australia', *International Law Review* 103, 412–52.

Zappala, G. 1992, 'The closed shop in Australia', *Journal of Industrial Relations* 34, 3–30.

INDEX

'Federal arbitration commission' is used as the generic term for the institutions of arbitration, as in the text.